SWINDOLL'S

NEW TESTAMENT

INSIGHTS

INSIGHTS ON

JAMES, 1 & 2 PETER

CHARLES R. SWINDOLL

SWINDOLL'S

NEW TESTAMENT

INSIGHTS

INSIGHTS ON

JAMES, 1 & 2 PETER

ZONDERVAN®

ZONDERVAN.com/
AUTHORTRACKER
follow your favorite authors

ZONDERVAN

Insights on James, 1 and 2 Peter
Copyright © 2010 by Charles R. Swindoll

This title is also available as a Zondervan ebook. Visit www.zondervan.com/ebooks.

Requests for information should be addressed to:

Zondervan, *Grand Rapids, Michigan* 49530

Library of Congress Cataloging-in-Publication Data
    Swindoll, Charles R.
        Insights on James, 1 and 2 Peter / Charles R. Swindoll
            p. cm. (Swindoll's New Testament insights)
        ISBN 978-0-310-28432-1 (hardcover)
        1. Bible. N.T. James—Commentaries. 2. Bible. N.T. Peter—Commentaries. I. Title. II. Title: Insights
on James, First and Second Peter
    BS2785.53.S95 2010
    227'.907—dc22   2009053272

Scripture taken from the *New American Standard Bible.* Copyright © 1960, 1962, 1963, 1968, 1971, 1972, 1973, 1975, 1977, 1995 by The Lockman Foundation. Used by permission.

Maps by International Mapping. Copyright © 2010 by Zondervan. All rights reserved.

Any Internet addresses (websites, blogs, etc.) and telephone numbers in this book are offered as a resource. They are not intended in any way to be or imply an endorsement by Zondervan, nor does Zondervan vouch for the content of these sites and numbers for the life of this book.

All rights reserved. No part of this publication may be reproduced, stored in a retrieval system, or transmitted in any form or by any means—electronic, mechanical, photocopy, recording, or any other—except for brief quotations in printed reviews, without the prior permission of the publisher.

Published in association with Yates & Yates, www.yates2.com.

Cover design: Rob Monacelli
Cover photography: PixelWorks Photography
Interior design: Sherri Hoffman

Printed in the United States of America

11 12 13 14 15 16 17 18 19 20 21 /DCI/ 24 23 22 21 20 19 18 17 16 15 14 13 12 11 10 9 8 7 6 5 4 3 2

CONTENTS

AUTHOR'S PREFACE

For almost sixty years I have loved the Bible. It was that love for the Scriptures, mixed with a clear call into the gospel ministry during my tour of duty in the Marine Corps, that resulted in my going to Dallas Theological Seminary to prepare for a lifetime of ministry. During those four great years I had the privilege of studying under outstanding men of God, who also loved God's Word. They not only held the inerrant Word of God in high esteem, they taught it carefully, preached it passionately, and modeled it consistently. A week never passes without my giving thanks to God for the grand heritage that has been mine to claim! I am forever indebted to those fine theologians and mentors, who cultivated in me a strong commitment to the understanding, exposition, and application of God's truth.

For more than forty-five years I have been engaged in doing just that — *and how I love it!* I confess without hesitation that I am addicted to the examination and the proclamation of the Scriptures. Because of this, books have played a major role in my life for as long as I have been in ministry — especially those volumes that explain the truths and enhance my understanding of what God has written. Through these many years I have collected a large personal library, which has proven invaluable as I have sought to remain a faithful student of the Bible. To the end of my days, my major goal in life is to communicate the Word with accuracy, insight, clarity, and practicality. Without resourceful and reliable books to turn to, I would have "run dry" decades ago.

Among my favorite and most well-worn volumes are those that have enabled me to get a better grasp of the biblical text. Like most expositors, I am forever searching for literary tools that I can use to hone my gifts and sharpen my skills. For me, that means finding resources that make the complicated simple and easy to understand, that offer insightful comments and word pictures that enable me to see the relevance of sacred truth in light of my twenty-first-century world, and that drive those truths home to my heart in ways I do not easily forget. When I come across such books, they wind up in my hands as I devour them and then place them in my library for further reference . . . and, believe me, I often return to them. What a relief it is to have these resourceful works to turn to when I lack fresh insight, or when I need just the right story or illustration, or when I get stuck in the tangled text and cannot find my way out. For the serious expositor, a library is essential. As a mentor of mine once said, *"Where else can you have 10,000 professors at your fingertips?"*

In recent years I have discovered there are not nearly enough resources like those I just described. It was such a discovery that prompted me to consider becoming a part of the answer instead of lamenting the problem. But the solution would result in a huge undertaking. A writing project that covers all of the books and letters of the New Testament seemed overwhelming and intimidating. A rush of relief came when I realized that during the past forty-five-plus years I've taught and preached through most of the New Testament. In my files were folders filled with notes from those messages that were just lying there, waiting to be brought out of hiding, given a fresh and relevant touch in light of today's needs, and applied to fit into the lives of men and women who long for a fresh word from the Lord. *That did it!* I began to pursue the best publisher to turn my dream into reality.

Thanks to the hard work of my literary agents, Sealy and Matt Yates, I located a publisher interested in taking on a project this extensive. I thank the fine people at Zondervan Publishing House for their enthusiastic support of this multivolume venture that will require over ten years to complete. Having met most of them over the years through other written works I've authored, I knew they were qualified to handle such an undertaking and would be good stewards of my material, staying with the task of getting all of it into print. I am grateful for the confidence and encouragement of both Stan Gundry and Paul Engle, who have remained loyal and helpful from the beginning. It is also a pleasure to work alongside Verlyn Verbrugge; I sincerely appreciate his seasoned wisdom and keen-eyed assistance.

It has also been especially delightful to work, again, with my longtime friend and former editor, John Sloan. He has provided invaluable counsel as my general editor. Best of all has been John's enthusiastic support. I must also express my gratitude to both Mark Gaither and Mike Svigel for their tireless and devoted efforts, serving as my hands-on, day-to-day editors. They have done superb work as we have walked our way through the verses and chapters of all twenty-seven New Testament books. It has been a pleasure to see how they have taken my original material and helped me shape it into a style that remains true to the text of the Scriptures, at the same time interestingly and creatively developed, and all the while allowing my voice to come through in a natural and easy-to-read manner.

I need to add sincere words of appreciation to the congregations I have served in various parts of these United States for almost five decades. It has been my good fortune to be the recipient of their love, support, encouragement, patience, and frequent words of affirmation as I have fulfilled my calling to stand and deliver God's message year after year. The sheep from all those flocks have endeared themselves to this shepherd in more ways than I can put into words ... and none more than those I currently serve with delight at Stonebriar Community Church in Frisco, Texas.

Finally, I must thank my wife, Cynthia, for her understanding of my addiction to studying, to preaching, and to writing. Never has she discouraged me from staying at it. Never has she failed to urge me in the pursuit of doing my very best. On the contrary, her affectionate support personally, and her own commitment to excellence in leading *Insight for Living* for more than three decades, have combined to keep me faithful to my calling "in season and out of season." Without her devotion to me and apart from our mutual partnership throughout our lifetime of ministry together, *Swindoll's New Testament Insights* would never have been undertaken.

I am grateful that it has now found its way into your hands and, ultimately, onto the shelves of your library. My continued hope and prayer is that you will find these volumes helpful in your own study and personal application of the Bible. May they help you come to realize, as I have over these many years, that God's Word is as timeless as it is true.

The grass withers, the flower fades,
But the word of our God stands forever. (Isaiah 40:8)

Chuck Swindoll
Frisco, Texas

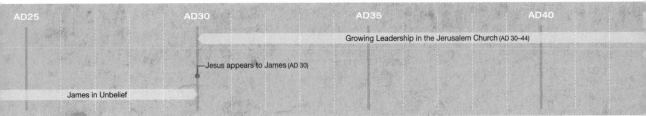

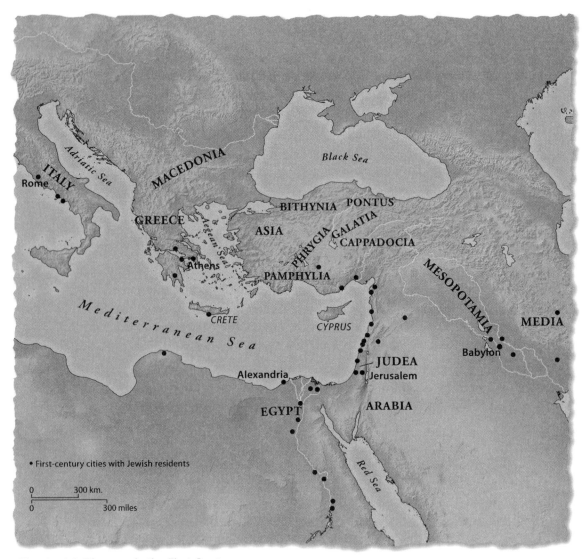

The Jewish Diaspora in the First Century

JAMES

Introduction

We live in a world where politics rules the day. In this world, a person's public reputation too often drowns out the private reality. *Whom* you know usually trumps *what* you know. Name-dropping often gets you further than talent or skill. These cynical sayings apply not only to the political realm, where quid pro quo is the status quo. Unfortunately, the "good ol' boy" system tends to corrupt most areas of business, academia, entertainment … and, yes, even the church.

This is why the opening words of the book of James are so refreshing. Like a cool spring breeze blowing through a musty room, the unassuming nature of these first few words drives out arrogance, ego, and presumption. Written by a man who could have dropped the Name above all names, this simple, straight-forward greeting sets the tone for a letter that assaults our natural human tendencies toward sin and selfishness with a radical message of authenticity and humility.

IDENTIFICATION OF JAMES

From the very first word, the name "James," this short letter presents us with a problem: which "James" wrote this letter? His humble self-identification as "a bond-servant of God and of the Lord Jesus Christ" doesn't get us far. And unless we were among those first recipients of the letter, we are left to some old-fashioned sleuthing to find out which James penned these words.

11

Overview of the Book of James

Section	Real Faith Produces Genuine Stability	Real Faith Produces Genuine Love
Themes	Joy in Trials Facing Temptations Responding to the Word	Partiality and Prejudice Faith at Work Bridling the Tongue
	Wisdom (1:5, 3:13, 15, 17) . . . Double-Minded	
Key Terms	Trials Perseverance Religion	Works Justify Tongue
Passage	1:1–1:27	2:1–3:12

Real Faith Produces Genuine Humility	Real Faith Produces Genuine Patience
Expressions of the Heart	
	Patience in Suffering
Settling Disputes	
	Sickness and Sin
Expressions of Desire	
	Carnality and Correction
Warning to the Wealthy	

(1:8, 4:8) . . . Faith (1:3, 6; 2:1, 5, 14–26; 5:15)

Jealousy	
	Persevere
Humble	
	Turn
Judge	

| 3:13–5:6 | 5:7-20 |

KEY TERMS

σοφία [*sophia*] (4678) "wisdom"

"Wisdom" has a rich meaning in the Hebrew Scriptures as well as in early Jewish Christianity. Wisdom involves far more than mere knowledge of facts and advances even beyond skillful living or the emphasis on practical virtue seen in Greek philosophy. Rather, "wisdom" in the Christian sense is a gift from God closely associated with the presence and working of the Holy Spirit, producing supernatural discernment and prudence. This explains why God, not human beings, is the ultimate source of true wisdom, which James repeatedly emphasizes (James 1:5; 3:13, 15, 17).

δίψυχος [*dipsychos*] (1374) "double-minded, wavering, doubting"

A simple compound of the words "two" and "soul," this word first appears in the Greek language in the book of James (James 1:8; 4:8). It doesn't appear again until the end of the first century in nonbiblical Christian books. Some scholars believe James himself coined the term. In any case, James uses the word to describe the wavering faith of Christians who claim to believe one thing but live in a way that betrays their confession. This term sums up in one word the heart of James's overarching message.

πίστις [*pistis*] (4102) "faith, confidence, reliance, trust"

For Christians, *pistis* is the means by which they relate to God. Depending on its context, the term can range in meaning from simple intellectual "assent" to demonstrable "faithfulness." For Christians, the entire range applies. Acceptance of core beliefs is essential for faith, but knowledge alone does not save. James develops the uniquely Christian concept of authentic, saving faith, which involves unwavering trust in and reliance on God. This authentic faith manifests itself through acts of faithfulness (James 1:3, 6; 2:1, 5, 14–26; 5:15).

If you run through the New Testament from Matthew to the book of James, you will come across four or — depending on how you count them — five men with this name (see chart, "Five Men Named James"). It's fairly easy to rule out a couple of these. James, the father of Judas (#1), never appears in the New Testament except in Luke 6:16. And James, the son of Alphaeus, is probably the same as "James the Less" (#3a and b). Though he is one of the Twelve, he disappears from the biblical account after the upper room experience on Pentecost (Acts 1:13). These two can be safely dismissed as candidates for authorship.

This leaves James, the son of Zebedee and brother of the apostle John (#2), or James, the half brother of Jesus (#4). Though the first James, one of the "Sons of Thunder," played a major leadership role in the infant church as one of Christ's inner three (Peter, James, and John), he was the first of the Twelve to suffer martyrdom

Five Men Named James

Four (or, perhaps, five) people with the name of James appear in the pages of the New Testament.

Identification	Scripture	Description
1. James, father of Judas (not Iscariot)	Luke 6:16	Nothing is known about this James. He is mentioned in the list of the original twelve disciples as the father of Judas (not Iscariot) to distinguish him from Judas the betrayer. This Judas is also distinguished by the name "Thaddeus."
2. James, son of Zebedee, brother of John	Matt. 4:21; 10:2; 17:1; Mark 1:19, 29; 3:17; 5:37; 9:2; 10:35, 41; 13:3; 14:33; Luke 5:10; 6:14; 8:51; 9:28, 54; Acts 1:13; 12:2	Brother of the apostle John and one of the "Sons of Thunder." He witnessed some of Jesus' private miracles, was present at Christ's transfiguration, and was invited to pray with Jesus in the Garden of Gethsemane. This James was the first of the twelve disciples to be martyred, put to death by the sword around AD 44.
3a. James, son of Alphaeus	Matt. 10:3; Mark 3:18; Luke 6:15; Acts 1:13	One of the twelve disciples, distinguished as the "son of Alphaeus" to keep him distinct from James #2. Many scholars believe #3a and #3b, "James the Less," are the same person.
3b. James the Less, son of Mary	Matt. 27:56; Mark 15:40; 16:1; Luke 24:10	The son of one of the women named Mary who witnessed Jesus' burial and resurrection. Many believe "James the Less" is the same as James, the son of Alphaeus (#3a).
4. James, son of Joseph and Mary, half-brother of Jesus	Matt. 13:55; Mark 6:3; Acts 1:14; 12:17; 15:13; 21:18; Gal. 1:19; 2:9, 12; 1 Cor. 15:7; Jude 1:1	The natural son of Mary and Joseph after the birth of Jesus. Though he did not believe in his brother, Jesus, during His earthly ministry (John 7:5), after the risen Lord made a special appearance to him, James became a believer and eventually the leader of the Jewish Christian church in Jerusalem until he was martyred around AD 62.

under Herod Agrippa I. That occurred around AD 44 in a persecution that resulted in further scattering the Jewish Christians throughout the Roman world (Acts 12:2). Shortly after this persecution, Jesus' half-brother James (#4) stepped in to lead the persecuted church in Jerusalem (12:17; 15:13; 21:18). This James, reared with Jesus in the home of Joseph and Mary, likely penned the letter that bears this name.

This identification of the author as the half-brother of Jesus goes back to the earliest centuries of Christian history. Most conservative New Testament scholars agree that both the tone and the content of the letter match the style one would expect from a well-known leader of the original Jewish Christian church.

A REVIEW OF THE LIFE OF JAMES

What do we know about James, the brother of Jesus, that will help us as we read his letter? Let's reconstruct a meaningful picture of his life.

No second-born son or daughter can possibly fathom what it must have been like to suffer second-child syndrome with an older brother who never sinned. But James did. Can you imagine? Jesus always came when His mother called Him the first time. He always washed His hands properly before supper. He always did His chores quickly and with delight. He always obeyed. Then there was James, born with a sinful nature like the rest of us, living in the shadow of a big brother who was God in the flesh. Being far from perfect, younger brother James had a built-in problem right from the start.

I suppose James would have been happy to see Jesus leave home when He did. But then his already "strange" older brother came back to their hometown saying, "I'm the Messiah!" How do you think James felt toward his older brother *then*? We don't have to wonder. John 7:5 says, "Not even His brothers were believing in Him." And Mark 3:21 tells us that His family "went out to take custody of Him; for they were saying, 'He has lost His senses.'" So, throughout the Gospels, we see James in a state of unbelief and skepticism over his older brother.

But things didn't stay that way.

In 1 Corinthians 15:7, the apostle Paul gives us a brief glimpse at an otherwise unknown event—the appearance of the resurrected Jesus to his brother James. We probably should avoid speculating about the nature of that visit, but I suspect it differed from Paul's much-needed Damascus encounter—the one that knocked him off his horse and blinded him with brilliant glory. Rather, I picture Jesus putting His arms around His younger brother, whispering words of encouragement and love in his ear ... words he had longed to hear all his life.

In any case, when the disciples of Jesus gathered in the upper room after their

Lord's ascension into heaven, James sat among them (Acts 1:14). He experienced the coming of the Holy Spirit on Pentecost (Acts 2) and the subsequent growth of the Jerusalem church in the midst of persecution (Acts 3–9). James was no doubt active in the Jerusalem church when Stephen was arrested and later martyred for his faith (6:8–7:60). Furthermore, James would have been aware that a young, zealous rabbinical student known as Saul of Tarsus supported the brutal death of Stephen and had begun "ravaging the church, entering house after house, and dragging off men and women" to put in prison (8:3).

Shortly after his conversion on the road to Damascus (Acts 9:1–18), Saul of Tarsus, later known as Paul the apostle, returned to Jerusalem to meet the leaders of the church he had once so viciously persecuted. It is noteworthy that he sought out James (Gal. 1:19) in that gathering. The account of this visit is recorded in Acts 9:26–28.

> When he came to Jerusalem, he was trying to associate with the disciples; but they were all afraid of him, not believing that he was a disciple. But Barnabas took hold of him and brought him to the apostles and described to them how he had seen the Lord on the road, and that He had talked to him, and how at Damascus he had spoken out boldly in the name of Jesus. And he was with them, moving about freely in Jerusalem, speaking out boldly in the name of the Lord.

Though initially suspicious of Paul's conversion, James quickly identified the marks of authentic faith in Paul's words and works. Perhaps James recalled his own stubbornness in accepting Jesus' messianic claims even though he had lived with Jesus all his life. But like Saul of Tarsus, James finally came around. God's work of grace had grabbed his heart, which resulted in his looking at his brother Jesus in a whole new light. As a result, not many years later, James wrote what is likely the very first book of the New Testament to be written, the short, practical manual of Christian living we call "James."

A dispute erupted in the church around AD 49, threatening to break the unity between Jews and Gentiles. Acts 15 tells us, "Some men came down from Judea and began teaching the brethren, 'Unless you are circumcised according to the custom of Moses, you cannot be saved.'" Naturally, this addition of circumcision to the gospel troubled Paul and Barnabas, who had been preaching a simple message of salvation by grace alone through faith alone apart from works (Gal. 2:15–21). Wanting to set the record straight, Paul and Barnabas immediately went to Jerusalem to consult with the apostles and elders, including Peter and James.

When Paul made his case to the leaders in Jerusalem, Peter concurred, reminding those assembled at the council that God had saved the Gentiles strictly by faith when he preached the gospel to Cornelius and his household (Acts 15:7–11; see 10:1–11:18). Following this, James himself stood up and supported Peter and Paul. Look closely at James's argument found in Acts 15:13–21:

> After they had stopped speaking, James answered, saying, "Brethren, listen to me. Simeon has related how God first concerned Himself about taking from among the Gentiles a people for His name. With this the words of the Prophets agree, just as it is written,
>
> > 'After these things I will return,
> > And I will rebuild the tabernacle of David which has fallen,
> > And I will rebuild its ruins,
> > And I will restore it,
> > So that the rest of mankind may seek the Lord,
> > And all the Gentiles who are called by My name,'
> > Says the Lord, who makes these things known from long ago.
>
> Therefore it is my judgment that we do not trouble those who are turning to God from among the Gentiles, but that we write to them that they abstain from things contaminated by idols and from fornication and from what is strangled and from blood. For Moses from ancient generations has in every city those who preach him, since he is read in the synagogues every Sabbath."

James's wise and convincing words became the basis for the Jerusalem council's decision to affirm Paul's gospel of salvation by grace alone through faith alone. In agreement with Paul and Barnabas, the Jerusalem apostles and elders firmly rejected the addition of works to the gospel (and aren't we grateful!). In order to maintain unity between the Jewish and Gentile believers, however, and to keep from offending Jewish Christians who felt compelled to keep the Law of Moses, Gentile converts were asked to avoid practices that would cause offense. Stated succinctly, James wanted to ensure that God-honoring works authenticated genuine faith.

James appears again in the book of Acts almost ten years later in AD 58. Shortly before being arrested and sent to Caesarea and later to Rome, Paul arrived in Jerusalem from his third missionary journey and met with James, who by then clearly had become the leader of the Jewish Christians in Jerusalem (Acts 21:15–19). In an attempt to exonerate Paul from charges that he had been encouraging Jews to abandon their customs after coming in faith to Christ, James and the other elders in Jerusalem encouraged Paul to participate in a purity ritual at the temple (21:23–24). From this we learn that James, a Jewish Christian living in Jerusalem and leading the Jewish believers, continued to keep the Law as a testimony to his fellow Jews. The last thing he wanted was for his genuine faith in Jesus as the

Messiah to be maligned because he and his people abruptly turned their backs on the Law of Moses. Though the Law was never a means of salvation, for James and many Jewish believers, the Law was a means of testimony to unbelieving Jews that their faith empowered them to do good works.

Ancient historians tell us that James continued to live and teach in Jerusalem, convincing many Jews and visitors that Jesus is the Messiah, the Son of God. Greatly esteemed for his piety, he spent so much time in the temple kneeling in prayer that he received the nickname "Camel Knees." Even his opponents, the scribes and Pharisees, could find no fault in him — except, of course, his "misguided" belief in the messiahship of Jesus.

James's authentic faith eventually brought about his death. His true faith in Christ — demonstrated through good works, strengthened through suffering, and seasoned with God-given wisdom — drew the ire of the increasingly zealous and jealous religious elite. His words and works attracted thousands of Jews to Christ, and the anti-Christian powers in Jerusalem eventually had enough of him. The ancient church historian, Eusebius, describes the events leading up to James's final confrontation with his opponents.

> But after Paul, in consequence of his appeal to Caesar, had been sent to Rome by Festus, the Jews, being frustrated in their hope of entrapping him by the snares which they had laid for him, turned against James, the brother of the Lord ... Leading him into their midst they demanded of him that he should renounce faith in Christ in the presence of all the people. But, contrary to the opinion of all, with a clear voice, and with greater boldness than they had anticipated, he spoke out before the whole multitude and confessed that our Savior and Lord Jesus is the Son of God. But they were unable to bear longer the testimony of the man who, on account of the excellence of ascetic virtue and of piety which he exhibited in his life, was esteemed by all as the most just of men, and consequently they slew him.[1]

Josephus reports that James was simply stoned,[2] but Eusebius recounts that he was thrown from the pinnacle of the temple, and then beaten to death with a club. Whatever the details of his brutal and unjust execution, James, the brother of Jesus, was martyred for his faith in AD 62.

A PREVIEW OF THE LETTER OF JAMES

In light of James's pedigree, position, kinship, and legacy, imagine how he could have started his letter:

"James, of the tribe of Judah, of the house of David, of the royal line of the kings of Judah ... , " or

"James, the eldest of the brothers of Jesus, the incarnate Son of God . . . ," or

"James, pastor of the First Christian Church of the world . . . ," or

"James, longtime associate of Peter, James, John, Paul, and the rest of the apostles . . ."

James could have dropped all kinds of names, pulled high rank, and impressed his readers with ego-inflating titles. But as we will see when we unpack his letter, that kind of pride is one of the things he rails against. That may be the style of this me-first world, but that wasn't the style of James. Instead, he began his letter simply, "James, a bond-servant of God and of the Lord Jesus Christ." James was a bond-servant (Greek *doulos*) — an indentured servant or slave, not a prized position in a class culture of the Roman world. But James did not regard his slavery to God and submission to Jesus Christ as burden or curse, but as a glorious honor.

After introducing himself, James then addresses the letter to his audience with a typical letter form at the time. He addressed his letter "To the twelve tribes who are dispersed abroad." Though most of the historical twelve tribes of Israel had lost their distinct identities centuries earlier in the Assyrian and Babylonian captivities, the term "twelve tribes of Israel" continued to be used as a figure of speech, referring to all children of Israel throughout the world. The phrase "who are dispersed abroad" reinforces the fact that James addressed primarily Jewish Christians, those he had likely known in Jerusalem, who had scattered as a result of persecution of the church by the unbelieving Jewish authorities. Several times throughout the book James calls his readers "brethren," indicating that he is addressing fellow believers in Jesus, not merely all Jews spread throughout the Roman world.

So, James was a Jewish believer writing to other Jewish believers in the first century who were "dispersed abroad." The Greek word is *diaspora*, meaning "scattered throughout," like seed sown throughout a field. When James wrote this letter, numerous exiles from the Holy Land already had established Jewish communities throughout the Roman world. Also at this time the Roman emperor Claudius had persecuted and driven Jews from Rome. Jewish businesses were boycotted. Jewish children were mocked and thrown out of schools. Times were harsh and life was grim.

At the same time, Jewish Christians, like the people to whom James wrote his letter, seem to have been living under a double *diaspora*. Not only were they subject to Roman ire because of their Jewishness; many had been driven out of the Jewish communities themselves because of their faith in the Messiah. More than any others, Jewish believers lived without roots and traveled outside Judea, looking for a place to call home. Many of these men and women found themselves in a social and religious limbo.

Though I believe suffering purifies and matures, I also believe that relentless, extreme suffering can confuse and crush. Many of these Jewish believers had begun to grow weary, tempted either to turn their backs on their Jewish roots or to defect from their faith in Christ. Many claimed that they believed the truth of God concerning the Lord Jesus, but because of the pressures of the day, they began to live a lie.

In this context of suffering, confusion, and defection, it is not surprising that James writes a letter of strong exhortation. Remember, this letter is not a doctrinal treatise, not a defense of the gospel regarding the person and work of Christ, not a retelling of the Christian story. This letter assumes his readers already know all those things. Instead, James pens a letter about authentic faith lived out in a hostile world.

The main theme of the book of James is that *real faith produces genuine works.* In other words, the person who has truly found the way genuinely walks in it. If you claim, "I have come to Jesus Christ; He is my Lord and Savior," James answers, "Then let your life give evidence of that truth. Let your outward acts reflect the inward reality. Justify your faith before others by your good works." When we realize this overarching theme, many of the individual sections and troublesome verses become clear.

We can now begin a brief overview of the book. You can use the chart on pages 12–13 to help you through the book of James; refer back to that chart throughout this study.

In the first major section, including all of chapter 1, James tells his readers that *real faith produces genuine stability.* When real faith gets stretched, it doesn't break; perseverance results instead. James supports this claim with three examples. First, in 1:1–12, he shows that trials and tribulations in life do not destroy faith, but actually deepen it and cause it to grow. In 1:13–18, James reminds us that we can face temptations through genuine faith. And in 1:19–27, he explains that true believers respond to God's Word positively, changing their lives to conform to its truth.

The second major section we will explore begins at 2:1 and runs through 3:12. In this section James argues that *real faith produces genuine love.* When true faith gets pressed by various circumstances, social challenges, and personal struggles, it does not fail. Instead, it produces a desire to put others first. Real faith takes a stand against prejudice (2:1–13), justifies itself through obedience and action (2:14–26), and bridles the beastly tongue (3:1–12). Genuine faith does not produce a passive, wimpy pushover, but a daring and durable force of love in action.

In the third section James asserts that *real faith produces genuine humility* (3:13–5:6). He contrasts worldly ambition with heavenly wisdom; one results in envy and strife, the other in righteousness and peace (3:13–18). James also lends practical advice on overcoming worldly behavior in the church, including behavior that brings division (4:1–10). He then exhorts his readers to overcome boasting by true humility before God (4:11–17). Finally, he warns the wealthy to live responsibly with their riches (5:1–6).

In the last section, James reaffirms the truth that *real faith produces genuine patience* (5:7–20). Jewish Christians distressed by their faith-challenging circumstances needed to hear that assurance over and over again. James exhorts his readers to be patient in suffering in light of the Lord's coming (5:7–12). He encourages them to seek physical and spiritual wholeness (5:13–18). And he ends his profoundly practical letters with an admonition to steer erring believers back onto the right path (5:19–20).

First-century Jewish Christians struggled with persevering through hardship, maintaining good works, promoting peace in their churches, and living patiently in anticipation of the Lord's return. They knew Jesus as the Way of life, but they needed a travel guide for walking in that Way through life. So do we! In the midst of the struggles of everyday life, we can all use a dose of James's hands-on Christianity.

Application

Which Path Are You On?

"There are two paths: the path of life and the path of death, and there is a vast difference between these two paths." (*Didache* 1:1)

These words begin what may be the oldest Christian writing outside the inspired New Testament. Like the book of James, the *Didache*, or "Teaching," is an early Jewish Christian writing. Parts of it probably were written around the time James penned his letter to the Jewish Christians throughout the world. It begins by describing the practical Christian life in terms of a journey on the "path of life."

For the believer, this journey begins with faith in Christ and continues until we reach our final destination: heaven. As John Bunyan portrays so vividly in his immortal work, *The Pilgrim's Progress,* it's a path laden with hardship, struggle, and suffering; but the path is also traveled with a company of joyous, confident, and victorious saints. The path swarms with persecutors, tempters, and discouragers; but the Lord Jesus Christ accompanies its travelers, bearing our burdens and providing His Holy Spirit to reinvigorate our weak steps. In Jewish Christian thought, the path of life, though narrow and difficult, led to a destination that would make any hazards, pitfalls, or setbacks along the journey well worth it.

James wrote his book to Jewish Christians who already had found the Way but were struggling to walk in that way. They had entered through the Door but now had to progress along the path. That's why James's practical manual for hands-on Christianity won't do us any good if we haven't set our feet on the path of life. But how does a person know if he or she is on the path of life leading to "the celestial city" ... or on the path of death, sliding ever so surely to destruction?

The answer from our culture is vague and uncertain. Ask anyone "on the street" and you'll hear a wide variation of opinions. As one of my mentors once described it, "the slimy ooze of indefiniteness" is everywhere to be found. The answer Jesus gave, however, is specific and simple: "I am the way, and the truth, and the life" (John 14:6). As *the* Way, He is Himself *the* path of life. As *the* Truth, He is *the* trustworthy One whose words and works can be trusted without reservation. And as *the* Life, He restores *the* vitality, meaning, purpose, and hope to those who formerly walked in darkness, confusion, fear, deception, and a deathlike existence.

Because of His great love for us sinners, God the Father sent His eternal Son to become human, to live a sinless life, and to die an unjust sinner's death on the cross. He died in our place, the just for the unjust, as our substitute. When we receive Him by faith, our sin and death are placed on Him, and His righteousness and life are transferred to our account.

If you are reading these words and you have never trusted in the finished work of the Lord Jesus Christ as your Savior — if you have never asked the resurrected Lord to come into your life — this would be the ideal time for you to do so. Here is a simple prayer for you to use: "Lord, I acknowledge Jesus Christ as my Savior. I believe He paid the complete payment for *my* sins and rose again, victorious over death, in order to grant me His life — eternal life. I acknowledge Him alone as the Door to the path of life, and today I willingly walk through that Door by faith."

If you have started your journey on the path of eternal life by faith in Christ, James's letter is for you. Read on!

NOTES: Author's Preface

1. Eusebius, *Ecclesiastical History* 2.23.1–2. English translation is from Philip Schaff and Henry Wace, eds., *Nicene and Post-Nicene Fathers,* 2nd ser.; vol. 1, *Eusebius: Church History, Life of Constantine the Great, and Oration in Praise of Constantine* (New York: Christian Literature, 1890).

2. Josephus, *Antiquities of the Jews* 20.9.1.

REAL FAITH PRODUCES GENUINE STABILITY (JAMES 1:1–27)

The two figures stood waist deep in the blue-green water that flowed easily around them. Light danced across the surface of the river as the sun peaked through the feathery clouds, illumining the two men who appeared to be arguing with each other. The one, dressed in a simple garment of camel's hair with a leather belt around his waist, held up his hands and shook his head in mild protest. His eyes closed, he patted his chest and pointed to himself.

The other man, also in his thirties and dressed in the robe and sash of the commoners, had stripped Himself in preparation for baptism and had been ushered by the prophet's younger disciples to the prophet John himself. After a brief exchange, John hesitated, and then, placing his hands on the young man named Jesus, immersed Him.

As Jesus rose from the water of the Jordan River, the Baptizer looked into the sky as the sunlight, briefly veiled by a passing cloud, broke through with brilliant light. But now his eyes fixed on something—something only he could see. He staggered backward in the water, losing his footing, but his disciples caught him.

"What, master? What did you see?"

"The Spirit of God descending like a . . . dove," John answered. "And a voice—a voice from heaven saying, 'This is My beloved Son, in whom I am well-pleased.'"

John and his disciples watched the man Jesus climbing out of the water on the opposite bank of the river—the one facing the wilderness. Instead of turning to follow the meandering Jordan, Jesus, still dripping with water, followed a fluttering dove eastward, toward the desert.

For forty days and forty nights Jesus was tempted, tested, and tried. Hungry, thirsty, and exhausted, He stumbled over the rocks, slept on gritty sand, and wandered aimlessly under a hot and brutal sun. But those physical troubles were nothing compared to the spiritual temptations He would face. Like a relentless warlord constructing a siege ramp to His soul, Satan tempted the Son of God to satisfy His human cravings (Matt. 4:1–4), to circumvent God's plan for salvation through suffering (4:5–7), and simply to fall down and worship him (4:8–11). Though Jesus endured an excruciating period of physical trials and temptations, He emerged victorious, His true qualities shining through—perfect Man and perfect God.

Yet Jesus' trials were not over. During the next three years of public ministry, He would continue to endure rejection, persecution, false accusation, abandonment, insults, mockery, beatings, and finally crucifixion before finishing His work.

KEY TERMS

πειρασμός [*peirasmos*] (3986) "trial, test, temptation"
Though the book of Revelation uses this term to refer to the coming period of global testing prior to the return of Christ (Rev. 3:10), the term generally refers either to tests that challenge the strength of one's faith (as in 1 Peter 1:6) or to "temptations" that challenge one's moral strength (Luke 4:13). James deals with both meanings in his letter: tests of faith in 1:2–12 and temptations to sin in 1:13–18.

ὑπομονή [*hypomonē*] (5281) "patient endurance, perseverance, steadfastness"
This term comes from two Greek words, *hypo* ("under") and *menō* ("abide"), with the basic meaning, "to abide under." It emphasizes the ability to bear the weight of difficult burdens or circumstances, as a beast of burden might abide under a heavy load without collapsing.

θρησκεία [*thrēskeia*] (2356) "religion, worship, piety, devout practices"
The Greek word for "religion" refers not to one's private convictions but to a well-defined religious community or system. Judaism was in this sense a "religion" (Acts 26:5), as was the angel-worshiping cult described in Colossians 2:18 (the "religion of angels"). In James, it refers to the orthodox Christian religion, emphasizing its fundamental beliefs and practices that distinguish it from other "religions."

Believers in Jesus Christ have followed Him in baptism, received the blessing of the Holy Spirit, and been called God's children by adoption. But we often forget that the faith-gift that saved us will continually be put to the test by trials and temptations. Like wanderers in a wilderness of hardships and allurements, we Christians face trials of life and temptations to sin. But like our Lord before us, we can face these harsh realities with confidence, responding to the truths of Scripture with faith and obedience rather than collapsing under temptations.

The book of James develops the overarching theme that *real faith produces genuine works.* In chapter 1, James will argue that when faith is put to the test, it perseveres. It results in stability. To demonstrate this point, he gives three examples. In 1:1–12, he argues that the normal trials that accompany life don't crush genuine faith—they produce endurance. Then, in 1:13–18, James notes the key to overcoming temptations to sin—drawing on God-given strength. Finally, in 1:19–27, James explains that, like the Lord Jesus' trials in the desert, genuine faith results in submission to God's Word, conforming the life of the believer to the image of Christ.

Trials of Life (James 1:1–12)

---

¹James, a bond-servant of God and of the Lord Jesus Christ,
To the twelve tribes who are dispersed abroad: Greetings.
²Consider it all joy, my brethren, when you encounter various trials,
³knowing that the testing of your faith produces endurance. ⁴And let endurance have *its* perfect result, so that you may be perfect and complete, lacking in nothing. ⁵But if any of you lacks wisdom, let him ask of God, who gives to all generously and without reproach, and it will be given to him. ⁶But he must ask in faith without any doubting, for the one who doubts is like the surf of the sea, driven and tossed by the wind. ⁷For that man ought not to expect that he will receive anything from the Lord, ⁸*being* a double-minded man, unstable in all his ways.

⁹But the brother of humble circumstances is to glory in his high position; ¹⁰and the rich man *is to glory* in his humiliation, because like flowering grass he will pass away. ¹¹For the sun rises with a scorching wind and withers the grass; and its flower falls off and the beauty of its appearance is destroyed; so too the rich man in the midst of his pursuits will fade away.

¹²Blessed is a man who perseveres under trial; for once he has been approved, he will receive the crown of life which *the Lord* has promised to those who love Him.

People don't need to march to the drumbeat of daily life or analyze its melody for very long before they realize that much of life's music is played in a minor key. Hurts, heartaches, pain, problems, disappointments, discouragements, sicknesses, suffering, disease, and death form a jarring bass line for what everybody wishes were an upbeat chorus. And however hard we try to conduct the often clamorous orchestra toward a sweeter song, the dissonant chords continually accost our senses.

This reality of suffering creates within us questions regarding God's justice and life's purpose. For millennia, the best philosophers and theologians have attempted to resolve the apparent discord between belief in an all-good and all-powerful God and the pervasiveness of wickedness, evil, and suffering in the world He created. At the same time, scientists and saints alike have struggled against the natural order of things, desperately trying to bring lasting relief to humanity's misery. In the end, many people in this world end up enduring through their short lives by dulling the torment with mind- or body-numbing methods that distract them from the pain but never deliver them from it—drugs, alcohol, entertainment, busyness, education, travel ... even world-denying religious pursuits. But while such things can provide a temporary means of escape, the floodwaters of adversity eventually rise above the highest hills of retreat. Trials of life—or death—eventually overtake everybody. Without exception.

In launching his overarching case that real faith produces genuine works, James begins with an opening argument that many preachers today would prefer to relegate to a closing remark—the problem of suffering and trials in life. But James couldn't have chosen a more relevant issue to begin to test his thesis of the durability of true faith. As we saw in the introduction and greeting, James's dispersed readers were enduring hardship as they tried to come to terms with their new identities as Jewish Christians in a culture that despised both Jews *and* Christians. In a social context like that, it's understandable that these trials would push many toward a more comfortable alternative—either go back to Judaism or stop living out their faith in Christ.

But this situation—or something similar—is not unique to first-century Christians. In fact, life's painful trials have touched every generation of Christians throughout history, including you and me.

— **1:1–4** —

As we discovered in the introduction to James, the recipients of this letter endured adversity. Having been "dispersed abroad," they felt disoriented, disillusioned, and probably downright depressed. They had become the brunt of criticism, brutality, and unjust treatment.

James addresses these beleaguered believers with a single word: "Greetings." Though a common form of official greeting at that time (Acts 15:23), the Greek word *chairein* literally means "to rejoice," as in Romans 12:15—"Rejoice (*chairein*) with those who rejoice!" This contrast between his readers' harried situation and James's exhortation to "count it all joy (*charan*)" in the very next line sets the tone for his letter.

Without hesitating, James leaps headfirst into his most pressing issue—trials. The Greek word James uses for "trial" is *peirasmos,* which appears a second time in 1:12. The word can refer to tests that challenge the integrity of one's faith (as in 1 Peter 1:6). But it can also refer to "temptations," things that appeal to our sinful tendencies and challenge our moral integrity (Luke 4:13). In verses 2–12, James deals with the first meaning—tests that challenge a believer's faith. Then, in verses 13–18, he treats the second meaning—temptations to sin. Before we address the testing aspect of these trials, let's look at two things James tells us in this verse about these tests of faith.

Two Trajectories in James 1

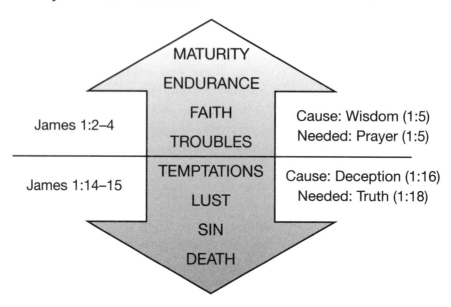

First, he tells us that trials are inevitable. Note that James doesn't say, "Count it all joy *if* you fall into various trials." Instead, he uses the word "when." Like death itself, trials are inescapable and unavoidable. Few things are certain in this world, but troubles, hardship, challenges to faith—count on it—they will come.

Second, James calls the trials "various." It may seem like a waste of time to dwell on such a seemingly unimportant word, but think about it. While we can expect trials to come, we have no idea what form they'll take. The Greek word for "various" (*poikilos*) can mean diverse, variegated, or many-colored. In other words, trials occur in all shapes and sizes. Like unwelcome guests, they burst into our lives unannounced and stay too long! Trials may be frequent and frustrating or epic and life-changing. We can never predict.

But James also pulls back the veil and lets his readers see the inner workings of trials, revealing that they have a purpose. As he cuts the pathway of the Christian journey through life, James declares that the trials produce both immediate and ultimate results.

First, *the testing of faith produces endurance* (1:3). That's the immediate result. The Greek word for "testing" is *dokimion*. It refers to a means of authenticating something. Like a prospector biting into a gold nugget to test its quality, God applies specific tests to each of His children, assessing their faith to reveal its true character.

Note that the object of God's testing is "your faith." Our heavenly Father is no mad scientist trying to torture his subjects to the breaking point. He's more like an expert trainer who knows which muscles to develop, what diet to follow, and what schedule to keep in order to bring about the best results. The goal is not to snap our faith muscles, but to stretch and strengthen them, producing *endurance*—a term derived from two Greek words that together literally mean "to abide under." We would say, "to hang in there."

Endurance is just the initial result. Endurance itself has an even greater purpose, a "perfect result" (lit., "perfect work"). God says, in effect, "In My sovereign plan I've lined up a chain of events that will take place, and My finger of testing pushes the first one—endurance." When endurance takes place, it bumps into maturity, which leads ultimately to a fully developed character.

The people I regard as having great Christian character invariably have learned how to handle life in the crucible. It's the mother who's lost a child and is able to say to God, "You gave, and You took away. Blessed be Your name." It's the father who, having given his best at the firm for years, loses his job and says to his family, "Let's get together tonight and thank God for this opportunity to trust Him." It's the teenager who says, "I won't surrender my principles. I'll maintain my standards even though I am shunned and treated like an outsider by my peers." That's the marvelous quality of maturity. A completeness and wholeness emerge when we patiently "hang in there."

James states that inevitable trials take various forms in our lives to bring about specific purposes—building the quality of endurance and leading His children toward maturity. In these verses he also answers the "how" question. How can Christians, neck-deep in troubles, rise above their situations without dropping out, giving in, or falling short? What can they do to handle the various trials that come their way? Verses 2–4 give specific commands James wanted his readers to follow: "consider" (1:2), "know" (1:3), and "let … have" (1:4). Each is worth a closer look.

The Greek word translated "consider" has an interesting background. The word comes from a root term that means to lead or guide, from which we get our word "hegemony," the leading influence or guide of something. The Greek term could be used for a person at the front of a line, leading a procession. James thus says our leading thought should be joy, behind which all our other attitudes and actions fall in line.

James uses a present participle for the word "knowing," which is his way of telling his readers how they can stay joyful, positive, even calm in the midst of trials. By knowing that God has a greater purpose in the testing, the believer is able to "consider it all joy."

Finally, James encourages his readers to "let endurance have its perfect result" (1:4). The language communicates the idea of cooperation with God's work. We find a similar idea of a passive cooperation with God's plan in 1 Peter 5:6: "Humble yourselves under the mighty hand of God, that He may exalt you at the proper time." Just as a potter may use her fingers to mold a work of art, so God's fingers work through various circumstances to bring about His perfect result of maturity and completeness in the lives of His people.

So, how do believers rise above troubles in everyday life? They face them with a deliberate attitude of joy, calling to mind the process that God is working out in their lives, and cooperating with Him throughout the entire process.

— 1:5–8 —

After giving a behind-the-scenes look at the ultimate purpose of trials and offering practical advice on how to endure them positively, James continues the theme by answering another lingering question: "Why do trials overwhelm us? Why do we sometimes cave in? What things block the joy of enduring life in the crucible?" The answer? *Our lack of wisdom.*

Therefore, whenever we feel ill-equipped to handle a trial, we have one option: ask God for wisdom. In this context, wisdom can be defined as the ability to view life from God's perspective. James says this kind of wisdom comes by prayer (1:5). It might be something as simple as, "Lord, in the midst of this loss or heartache or failure, I ask You for wisdom. Help me, first to see what I'm going through from Your viewpoint, and then I ask for faith not to give up."

Of course, when we feel overwhelmed, faith can be hard to come by. Just as a lack of wisdom can cause us to become overwhelmed, so a lack of faith can result in our caving in. James isn't referring to saving faith in verse 6. He has in mind sustaining faith—the kind of faith that allows us to endure trials, to align our will and our attitude with a divine perspective, abandoning ourselves to God and His mighty hand.

The opposite of faith is doubt. James compares a person who doubts to the "surf of the sea," driven by the wind. The word "surf," *klydōn*, is used in the gospel of Luke when the disciples thought they would perish in the storm on the Sea of Galilee. They awakened Jesus, who immediately "rebuked the wind and the surging waves [*klydōn*]" (Luke 8:24). Interestingly, the first words out of Jesus' mouth after calming the storm were, "Where is your faith?" (8:25).

James describes this kind of deep-seated doubt as being "double-minded" (James 1:8). The word *dipsychos* literally means "two-souled." It appears here in the book of James for the first time in all of Greek literature, and James may even have invented the word.[1] By the way, if you invent a word, you get to define it — so let's let James define it for us. James uses the term again in 4:8 — "Purify your hearts, you double-minded." It indicates an impurity of our inner person. Where there should be one thought, goal, attitude, or devotion, we find two competing thoughts. Consequently, a double-minded person is one who wants his or her will and at the same time God's will. That kind of person is unstable in *everything* he does. Pause and imagine what happens when a double-minded individual faces a double-barrel trial in life!

I've never done this — and I probably should warn you not to try this without professional supervision — but I've heard it said that one of the cheapest and easiest ways to catch a monkey is to cut off the end a hollow, long-necked gourd, fill it with rice, and tie it to a tree. The hungry monkey will push his scrawny little hand into the thin neck of the gourd to grab the rice. He'll clutch it with his hand and try to pull it out, but the monkey's fist is bigger than the gourd's neck. He's trapped, because that hungry, shortsighted monkey won't release the rice to remove his fist. He simply lacks the wisdom to decide that freedom without the rice is better than captivity with a meal.

That's the double-minded Christian. Inside the gourd is my will. Yes, part of me wants to live in God's will; but the other part wants it on my terms. And when a trial comes, I refuse to release my grip and trust that the purpose and plan of God will bring true freedom.

— **1:9–12** —

Trials affect everybody — even the wealthy, who sometimes believe they have a shield of protection, or at least a cushion to blunt the fall. But wisdom and faith are required for both poor and rich. For the poor person, who continues to endure the challenges of lacking worldly wealth, God's wisdom can remind him of his high position. What high position is this? James probably has in mind the position believers have in Christ. Paul describes it this way: "[God] raised us up with Him [Christ], and seated us with Him in the heavenly places in Christ Jesus, so that in the ages to come He might show the surpassing riches of His grace in kindness toward us in Christ Jesus" (Eph. 2:6–7).

For the wealthy, the worst trials come when they lose their worldly riches or when troubles enter their lives that money can't deflect. A rich person, too, is then reminded of the fragility of life (James 1:10). If such an individual fails to cooperate with the work of God, but instead, like a monkey grasping the rice, is determined to have his own will, he will fade away, as James says, "in the midst of his pursuits" (1:11).

But the one who stands up under the weight of trials will be blessed. The word "blessed" (*makarios*) means "genuinely happy." Jesus repeated the word some nine times in the introduction to His Sermon on the Mount (Matt. 5:3–11). Quite likely, the last couple of those beatitudes form the background of James's own teaching:

> "Blessed are those who have been persecuted for the sake of righteousness, for theirs is the kingdom of heaven.
> Blessed are you when people insult you and persecute you, and falsely say all kinds of evil against you because of Me. Rejoice and be glad, for your reward in heaven is great. (Matt. 5:10–12a)

James describes the reward in heaven as "the crown of life" (James 1:12). Without denying the future reward in store for those who endure trials and tests, I think there's a temporal crown, too. I believe the person who truly lives in the Christian life is the one who perseveres under the trial. They are rewarded in this life with maturity, wisdom, and insight into God's purposeful plan. That's real life at its best!

Application

Rising Above Trials

It seems so easy to whistle songs of praise when the sun shines on us, when a glorious dawn breaks, and when life's forecast looks bright and clear. It's quite another thing to praise our heavenly Father when a dark sky frowns at us, thunder rolls in, and violent storms of trouble break over our lives. How can anyone sing when days grow dark and nights are long? But this is exactly what James calls us to do, to respond to life's inevitable trials with joy, with wisdom, and with firm confidence in Him.

With an eye toward our personal response to God's truth, let's revisit two ways we can handle adversity.

First, *when troubles come, it's essential that we respond with wisdom*. This insight into trials doesn't come naturally. Wisdom for handling trials can come only from God; and the primary means He uses to give us wisdom is His Word. Calling to mind specific statements from Scripture that address this issue will help you respond appropriately in times of trouble. Let me offer three passages to chew on. I suggest you turn to each one and linger there. Romans 8:28 tells us that "all things" work out in God's sovereign plan for our good. Hebrews 12:1–3 turns our attention on Jesus and other fellow sufferers who have gone before as models of endurance. And 1 Peter 1:6–7 reminds us that endurance will ultimately result in praise, glory, and honor. Meditate on those passages to gain God's wisdom on trials.

Second, *when troubles come, we should respond in faith.* In the context of trials, faith means having absolute confidence in God's promises in the midst of circumstances that appear to contradict those promises. In the middle of a trial, it may appear as if God has allowed everything to crumble. To those who lack the insight and faith to see beyond their circumstances, it may appear as if our lives are in a tailspin, heading for catastrophe. But single-minded, focused faith means making a conscious decision, with God's help, to choose our attitude. It means surrendering fully to God because we trust Him, resisting the natural tendency to abandon hope.

This is where we can help each other. God's Spirit strengthens personal faith in the community of faith. Paul sent Timothy to Thessalonica to "strengthen and encourage" their faith (1 Thess. 3:2). The author of Hebrews exhorts his readers to hold fast their confession of hope by meeting together frequently to "stimulate one another to love and good deeds" (Heb. 10:24). Remember that God has not left us on our own to endure these things. He has given us a whole body of believers to strengthen and encourage our faith. Accept the gift He has given.

If you are wounded and hurting, undergoing seasons of deep sorrows and pain, I pray that you never forget the importance of endurance — of "abiding under." May God grant you, by His Spirit and through His Word, both wisdom and faith to reap the blessing of maturity He is working in you.

Temptations to Sin (James 1:13–18)

¹³Let no one say when he is tempted, "I am being tempted by God"; for God cannot be tempted by evil, and He Himself does not tempt anyone. ¹⁴But each one is tempted when he is carried away and enticed by his own lust. ¹⁵Then when lust has conceived, it gives birth to sin; and when sin is accomplished, it brings forth death. ¹⁶Do not be deceived, my beloved brethren. ¹⁷Every good thing given and every perfect gift is from above, coming down from the Father of lights, with whom there is no variation or shifting shadow. ¹⁸In the exercise of His will He brought us forth by the word of truth, so that we would be a kind of first fruits among His creatures.

Marcus Antonius — better known as simply Mark Antony — was a famous Roman statesman from 83 to 30 BC. A supporter of Julius Caesar and eventually one of three co-rulers of the empire, that silver-tongued orator could sway the masses like no other man in his day. Not only did he have the gift of dynamic public speaking, but he also was a cunning general and a brilliant thinker. Yet his military and intellectual skills lacked the power to conquer his moral weakness. In fact, an exasperated tutor—frustrated with the prospect of such a gifted youth being spoiled by moral failure—shouted in his face, "O Marcus! O colossal child! Able to conquer the world ... but unable to resist a temptation!"

That indictment could be made against far too many "Mark Antonys" today. Many Christians are supersaturated with education, biblical knowledge, inspiring examples of moral successes, and sobering warnings from moral failures. Yet far too many have driven headlong into temptation, suffering disaster at work, church, and the home. Temptation knows no limits. It respects no title. It plays no favorites. It ignores all human obstacles, cares nothing about the time of day or night, and camouflages itself in any situation, prepared to pounce at any moment. Temptation has many faces—stealing, lying, gossiping, cheating, envying, striving for popularity, vying for power ... the list seems endless.

In the previous section, James dealt with the kind of "trials" of life that test a person's ability to keep the faith, despite extreme pressure to give in. In this section, James explores the other meaning of that word *peirasmos*—a test of moral endurance. In six short verses he presents the truth about temptation in a straightforward manner. Rather than skimming the surface of temptation, as many preachers and teachers tend to do, James probes deeply below the surface to reveal the inner workings of temptation. But less like a psychologist and more like a physician, James begins with certain facts that describe temptation (1:13–16); from there he moves to a focus that determines victory (1:17–18).

— **1:13** —

James wants his fellow believers to understand at least four things about temptation. First, temptation is always present; "no one" is exempt from it. Like tests of faith, temptations are inevitable. There is no spiritual vaccine, no "get out of temptation free" card, no alternate route to avoid the traps along the trail. Not a person reading these words is immune or innocent. The aging monk in the monastery is no more safe from temptation than the young man at the mall. The saint in prayer wrestles with temptation just as much as the salesman in his Porsche.

Second, temptation is never prompted by God: "Let no one say ... 'I am being tempted by God'" (1:13). A small but important detail appears in the Greek text. The word translated "by" in this verse is *apo*. James had a couple options for expressing the way in which temptations might come from God. The preposition *hypo* would have meant direct agency, used of Satan, who directly tempted Jesus to sin (Matt. 4:1). Clearly God doesn't whisper evil thoughts into our minds or create an alluring mental image. But James's use of *apo* goes even further at exonerating God. The preposition refers to the origin of something—temptation to sin doesn't have its ultimate origin in God. God isn't even *indirectly* involved in temptation. While God uses trials and troubles in life to bring about His work of maturing us (James 1:1–12), God is never the author of temptation or evil. Never!

God's absolute goodness and holiness guarantee the truth of James's statement. To be holy means to be separate from evil, set apart, unaffected. Holiness has two sides—the inability to be affected by evil and the inability to cause evil. For God, who is the absolute standard of holiness, both are true. James says God is not able to be tempted, nor does He tempt. He's holy!

—1:14–15—

The third fact to understand about temptation is that temptation always follows a consistent process. James introduces his statement with "but," indicating a contrast. In contrast to the wrong view that God is the author of temptation, James reveals the true source. In verse 14, James implies that temptation originates in some kind of external object. In the same verse, he clearly states that the one tempted is "enticed by his own lust." The term "enticed" is a fishing term, meaning "to bait." So, a lure gets dropped into our lives—something external. That, in itself, is not sin. Our problem is that deep within us a hunger stirs, a desire to take the bait: *lust.* Through persuasion of curiosity mixed with a big dose of rationalization, we find ourselves drawn toward the lure, motivated by our own desire to *have.*

At this point James uses the preposition *hypo*—we are tempted "by the direct agency of" our own lust. Note the contrast! Whereas God is not even remotely a part of the temptation, not even indirectly, our lustful desire is the *direct cause* of our sin. In fact, we can't even blame the alluring bait! The temptation itself is a necessary cause, but not a sufficient cause. The point? We, *alone*, are culpable.

Dietrich Bonhoeffer, the courageous German theologian put to death by the Nazis for taking a stand against Hitler's evil regime, articulates the process of temptation as clearly as I've ever found it explained:

> In our members there is a slumbering inclination towards desire which is both sudden and fierce. With irresistible power desire seizes mastery over the flesh. All at once a secret, smouldering fire is kindled. The flesh burns and is in flames. It makes no difference whether it is sexual desire, or ambition, or vanity, or desire

for revenge, or love of fame and power, or greed for money, or, finally, that strange desire for the beauty of the world, of nature. Joy in God is in course of being extinguished in us and we seek all our joy in the creature. At this moment God is quite unreal to us, he loses all reality, and only desire for the creature is real; the only reality is the devil. Satan does not here fill us with hatred of God, but with forgetfulness of God.[2]

In sum, James 1:14 describes the essential ingredients for temptation: an alluring outward bait plus our inward desire. When these two are combined with a will that yields to the temptation, the result is disaster, described in verse 15.

James begins verse 15 with the word "then." The order of steps in the process is clear. The word "conceived" is literally used for the conception of a child and comes from two Greek words, *syn* and *lambano*, "to take together." In this context, James emphasizes that when the two necessary ingredients join—the object of temptation and the internal lust—then temptation is conceived. A cycle is set in motion that, if allowed to run its course, results in a sinful act.

King David illustrates James 1:14–15 in a radical way. While his armies were out fighting, David stayed in Jerusalem, lounging and lingering at the palace (2 Sam. 11:1). Had he been with his army where he was supposed to be, he could have avoided the downward plunge into immorality. But instead of waging physical war on the battlefield, David fought a spiritual war against temptation—and lost. It started out innocently enough. As he meandered on the palace roof, the king's wandering eyes caught a woman bathing (11:2). This accidental glance was not itself a sin. But mixed with David's restless urges, that unintentional glance quickly became a willful stare. He noticed she was "very beautiful" (11:2). The focus of his gaze and his internal desires conceived a powerful temptation that few men in David's position could resist. Like a victim dropping through a trap door, David's plunge from temptation to sin followed in a break-neck progression. He inquired about her (11:3) . . . sent for her (11:4) . . . and slept with her (11:4)—all the while knowing she was Bathsheba, the wife of Uriah the Hittite (11:3).

David's sin didn't end in adultery. His immorality turned into desperate attempts at cover up, leading ultimately to two deaths—the death of Uriah the Hittite and the death of his son, the product of his one-night stand (2 Sam. 11:5–12:14). From lust to death, David's temptation becomes a textbook example of temptation and sexual lust, almost as if he took the slippery slope of sin in James 1:14–15 as a script.

The most frightening thing about David's sin is that it happened to "a man after [God's] own heart" (1 Sam. 13:14). If such a great man of God can fall so suddenly and so severely, we shouldn't think for a moment that it can't happen to us. That's the bad news about temptation.

The good news is, any temptation can be resisted. A person can resist the desire, turn from the bait, and retrace his or her steps, thus canceling the process. But if the one tempted coddles the desire, embraces the enticement, and runs (or even wanders) into the trap, the result is the act of sin. Don't miss the progression. When some allurement carries us away, we move into the realm of temptation. When we allow temptation to linger, we eventually sin. And when sin continues without repentance, it results in death—a deathlike existence (James 1:15). Sin, that monstrous offspring of depravity, has gone through its conception, development, birth, growth, and finally death. That's James's life cycle of sin.

It would help to linger over the word "death" in James 1:15. Sometimes people can die as a result of sin, such as those infected with diseases through sexual sin or those whose alcoholism or drug addiction leads to premature death. Paul, James, and John all refer to sins that can lead to sickness or even death, apparently a result of God's temporal discipline of saints for the sake of their ultimate sanctification (1 Cor. 11:30; James 5:15; 1 John 5:16–17). James 1:15, however, cannot refer primarily to physical death as a result of temptation and sin. If it did, then all of us would be corpses within days. We wouldn't be able to live through it. James doesn't mean spiritual death, either. Our good works don't save us, nor do our bad works condemn us. Paul says we are saved by grace through faith apart from works (Eph. 2:8–9). There is now "no condemnation for those who are in Christ Jesus" (Rom. 8:1). So, if James isn't talking about physical death or spiritual death as a result of sin, then to what death is he referring?

This is where recognizing James's Jewish background becomes helpful. In Jewish thinking, death was often seen more as a trajectory than a destination. To be "dead" was often a description of the poor quality of life rather than the cessation of being. Deuteronomy 30:15 says, "See, I have set before you today life and prosperity, and death and adversity." We also see this choice between "life existence" and "death existence" in Proverbs: "In the way of righteousness is life, / And in its pathway there is no death" (Prov. 12:28); "The teaching of the wise is a fountain of life, / To turn aside from the snares of death" (13:14).

Jewish Christians saw people as either traveling the path of life (walking with Christ by the Spirit) or the path of death (walking apart from Christ in the flesh). This "death-like existence" is the opposite of the "abundant life" Christ promised (John 10:10). No longer can the sinner, walking in death, live out the true life in the Spirit—"love, joy, peace, patience, kindness, goodness, faithfulness, gentleness, self-control" (Gal. 5:22–23). For those walking in death, gone are the signs of spiritual vitality, like fading memories of estranged friends. That's the kind of death James has in mind.

From My Journal

Focus and Flee

During the sixteen months I spent on the island of Okinawa as a twentysomething young man in the Marine Corps, thousands of miles away from my wife and family, I learned the value of focusing on God's Word. I was involved in a Bible study with other guys in the military service. We came from different bases on the island every Friday night and made our way to the home of The Navigators' representative, Bob Newkirk, who lived in Naha, the capital city. Between my base (Camp Courtney) and Bob's home lay several villages, each having numerous bars and brothels. The prostitutes on the island were both plentiful and available ... always willing to give themselves to young and lonely men. Bob knew of the strong temptations all of us faced every Friday night as we made our way to his home, week after week.

He taught us a simple formula: *"Focus and flee,"* he would say. We learned to walk straight ahead, never looking to the left or right, as we focused on specific "victory verses" we had memorized. In addition, one learned to keep a fast pace—he even suggested to *run* at times. (I discovered that it's impossible to run and lust at the same time.) Looking back on those months, I am *so* grateful for Bob's counsel. More important, I am thankful that God's Word really can keep a young man (and older ones, too!) pure, as we read in Psalm 119:9–11,

> How can a young man keep his way pure?
> By keeping it according to Your word.
> With all my heart I have sought You;
> Do not let me wander from Your commandments.
> Your word I have treasured in my heart,
> That I may not sin against You.

Now that I have grandsons in their teen years, I am passing along the same counsel to them as we spend time together reading and discussing the Scriptures. The same focus on the "victory verses" that once worked for me is now working for them.

We have seen that temptation is always present (1:13) and that God never prompts it (1:13). We also have explored the consistent process that temptation follows (1:14–15). The fourth fact James notes regarding temptation is that it flourishes on inconsistent thinking (1:16).

—1:16—

James abruptly breaks into his description of temptation, sin, and its consequences with a clear command: "Do not be deceived, my beloved brethren." Do not be led astray. The lures of temptation will come in many forms and at different times. Don't let your thoughts stray away from the truth toward the deception of false-hood. Because the process of temptation begins in the mind, we must force our-selves to face the facts, to apply the truth, and to review the consequences of our lustful actions in advance. Allurement builds its case on deceptive thoughts and empty promises. Don't buy it.

—1:17–18—

Having vividly described the facts of temptation, James then turns his readers' attention in these final two verses to the source of victory: God.

God provides the means of victory over the subtle allurements of temptation and sin. Anything good and perfect comes from the One who is Himself good and perfect. He is "the Father of lights," who dispels the darkness of deception. And He is the unchanging one, in whom there is no "variation or shifting shadow," unlike the allurements of temptation. We should note a contrast between the irresponsible sinner James quoted in 1:13 ("I am being tempted by God") and the reality of God's role in the lives of believers—goodness and perfection (1:17).

The One who creates things good and perfect is the One who "brought us forth by the word of truth" (1:18; see Col. 1:5; 2 Tim. 2:15). The work He continues to do in us is done by that same word. We were designed to be "first fruits" among His creatures, not spoiled fruit rotting on the vine.

In the previous section (1:1–12), James argued that trials of our faith were given for our good—to mature us. But God's wisdom can help bring about their intended result. In this section (1:13–18), James has explained that temptations to sin come not from God but from our own sinful nature. But God's good and per-fect gifts can bring victory through His Word. James contrasts two trajectories in the lives of believers—one toward maturity, the other toward sin; one by enduring trials, the other by succumbing to temptations; one upward on the path of abundant life, the other downward on the slippery slope of death. (See the chart, "Two Trajectories in James 1" on page 28 above.) James implies a question for all who read his inspired words: Which path are you on?

Application

Focus That Determines Victory

Sow a thought, you reap an act;
Sow an act, you reap a habit;
Sow a habit, you reap a character;
Sow a character, you reap a destiny.
—Author Unknown

Those words poignantly reflect the warning of James. The "insignificant" thoughts, the "minor" transgressions, the "harmless" habits — all these can snowball into lifestyles that will obliterate the testimony of the most respected saint. And they force the obvious question: How can we avoid the slippery slope of sin and stand victorious against the allurement of temptation?

First, *victory comes through dwelling on the good*. James notes that good and perfect gifts come from God the Father (1:17). Surely, He gives these good things for a reason. You can't harbor evil in your mind and reap good results, nor can you nurture good and wholesome thoughts in your heart and constantly produce evil. So, not surprisingly, you must dwell on the good in order to reap the good. While addressing the value of allowing the peace of God to guard our hearts and minds, Paul writes, "Finally, brethren, whatever is true, whatever is honorable, whatever is right, whatever is pure, whatever is lovely, whatever is of good repute, if there is any excellence and if anything worthy of praise, dwell on these things" (Phil. 4:8).

Honestly now, do you do that? When you feel overwhelmed by a particular problem, what do you think about? What do you read? To whom do you listen? What do you dwell on? Take some time to evaluate the kinds of seeds you sow in the fertile garden of your mind. Are they seeds that grow into thoughts that are true, honorable, right, pure, lovely, good, excellent, and worthy of praise? Or are you slowly poisoning your mind and setting yourself up for failure when the inevitable tempests of temptation blow through your life?

Second, *victory comes through living in the truth*. James says that we have been brought forth "by the word of truth" (1:18). That same motherly word that gave birth to us will also nurture and protect us, giving us all we need to grow. And when those inevitable and appealing temptations come, God's Word can literally deliver us from evil. King David said, "Your word I have treasured in my heart, / That I may not sin against You" (Ps. 119:11).

How are you treasuring God's Word in your heart? Do you merely dabble in Scripture now and then, or do you immerse yourself in its purifying, refreshing waters? Do you search through it mechanically to satisfy your curiosities, or do you allow it to search you in order to cleanse your heart and mind? Reading, memorizing, and meditating on God's Word—the greatest and most perfect gift from above—will help you to stand strong in the moment of temptation.

Take this opportunity right now to ask the Holy Spirit to do soul surgery in your life. Pray the prayer David once prayed:

Search me, O God, and know my heart;
Try me and know my anxious thoughts;
And see if there be any hurtful way in me,
And lead me in the everlasting way. (Ps. 139:23–24)

Whatever your particular temptations may be, no matter how relentless they are, the Father is ready to provide the good and perfect gifts that will strengthen your heart with His life-giving power and personal victory. I can tell you from my own, personal experience, focusing on God's Word *works*.

Response to Scripture (James 1:19–27)

---

[19]*This* you know, my beloved brethren. But everyone must be quick to hear, slow to speak *and* slow to anger; [20]for the anger of man does not achieve the righteousness of God. [21]Therefore, putting aside all filthiness and *all* that remains of wickedness, in humility receive the word implanted, which is able to save your souls. [22]But prove yourselves doers of the word, and not merely hearers who delude themselves. [23]For if anyone is a hearer of the word and not a doer, he is like a man who looks at his natural face in a mirror; [24]for *once* he has looked at himself and gone away, he has immediately forgotten what kind of person he was. [25]But one who looks intently at the perfect law, the *law* of liberty, and abides by it, not having become a forgetful hearer but an effectual doer, this man will be blessed in what he does.

[26]If anyone thinks himself to be religious, and yet does not bridle his tongue but deceives his *own* heart, this man's religion is worthless. [27]Pure and undefiled religion in the sight of *our* God and Father is this: to visit orphans and widows in their distress, and to keep oneself unstained by the world.

A debilitating "disease" is crippling the body of Christ—a syndrome so common that it seems to affect every believer with either a mild or acute case. This insidious condition neutralizes the church's impact and nullifies her testimony. It can diminish effectiveness and paralyze production. The problem? A rupture between confession and deed ... theology and action ... hearing and doing. For too many of us Christians, God's Word fails to make it from the head to the heart. And for many more, His Word gets lodged between the heart and the hands.

A. W. Tozer vividly portrays the situation:

> So wide is the gulf that separates theory from practice in the church that an inquiring stranger who chances upon both would scarcely dream that there was any relation between them. An intelligent observer of our human scene who heard the Sunday morning sermon and later watched the Sunday afternoon conduct of those who had heard it would conclude that he has been examining two distinct and contrary religions....
>
> It appears that too many Christians want to enjoy the thrill of feeling right but are not willing to endure the inconvenience of being right. So the divorce between theory and practice becomes permanent in fact, though in word the union is declared to be eternal. Truth sits forsaken and grieves till her professed followers come home for a brief visit, but she sees them depart again when the bills become due.[3]

In developing his overarching lesson that *real faith produces genuine works*, James has already dealt with the Christian's perseverance through trials, which proves our faith (1:1–12) and the believer's victory over temptation, which demonstrates our character (1:13–18). In this final section of chapter 1, James zooms in on the believer's appropriate response to God's Word. The break in the relationship between belief and behavior may be pandemic among Christians, but James reminds us that the two estranged partners of the Christian walk *can* be reconciled.

— 1:19–20 —

James begins with a reminder: "This you know, my beloved brethren." He's writing, unquestionably, to believers, to brothers and sisters in Christ. And he begins by acknowledging that they already know what he's about to say. James is saying, "Yes, I know you're aware of what I'm about to cover, but you need to hear it again. I feel the need to review it, to revisit some basics." In that sense, the phrase "you know" serves as a mild command: "Remember!" As we will soon see, it's also a rebuke: "You've forgotten!"

What is the content of this knowledge? Three important things fertilize the soil of the heart in preparation for receiving the planting of God's Word in our hearts (1:21). First, James urges us to be "quick to hear" (1:19). The command means more than merely listening intently. James wants us to genuinely receive the words spoken.

Let me give you an illustration. You probably know from experience that there are two ways of reading a book. The first kind of "reading" — if it can be called that — is the assigned reading in school or college. The eyes scan the pages of words, sentences pass across the retina, but the ideas don't seem to make it into the brain. The goal of that kind of reading is to place a check box in the reading report. But another kind of reading — authentic reading — includes highlighting or underlining important points, taking notes, even incorporating the ideas in discussions or reports. It should be obvious which student actually *read* the book. The same is true for listening.

Jesus Himself complained about hypocrites in His day: "You will keep on hearing, but will not understand" (Matt. 13:14). And He followed this sentiment with an interpretation of His parable of the sower: "The one on whom seed was sown on the rocky places, this is the man who hears the word and immediately receives it with joy; yet he has no firm root in himself, but is only temporary, and when affliction or persecution arises because of the word, immediately he falls away" (13:20–21). Jesus' teaching forms the background of James's letter. Having just discussed the need to endure through trials of life and overcome temptations to sin (James 1:1–18), he warns that failure to receive the Word of God with a ready heart can lead to disaster (1:19–27).

The second ingredient of preparing the heart to receive God's Word effectively includes putting a damper on the tongue. That's the other side to listening well. Keeping our mouths shut makes room for thinking, pondering, meditating, considering — all the elements necessary for true listening (and learning).

Finally, right on the heels of "slow to speak," James attaches the phrase "slow to anger." In the Greek text, James doesn't include a conjunction like "and" between these admonitions. All three are so closely related to preconditions for receiving the planting of the Word that James conceives of them as links in a chain.

How does being "slow to anger" relate to the reception of the Word? It relates in part to the function of the Word in the lives of believers. Paul tells us, "All Scripture is inspired by God and profitable for teaching, for reproof, for correction, for training in righteousness" (2 Tim. 3:16). When the Word hits close to home, a sinner most naturally responds with defensiveness, indignation, even anger. Nobody likes their crookedness held up to a perfect standard, but that's just what happens when we let God's Word expose our innermost thoughts and actions. Instead of allowing the typical response of anger, James calls us to respond in peace, "for the anger of man does not achieve the righteousness of God" (1:20). Anger rejects rebuke; peace accepts it. Anger dismisses correction; peace embraces it.

—**1:21**—

After preparing to receive the truth by opening the ears of the heart, zipping the lips, and suppressing the urge to strike back (1:19–20), we are ready to properly receive the truth (1:21). Nestled in the center of this short verse is a simple command that ties the whole section together: *receive*. The word *dechomai* usually means more than to passively "accept." It often includes the idea of fully embracing, making the thing part of oneself. The word is used of people "receiving" Jesus hospitably (John 4:45). More appropriate for the usage in James, the Bereans "received [*dechomai*] the word with great eagerness, examining the Scriptures daily to see whether these things were so" (Acts 17:11). Similarly, the Thessalonian believers not only "received the word in much tribulation with the joy of the Holy Spirit" (1 Thess. 1:6), but they also received it "not as the word of men, but for what it really is, the word of God" (2:13). These passages illustrate the eagerness, the earnest reception James has in mind in 1:21.

With the conjunction "therefore," James rests this command on his previous admonishment to be quick to listen, slow to speak, and slow to anger (1:19–20). *Because* an angry response to the Word does not achieve God's righteousness, we must *therefore* receive the Word a certain way. James describes the conditions that must accompany this reception: putting aside all filthiness, putting aside all that remains of wickedness, and putting on humility. Filthiness in life plugs our hearing. Wickedness slows our response time. Pride keeps us from exposing our true selves to the light of the Word. But humility means submitting to whatever the Word has to tell us, ready to put off the thoughts and deeds of the old lifestyle in favor of the attitudes and actions of the new.

—**1:22–25**—

The logic in James's progression of preparing for, receiving, and responding to the truth is simple and elegant. First, the soil of our souls should be prepared (1:19–20). Second, the seed of truth must be planted (1:21). And third, the smothering weeds of anger, filth, and wickedness must be uprooted (1:19–21). But having gotten this

From My Journal

My Years as an Auditor

For many years I was simply an "auditor," not an "actor" … a "hearer," not a "doer" of the Word. Though I take full responsibility for my former condition, it didn't help that I attended a church where the Bible was opened and dealt with like a textbook. I got so much information my ears could hardly stay together as my head swelled with all sorts of new truth that never made that all-important journey down to my heart and out into my hands. Sunday after Sunday the lectures from the pulpit stacked fact upon fact until I thought I knew it all.

God had to get me out of that classroom Christianity to break the auditor mentality. And that's just what He did. One man—a true mentor—was honest enough to look me in the eye and set me straight. "Chuck, you know more truth than our whole group of Christians put together, but it sure doesn't show. That's called hypocrisy!" He got my attention. As time passed, I began to see the Scriptures not as a textbook of information, arguments, and logical propositions to satisfy my intellectual curiosity, but as the living Word of truth, given by God to alter my attitudes and change my actions.

A lifetime of pastoral ministry has shown me that the church has too many "auditors" of the Word. I see the old me in the faces of so many people in the pews. They have their notebooks packed full of notes, but they would be hard-pressed to show any significant changes they made based on those notes. I can no longer settle for that kind of Christianity. I want well-grounded faith, and I long for it to result in well-rounded living.

far in the process, God's Word still hasn't borne fruit in our lives. This requires a proper response (1:22–27).

James begins with a command: "Prove yourselves doers of the word, and not merely hearers" (1:22). If one phrase in James's letter could be called a key phrase, this is it. That phrase sums up the whole theme of the book—*real faith produces genuine works.* Those who hear without doing may be guilty of "fake faith," but those who hear and do demonstrate their authenticity. Note that James doesn't simply tell his readers to be "doers." He pairs it with the other side of the coin—not merely "hearers." Hearing, listening, and receiving the word is a necessary first step. The word must be understood and lodged in our hearts. That's the key. But James contrasts the one who hears and acts with the one who simply hears.

Let me illustrate this with something you frequently run across in colleges or universities, though you may not realize it immediately. In many classes you have what they call "auditors." They are merely *hearers* of the instruction. They sign up for the class, pay a nominal auditor's fee, and then sit through the lectures. But beyond that, everything is optional. Some may take notes, but they're not required to do so. Some might read the textbook, but that's optional, too. Auditors don't write papers or take tests. They're not in it for course credit because they are merely *hearers* of the instruction, not doers. In contrast, James says the Christian life is one not only of hearing, but of doing. Those who merely hear the Word without acting on it "delude themselves" (1:22).

James follows this exhortation to be doers of the Word with an illustration (2:23–25). He describes two kinds of Christians who show up for church. Believe me, four decades of pastoral ministry have shown me that the same thing is true today! I see these different brands of Christians in every church. The first is what we call the "forgetful hearer" (1:23–24). James uses the illustration of a man who glances in the mirror, sees what he looks like (which apparently isn't attractive), then shrugs, walks away, and does nothing about it. Similarly, God's spiritual mirror shows you what kind of person you are. James pictures a man who glances at the Scriptures, looks at words on the page, and then closes it and goes his way, forgetting what God said about his condition.

The second kind of Christian is the "effectual doer" of the Word (1:25). What characterizes this person? He gives careful attention to the Scriptures, called by James the "perfect law, the law of liberty." He thinks deeply, obeys willingly, responds positively, and abides by its principles. Instead of hearing and forgetting, he hears and does. This person will be blessed in what he does—made genuinely happy in his pursuit of doing what is right.

— **1:26 – 27** —

James describes a true adherent of his or her religion. The Greek word for "religion," *thrēskeia*, used twice in these verses, refers not to one's personal convictions or principles, but to a well-defined religious community or organization. Judaism was in this sense a "religion" (Acts 26:5), as was the angel-worshiping cult described in Colossians 2:18 (the "religion of angels"). James is therefore referring to Christianity as a distinct body of believers. This is important to note, because James says a person who does not control his tongue, but who says one thing and does another, actually makes his or her religion worthless (James 1:26). How many times have we seen this to be true! When unbelievers witness the hypocrisy of Christians, it too often makes the whole *religion* look bad, not just the person claiming the name.

In his typical way, James provides a positive example to contrast his negative. Those who live consistently with their religion give attention to the needs of others. Visiting orphans and widows and keeping oneself unstained by the world — these clear examples of genuine faith demonstrate the uniqueness and truthfulness of the Christian message.

NOTES:

1. Stanley E. Porter, "Is *Dipsychos* (James 1,8; 4,8) a 'Christian' Word?" *Biblica* 71 (1990): 469–98.
2. Dietrich Bonhoeffer, *Creation and Fall; Temptation: Two Biblical Studies* (New York: Collier, 1959), 116–17.
3. A. W. Tozer, *The Root of the Righteous* (Camp Hill, PA: Christian Publications, 1986), 51–53.

REAL FAITH PRODUCES GENUINE LOVE (JAMES 2:1–3:12)

I'll never forget my first week in boot camp. When I arrived, I had an idea about the Marine Corps that was altogether false. It took about sixty seconds for reality to shatter my fragile image. During our first orientation class, with our heads shaved, our bodies aching, and our egos stripped, I distinctly remember the instructor shouting, "Look to your right! Look to your left! In fourteen weeks one of those guys won't be here!" And I thought, "Are they gonna shoot 'em?" Of course not, but at that point we were all scared half to death. We just wanted to survive. As those petrified recruits pivoted their heads left and right, I thought, "Hey! The guys on my right and my left are looking at *me*!" And I realized that I could very well be one of those men who wouldn't measure up.

It was no bluff. Our training started with eighty-five and we graduated forty-two. So that instructor didn't exaggerate. That intense training thinned the ranks. We all had a naïve, even romantic, idea of life in the Corps, as if it were a fourteen-week summer camp or a Boy Scouts for adults. But a few months later and forty-three men fewer, I learned what it was really all about. We learned what it meant to be among "the few, the proud." We discovered the meaning of submission, taking orders, and going above and beyond the call of duty. And we learned the true meaning of the Marine Corps motto, *Semper Fidelis*—"Always Faithful."

Like that life-changing experience in boot camp, a serious reading of the book of James thins the ranks. It sifts the Christian crowd of religious phonies. He's looking for a few good men and women who will remain "always faithful" in word and deed. The tough words of James assault the inauthentic faith of wannabes. Some onlookers may even say, "That's just not for me." But that's the job of the book. James is asking, "If you say you believe like you should, then why do you live like you shouldn't?" People who naïvely embrace a sit-back-and-watch kind of comfy Christianity will have a hard time with our drill instructor, James.

The first section of this letter has already introduced a number of profoundly practical themes—enduring life's tests and temptations (1:2–8), the struggle between rich and poor (1:9–11), the need to be authentic doers of the Word (1:22–26), guarding the tongue (1:26), and investing in those who could never repay (1:27). He introduced these as examples of how to submit to the "perfect law" of liberty in Scripture, answering the question, "What does authentic faith look like?"

KEY TERMS

ἔργον [*ergon*] (2041) "work, deed, completion of a task or duty"

This Greek term, like the English noun "work," describes both the act of labor and its result. If a person were to build a house, the structure is said to be his or her "work." That is, the house represents both the effort and the result of the builder's activity. For James, the term *ergon* emphasizes the practical effects of a person's inward convictions — the visible manifestations of invisible thoughts.

δικαιόω [*dikaioō*] (1344) "to justify, to declare righteous, to prove innocent, to vindicate"

In the New Testament, this verb almost always bears a legal connotation that grants a person the status of "not guilty," an official pronouncement that may or may not reflect the actual guilt or innocence of the subject. An innocent person may be vindicated, such that the governing authority officially affirms his or her righteousness; or one may be declared righteous despite actual guilt, so that he or she receives the same rights and privileges as a genuinely innocent person.

γλῶσσα [*glōssa*] (1100) "tongue, language"

Throughout the Old Testament and especially in wisdom literature, Scripture addresses the "tongue" in both positive and negative terms. In fact, Proverbs 18:21 says, "Death and life are in the power of the tongue." James, seeped in Jewish wisdom imagery, draws on this concept of the "tongue" as a tool of both blessing and cursing, life and death. Though the word refers specifically to the physical organ, most of its uses are metaphorical, indicating a person's words or language.

But now, in the second major section of this manual of hands-on Christianity, James shatters the fantasy world of a flimsy faith. He sets out to deal with the nitty-gritty of the Christian life, burrowing deeply into issues of partiality and prejudice (2:1–13), faith and works (2:14–26), and bridling the tongue (3:1–12). Fully developing matters that were merely touched on in the first section, James intends to transform his readers from a ragtag bunch of naïve recruits into a cadre of spiritual warriors who set the standard of faithful living in a world of corruption and compromise.

Partiality and Prejudice (James 2:1-13)

¹My brethren, do not hold your faith in our glorious Lord Jesus Christ with *an attitude of* personal favoritism. ²For if a man comes into your assembly

with a gold ring and dressed in fine clothes, and there also comes in a poor man in dirty clothes, [3]and you pay special attention to the one who is wearing the fine clothes, and say, "You sit here in a good place," and you say to the poor man, "You stand over there, or sit down by my footstool," [4]have you not made distinctions among yourselves, and become judges with evil motives? [5]Listen, my beloved brethren: did not God choose the poor of this world *to be* rich in faith and heirs of the kingdom which He promised to those who love Him? [6]But you have dishonored the poor man. Is it not the rich who oppress you and personally drag you into court? [7]Do they not blaspheme the fair name by which you have been called?

[8]If, however, you are fulfilling the royal law according to the Scripture, "You shall love your neighbor as yourself," you are doing well. [9]But if you show partiality, you are committing sin *and* are convicted by the law as transgressors. [10]For whoever keeps the whole law and yet stumbles in one *point*, he has become guilty of all. [11]For He who said, "Do not commit adultery," also said, "Do not commit murder." Now if you do not commit adultery, but do commit murder, you have become a transgressor of the law. [12]So speak and so act as those who are to be judged by *the* law of liberty. [13]For judgment *will be* merciless to one who has shown no mercy; mercy triumphs over judgment.

Through most of my Christian life, I've wrestled against a form of Christianity obsessed with externals. Almost as if they had completely forgotten that "man looks at the outward appearance, but the LORD looks at the heart" (1 Sam. 16:7), too many believers draw quick conclusions about people based merely on what they first see or hear.

- Her hair is too short.
- He shouldn't wear *that* to church.
- What's with those tattoos?
- That car is too expensive.
- Their house is too big.
- Why did she wear *that* to church?
- He has a PhD.
- She didn't even graduate from high school.
- They go to public school.
- They're homeschoolers.

Prejudice. Our English word stems from a Latin noun that emphasizes a prejudgment of someone, causing us to form an opinion before knowing all the facts. And once we've raced to our conclusions, ignoring those essential facts, we're well on our way to irrational thinking—thinking that results in an insidious attitude buried deep inside that says, "My mind's made up. Don't confuse me with the facts."

The whole point of James 2:1 – 13 is to diffuse that kind of faulty thinking. As a master communicator, James first states his principle (2:1), then provides a real-life illustration of the principle (2:2 – 4). Next he explains the reasons why such behavior is inconsistent with authentic Christian faith (2:5 – 11) and ends with a final exhortation to do what's right (2:12 – 13).

— **2:1** —

James begins by saying, in essence, "Faith in Christ and partiality are incompatible." The command in this verse is straightforward: literally, "do not have." James is clearly addressing Christians, whom he calls "brethren," those who already have faith in Christ. The issue is not what they believe or in whom they trust. In fact, James uses some of the most exalted language for Christ in this brief statement — "our glorious Lord Jesus Christ." So, these people have solid theology. They are part of God's forever family.

But something is wrong. The attitude that accompanies their faith doesn't fit. The Greek word translated "personal favoritism" is *prosōpolēmpsia*, a compound word that communicates the idea of "receiving the face." What a great way to put it! You see a person's outward appearance (his or her "face"), and you receive that image as if it's the real thing. The word is used in the New Testament in reference to God. In Acts 10:34, Peter uses a related word, "I most certainly understand now that God is not one to show partiality." God judges the truth of a matter by the heart, not the face. And we as Christians are called to reflect this quality in our own lives.

A word of clarification is in order. Partiality and prejudice can go in one of two directions: positive or negative. On the one hand, by merely looking at outside characteristics, we can miss fatal character flaws in a person masked by attractive attire, smooth talk, and a firm handshake. On the other hand, we can too quickly condemn a person based on outward appearance, failing to see the Christlike character and abundant spiritual fruit that compose the person's true identity. So, James isn't questioning the importance of wise character study to discern whether we should be involved with a person. We should all exercise that kind of discernment. James is addressing the problem of prejudice shown in our first encounter.

— **2:2–4** —

Like windows of light flooding a home with beauty, illustrations open the truth to our minds and let it shine in our hearts. James is a master illustrator. He doesn't leave his readers with a mere rule to follow; he tells them a story to which they can relate.

The setting of the illustration is the "assembly." The word here isn't *ekklēsia*, "church," but *synagōgē*, "synagogue." In the earliest days of Christianity, especially for Jewish believers, the place of meeting was still called a "synagogue." In some cities, Jewish Christians were able to meet in the Jewish synagogues, but before long the unbelieving Jews decided that they couldn't tolerate fellow Jews who believed in Jesus as the promised Messiah, and so they expelled them from their synagogues. Although most Jewish Christians likely met in homes or other convenient locations, they often retained the term "synagogue" to describe their assemblies. As we apply this story to our day, the "assembly" represents our place of worship ... the church.

In James's illustration, two men stand out as the church is gathering for worship. One is dressed to the nines — from fancy jewelry to expensive, elegant clothing. In the ancient Near East, it was customary for a person of great wealth or nobility to wear jewel-studded garments of fine fabric like silk. Their garments announced them as influential, powerful men who could change your life with the nod of their heads. But something about this illustration would probably strike James's first-century readers as odd. At the time James wrote this letter, the story was usually reversed — Christians were often brought into the assemblies of the rich and powerful for interrogation and judgment. It wasn't common for the wealthy and respectable to show up at church! So, having caught his readers' imagination, James introduces the second character in his illustration.

A poor man in grubby, soiled clothes wanders into the assembly. He looks like a hobo who just hopped the train at a whistle stop. Dirty, shabby clothes hang from his scrawny form. No jewels, no silk, no entourage to protect him from thieves or assassins ... and no influence over anyone. Please note that this isn't just an average man off the street coming to church out of curiosity. This one stands out to normal people as exceptionally poor, just as the wealthy man stood out as enviably rich.

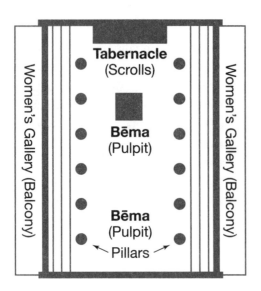

A floor plan of a first-century synagogue, indicating the seating arrangement and the location of the *bēma* and lectern.

This leaves the usher with a decision to make and no time to think. In cases like this, a person's true character shines through. What does he do? In James's illustration, the usher is blinded by the bling (2:3) and so the rich man gets V.I.P. treatment: "You sit here in a good place." Where was that? Matthew 23:6 mentions "chief seats in the synagogues," so there must have been preferred seating for people of importance. In an ancient synagogue, the pulpit stood near the center of the meeting hall, while the tabernacle, where the scrolls were kept, was toward the front. Seating for men ran along the two sides and women and children sat in a balcony. The best seats in the house were nearest the lectern.

While the rich man is shown to a seat of honor, the poor man doesn't even get a seat! Instead, with a wave of the hand or an impatient huff, the usher barks, "You stand over there, or sit down by my footstool" (2:3). In other words, "Stay out of the way!"

Now, let me make something clear about what James is *not* saying in this passage. The illustration is about the one judging the rich man as being better than the poor. It's *not* about the rich or poor man. There's nothing necessarily wrong with being rich, and there's nothing necessarily wrong with being poor. The problem James is addressing is the *motive* that affects the *behavior*.

In verse 4, James announces his verdict: the usher is guilty of discrimination. He has "made distinctions" and become a judge not with objective clarity, but with "evil motives." Maybe he played favorites for personal gain, thinking it would win him favor with an influential politician. Maybe less personally—but just as wrong—the usher envisions the great financial contribution that could come to the church through such a wealthy man.

James couldn't be clearer. *This kind of prejudice is sin.* If there's one place where class distinctions have no place, it's in our places of worship. Color, political persuasion, financial status, fashion, appearance—we should leave these things at the door.

—2:5–11—

James shifts into low gear and explains why prejudice and partiality are unfit for Christians. He gives three reasons: theological, logical, and biblical.

A theological reason (2:5). God shows no partiality, so neither should His children. The apostle Paul develops this principle in 1 Corinthians 1:26–29:

> For consider your calling, brethren, that there were not many wise according to the flesh, not many mighty, not many noble; but God has chosen the foolish things of the world to shame the wise, and God has chosen the weak things of the

From My Journal

General Seating No Longer Available

When I was stationed on the island of Okinawa, our general liked to sit down in front during chapel services. There was always a place reserved for him and his entourage of aides and all those guys that waited on him hand and foot. He usually arrived about five minutes after the worship started and you could hear them all marching in step and sitting down in that one spot everybody knew belonged to them.

We had a fine Christian chaplain, a real maverick, a strong preacher, and a courageous fellow. He was one of the only chaplains I knew who was genuinely born again. One Easter Sunday morning the chapel was packed. Guys outside couldn't get a seat. The chaplain wanted to make as much room as possible for all the troops, so he packed them in wherever he found space. He told the ushers, "Bring 'em down." And guess who sat in the general's seat? *A private.* Now, in the Marine Corps, trust me, *no one* else sits where generals are supposed to sit ... especially buck privates!

But this Easter Sunday, one did.

Then in came the general. He surveyed the chapel and saw no place available. The general obviously didn't like it, because in less than three months, our fine chaplain got shipped off the island. The chaplain paid a big price for a valuable virtue. He refused to show partiality, even if it meant seating an on-time private over a tardy general.

But God works in mysterious ways. I found out months later that our chaplain who got booted off Okinawa wound up being stationed on Hawaii. How good is *that!*

world to shame the things which are strong, and the base things of the world and the despised God has chosen, the things that are not, so that He may nullify the things that are, so that no man may boast before God.

A logical reason (2:6–7). James asks two rhetorical questions, which reveal much about the situation in which the Jewish Christians found themselves. First, the rich and powerful were persecuting Christians, dragging them before the authorities (2:6). Second, the rich and powerful were blaspheming Christ's name. Reading between the lines, we can tell that the poor were not involved in this kind of persecution. Indiscriminately showing favoritism toward the rich and mistreating the poor, therefore, made no logical sense.

A biblical reason (2:8–11). Finally, James points his readers to Scripture, which excludes all partiality. His text comes from Leviticus 19:18: "You shall love your neighbor as yourself." James's readers immediately would have recognized this as a key Old Testament verse Jesus used in His own teaching (Matt. 19:19). In fact, it's the basis for His "Golden Rule": "Treat people the same way you want them to treat you" (7:12). Christ called this the second of the two greatest commandments, together with loving God with all our heart, soul, mind, and strength (Mark 12:31). Paul says that every commandment in the Law of Moses "is summed up in this saying" (Rom. 13:9) and that "the whole Law is fulfilled in one word, in the statement, 'You shall love your neighbor as yourself'" (Gal. 5:14).

Given the fundamental importance of this "royal law"—or, "king of the law"— to break this one law is like breaking all of them; and vice versa, if you break any of the others, you've broken this one (James 2:11). For this reason, prejudice—which refuses to love all equally—transgresses the great commandment.

— **2:12–13** —

James wraps up his indictment against partiality with an exhortation to apply his teaching. Let Scripture be your standard! Let love be your law! Let mercy be your message! Do not speak and act out of natural, superficial, cultural conditioning. To speak and act that way makes believers into lawbreakers, subjecting them to God's discipline. Believers will never fall under condemnation by God (Rom. 8:1), but they will be judged and rewarded on how they conduct themselves in this life. James reveals the standard by which all believers will be judged: "by the law of liberty" (2:12). In the context of 2:8–11, we know the law James had in mind—the liberating, royal law that excludes all prejudice and puts away all partiality: "You shall love your neighbor as yourself."

Application

Prejudice Is a Sin

As the adage goes, "birds of a feather flock together." How true that is, even in our churches. I'm tempted to say, *especially* in our churches. We have large churches, small churches, downtown churches, suburban churches, inner-city churches, young churches, old churches, formal churches, informal churches—all of them composed of people who look the same, think the same, talk the same, act the same. Oh, and they often mistrust, dislike, or alienate "others" on the outside of their culture.

Why has it been so difficult for Christians to take seriously James's words about partiality and prejudice? We're okay with loving our neighbors, so long as we get to pick the neighborhood! But James's words concerning prejudice and partiality should challenge our attitudes—*and change our actions*. At the close of 2:1 – 13, James leaves us with some ways to apply his principles against prejudice in our own lives.

First, *let the Scriptures be your standard rather than your habits* (2:12). I was raised in the South. I inhaled the prejudice propaganda from the moment I took my first breath. I was taught it in school. I saw it among my friends. I even heard it in pulpits. But I have to call it what the Bible calls it—*sin*. We often hide behind excuses like, "That's just how I was raised," or "Those people have their own ways of doing things." As James said, prejudice and faith in Christ do not mix (2:1).

So, stop holding on to your prejudices and hiding behind flimsy excuses. Whether your particular group is black, white, Hispanic, Arab, Asian, Palestinian, Jewish, or Indian, you need to get over it! Decide right now to agree with Scripture and call sin what it is.

Second, *let love be your law* (2:12). James calls the command to love your neighbor as yourself the "royal law" (2:8) and "the law of liberty" (2:12). When we encounter people who are different from us—older or younger, lighter or darker, richer or poorer—we need to resist the question, "How can I get as far away from this person as possible?" We must answer the question, "How can I best love this person in word and action? How can I help her? How can I build this person up? How can I show grace and mercy instead of discrimination and partiality?"

As you seek to apply James's message, ask God to reveal where you may be guilty of favoritism and partiality. Do you target certain groups for evangelism and exclude others? Do your church programs focus on a particular demographic that will bring in more converts and more money, ignoring the smaller, poorer populations in your neighborhood? We need to be strategic in ministry, but we can't be prejudiced.

At the same time, ask for discernment to make accurate distinctions about how to love, whom to trust, and when to confront. James isn't saying we must treat every soul on earth exactly the same, but we can't treat people unfairly simply based on our superficial prejudices. If we approach each person we meet as opportunities to demonstrate love, we'll make good progress at putting away prejudice from our midst.

Faith at Work (James 2:14–26)

---

¹⁴What use is it, my brethren, if someone says he has faith but he has no works? Can that faith save him? ¹⁵If a brother or sister is without clothing and in need of daily food, ¹⁶and one of you says to them, "Go in peace, be warmed and be filled," and yet you do not give them what is necessary for *their* body, what use is that? ¹⁷Even so faith, if it has no works, is dead, *being* by itself.

¹⁸But someone may *well* say, "You have faith and I have works; show me your faith without the works, and I will show you my faith by my works." ¹⁹You believe that God is one. You do well; the demons also believe, and shudder. ²⁰But are you willing to recognize, you foolish fellow, that faith without works is useless? ²¹Was not Abraham our father justified by works when he offered up Isaac his son on the altar? ²²You see that faith was working with his works, and as a result of the works, faith was perfected; ²³and the Scripture was fulfilled which says, "And Abraham believed God, and it was reckoned to him as righteousness," and he was called the friend of God. ²⁴You see that a man is justified by works and not by faith alone. ²⁵In the same way, was not Rahab the harlot also justified by works when she received the messengers and sent them out by another way? ²⁶For just as the body without *the* spirit is dead, so also faith without works is dead.

Many years ago I was driving through our town with a couple of my young kids in the back seat. As children do, they were singing a song they had learned in Sunday school. Now, this was long before they made kids in the backseat wear seatbelts, so one was lying on the seat, the other on the floor. That kind of thing today makes us cringe, but you may be old enough to remember when that was typical. I couldn't see them back there, but I could sure hear them belting out that song at the top of their little voices: "If you're saved and you know it, say 'Amen!'" And they'd shout, "Amen!"

Eventually they wrangled me into singing along. As we got to the last verse where we're supposed to "do all three," I stopped at a red light. With the window rolled down I was shouting, "If you're saved and you know it, do all three!"

And I stomped, shouted, "Amen," and clapped my hands. Just then I realized two sophisticated-looking people in the car beside us were watching us. Well, I should say *I* was being watched—because they couldn't see the two kids singing with me, lying down on the backseat!

I could see the shock on their faces. They must have thought I was nuts, intoxicated, high, or worse; but they weren't going to stick around to find out. Their car took off as soon as the light turned green. I wanted to chase them down and explain, "There are two kids in the back seat that got me into this!" But I shrugged my shoulders and thought, *Who cares?* Then, as I accelerated through the green light, we came to the part of the song where we sang, "If you're saved and you know it, then your life will surely show it." They kept on, but I stopped singing.

Immediate conviction set in. I thought, *Lord, does my life really show it?* I sure showed something to those people in the next car over, but I felt only a little embarrassed about that minor social infraction. What about all the things I'm called to do daily as a believer in Christ—all those things that cut crosswise against cultural norms and society's expectations? So I began to quickly review the past week ... months ... and years, trying to determine if my life really showed my faith. That simple children's song got to me.

Someone once said that faith is like calories: you can't see them, but you can always see their results! That's the major theme resonating throughout James's letter. We can boil it down to one word—*results*. Real faith results in genuine works. And nowhere does James more passionately argue and illustrate this theme than in James 2:14–26. This passage forces us to answer that penetrating question: "If you say you believe like you should, then why do you behave like you shouldn't?"

— **2:14** —

This section is the main thesis of the book. Everything before this passage is like an arrow pointing forward to it. Everything after is like an arrow pointing back. It's the apex of a pyramid, in James's mind. He asks two rhetorical questions, not expecting an answer but about to give one: "What use is it, my brethren, if someone says he has faith but he has no works? Can that faith save him?"

James's question is like asking, "What good is it to carry around a driver's license if you can't actually drive?" People may be called Christians and claim to be part of the faith, but do they have any genuine results that prove to those around them that their confession is authentic? That's what James is asking. And frankly, James says that if somebody claims to have faith in Christ but his or her life doesn't show results of faith, that faith might very well be phony.

The second question, "Can that faith save him?" refers to a certain *quality* of faith—a faith that produces no fruit. The implied answer, of course, is a resounding *no*! In fact, the form of the question in Greek shows that James is asking a question that *anticipates* a negative answer.

For the rest of the section, James digs deeper into this basic assertion that phony faith devoid of works is not genuine, saving faith.

—2:15–20—

In verses 15 to 20, James gives a series of four characteristics of genuine faith.

(1) *Genuine faith is not indifferent, but involved* (2:15–16). Carefully consider this illustration. James is making it easy for his readers to decide whether they should help these people in need. They're not being asked to throw charity at ungrateful heathens or wicked blasphemers. These needy folks are genuine "brothers and sisters" who have genuine needs: food and clothing (2:15). In 1 Timothy 6:8, Paul said, "If we have food and covering, with these we shall be content." The people in James's example didn't even have the basics of life! They were in dire need, but instead of providing them with clothing or food, James's hypothetical feigners of faith send the needy believers away with nothing but a hollow cliché: "Go in peace, be warmed and be filled" (2:16).

My guess is that everybody reading this has experienced something like this from so-called brothers and sisters in Christ. Maybe you haven't missed meals or clothing, but perhaps you've endured pain and desperately needed comfort ... or you've had a specific need that required at least a caring ear, a shoulder to cry on. Instead, you felt a pat on the head and you heard a hasty platitude. Instead of reaching out with real help, those who could (and should) have stepped up did nothing to meet your need. That's James's indictment.

James isn't alone in these sentiments. The apostle John says the same: "But whoever has the world's goods, and sees his brother in need and closes his heart against him, how does the love of God abide in him?" (1 John 3:17). The implication? *It doesn't*. If there's genuine love, it reaches out to others. And if there's real faith, it produces acts of compassion. In James's definition, genuine faith is not indifferent, but involved.

(2) James urges that *genuine faith is not independent, but in partnership* (2:17). James says that genuine faith is always accompanied by results. If it doesn't have results, it's "dead." By "dead" James means "useless, ineffective, impotent." It's the opposite of a living, effective, vibrant faith. In this verse, we might even put quote marks around "faith," because in James's mind the so-called "faith" that has no works is phony.

(3) *Genuine faith is not invisible, but on display* (2:18). James puts words in the mouth of a hypothetical person who says, "You have faith and I have works; show me your faith without the works, and I will show you my faith by my works." The subtle argument imagines somebody who agrees with James but claims to have a quiet, invisible, private faith. You've met people like that. "I keep my faith to myself," they say. "I don't wear my religion on my shirt sleeve." To a person like that, anybody who actually lives out his or her faith looks like a fanatic. But James directly challenges the idea of a private, passive faith: genuine faith displays itself. If you can't actually see it, how can anyone know it actually exists?

(4) *Genuine faith is not intellectual, but from the heart* (2:19–20). James imagines yet another kind of person—the religious intellectual. Such a person knows the facts and can recite the truth, but he lacks a life that matches the facts. He believes that "God is one" (2:19). This statement comes straight out of the ancient confession of Judaism called the *Shema*—"Hear, O Israel! The LORD is our God; the LORD is one!" (Deut. 6:4). This guy has his basic theology down. He gives intellectual assent to the truth. But it hasn't penetrated the heart or made its way to the hands and feet. Those whose faith is merely intellectual have that much in common with demons! Only those who exhibit genuine faith by visible works are better off than demons, who have impeccable theology but abhorrent works.

By the way, we encounter another kind of "religious intellectual" in our own day, and that's the intellectual skeptic. You've seen them interviewed in documentaries on the historical Jesus or waxing eloquent on the "truth" behind the "myths" of the Bible. They boast all kinds of scientific and historical credentials. They want to talk about religion as a social, psychological, or philosophical phenomenon. They claim to remain objective, analyzing and reinterpreting faith for the modern mind. But the truth is *they don't actually have faith*. And to make matters worse, they aren't interested in getting it! That's a radical intellectual disconnect that goes even further than what James had in mind, but it's a new reality we have to cope with today. Studying the idea of God or analyzing belief systems is light-years away from receiving the Lord Jesus Christ by authentic faith, then living out that faith with real action.

Finally, driving his case home by repeating his thesis, James writes, "But are you willing to recognize, you foolish fellow, that faith without works is useless?" (2:20). This rephrasing of the statement helps us understand what James means by referring to faith without works as "dead." Note that James doesn't say that a person without faith is dead, but that such a "faith" is useless, as good as dead. Though James doesn't address the issue directly, behind this description of fake faith may stand a suggestion that such a person has not truly experienced the gift of salvation by grace through genuine faith.

Let me put this in practical terms. Suppose a member of your adult home group has lost his job and can't buy school clothes for his family. You just got a big raise. But instead of opening your hand to your brother, you merely pat him on the back and say, "We'll be praying for you." Or put yourself in the other place. An unexpected illness hits your family and the medical bills have made it difficult to stay afloat. Instead of tapping into their benevolence fund to help you through this tough time, you get nothing but a card from your pastor that says, "God causes all things to work together for good to those who love God" (Rom. 8:28). In each of these cases, we see a specific need and an ability to meet the need ... but a useless, dead response.

In light of James's indictment, do these responses exemplify genuine faith? No!

— **2:21–25** —

As a master teacher, James drives his point home with two biblical examples of true, inward faith demonstrated by obvious, outward actions. Though he has at his disposal a host of examples of faith and faithfulness from the Old Testament, James selects two extremes: Abraham and Rahab. What a difference!

Abraham, the father of the Hebrews	Rahab, a Gentile harlot
Abraham, a man of power and respect	Rahab, a woman of ill-repute
Abraham, the recipient of God's promises	Rahab, the breaker of God's moral laws

Yet in selecting these polar opposites to prove his point, James casts a broad net that captures every one of us reading his words. Every Christian finds himself or herself somewhere between Abraham and Rahab. So James's message about faith and works applies to all of us.

The author of Hebrews, too, marvels at the faith exhibited by the actions of Abraham and Rahab. Hebrews 11:17 says, "By faith Abraham, when he was tested, offered up Isaac, and he who had received the promises was offering up his only begotten son." And in 11:31 we read, "By faith Rahab the harlot did not perish along with those who were disobedient, after she had welcomed the spies in peace." James was not the only New Testament writer to see in both Abraham and Rahab examples of true faith! And both Hebrews and James emphasize that these works were done *by faith*. This means the actions were the result of a genuine faith within each believer, working themselves out in practical, hands-on actions.

At this point all those familiar with the letters of Paul will see an apparent problem pop off the page. In verse 21, James writes, "Was not Abraham our father justified by works when he offered up Isaac his son on the altar?" Hold it! *Justified by works?* Doesn't this contradict what Paul says in Romans? Paul wrote, "For we maintain that a man is justified by faith apart from works of the Law" (Rom. 3:28). How, then, can James say, "You see that a man is justified by works and not by faith alone" (James 2:24)? Is James denying the heart of the gospel of grace? Or did Paul get it completely wrong?

Neither! James is not disputing Paul, nor is Paul correcting James. We might remind ourselves that James fully supported Paul's preaching of salvation by grace through faith (Acts 15:13 – 21). Later, James defended Paul's reputation among the Jewish believers in Jerusalem (21:15 – 24). Nowhere do we see Paul and James wrangling over the core essentials of the gospel; we always see them agreeing on foundational truths! James and Paul had no need of reconciliation in the first century, so how do we reconcile their apparent differences in our own minds here in the twenty-first?

The answer involves two nuances of the word "to justify." The Greek verb is *dikaioō*. Depending on context, the word can mean either "to declare righteous," as in a legal proceeding; or "to demonstrate as righteous." The legal definition can simply be a verdict of "not guilty," even if a person is in fact guilty as charged. In the second case, a person demonstrates his or her rightness by actions observable to everybody. Paul and James pick up these two uses of "justify," so that the same word forms two sides of the same coin.

Paul looked at the root of salvation. At the moment of salvation, you are saved through faith plus nothing. On the other side of the coin, James looked at the fruit of salvation. After salvation—after the root of faith gets planted—our lives will bear the fruit of good works.

Another contrast involves two perspectives. Paul looks at life from God's perspective; James looks at life from the human perspective. Paul uses the word "justified" to mean "declared righteous in the sight of God, even though I am still in my state as a sinner." That's a gift. James addresses believers who already have experienced this gift of salvation, so he uses the word "justified" to mean, "I demonstrate myself to be righteous in the sight of people to show that I have received God's gift of eternal life." The accompanying chart, "Paul and James: Two Sides of the Same Coin" can help distinguish the two complementary (not contradictory!) aims of Paul and James.

Paul and James: Two Sides of the Same Coin

Paul	James
"For we maintain that a man is *justified by faith* apart from works of the Law." (Rom. 3:28)	"You see that a man is *justified by works* and not by faith alone." (James 2:24)
Uses "justified" to mean "pronounced righteous in the sight of God"	Uses "justified" to mean "proved righteous in the sight of others"
Shows how an unbeliever becomes a Christian	Shows how a believer lives as a Christian
Emphasizes the root of salvation	Emphasizes the fruit of salvation
Stresses inward disposition	Stresses outward actions
Demonstrates God's part with human participation	Demonstrates human part with God's help

Once we understand James's different approach, his illustrations from the actions of Abraham and Rahab make sense. We know Abraham was a man of faith because we can see his ultimate act of faith in obeying the commands of God, even when they made absolutely no sense to him. To this day, we squirm as we read of God's test of Abraham's faith when He ordered him to offer Isaac as a sacrifice. Knowing beforehand that God fully intended to stay Abraham's hand and provide a ram as a substitute doesn't help. *Abraham* didn't know that! Yet he trusted in the absolute goodness and power of God, in spite of the incomprehensible command.

Just think of it! Isaac was Abraham's only son of the promise and the one through whom God intended to make Abraham's descendents into a great nation. Yet *this* is the one to be offered as a sacrifice to God! The book of Hebrews tells us that while he was offering Isaac to God, Abraham "considered that God is able to raise people even from the dead" (Heb. 11:19). Though he didn't know *how* God could keep His promises through Isaac, Abraham exhibited for generations to come an absolute, unswerving trust in God's goodness and power. So James concludes, "You see that a man [in this case, Abraham] is justified [shown to be a person of faith] by works and not by faith alone" (James 2:24).

Rahab serves as James's second example. She was not an Israelite and therefore not a member of God's covenant people. Yet she went out on a limb and believed that the God of Israel would keep His promises to Israel and deliver her city of

Jericho into their hands. Having lost all confidence in Jericho's local deities to protect the city, Rahab changed allegiances and demonstrated her change in faith from false gods to the one true God. We read in Joshua 6:17, 22–23 that when the Israelites defeated Jericho, Rahab and her household were spared because of her courageous act of faith. And we learn that Rahab herself became an Israelite. In fact, she became one of four Old Testament women mentioned in the genealogy of Jesus (Matt. 1:3–6). What a remarkable example of the lasting fruit of authentic faith!

—2:26—

James concludes this section on faith at work with a reiteration of his thesis: "For just as the body without the spirit is dead, so also faith without works is dead." Wherever you find separation, you find death. It's true in physical life when the soul is separated from the body. It's also true in the Christian life. When you have a life you call "faith" but have nothing to demonstrate it as authentic over the long haul, then an abnormal separation has occurred between faith and works. The result is a hollow, useless faith.

A life without works means one of two things. If the person is a genuine believer, the result will be a slide toward a deathlike existence. We saw James deal with that when he explained the slippery slope toward sin (1:13–15). The answer for true believers? Repent and get back on the path of spiritual life and growth.

The other kind of person can't produce real fruit because he or she lacks the root of faith. It may be that such a person has fake faith. It may be that he or she never understood that salvation comes as a gift from God through simple faith in Christ's death and resurrection for us. They have no works because they have no true faith. The solution to that kind of spiritual death is not to try to make yourself better through more works, but to admit that apart from Christ, you can do nothing. Only when the root of faith gets firmly planted can a life produce authentic fruit that pleases God and is apparent to others.

Application

Feeding a Living Faith

James's puzzling phrase "justified by works" can sometimes distract us from the extremely practical principles in this section. Instead of dissecting his words, how about digesting them? Let's move from the study into the dining room and let me offer you a five-course meal for making James's message part of a balanced spiritual diet.

Instead of rushing through your meals this week, how about nourishing your soul with some spiritual food around the table? Choose the best mealtime for discussion and chew on these questions with family members, with friends, and with whomever you regularly share meals. Or carve out a little time alone each day during the week to think through the practical implications of James's emphasis on the fruit of genuine faith.

Day 1. Define clearly the issue in James 2:14. Why would people *claim* to have genuine faith if they don't? What might motivate this kind of deception (or self-delusion) in our world today? How would you know for sure if another person is truly born again ... or *can* you?

Day 2. Read James 2:15–16. Does this mean that we should help everyone in need? What if they aren't "brothers or sisters" in Christ? Isn't discernment needed? What constitutes a real need, according to this passage? How can we discover real needs in our own church or community? What are these?

Day 3. James attacks cold, intellectual belief in James 2:19–20. Illustrate this kind of "heady" approach to Christianity with a couple of modern examples. Why is it wrong to assent to the facts without having it affect your life? In what ways do you tend to *intellectualize* rather than *actualize* your faith?

Day 4. Look at James 2:21–25. Abraham and Rahab—*what a combination!* Think about the differences between those two examples of fruitful faith and discuss why James would use them as illustrations. Their stories are found in Genesis 22 and Joshua 2 and 6. Put yourself in their places and describe how difficult it would be for you to exhibit faith in those circumstances. What circumstances in your life make it difficult for you to live out your faith?

Day 5. Looking back to the time when you were saved, can you think of specific "works" that soon occurred, demonstrating to others that you had a genuine faith in Christ? Share a few of the changes God has brought about in your life. On the basis of James 2:20 and 26, would you describe your faith as "living" or "dead"—profitable or useless?

Before clearing the table, discuss what you need to *do* in response to your answers to these questions. The book of James is all about hands-on Christianity. He's telling each of us to stop sitting on our hands and start using them to do God's work!

Bridling the Tongue (3:1–12)

> [1]Let not many *of you* become teachers, my brethren, knowing that as such we will incur a stricter judgment. [2]For we all stumble in many *ways*. If anyone

does not stumble in what he says, he is a perfect man, able to bridle the whole body as well. [3]Now if we put the bits into the horses' mouths so that they will obey us, we direct their entire body as well. [4]Look at the ships also, though they are so great and are driven by strong winds, are still directed by a very small rudder wherever the inclination of the pilot desires. [5]So also the tongue is a small part of the body, and *yet* it boasts of great things.

See how great a forest is set aflame by such a small fire! [6]And the tongue is a fire, the *very* world of iniquity; the tongue is set among our members as that which defiles the entire body, and sets on fire the course of *our* life, and is set on fire by hell. [7]For every species of beasts and birds, of reptiles and creatures of the sea, is tamed and has been tamed by the human race. [8]But no one can tame the tongue; *it is* a restless evil *and* full of deadly poison. [9]With it we bless *our* Lord and Father, and with it we curse men, who have been made in the likeness of God; [10]from the same mouth come *both* blessing and cursing. My brethren, these things ought not to be this way. [11]Does a fountain send out from the same opening *both* fresh and bitter *water*? [12]Can a fig tree, my brethren, produce olives, or a vine produce figs? Nor *can* salt water produce fresh.

If you ever see a wild animal prowling your neighborhood, you can call your local animal control agency to round it up and haul it off. The dogcatcher can take stray dogs to the pound or return loose dogs to their owners. Feral cats can be caught; skunks chased off; raccoons lured away. We can round up all these wild and roaming animals.

So why not a catcher and a pound for stray words? Now *that's* an occupation that could earn a decent living in *any* economy!

Imagine a razor-toothed invective cornered by a couple of word catchers: "Careful now, careful ... that's a mean one!"

"Who would let such a thing loose?"

"Aw, some guy got worked up and unleashed it on his poor wife."

"I'd hate to see what that gal feels like now."

"Like shredded wheat, probably."

"Well, let's get this pit bull of a word off the street before it bites somebody else."

Now then, let's say you're home and these same word catchers suddenly ring your doorbell. "Excuse me, sir," they ask, "does this word belong to you? We caught it running loose out there, backbiting everyone where you work. Your boss said it sounded like it was one of yours." You take a long look at their catch and, sure enough ... you let that little gossip out on Wednesday, and by Saturday it's ruined a dozen weekends. Red-faced, you claim your nasty words and send the word catchers away.

Of course, word catching is an imaginary profession. But my guess is that if you could find a way to round up and return people's words in time to stop their damage, you would create a lucrative business in our world of loose lips and unrestrained tongues. I know I've let loose a few nasty ones in my life that I would have paid almost anything to take back. I'm sure you have your list, too.

In James 2:14–26, the half brother of our Lord zoomed in on his central message — real faith produces genuine works. Throughout the book of James, a probing question holds his whole theme together: "If you say you believe like you should, then why do you behave like you shouldn't?" In James 3:1–12, he develops this general theme in a specific direction: controlling the tongue. No other section of the Bible speaks with greater clarity and impact on the potential destructive power of our words. We might summarize this powerful passage in the form of a question: "If you say you believe like you should, *then why do you say things you shouldn't?*"

— 3:1–2 —

James begins his indictment against the tongue with a surprising introduction. At first glance it looks as though he's attacking and condemning the ministry of teaching in the church. But on closer examination, we realize he's trying to protect it. James begins with a direct imperative to his readers, as if to say: "Don't run quickly to the role of teaching." It's a warning, not a condemnation. The reason? Because teachers — those who have the responsibility of speaking God's truth fully and accurately — will fall under stricter judgment.

Why does a teacher receive stricter judgment than the learner? Several reasons come to mind.

1. A teacher is responsible to *speak the truth*, not personal opinions. You and I have seen teachers who have strayed from the truth into the realm of their own speculations.
2. What a teacher says *affects many lives*. Sometimes it's an overwhelming feeling that I experience before a message on Sunday morning. The responsibility to handle God's Word accurately can't be taken lightly. Too many people's lives are at stake to just wing it.
3. Teachers fall under stricter judgment because we are expected to *live the truth*, not just teach it. You see, the real test of a teacher isn't what he says, but what his family says. The extent of a person's ministry isn't the size of his church, it's the depth of his family life. Teachers must never forget that.

Verse 2 especially applies to the teacher. Nobody is infallible. Everybody stumbles in many ways. But when a teacher stumbles, he can cause a whole crowd of people to stumble with him. The tongue is the teacher's indispensable tool. But an ignorant, deceptive, or wicked tongue can become a disastrous weapon. If you have the responsibility of teaching but have a loose tongue, James says you'll become the object God's judgment. Every teacher should take to heart the fact that James states with uncompromising clarity: "If anyone does not stumble in what he says, he is a perfect man" (3:2). Because there was only one perfect Man, the logical conclusion is that every one of us will stumble in what we say. So the warning must be taken with utmost seriousness.

A couple of clarifying remarks are necessary before we dig into the meat of the passage. First, James is not condemning teaching. The church needs willing, gifted, trained, and qualified teachers. James is warning against hurrying into teaching without realizing what a serious responsibility it is. Second, James is not condoning or promoting silence. He's urging self-control. And this self-control begins not with the tongue, but with the heart.

Jesus' words in Matthew 15 set the proper theological background for James's practical teaching about the tongue. Jesus tells us that the basic problem is not the tongue, but the heart. The tongue is merely the messenger that carries the words from the heart. It's the bucket that dips into the well and pours out either fresh water or poison.

In fact, Christ addressed the serious responsibility of teachers, calling the Pharisees "blind guides of the blind," who were leading their followers into a pit (Matt. 15:14). This suggests that James had this specific teaching of Jesus in mind as he penned his own words to his Jewish Christian audience. Listen to Jesus' words:

> It is not what enters into the mouth that defiles the man, but what proceeds out of the mouth, this defiles the man ... Everything that goes into the mouth passes into the stomach, and is eliminated[.] But the things that proceed out of the mouth come from the heart, and those defile the man. For out of the heart come evil thoughts, murders, adulteries, fornications, thefts, false witness, slanders. (Matt. 15:11, 17–19)

Now that we understand this root problem of the heart, let's observe how James develops his thoughts regarding the tongue.

— **3:3–5** —

Leonardo da Vinci's giftedness as a master sculptor led him to study the human body in as much detail as any physician of his day. When he began describing the tongue (which rarely appears in either his paintings or his statues), he noted, "No member needs so great a number of muscles as the tongue; this exceeds all the rest in the number of its movements." Indeed, the tongue is very small but extremely powerful. James wants to impress this fact on our minds so we won't underestimate the effects it can have—both positively and negatively. To do so, he gives us three analogies for the power of the tongue.

First, the tongue is like a bit in a horse's mouth (3:3). A small piece of rope, a few straps of leather, or a uniquely shaped strap of metal can control the movement of an entire horse. Similarly, the tongue can steer the direction of a person's life.

Second, the tongue is like the rudder on a ship (3:4). Just think of a giant cruise ship—a towering, floating hotel, really. But that massive hulk of steel can be steered by a comparatively small flap of metal, determining the course of that ship. In the same way, the tongue, though small, determines the course of a person's life.

These first two illustrations are neutral. They could have either positive or negative results. But James's third analogy reminds us of the potential danger of the tongue: "See how great a forest is set aflame by such a small fire" (3:5). If you take a spark, a glowing ember, or a smoldering ash and drop it in the wrong place, hundreds of thousands of acres of forest can go up in flames. By analogy, the tongue is a tiny spark, but it can set hundreds of people's lives ablaze. An unchecked tongue can assassinate a person's character ... destroy a reputation ... even ruin a church.

I visited a church years ago that suffered the devastating effects of backbiting, bickering, gossip, and slander. No major heresy, no natural disaster, no great financial collapse. Instead, a hundred fiery tongues had lit those hearts on fire, and by the time the flames of controversy had swept through, about thirty-five members were left stumbling through the ashes.

Our words can build unity ... or demolish it. The tongue can encourage fellowship ... or destroy it. Our mouths can form community ... or fracture it. The tongue is a small but powerful member. Yes, it has the ability to do tremendous good. But it also has the potential to do incalculable harm.

— 3:6–8 —

James moves to an even more direct picture to demonstrate both the necessity and the danger of the tongue. He further develops the image of the tongue as fire. Please observe a couple of things about the vivid terms James uses to describe this tiny muscle tucked behind our teeth. First, look at those intriguing phrases in 3:6:

- It's a world of iniquity.
- It defiles the entire body.
- It sets on fire the course of our life.
- It's set on fire by hell.

What harsh words! James is saying that the full range of iniquity finds an outlet through the tongue. Think about that. It's virtually impossible to seethe with anger without expressing our rage in words. Bitterness sours our speech. Pride prattles on and on. Hate explodes from the lips. The tongue can suddenly turn an otherwise gentle person into a monster. It's a "world of iniquity."

The tongue also has some connection to hell. Isn't that interesting? Look at the relationship. The tongue is set on fire by hell, and then it sets the entire course of our lives on fire. In Greek the word translated "hell" here is *gehenna*. This word appears only in Jesus' teaching in the Gospels and here in James. Since the word finds its origin and most common usage among Jews familiar with Jerusalem, James's Jewish Christian audience would have caught his meaning instantly.

Gehenna refers to the Hinnom Valley, which runs along the south side of Jerusalem. In the days of Jesus and James, residents of Jerusalem stacked all their garbage and filth in the Hinnom Valley, where it was often burned. It's as though James were saying, "You know that stinky, smoldering trash dump south of town? Our tongues are just like that. When we start our uncontrolled blathering, the garbage in our hearts is set ablaze. And like the putrid smoke that reminds us that garbage is burning in Hinnom Valley, our tongues let everybody hear the wickedness in our hearts.

James also refers to the tongue as an untamed beast (3:7). It seems we can train any kind of animal—from snakes to elephants, from tigers to dolphins—but the wild tongue resists taming. We can't seem to break that beast.

Here is a truth to be remembered. Verse 8 says literally, "The tongue no one of human beings has the power to tame." James is talking about subduing our sinful speech by our own power. He says human beings, on their own, do not have the ability to keep their tongues in check. But if you know Christ personally, God's power through the Holy Spirit's presence can transform your heart and take full control of the tongue. As Christ said regarding another impossibility: "With people this is impossible, but with God all things are possible" (Matt. 19:26).

James also pictures the tongue as "full of deadly poison" (3:8). It's as though we have a capsule of cyanide behind our teeth, ready to break open and spread words of death wherever we go. I once lodged at a hotel that was hosting a convention of military officers—several colonels, majors, a number of lieutenant colonels, captains. A lot of rank in that crowd. At one evening meal a large number of officers—both men and women—sat near our table. So near, in fact, that my ears caught a steady flow of profanity from their mouths. The men had no respect for the mixed company. They had no regard for the "civs" at the tables around them. And they had no concern about the decorated uniforms they wore. Instead, it seemed like every sentence produced a steady stream of cursing, constant as machine gun fire.

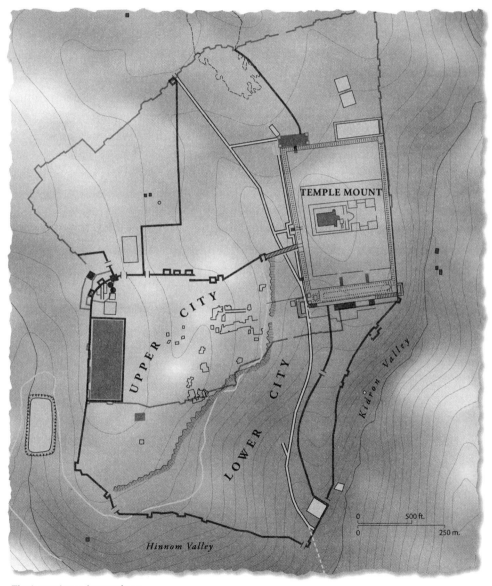

First-century Jerusalem

As I listened, I thought of Romans 3:13 – 14: "Their throat is an open grave . . . The poison of asps is under their lips; whose mouth is full of cursing and bitterness." Now, their words didn't hurt me or anybody else in that room. They weren't directed at us or to anybody in particular. But they certainly soiled their image. Any respect one might have for their uniforms or their ranks was diminished by their vile verbiage.

— **3:9–12** —

After likening the tongue to a fire, a wild beast, and a deadly poison, James backs up his argument with two illustrations. The first comes from human experience (3:9 – 10). The second comes from nature (3:11 – 12). Together these examples demonstrate that the tongue is necessary but inconsistent.

I think all of us can relate to James's first illustration from human experience. You're driving along, singing a joyous song of praise to the Lord: "This is the day that the Lord has made / Let us rejoice and be glad in it." Suddenly some bozo cuts you off, forcing you to slam on your breaks, leaving skid marks on the highway. But worse than that, the tongue you just used to praise God suddenly switches gears and you find yourself cursing the guy who couldn't find a free hand to signal because of his gabbing on the cell phone! "From the same mouth," James says, "come both blessing and cursing. My brethren, these things ought not to be this way" (3:10).

This can happen just as easily in a family setting. After a long Sunday morning service, a family sat down to eat lunch. The father bowed his head and led the children in the blessing. He thanked the Lord for the food, for the day, and for their home. Shortly after saying, "Amen," he proceeded to fuss about the preacher, the church, his job. Nothing but complaints poured from him lips. Following all that, his little daughter tapped him on the shoulder and said, "Daddy, did God hear you when you said the blessing?"

Switching to theological authority, Dad answered, "Yes, darling, He did."

"Well," asked his daughter, "did God hear you when you fussed right after you prayed?"

"Well . . . uh, yes, honey, I suppose He did."

"Then, Daddy," she said, "which one did God believe?"

James concludes with two illustrations from nature. A fountain doesn't produce both fresh and contaminated water. Neither does a fig tree produce olives, nor does a grapevine produce figs. If our hearts fill to the brim with grace, shouldn't our lips overflow with goodness?

In 3:11–12, James says the product is consistent with the source. A man who speaks out of two sides of his mouth reflects the heart of a double-minded man. As Jesus said, "A good tree cannot produce bad fruit, nor can a bad tree produce good fruit" (Matt. 7:18). This sobering thought forces us to ask ourselves: From where is this inconsistent speech coming? Or if we're consistently negative, deceitful, or bitter, we have to consider what our tongue reveals about our hearts. Think about that. Don't just shrug this off and move on to the last paragraph. Let that sink in.

Allow me to drive this home with three simple statements that sum up James's practical concern. First of all, *the tongue defiles.* Jesus said that in Matthew 15, and James says it in the first several verses of this passage. With just a syllable your tongue can stain your clean-cut image. The tongue is *that* powerful.

Second, *the tongue defies.* It resists merely natural attempts at self-control — resolutions, self-improvement gimmicks, whatever. In our own strength, those techniques simply will not work, at least not permanently.

Third, *the tongue displays* what you really are. That inner person, hiding behind the nice image we project to others, always seems to find opportunities to reveal itself through the tongue. The fruit of our lips finds its source in the root of our soul.

I've seen the countenance of children's faces wilt under the rage of a father's tongue. I've seen the spirit of a new Christian crushed because of the demeaning and debilitating words of an impatient, older Christian. I've seen characters assassinated, reputations ruined, marriages ripped apart because of an uncontrolled, wicked tongue. The tongue can be a devastating force of enormous destruction!

The answer? Stop all attempts at self-control and surrender to God's control. He can quench the raging fire. He can tame the snarling beast. He can provide the antidote to the poison of hellish, hateful speech. James does not rail against the tongue to condemn us for what we've all done in our past; rather, he wants to prevent us from allowing this behavior to go on into our future. This would be an appropriate time to pause and pray. Ask God to change your heart and your tongue today.

REAL FAITH PRODUCES GENUINE HUMILITY (JAMES 3:13 – 5:6)

One of the most desolate places in all the world is the Libyan desert in North Africa. Picture a desolate, unproductive, barren, scorched, useless mass of land. It's fit for little more than wandering nomads who stroll from oasis to oasis, driving scraggly herds day after day.

I remember a documentary several years back that featured a flyover shot of this vast desert. Beautiful ... but bleak. Miles and miles of shimmering waves of sand. But then something remarkable comes into focus. In the center of that wasteland, a patch of green appears—a paradise island in the midst of an ocean of sand. As the camera draws closer, we make out details. This is more than an oasis of palm trees; we see deep green plants, luscious fruit trees, thriving vegetation. When we finally calculate the scale of the massive oasis, we realize it runs through the desert for miles. Obviously, that track of green landscape has something the rest of the desert doesn't: *water ... lots and lots of water.* Engineers had sunk deep wells and pumped massive amounts of water to the surface, in the process quenching that parched land and producing an Eden-like paradise in what was once a barren, fruitless desolation.

This image vividly illustrates the Christian life. Left to our natural state, we humans are like deserts: rough, barren, dry, and fruitless. We have nothing to offer the world but dust and death. That's the natural condition of the soul apart from God's grace. But when the Spirit of God invades the otherwise desolate human heart, it teems with new life. A spring of living water satisfies the soul, and soon spiritual fruit begins to emerge.

James has already told us that "every good thing given and every perfect gift is from above, coming down from the Father of lights" (1:17). He has reminded us that God "brought us forth by the word of truth, so that we would be a kind of first fruits among His creatures" (1:18). This new birth from above—spiritual birth by the Holy Spirit—transforms the lives of believers from within. Throughout his letter, James encourages us believers to cultivate that implanted word (1:21). When we do so, it leads to living works of faith produced in us by God's Spirit.

In the first section, James argues that *real faith produces genuine stability* (1:1 – 1:27). It endures trials (1:2 – 12), resists temptations (1:13 – 18), and responds to God's Word (1:19 – 27). In the second section, James tells us that *real faith produces genuine love* (2:1 – 3:12). Faith rejects prejudice (2:1 – 13), acts kindly toward those in need (2:14 – 26), and refrains from harming others with the tongue (3:1 – 12).

KEY TERMS

ζῆλος [*zēlos*] (2205b) "jealousy, zeal"

In James the concept is closely related to "selfish ambition." Though the word can have positive connotations — being "zealous" or "jealous" for God (Rom. 10:2) — most often the zeal is portrayed as misguided and misplaced. In this case, the idea is self-centered zeal or self-serving acts of jealousy.

ταπεινόω [*tapeinoō*] (5013) "to humble, lower, make low"

Though James uses the word only once in his letter (4:10), the concept of humbling one-self can be found throughout his exhortations. The concept of humbling means to make oneself lower than his or her normal stature. In the ancient world, "humbling" was often associated with the physical act of bowing or lying down on the ground, demonstrating inner humility before someone of greater rank.

κρίνω [*krinō*] (2919) "to judge, divide, assess, decide"

The literal meaning is "to sift and separate" in order to isolate the components of a mixture. The primary use is metaphorical in the sense of "sifting through the details to arrive at a conclusion." In terms of a person, the idea is to sift the details of one's life in order to examine them and render a decision about a person's character. "Judgment," then, is the result of this sifting.

In this third section of his letter, James reminds us that *real faith produces genuine humility* (3:13–5:6). He reminds us that our goodness comes from God-given wisdom, not our own human wisdom (3:13–18). He calls us to turn to Him, not ourselves, for peaceful relationships (4:1–10). He then warns us against boasting about our lives instead of submitting to God's sovereignty (4:11–17). And he rails against the pride that so easily deludes the rich of this world (5:1–6). In each case, James encourages God-enabled humility, for apart from God's grace working in our hearts to produce godly wisdom and good works, we will be as fruitless as the parched Libyan desert.

Wise, Unwise, and Otherwise (James 3:13–18)

¹³Who among you is wise and understanding? Let him show by his good behavior his deeds in the gentleness of wisdom. ¹⁴But if you have bitter jealousy and selfish ambition in your heart, do not be arrogant and *so* lie against the truth. ¹⁵This wisdom is not that which comes down from above, but is earthly, natural, demonic. ¹⁶For where jealousy and selfish ambition

exist, there is disorder and every evil thing. [17]But the wisdom from above is first pure, then peaceable, gentle, reasonable, full of mercy and good fruits, unwavering, without hypocrisy. [18]And the seed whose fruit is righteousness is sown in peace by those who make peace.

A woodman's old proverb says, "A tree is best measured when it's down." The true size and quality of a tree's lumber can best be determined after it's been felled. So, too, the true measure of a person's accomplishments can be seen at the end of his or her life. This proverb is especially true of the life of Solomon, son of David. During his reign, Solomon thrived as an author, diplomat, poet, politician, philanthropist, architect, and engineer. At his zenith, Solomon had no equals.

How could Solomon accomplish so much during his lifetime? Second Chronicles 1 provides the answer. When he inherited the kingdom from his father, God appeared to him in a vision, saying, "Ask for whatever you want me to give you" (1:7 NIV). Can you imagine that offer? What would you ask for if the Lord of heaven and earth offered *anything you asked*?

Well, Solomon revealed his true character when he answered, "Give me now wisdom and knowledge, that I may go out and come in before this people, for who can rule this great people of Yours?" (2 Chron. 1:10). In essence, he said, "I've inherited an overwhelming task! More than anything else, I need wisdom! I need practical insight into the subtleties of life so I can govern Your people well. *This* I ask, and nothing more." Now, that's a response of humility! With open hands, he turned to God to give him what he needed to accomplish what he needed to do.

About a thousand years after Solomon asked for wisdom from God to accomplish his calling, another descendent of David named James wrote, "But if any of you lacks wisdom, let him ask of God, who gives to all generously and without reproach, and it will be given to him" (James 1:5). In fact, one might say that the book of James is the New Testament version of Old Testament wisdom literature. Like Solomon's own contrast between Madam Folly and Lady Wisdom in the opening chapters of Proverbs, James 3:13 – 18 contrasts the unwise and the wise. These six short verses paint two pictures with a palate of colorful words: one the portrait of someone who lacks God's wisdom, and the other of a person who has received the wisdom from above.

— **3:13** —

James kicks off with a question: "Who among you is wise and understanding?" James isn't really looking for a show of hands. Obviously, most people reading this

Unwise versus Wise (James 3:13–18)

	The Unwise	The Wise
Signs (3:13–14)	1. Bitter jealousy 2. Selfish ambition (3:14)	1. Good behavior 2. Gentle deeds (3:13)
Characteristics (3:14–15, 17)	1. Arrogant 2. Dishonest 3. Worldly 4. Natural 5. Demonic (3:14–15)	1. Pure 2. Peaceable 3. Gentle 4. Reasonable 5. Merciful 6. Bountiful 7. Unwavering 8. Sincere (3:17)
Results (3:16, 18)	1. Disorder 2. Every evil (3:16)	1. Righteousness 2. Peace (3:18)

want to think of themselves as wise and knowledgeable. It's like that once popular game show, *Who Wants to Be a Millionaire?* Dumb question. Almost anybody you ask would raise both hands! The real challenge is demonstrating the lengths and depths of your knowledge—how much you know about obscure and trivial things. Few measure up. That's the point of James's question. "You think you're wise and understanding? Well, we'll see about that. Let's take a look at a couple things that will test the quality of your wisdom."

James instructs the wise person to demonstrate wisdom by good behavior and gentle deeds (3:13). The first refers to the changed lifestyle of a believer, a topic James already has treated in great depth (see 2:14–26). The life of a wise person changes toward the good, exhibiting ready obedience to God's Word. This relates directly to the main message of James's letter: *real faith produces genuine works*. Smarts, wits, and education do not make a person wise; what does make a person wise is how well his or her lifestyle reflects the truth.

Second, "deeds in the gentleness of wisdom" refers to wisdom-inspired humility and meekness. People today view "meekness" and "gentleness" as marks of weak, spineless folks who let others walk all over them. Not so in Scripture! "Gentleness" is an aspect of the fruit of the Spirit in Galatians 5:23 and it's closely tied to "self-control." It's a word used to describe a high-spirited horse brought under control. He hasn't lost his natural strength, but he carries that strength with gentleness and humility. That's biblical wisdom.

This has profound practical implications. Are you looking for a good teacher or preacher? Invariably you'll gravitate toward the most intellectually astute person, preferably seminary trained. The more letters after his name, the better ... right? That's fine. Degrees and training are great, provided they're accompanied by a lifestyle patterned after the truth with an ego under control. Far too many credentialed teachers and eloquent preachers tend toward rash, foolish extremes. But wise leaders and mentors know when to put on the brakes and when to accelerate. It's not by accident that in his profile of church leaders, Paul sandwiches "able to teach" between the need to be "kind" and "patient" (2 Tim. 2:24).

— 3:14–16 —

Having introduced the idea of a wise person marked by a good way of life and gentle works, James shifts gears and spends some time describing the signs of an unwise person. He starts off in verse 14 with two heart-level characteristics: bitter jealousy and selfish ambition. These dispositions overflow into a person's life, which James describes in verses 14–15; he mentions the ultimate results of such actions in verse 16.

"Bitter jealousy" likely refers to jealousy that harbors hard feelings. Jealousy refers to a person with full hands who feels his or her own belongings or accomplishments are threatened by another's success. This first vice usually accompanies the second: selfish ambition. The heart of an unwise person carries an insatiable hunger to push himself or herself to the top.

By the way, don't think for a second that Christian circles are free from jealousy and selfish ambition. If you attend enough Bible conferences, visit enough churches, or hang out long enough in Christian academia, you'll find a lot of petty jealousy and unbridled ambition. You'll also see it among singers, preachers, missionaries, and educators—saints jockeying for higher positions and jostling to stay on top.

James gives five characteristics of counterfeit wisdom dominated by the flesh, the opposite of wisdom given from above. The human heart generates this fleshly wisdom.

1. *Arrogant* (3:14). The Greek word used here basically means to exult over others. For wicked people, it means proudly justifying one's own sinful actions. This is contrary to God-inspired humility. The great theologian Charles Hodge said it best: "The Bible doctrine concerning man ... is eminently adapted to make him what he was designed to be: to exalt without inflating; to humble without degrading."[1]

2. *Lying against the truth* (3:14). Despite what a lot of philosophers, theologians, and, yes, preachers, are saying today, truth remains an immovable standard. Forget

From My Journal

Unbridled Zeal

Back in the 1950s I worked my way through school in a machine shop, which I regarded as my personal mission field. I remember witnessing to a man who happened to be a member of a denomination vastly different from mine. Naturally, I targeted him for conversion. After all, I had a firm footing on the truth, while this guy was neck-deep in error! I wasn't aware of it at the time, but I came across as a raving zealot. I had Bible verses, facts, answers, provocative questions—an entire arsenal of spiritual weapons to slaughter my opposition. And I was using everything I had. I wasn't just witnessing; the way I swung the Sword of Truth against infidels back then probably would have put medieval crusaders to shame!

I hammered away at that misguided fellow day after day, shift after shift. Relentless, merciless evangelism. Finally he'd had enough! He grabbed me by the arm, looked me in the eye, and said, "Listen to me. You've convinced me by the facts that I'm wrong, but I will never change ..." Just as my mind was rushing to come up with a good response to such a stupid, foolish statement, he added, "... because I can't stand you!"

Those words still sting as I think about how foolish I had been. It was like somebody throwing a rock through the window of my soul, a rock carrying a message I desperately needed to hear ... and would never forget. You can have all the facts on your side, but if you don't have the wisdom to know how to share those facts without assaulting a person, keep your mouth shut. I had put that coworker down time and time again, beating him black and blue with the facts. As a result, he couldn't stand me. I was worse than annoying—*I was downright obnoxious.*

The great Howard Hendricks of Dallas Seminary summed up this message in one of his pithy proverbs, for which he's a legend. I'm sure these words still ring in the ears of thousands of his former students: "They won't care how much you know until they know how much you care." Those wise words reflect the kind of gentle words and deeds urged in James 3:13.

postmodern concepts of relative truth or the uncertainty of truth. God's revealed truth corresponds to the way things really are. The unwise, however, change their truth standard to match their beliefs or lifestyles.

I learned this lesson the hard way many years ago. I had been deeply impressed with the life of a Bible teacher. I dearly loved and respected him. I knew of no one who could handle the Word like that particular scholar. I quoted him, followed him, studied with him, and longed to be like him. A lot of us did. But gradually I began to discern certain things in his teachings that didn't seem to square with the Bible. So I went to him and said, "Look, this verse says so-and-so. How does that fit with what you're saying?" Instead of explaining the passage, he pulled rank on me. In his reaction and verbal rebuke, I witnessed arrogance, defensiveness, and self-justification. Eventually the situation came to a head and he put me down, castigating me for my disagreement—just for asking about inconsistencies between his words and *the* Word. That teacher exhibited a pride that led him to clutch his self-made doctrines even when they failed to align with God's truth.

3. *Earthly* (3:15). The word means "of the earth," and James contrasts it with wisdom "from above." It's a purely horizontal perspective—worldly measures of truth, earthly standards of success, material motives, and temporal priorities.

4. *Natural* (3:15). This fourth characteristic of the unwise literally means "soulish." The Greek word *psychikos* is related to our word "psyche," which applies to the self—the inner human motives. The source of this wisdom is our own thoughts, attitudes, interests, and pursuits, not the Spirit's wisdom from above.

5. *Demonic* (3:15). This doesn't necessarily mean their worldly wisdom comes straight from demonic beings, though in some cases that may be so. Rather, the emphasis is on wisdom that reflects a philosophy or pattern of thinking so contrary to God's truth that Satan himself could endorse it.

So, we see the heart of the unwise marked by bitter jealousy and selfish ambition (3:14). Such a person is arrogant, dishonest, worldly, natural, and demonic in his or her

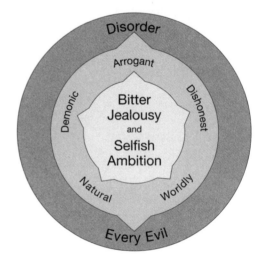

Fruits of the Unwise

character (3:14–15). James ends his portrait of the unwise with a brief description of the end result: "For where jealousy and selfish ambition exist, there is disorder and every evil thing" (3:16). In the wake of the unwise we see waves of chaos, confusion, disharmony, antagonism, and pettiness—certainly not an example to follow!

—**3:17–18**—

Having described wisdom from below in frank terms in 3:14–16, James ends with the stark contrast of "wisdom from above" (3:17–18). He has already mentioned the truly wise person as demonstrating this wisdom by his good behavior and deeds done in gentleness (3:13). Now he revisits the person with this kind of heart, showing the characteristics that mark his or her life (3:17) and the results that follow (3:18).

1. *Pure.* Wisdom from above is "first pure." The word "first" means more than merely first on a list. It indicates first in order of importance. God-given wisdom produces purity of internal motives as well as external actions. This kind of lifestyle has a built-in promise, as Jesus said: "Blessed are the pure in heart, for they shall see God" (Matt. 5:8). Purity of thought and deed helps us see God working in all of our circumstances.

2. *Peaceable.* In contrast to the "bitter jealousy" and "selfish ambition" of the unwise, God-given wisdom produces peaceful relationships. The natural tendency is to be argumentative, quarrelsome, belligerent, and quick-tempered. But God's supernatural life within us guards against alienating others. Rather, it seeks to remove ill will. Jesus has a promise for the peaceable: "Blessed are the peacemakers, for they shall be called sons of God" (Matt. 5:9).

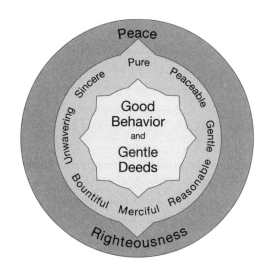

Fruits of the Wise

Peace · Pure · Peaceable · Sincere · Gentle · Unwavering · Good Behavior and Gentle Deeds · Reasonable · Bountiful · Merciful · Righteousness

3. *Gentle.* The third characteristic of a wise person is gentleness. This is a different Greek word than the word translated "gentleness" in 3:13. That verse emphasized humility. In verse 17, the meaning is "equitable, moderate, yielding." It describes a person who surrenders his rights for a higher ideal. In our day, when

people feel their rights have been violated, they strike out with a lawsuit over the most insignificant offenses. That's the world's wisdom: petty, contentious, selfish, bitter. But with God's wisdom, we meet petty infractions of our "rights" with a different kind of ethic: "Whoever slaps you on your right cheek, turn the other to him also. If anyone wants to sue you and take your shirt, let him have your coat also" (Matt. 5:39 – 40).

4. *Reasonable*. This Greek word appears only here in the New Testament. It comes from two Greek words, "well" and "persuadable." Together they mean, "easily persuaded." But don't get the wrong idea. This doesn't mean a wise person is a naïve pushover! Rather, it has the sense of "teachable," somebody who puts aside stubbornness and readily yields to the truth. It can refer to a person who is conciliatory, flexible, and open to change. When the Spirit of God captures the heart and does His work deep within, He softens us.

Abraham's relationship with Lot in Genesis 13 exemplifies this kind of conciliatory attitude. God had blessed these two men with so much livestock that the same fields could no longer sustain their herds. Now remember, Abraham was the older of the two, and he was the one to whom God had promised all the land of Canaan. He could have said, "Lot, take your herdsmen and your flocks and move on." But he didn't. According to Genesis 13:8 – 9, "Abram said to Lot, 'Please let there be no strife between you and me, nor between my herdsmen and your herdsmen, for we are brothers. Is not the whole land before you? Please separate from me; if to the left, then I will go to the right; or if to the right, then I will go to the left.'" Now, that's a man of wisdom — *reasonable ... cooperative ... flexible.*

5. *Merciful.* The fifth character trait of those who exhibit wisdom from above is mercy. If grace is giving a person a blessing he or she doesn't deserve, mercy is withholding a just punishment a person *does* deserve. Mercy implies looking on somebody with compassion when they probably deserve punishment. While worldly wisdom would heap on ridicule or judgment, mercy shows kindness and benevolence.

6. *Bountiful.* Wise people are filled with "good fruits." James ties this closely with the previous quality, "mercy." It probably refers to the outward actions that accompany the attitude of pity for others. A person who has genuine mercy will give bountiful blessings to others. In the last chapter, James used the example of the useless "faith" of those who saw a brother or sister in need but who refused to do anything about it (2:15 – 16). Godly wisdom, however, puts mercy to work, abounding in fruitful deeds.

7. *Unwavering.* This term suggests a person with fixed principles, who will never violate biblical standards regardless of the situation. This steadfast person is never willing to compromise on the truth of Scripture. Never! Now, this doesn't

Erich Lessing/Art Resource, NY

Theatre masks worn by a Greek *hypokritēs* ("actor").

contradict the earlier characteristic of "reasonableness." Rather, James indicates the balance that true wisdom brings. A wise person does not take the virtue of steadfastness to the extreme of ornery legalism, nor does he or she take flexibility to the extreme of compromising on absolute truth. That kind of balance takes true wisdom … and that comes only from above.

8. *Sincere.* Finally, James describes wisdom from above as "unhypocritical." The Greek word *hypokrisis* comes from a term used to describe an actor playing two parts. In Greek plays one actor would often switch masks, costumes, or props to take on different roles. (The fewer actors who put on a play, the larger the cut from the ticket sales!) When the actor played a comedic role, he would wear a mask with a big smile. For a tragic character, the mask would change to sorrow. He'd then run off the stage and come out with an angry face for the villain. That's the essence of hypocrisy—a shiftiness, instability, unpredictability. But believers endowed with the Spirit of wisdom will live a life of sincerity. All the masks come off and they follow the WYSIWYG principle: "What You See Is What You Get."

Following the eight characteristics of a wise person, we see the results in verse 18: "The seed whose fruit is righteousness is sown in peace by those who make peace." The word "peace" refers to relational harmony, peace with one another. Remember the outcome of false "wisdom" in James 3:16 — "disorder and every evil thing"? The polar opposite lifestyle produces the opposite result: order (peace) and every good thing (righteousness).

James makes his point crystal clear. *If you claim to have wisdom like you should, then why do you live like you shouldn't?*

Application

Trapped between Two Portraits

Imagine yourself sitting in the center of a small art gallery. The brightly lit room appears empty except for two contrasting portraits on opposite walls. On the one side hangs the portrait of an arrogant, worldly, devilish fellow, featured on a dark backdrop that stirs emotions of anger and envy. A scraggly beard and mustache veil his features, and a large hat casts a shadow over his shifty eyes. He leaves chaos and destruction in his wake as he advances, unflinching, toward the pursuit of his goals, driven by jealousy and ambition. The caption beneath the portrait reads: "The Unwise," painted by "Self."

The portrait on the facing wall couldn't be more different. That man sports a gentle demeanor, his posture relaxed and his expression serene. His eyes feel inviting and his hands appear ready for service. Behind him people follow, eager to hear his words and mimic his actions. Children celebrate his arrival, delighted to see what gifts he might bring. Clearly respected, he shows no signs of pride, and in his path are joy, peace, and prosperity. Below this portrait the caption says: "The Wise," painted by "The Spirit of God."

In light of the two contrasting pictures of the wise and unwise in James 3:13 – 18, with which portrait do you align? Do you struggle with jealousy of others' successes? Is your life motivated by personal pursuits at the cost of peace? How have these inward feelings and outward actions affected those around you? Do disorder and pettiness mark your life? Do you pursue the things of the world rather than the things of God?

Or is your life characterized by gentleness and humility? Do people know you as a person of mercy, authenticity, and peace? Do you act the same way at home as you do at work ... or at church ... or in public? Do you build others up, rejoice at their successes, and place the needs and interests of others ahead of your own? Do you leave harmony and joy in your wake?

As you seriously think through these questions, avoid answering the way you *wish* things were. Answer the way things really *are*. Try to defend your answer with actual evidence from examples that come to mind. Ask yourself whether your closest family members or friends would answer these questions about you in the same way.

After you've identified with either the portrait of the wise or the unwise, think through your response. For the wise, respond to God with thanksgiving, praising Him for molding you through the unfolding years of your life. You're not wise by your own making, but by the inner working of God's Spirit. For the unwise, ask God for wisdom, then determine which character problems you need to address specifically by God's help. Do you need to mend a particular relationship? Do it. Need to forsake a certain selfish pursuit? Stop it. Need to start a neglected spiritual exercise like prayer, worship, or Scripture reading? Get started now. It's never too late to start doing what's right.

Don't let the effects of folly spiral out of control. Allow God to begin repainting your portrait with life-transforming colors. You'll begin to reflect not your own frail character, but the character of His Son.

How Fights Are Started ... and Stopped (James 4:1–10)

---

¹What is the source of quarrels and conflicts among you? Is not the source your pleasures that wage war in your members? ²You lust and do not have; *so* you commit murder. You are envious and cannot obtain; *so* you fight and quarrel. You do not have because you do not ask. ³You ask and do not receive, because you ask with wrong motives, so that you may spend *it* on your pleasures. ⁴You adulteresses, do you not know that friendship with the world is hostility toward God? Therefore whoever wishes to be a friend of the world makes himself an enemy of God. ⁵Or do you think that the Scripture speaks to no purpose: "He jealously desires the Spirit which He has made to dwell in us"? ⁶But He gives a greater grace. Therefore *it* says, "God is opposed to the proud, but gives grace to the humble." ⁷Submit therefore to God. Resist the devil and he will flee from you. ⁸Draw near to God and He will draw near to you. Cleanse your hands, you sinners; and purify your hearts, you double-minded. ⁹Be miserable and mourn and weep; let your laughter be turned into mourning and your joy to gloom. ¹⁰Humble yourselves in the presence of the Lord, and He will exalt you.

Ever eat grass?

In the neighborhood where I grew up, that was the standard punishment for anybody who lost a fight. Victor and spectators jeered and howled while the vanquished grazed. Then we would all go play again … until the next fight. You probably had your own unwritten protocol that integrated fighting into the fabric of adolescent subculture. Our cycle of "fighting, eating grass, playing, fighting, eating grass, playing" sure sounds silly, doesn't it? And it was.

I just wish we had grown out of it by our adult years.

No, we don't eat grass any more, but we still seem to work fighting into our lives. Fighting comes naturally to most people — especially men. Why? Because we're each born with a scrappy nature that prefers going for the jugular instead of giving in. It all started after the fall, recorded in Genesis 3. The first fight between Cain and Abel ended in murder (Gen. 4:1 – 8). Since then we can chart history easily by its conflicts and wars. It isn't surprising, then, that James addresses the cycle of conflicts among Christians. Worshiping, fighting, praying, worshiping, fighting, praying — it was the same two thousand years ago as it is today. That's the specific problem James addresses in 4:1 – 10.

The chapter break between James 3:18 and 4:1 is unfortunate. Remember, James didn't number chapters or verses — those were added centuries later for convenience. The fourth chapter continues to develop the same thoughts as those in chapter 3. In fact, the initial comments he made regarding the destructive nature of the tongue in 3:6 – 10 build to a climax in the beginning of chapter 4 as he deals with open conflicts among Christians. And he further unpacks the effects of bitter jealousy and selfish ambition introduced in 3:13 – 15. So, in these first ten verses of chapter 4, James sets forth the reasons for fights among believers, as well as their tragic results. But James doesn't leave us without some answers on how to stop these conflicts that have taken their toll within our ranks. His diagnosis includes a prescription for handling all kinds of conflict.

— **4:1** —

We should expect the world, with its back to God and devoid of His Word and Spirit, to be characterized by fighting. People fight in business, in politics, in religion, in education, in marriage, and in sports. But sad to say, believers also fight in church. In fact, this is the specific arena of conflict James has in mind in the first part of verse 1: "What is the source of quarrels and conflicts *among you*?" Throughout his letter he's addressing Jewish Christian believers (3:1; 4:11). This section reveals that they are obviously having problems getting along.

Their problem? "Quarrels and conflicts." The Greek word translated "quarrels" is a general word for fights or warfare from which we get our word "polemics." The word for "conflicts" is a more narrow term for skirmishes, individual attacks. In terms of physical warfare, the first term would refer to the war; the second would signify a specific battle. These Christians were in an ongoing state of quarreling that exploded into open conflict.

Where do these wars and skirmishes come from? We might be tempted to say, "From Satan!" or "From false brethren!" or "From heretics who crept in secretly!" Wrong! James answers, "Is not the source your pleasures that wage war in your members?" James is good at rubbing our nose in our own depravity when we need it. It may seem harsh at times, and if you dwell there every minute of the day, it can be.

But frequent reminders of our own wicked natures apart from God's grace can do us great good. Remember that James named the source of temptation and sin as our "own lust" (1:14). And disorder and wickedness result from our own "jealousy and selfish ambition" (3:16). In the same way, we are primarily responsible for our own infighting. Satan may have a field day and unbelievers may feel pleased to see us go at it, *but we are the ones to blame.*

James 4:1 uses a more neutral term for "pleasures." It literally means "enjoyments." This may include the desire to be successful, the desire to use your gifts and talents, or the desire for relationships, for food, for leisure, and or the necessities of life. The problem comes when the world frustrates our achievement of these desires. Then the "pleasures" of life become sources of conflict. When something steps in the way of fulfilling our desires, we tend to fight until we get our way.

— 4:2–4 —

Those who lust for things they don't have commit "murder" (4:2). Of course, few people actually commit murder in a literal sense, but we are all guilty of murder in our hearts and with our lips. Remember Christ's interpretation of the Law: "You have heard that the ancients were told, 'You shall not commit murder' and 'Whoever commits murder shall be liable to the court.' But I say to you that everyone who is angry with his brother shall be guilty before the court" (Matt. 5:21). Similarly, John succinctly noted: "Everyone who hates his brother is a murderer; and you know that no murderer has eternal life abiding in him" (1 John 3:15).

Those who fight out of frustration fail to turn to God for their provision. Jesus said, "Until now you have asked for nothing in My name; ask and you will receive, so that your joy may be made full" (John 16:24). Fighters fail to pray. "But," some may object, "I've prayed and prayed for such-and-such, but He still hasn't given me what I want!" James has an answer for this: "You ask and you do not receive, because you ask with wrong motives, so that you may spend it on your pleasures" (James 4:3).

God's promise of answering our prayers and giving us what we ask for must be governed by all the Bible's teachings about prayer. This isn't a "name-it-claim-it" kind of deal, or a "gab-it-grab-it" theology. The apostle John helps balance our perspective on prayer.

> Whatever we ask we receive from Him, because we keep His commandments and do the things that are pleasing in His sight ... This is the confidence which we have before Him, that, if we ask anything according to His will, He hears us. (1 John 3:22; 5:14)

Did you catch that? James warns against pleasure-motivated prayer; John encourages God-pleasing prayer. Spiritualy minded Christians pray for things that please God, not for things that fuel their own envious, selfish desires.

James addresses his readers in verse 4 as severely as any passage in Scripture: "Adulteresses!" *That* is bound to grab their attention. Why does he call some of his readers "adulteresses?" Because they're cheating on God! Their attention, affection, and allegiance are not toward God and His people, but toward themselves and the world.

The word "world" here is the Greek word *kosmos*. It refers to the world system at odds with God. It's fallen humanity collectively shaking its fist at God, turning its back on the Creator. God calls people "adulterers" only if they're supposed to be faithful to Him but aren't. The unsaved person is not an adulterer. But the saved person who cozies up with the cosmos is committing adultery and therefore making himself or herself an enemy of God.

So James refers to Christians committing spiritual adultery. This worldliness in the church causes quarrels and conflicts. It comes when we play politics, place economics before ministry, or try to entertain rather than discipline. It surfaces when we replace unchanging truth with cultural fads or turn a relationship with Christ into just another world religion. Those moves split churches and destroy ministries.

To sum up, frustrated inner desires lead to murderous thoughts, arguments, failure to pray, and prayer with wrong motives (4:1–3). A heart beating to the rhythm of the world leads to anger with God and opposition to His words and works (4:4). Both of these conditions lead to quarreling and fighting among believers.

—4:5–6—

Thankfully, James doesn't drop the problem on us without a solution. Like a good physician, he follows the diagnosis of our ailment with a prescription. He presents a synopsis of the solution, a treatment for infighting that includes pointing out the power and then laying out a principle.

Verse 5 is notoriously difficult to translate and interpret. One scholar calls it "one of the most difficult verses" in the whole New Testament![2] James alludes to some Old Testament passage or teaching—"Or do you think that the Scripture speaks to no purpose?" But the actual statement is difficult to render into English without making all kinds of interpretive decisions. A quick comparison of a few Bible translations demonstrates how tough this verse can be.

> ... He jealously desires the Spirit which He has made to dwell in us. (NASB)
> ... The spirit he caused to live in us envies intensely. (NIV)
> ... The spirit that dwelleth in us lusteth to envy. (KJV)
> ... The spirit that God caused to live within us has an envious yearning. (NET)
> ... God yearns jealously for the spirit that he has made to dwell in us. (NRSV)

So, which is it? The problem is that the words James uses for "jealously" and "desires" are neutral terms that can have either a positive or negative connotation. Also, the word "spirit" can refer either to the human spirit or the Holy Spirit. Further confusing the problem, the form of the word "spirit" in Greek can be either the subject of the phrase or the object! So, is James saying that the human spirit, given to us when God created Adam, "envies intensely" ... or that God is intensely jealous for us to honor Him with our spirits ... or that God's Spirit within us is intensely jealous for our faithfulness ... or that God is intensely jealous for us to honor Him by the Holy Spirit living in us?

I think the context of this phrase helps us clear up the confusion. Remember that James 4:4 accuses believers of being "adulteresses," those who cheat on God and His ways in favor of the world and its ways. Then James follows up with God's response to believers' unfaithfulness. We might render this phrase, "The Spirit that dwells in us is longing jealously."

If this is the meaning of the phrase, James probably has dozens of Old Testament passages in mind when he says, "the Scripture speaks." God's jealousy for His people's faithfulness is like a husband's longing for his wife's fidelity. We see this theme best developed in the book of Hosea, where God's relationship to Israel is illustrated by the prophet's relationship to his prostitute wife, Gomer. This background fits the image of God as a husband justly jealous for the faithfulness of His bride, the church. So, the first solution to the problem presented by James is the power of the Holy Spirit. God wants control of your life by His Spirit, and that means relinquishing your own control.

Years ago when my children were little, they wanted to drive the car. On occasion, I let them. But I didn't just hand my six-year-old the keys and say, "Be back by seven." No way! I sat them on my lap, shifted into drive, and let them "steer" a few feet right or left in the safety of the driveway. Oh, they thought they were driving … and in a certain sense, they were. But the reality is, I had my foot poised on the brake, my hands near the steering wheel, and a close eye on my surroundings. I was in complete control — and my son or daughter cooperated with me. That's the kind of control God wants to have in our lives. If we release our grip and our selfish demands, He'll make sure we're steering straight.

This kind of humble surrender to God's control is the key principle described in verse 6: "But He gives a greater grace." Greater than what? Greater than our wills, our selfishness, our inability to relinquish control. That's the primary work of the Holy Spirit. It's not easy to turn from the self-centered pride of life and humble ourselves before God. But when we do, we'll find a storehouse of God's grace ready to be poured out on us. The nearly forgotten hymn of Annie Johnson Flint puts it well:

> He giveth more grace when the burden grows greater;
> He sendeth more strength when the labors increase.
> To added affliction He addeth His mercy;
> To multiplied trials, His multiplied peace.[3]

— 4:7–10 —

James ends with practical advice on how to put the principle of humility into practice through the power of the Spirit. Our frustrated pursuit of pleasure causes our propensity to fight (4:1 – 4), and God's Spirit of grace is the prescription (4:5 – 6). James now spells out the way we can apply the cure to our lives (4:7 – 10). It's the daily regimen — the proper dosing, if you will — that describes how to make God-given humility a part of our character.

Initially, we must submit to God (4:7). This is an imperative — a command. Don't fight, resist, or push. Instead, surrender, resign, and relinquish. Yes, it goes against the grain of our natural tendency to fight; but God gives grace to do it. Say, "Lord, I give up. I'm beaten."

This goes hand in hand with resisting the devil. Don't take that statement out of context. James isn't suddenly shifting into a lesson on casting out demons. He's saying the proud pursuit of our own "I wills" looks a lot like Satan's rebellious conceit that led to his downfall (Isa. 14:13 – 14). To follow the philosophy of the world is to follow the demonic worldly wisdom (James 4:15). It's the opposite of following God.

Verse 8 tells us, "Draw near to God and He will draw near to you." In terms of salvation, we can't draw any nearer to God than we already are. When we place our faith in Christ alone to save us, we are immediately baptized by the Spirit into the body of Christ (1 Cor. 12:13). The Spirit sealed us for redemption (Eph. 4:30), and we have been given "everything pertaining to life and godliness" (2 Peter 1:3). We *have been saved* (past tense) by God's grace through faith alone (Eph. 2:8–9). All of this describes our *position* in Christ, which can never change.

But James 4:8 is speaking about our daily relationship with God — our experiential growth in knowing Him and progressively becoming more like His Son. Then, how do we "draw near to God" in our personal relationship with Him? The rest of 4:8–10 provides that answer in rapid-fire fashion:

- Cleanse your hands (Stop doing evil!)
- Purify your hearts (Stop thinking evil!)
- Be miserable and mourn and weep (Feel remorse for your wickedness!)
- Let your laughter be turned into mourning and your joy to gloom (Don't make a joke out of your wickedness!)

All these commands reflect the inner thoughts and outward effects of *repentance*. If we clench our fists and we turn our backs to God in proud rebellion, then drawing near to God means turning our faces toward Him and opening our hands to whatever He has for us. Then, in the arms of the One who cares about us most, we receive from Him what we had been trying to gain for ourselves: "Humble yourselves in the presence of the Lord, and He will exalt you" (4:10).

James's message is clear. Instead of putting up a fight, put on faith. Instead of causing conflict, nurture contentment. Instead of stomping and stonewalling, willingly submit to God. When you do, He will give you the grace to handle whatever circumstance you're facing.

Application

Slaying the Green-Eyed Monster

O, beware, my lord, of jealousy;
It is the green-eyed monster which doth mock
The meat it feeds on.[4]

Those words from Shakespeare's *Othello* are the background for the English idiom, "green with envy." The ancient Greeks thought that feelings of envy and its sister sin, jealousy, caused an overproduction of bile, turning that person a pale, putrid green. The idea of being sick with jealousy comes from that deep, nauseous feeling we get when we're jealous or envious. James blames uncontrolled envy for all kinds of problems when he writes, "You are envious and cannot obtain; so you fight and quarrel" (4:2).

What exactly is envy? How does it differ from its sibling, jealousy? Envy is a painful and resentful awareness of an advantage enjoyed by someone else, accompanied by a strong desire to possess the *same* advantage. Envy sheepishly wants to have what someone else possesses. Jealousy exclusively wants to possess what it already has. Jealousy is coarse and cruel. Envy is sneaky and subtle. Jealousy clutches and smothers. Envy is forever reaching, longing, squinting, pondering, and saying sinister things.

Envy finds socially acceptable ways of expressing personal resentment. One favorite method is the "but" approach. When I talk of someone I envy, I may say, "He is an excellent salesman, *but* he really isn't very sincere." Or "Yeah, she has a brilliant mind, *but* what a dull teacher!" Or "The man is an outstanding surgeon, *but* he doesn't mind charging an arm and a leg!"

Another favorite avenue of expressing envy is the "reversal" approach. Somebody does a good job and I cast a shadow over it by questioning the motive. An individual gives a truly generous gift, and we mutter, "He's obviously trying to impress us." A Christian couple buys a new car and a few pieces of furniture. Watch out! There will be somebody who will squeeze out an envious comment like, "Hmmmm. I wonder how many missionaries could have been supported with that car payment?"

The "unfavorable comparison" approach is equally cynical. The baritone does a commendable job on Sunday as an envious pew-warmer thinks, *Yeah, he was all right. But you should have heard So-and-so sing that piece.* Or, "If you think my neighbor has a nice lawn, you should see that house down on First Street!" Or "That's a nice car, all right, but *Consumer Reports* gave it only an average rating."

It's a curious fact that envy is a tension often found among professionals, the gifted, and the highly competent. You know the sort: doctors, singers, artists, lawyers, entrepreneurs, authors, entertainers, preachers, educators, athletes, politicians. Strange, isn't it? Such capable folks find it nearly impossible to applaud others in their own field who excel a shade or two more than they. Envy's fangs may be hidden, but take care when the creature coils. No matter how cultured and dignified it may appear, the "green-eyed monster" can rip a person to shreds and leave a whole community in chaos.

Look at the monster in Scripture. It sold Joseph into slavery, drove David into exile, threw Daniel into the lions' den, put Christ on trial, and nearly split the church at Corinth. Paul tells us envy is one of the prevailing traits of depravity (Rom. 1:29). And it hangs around with other beasts like profanity, suspicion, and conceit (1 Tim. 6:4).

Are you struggling with envy? Ask yourself these questions: When somebody at work gets a commendation or promotion for which you, too, are eligible, how do you respond? When somebody at church gets recognition for an accomplishment, what's your reaction? Do you share the news with a "but" attached? Do you try to discern wrong motives that might be driving the recognition? Do you try to "put it into perspective" by comparison? If so, you've been bitten by the green-eyed monster. Feeling sick yet?

What's the cure? *Contentment.* Feeling comfortable and secure with who you are and where you are. Not having to "be better" or "go further" or "own more" or "prove to the world" or "reach the top." Contentment means surrendering your frustrated hopes and missed goals to God, who alone "makes poor and rich; He brings low, He also exalts" (1 Sam. 2:7). Having some struggles with envy? Eating your heart out because somebody's a step or two ahead of you in the race and gaining momentum? *Relax.* You are *you*—not him or her! And you're responsible to do the best you can with what you've got for as long as you're able.

The choice is yours—*contentiousness* or *contentment.* If you want the peace that comes with contentment, why don't you spend some time committing Philippians 4:11–13 to memory? Then turn to God and ask for strength to slay the green-eyed monster.

The Perils of Playing God (James 4:11–17)

---

[11]Do not speak against one another, brethren. He who speaks against a brother or judges his brother, speaks against the law and judges the law; but if you judge the law, you are not a doer of the law but a judge *of it.* [12]There is *only* one Lawgiver and Judge, the One who is able to save and to destroy; but who are you who judge your neighbor? [13]Come now, you who say, "Today or tomorrow we will go to such and such a city, and spend a year there and engage in business and make a profit." [14]Yet you do not know what your life will be like tomorrow. You are *just* a vapor that appears for a little while and then vanishes away. [15]Instead, *you ought* to say, "If the Lord wills, we will live and also do this or that." [16]But as it is, you boast in your arrogance; all such boasting is evil. [17]Therefore, to one who knows *the* right thing to do and does not do it, to him it is sin.

Without question, Jesus Christ best demonstrates true humility. He voluntarily gave up His heavenly position, came into the world and became a blue-collar laborer, lived in perfect obedience to God and the Law, and willingly sacrificed His life on the cross for the sins of all (Phil. 2:6–8). This perfect humility of God the

Son becomes a model for us in our own pursuit of humility. Paul said, "Have this attitude in yourselves which was also in Christ Jesus" (2:5).

And to back up a little more, Paul warned the Philippians against the very same kinds of egocentric arrogance that James rails against throughout his own letter. Paul writes, "Do nothing from selfishness or empty conceit, but with humility of mind regard one another as more important than yourselves; do not merely look out for your own personal interests, but also for the interests of others" (Phil. 2:3–4).

In James 3:13–5:6, James develops the theme that *real faith produces genuine humility*. In 4:11–17, James takes us deeper, revealing more ways we assert an arrogant spirit. The first has to do with the way we often view others (4:11–12). He deals with our tendency to take the place of God in other peoples' lives as we judge or criticize them. The second has to do with the way we often view ourselves (4:13–16). In these verses, he deals with our tendency to take the place of God in our own lives as we presume or boast in ourselves. In both cases—whether playing judge over others or playing king for ourselves—we err by playing roles reserved for God alone.

— **4:11–12** —

The objective of playing God in the lives of others is to imagine yourself superior to other Christians and to put them down in various ways. The one who takes on God's role becomes a qualified critic, somebody who stands over a fellow, assuming a position of superiority.

We find the two simple rules of the game in verse 11. The first is to "speak against" a brother or sister in Christ. What does this look like? Scripture gives several examples using the same Greek word, *katalaleō* ("to talk down"), both in the Greek translation of the Old Testament as well as in the Greek New Testament.

- Aaron and Miriam *spoke against* Moses for marrying a Cushite woman (Num. 12:8).
- The people of Israel *spoke against* God by complaining about their conditions in the wilderness (Num. 21:5).
- The psalmist says a wicked person will *speak against* his brother, slandering him with lies (Ps. 50:20).
- Job's friends *spoke against* Job, insulting him and crushing him with their words (Job 19:1–3).
- Unbelievers *speak against* Christians, slandering them as evildoers (1 Peter 2:12; 3:16).

What does this recounting of *katalaleō* tell us? Let me put it bluntly. James is suggesting that Christians who "speak against" their brothers or sisters in Christ include themselves in that biblical register of rebellious mumblers, moaning grumblers, deceitful slanderers, crushing insulters, and wicked slanderers. (Not exactly the best company!)

Let me show you how this game works. You talk down against the other person in the ears of the hearer, hoping to lower their estimate of the person (and in the process you hope to make yourself look all the better). Of course, you have to cover up your malicious intent with creative sentimentality. So, you begin your statements with "Now, stop me if I'm wrong, but …" Or, "Now, I don't mean to be critical, but …" Or, "Perhaps I shouldn't say this about him or her, but …" Or even, "I really like So-and-So as a person, but …"

James also brings up the horrible habit of judging believers. These two go hand in hand—speaking against a sister and judging her; slandering a brother and condemning him. The Bible repeatedly condemns judgmental attitudes and actions. Jesus said, "Do not judge so that you will not be judged" (Matt. 7:1). And Paul wrote, "You have no excuse, everyone of you who passes judgment, for in that which you judge another, you condemn yourself" (Rom. 2:1).

The idea of withholding judgment is certainly biblical. At the same time, though, we need to note the context. Jesus spoke of a pharisaical, legalistic judgmentalism with a "more-righteous-than-thou" attitude: "Or how can you say to your brother, 'Let me take the speck out of your eye,' and behold, the log is in your own eye?" (Matt. 7:4). Paul adds, "But do you suppose this, O man, when you pass judgment on those who practice such things and do the same yourself, that you will escape the judgment of God?" (Rom. 2:3).

In short, the Bible targets self-serving, malicious judgment while actually encouraging wise, righteous discernment. Jesus said, "Do not judge according to appearance, but judge with righteous judgment" (John 7:24). And Paul said, "What have I to do with judging outsiders? Do you not judge those who are within the church? But those who are outside, God judges. Remove the wicked man from among yourselves" (1 Cor. 5:12–13). So, let's be clear. James isn't suggesting we be gullible and permissive, letting people get away with anything. Remember, in his own letter James confronts fellow Christians about their sins. But there's a difference between confrontation for the purpose of building up and condemnation for the purpose of tearing down.

James says that if you tear down and judge your fellow Christian, you become a lawbreaker. Which law does James refer to? This isn't the Law of Moses, and certainly not the additional laws of Judaism. James refers to the law he's been

Fact-Check

An event back in seminary still haunts me. We had a guest missionary speaker who did a lousy job in his presentation. Afterward a group of us stood in the back and bad-mouthed the message. We ripped him apart with a smug, critical spirit. And we weren't concealing our scorn, because an underclassman overheard us. He targeted me for censure because—I hate to admit it—I was one of the officers of the student body. I should have known better.

That younger man grabbed me by the arm and said, "Chuck, you don't know all the facts."

"What do you mean?" I said, "That was a pitiful message!"

He responded: "Did you know that two hours before the message, his wife called and told him his youngest son had been killed? Did you know that three months before, his wife was diagnosed with terminal cancer? And in spite of all that, he still came and delivered his message."

The younger student had every right to confront me. You can't imagine the shame I felt. I had judged—and spoken against—a brother in Christ who delivered his poor message under unimaginably difficult circumstances. I didn't know the facts.

Far too often Christians criticize others before we get all the facts. We observe an event, catch a few words of a conversation, or gather a handful of random facts. We then leap to conclusions and start flapping our jaws about it. The jabbering catches on and spreads, and before you know it the "gossip" becomes "news." There's nothing more contagious in a church, student body, business, staff, organization, or home than a negative spirit. That infection is contagious; it spreads like a cold in a kindergarten.

Thankfully, the younger seminarian had the guts to confront me about my judgmental attitude before it got out of control. He appropriately reminded me that I wasn't qualified to pass judgment on that missionary.

The principle bears repeating: only God is qualified to judge … because only He has all the facts.

advocating throughout his letter. He describes it as the "perfect law, the law of liberty" (1:25). It's the royal law, "love your neighbor as yourself" (2:8). In fact, James revisits the theme of standing in judgment over others, which he introduced in 2:4–13 when discussing the problem of partiality and prejudice. So, a judgmental attitude manifests itself in all sorts of ways. But in all cases the self-made judge breaks the law of love.

The real problem with judging others is that it comes perilously close to playing God. James 4:12 reminds us that "there is only one Lawgiver and Judge." Only God can pass judgment on a person's actions *and* motives without fault, without hypocrisy, and without spite. The final indictment in verse 12 packs a personal punch in Greek. He's saying, "You there! Who are you to judge your neighbor?" We might paraphrase the indictment in verse 12 this way: "Who do you think you are?" Or even, "Who made *you* God?"

— 4:13–16 —

Verses 11 and 12 addressed the problem of playing God in the lives of others. Verses 13–16 look at playing God over our own lives. The objective of this game is to imagine ourselves as the final authority over our own lives, and then to live like it. You sequester God in His own compartment of your life and keep Him there, except in a rare instance when you're really in a bind. Now, most people wouldn't admit to banishing God to the back room of their lives. But many of us assign Him sovereignty over certain tasks, keeping the daily and mundane for ourselves. God becomes the boss of religious issues, moral matters, international conflicts, questions of faith. That's His realm. But we'll handle things like finances, relationships, business decisions — those things God couldn't care less about, so long as He has our hearts.

At the core of this false philosophy, though, is the idea that we are the masters of our own destiny. Such people recite the hymn of self-reliance encapsulated in the verse of William Ernest Henley's poem "Invictus":

> It matters not how strait the gate,
> How charged with punishments the scroll,
> I am the master of my fate:
> I am the captain of my soul.[5]

That's the philosophy of the person who plays God in his or her own life. Pray only for important things. Pull yourself up by your own bootstraps! Call your own shots!

The rules for this game are found in James 4:13. Let me break it down, step by step.

Rules for Playing God ... according to James 4:13	
1. Set your own schedule.	"Today or tomorrow . . ."
2. Select your own path.	". . . we will go to such and such a city . . ."
3. Place your own limits.	". . . and spend a year there . . ."
4. Arrange your own activities.	". . . and engage in business. . ."
5. Predict your own outcome.	". . . and make a profit . . ."

Now, notice that none of the activities James describes is negative in and of itself. There is nothing wrong with planning ahead, nothing evil or peculiar about setting a schedule, nothing abnormal about engaging in business, and nothing sinful about making a profit. In fact, James describes the everyday affairs of normal life. *But that's precisely his point.* Because God is our sovereign Lord, His will must be considered in every aspect of our lives.

James begins pointing out problems with a go-it-alone attitude toward life in verse 14. First, *as mere mortal humans, we have no idea what the future will bring.* We don't know what will happen today, much less what the next year or two will look like. Every one of us is one heartbeat away from the end of our lives. One rude intrusion of an unexpected event could put an end to all our plans. We could live into our nineties ... or die tonight. Nobody knows. Only God knows.

Second, *playing God with our own lives is risky because we have no assurance of a long life.* James describes our lives as a "vapor" that appears suddenly and dissipates quickly. Imagine yourself outside in the middle of a subzero winter day. You're bundled in your thick coat, stocking cap, and gloves ... with a scarf wrapped twice around your neck. As you exhale, what happens? Your warm breath forms a small puff of white vapor that lingers for a second, then vanishes. Gone. That's life—and not just the life of somebody who dies young. Even a relatively long life flies by. People in their nineties say they feel as if it was just yesterday that they graduated from school. But youth doesn't last. Before your know it—poof!—the vapor of life dissolves—and it happens fast. About the time your face clears up, your mind gets fuzzy!

Third, *we have no right to ignore God's will in every aspect of our lives.* In verse 15, James provides the necessary corrective to the folly of playing God: "Instead, you ought to say, 'If the Lord wills, we will live and also do this or that.'" For many believers those two words, "God willing," have become almost a cliché, an obligatory tag-on that we superstitiously attach to our plans to make sure we're not perceived as presumptuous.

James's instruction to say, "If the Lord wills," reflects an attitude and orientation toward life. It means submitting ourselves humbly before the one true God who is entitled to be Lord of all things in our lives, not just a few things. It means erasing from our minds the sacred–secular, heavenly–earthly, spiritual–physical dichotomies that delegate some things to God and some to us. God governs *all* things, even the "mundane" daily decisions. He owns it all. The alternative to submitting all things to God is an evil, boastful arrogance—living life as if we are the masters of our fate or the captains of our souls (4:16).

— **4:17** —

James concludes by pointing out two ways to stop playing God. Both relate to humility that flows from authentic faith: first, *know the right thing to do*; second, *start doing the right thing.* God has a standard of right living that transcends our own interests and pursuits, and He wants to guide us along a path He's set for us. To make that happen requires staying close to His Word and shaping our path according to its wisdom.

But that's only half the solution. When we know what God wants from us, we must do it. If we continue to live as though God isn't interested in certain areas of our lives, it's sin. If we try to call our own shots, make our own plans, and independently do our own thing, we're not doing what God wants us to do. That's the point of James's final warning. Know the right way; then humbly submit to it.

Application

"Take My Will and Make It Thine"

Psalm 14:1 says, "The fool has said in his heart, 'There is no God.'" I suppose something worse than pronouncing that there is no God and living accordingly would be to *know* and *believe in* the true God, and then act as if He's not God. And to add idolatry to blasphemy, the worst case is to set ourselves up as "god" in place of the only One who has the right to be both Judge and Lord over our lives. This is the point of James 4:11 – 17. When we stand in judgment over our brothers and sisters in Christ, we're playing the part of divine Judge. And when we plan our lives as if God were uninterested or uninvolved, we're playing the part of divine Lord.

James 4:17 is especially practical for those of us who have a tendency to encroach on God's territory: "Therefore, to one who knows the right thing to do and does not do it, to him it is sin." In this short verse, James gives us two simple rules to follow. First, *you must know the right thing to do.* Whatever the cost, you must evaluate your life and pattern it according to God's Word, not according to your habits or traditions. Second, *you must start doing the right thing.* Instead of doing the wrong thing, replace it with the right thing. First, *know* . . . then, *do.*

Let me lay it on the line here. If you are a negative, petty, gossipy person and you have been confronted with this message from God's Word, you're responsible to change. If you don't, it's sin. To phrase it otherwise: slanderous judgment, malicious criticism, mean-spirited denigration — these things are unbecoming of a Christian. It's damaging to the body of Christ and to yourself. Stop! Reread James 4:11 – 12 and consider these probing questions:

- Have I been speaking against a brother or sister in Christ in a judgmental way?
- Have I hypocritically pointed the finger at others out of self-serving motives?
- Have I confronted others under the guise of looking out for their interests, while masking a heart of envy or jealousy?
- What must I do to stop this pattern of behavior?

But there's another side of playing God, probably more common. If you've slipped outside the absolute lordship of Christ over every aspect of your life, it must stop. If you're calling your own shots, being your own umpire, making your own plans, it's sin. I can't put it any clearer. It *has* to stop. Ask yourself these questions:

- In what specific areas of my life do I tend to "go it alone"?
- What decisions have I made lately in which I failed to include God's perspective?
- What decisions are on the horizon that I need to set before God and seek His will?

To some degree, we are all guilty of the sin of playing God. We play God with others when we talk down and judge them. We play God with ourselves when we leave

Him no room to guide our steps. Rather than the me-centered philosophy of Henley's "Invictus," how much better to emulate the lyrics of Frances Ridley Havergal:

> Take my life and let it be
> Consecrated, Lord, to Thee,
> Take my moments and my days—
> Let them flow in ceaseless praise,
> Let them flow in ceaseless praise.
>
> Take my voice and let me sing
> Always, only, for my King;
> Take my lips and let them be
> Filled with messages from Thee,
> Filled with messages from Thee.
>
> Take my will and make it Thine—
> It shall be no longer mine;
> Take my heart—it is Thine own,
> It shall be Thy royal throne,
> It shall be Thy royal throne.[6]

Is something keeping you from making this hymn of surrender your prayer today?

Warnings to the Wealthy (James 5:1–6)

> [1]Come now, you rich, weep and howl for your miseries which are coming upon you. [2]Your riches have rotted and your garments have become moth-eaten. [3]Your gold and your silver have rusted; and their rust will be a witness against you and will consume your flesh like fire. It is in the last days that you have stored up your treasure! [4]Behold, the pay of the laborers who mowed your fields, *and* which has been withheld by you, cries out *against you*; and the outcry of those who did the harvesting has reached the ears of the Lord of Sabaoth. [5]You have lived luxuriously on the earth and led a life of wanton pleasure; you have fattened your hearts in a day of slaughter. [6]You have condemned and put to death the righteous *man*; he does not resist you.

In 1923 an elite group of businessmen met at the luxurious Edgewater Beach Hotel in Chicago. The roster included some of the most influential, famous, and wealthy moguls of the early twentieth century. Some of the names included:

- Charles M. Schwab—president of Bethlehem Steel Corporation
- Richard Whitney—president of the New York Stock Exchange

- Albert Fall—Secretary of the Interior under President Harding
- Jesse Livermore—Wall Street tycoon
- Ivar Kreuger—head of a global monopoly of match manufacturers

These heavy hitters controlled more wealth than the total assets of the United States Treasury at the time. Surely these men would become models of the entrepreneurial spirit and stellar examples of financial success. But fast-forward about twenty-five years or so and look back on the courses of their lives:

- Schwab—died $300,000.00 in debt in 1939
- Whitney—served time at Sing Sing prison for embezzlement
- Fall—served time for misconduct in office, leaving behind a ruined reputation
- Livermore—committed suicide in 1940, describing himself as "a failure"
- Kreuger—shot himself in 1932 after his global monopoly collapsed[7]

Buried beneath the rubble of humiliation, defeat, crime, sickness, and financial collapse, these men—along with a number of their colleagues—died in a depressing, pitiable condition. Their wealth, power, and prestige did nothing to sooth the personal anxiety and guilt they suffered in life. The reality is that great intelligence and hard work can make a person wealthy. But it takes God-given wisdom and supernatural humility to be able to manage wealth and influence.

—**5:1**—

James begins by calling his wealthy readers to attention: "Come now!" He used the same phrase when addressing the autonomous businessman in 4:13. It's almost as though James expects certain people to be so distracted by their own worldly pursuits that he needs to snap them out of their daze: "Listen up!" In 4:13, he addressed those who *spent their days* as if God weren't their Lord. In 5:1, he addresses those who *spend their money* as if God weren't their Master.

This is the first time in his letter that James directly addresses wealthy people, though he has mentioned them twice before. In James 1:10–11, he noted that the rich man should "glory in his humiliation," because he will fade away in the midst of his pursuits like grass withering in the scorching wind. And in 2:5–6, he scolded those who favor the wealthy over the poor, because the rich and powerful are the ones who tended to persecute Christians. Based on these passages, it would be easy to conclude that James has it in for the rich. One might walk away from James's apparent ridicule of the rich and conclude that the poor go to heaven while the rich

Four Kinds of Wealth and Poverty

Physical condition	Spiritual condition	Description	Prescription	Biblical example
Poor	Poor	Having few of the world's goods and not living in God's love, the doubly poor are in a most miserable condition.	Provide essential physical needs to express God's love; *for unbelievers*, point them to salvation in Christ; *for believers*, exhort them to trust in Christ to provide both physically and spiritually.	Those who are both physically and spiritually afflicted (Isa. 61:1)
Rich	Rich	Having been blessed in both material wealth and heavenly riches, the doubly rich use their prosperity to help others.	Provide opportunities for giving and serving others with time and resources.	Job before and after his trials (Job 1:1–3; 42:10); Joseph of Arimathea (Matt. 27:57)
Poor	Rich	Having few of the world's goods, the externally poor are often in need of food, clothing, and shelter; but they have a strong faith and often give what little they have.	Provide essential physical needs and give opportunities to minister to the spiritual needs of others.	The poor widow (Mark 12:42–44); the poor of this world who are rich in faith (James 2:5); the church in Smyrna (Rev. 2:9)
Rich	Poor	Having an abundance of the world's goods, the spiritually poor forget that their blessings come from God in order to bless others.	Provide correction; *for unbelievers*, exhort them to trust in Christ instead of riches; *for believers*, encourage them to submit their wealth to the lordship of Christ.	Unbeliever: the rich young ruler (Mark 10:21); believers: the church of Laodicea (Rev. 3:17)

go to hell. But let's not go there. Clearly, Scripture teaches that it's not a person's financial wealth or poverty that determines one's relationship with God, but the person's *spiritual* condition.

Being *outwardly* rich or poor refers to how much of the world's goods a person has at his or her disposal. *Inward* wealth or poverty refers to a person's relationship (or lack of such) with God, expressed through his or her love for others. When we look at things this way, there are really four classifications. The chart on page 103 may help explain this more simply. I have included a description, a prescription for how to minister to people in each category, as well as a biblical example or two for each type.

Do you see yourself as fitting into the third category — poor in this world, but spiritually rich in Christ? If so, let me challenge you by suggesting that, for the most part, our definition of "poor" is far different than the Bible's. Poor people in the Bible were homeless, helpless, destitute, and hopeless. They often had nothing to eat, nothing to wear, and nowhere to stay. By biblical standards, even most people living by our society's standard of "poverty" wouldn't have been regarded as truly "poor." The reality is that most of us are blessed with more than we need and are therefore in the position to bless others, if we assume, of course, that we haven't fallen into the fourth category of the spiritually poor.

It is to the physically rich and spiritually poor that James addresses his rebuke. Although believers can be outside of God's will with regard to their finances, in 5:1 – 6, James primarily targets the unbelieving rich who oppress the poor. These are the same people he mentioned in passing in James 2:6 – 7. What does he say to this group? "Weep and howl for your miseries which are coming upon you" (5:1). Behind this general warning lies a long history of crying and wailing because of judgment that comes upon the ungodly (Isa. 13:6).

This is the same context in which James addresses the oppressive rich. He mentions "the last days" in James 5:3 and then discusses how believers should live "until the coming of the Lord" in 5:7. The warning is clear: trusting in the strength of riches instead of trusting in Christ will end in disaster. As Psalm 62:10 says, "Do not trust in oppression and do not vainly hope in robbery; if riches increase, do not set your heart upon them."

— **5:2-6** —

After that general rebuke, James turns to some specific reasons for it. James paints a grim picture of the wealthy unbelievers' dark spiritual condition. Along the way he also points out the divine retribution that comes with this kind of behavior.

First, James rebukes the rich *because they are guilty of hoarding their riches* (5:2–3). In those days a person could display his or her wealth in three ways: by feasting lavishly, by dressing extravagantly, and by spending wildly. (Some things never change!) James targets these three areas of the flamboyant lifestyle of the rich, pointing out how foolish it is to center their lives on these things. Through time and disuse, food goes bad, garments get eaten by moths, and precious metals tarnish. By hoarding rather than sharing, the wealth of the rich rots and rusts.

Second, James rebukes the rich *because they are guilty of cheating others* (5:4). Instead of giving a fair wage to those who work their fields, the rich cheat them. One sign of the selfish rich is their reluctance to pay their bills. During the financial crisis that began in 2008, the world witnessed numerous superrich reward themselves with bonuses while their employees lost their jobs. It's an amazing reality that some of the greediest people are also some of the wealthiest—and some of the most generous people will give away their last dime!

Third, James rebukes the rich *because they are guilty of a selfish lifestyle* (5:5). The wealthy wicked live in the lap of luxury, indulging in pleasures and fattening not just their bellies, but their hearts, too. James paints a picture of a person trying to satisfy the deepest longings of his heart by a playboy lifestyle. Like a pig fattened for slaughter, these wealthy don't even know that as they selfishly gorge on the pleasures of life, they are eating and drinking judgment upon themselves.

Fourth, James rebukes the rich *because they are guilty of taking unfair advantage of the righteous* (5:6). Echoing a charge already mentioned in 2:6, James takes his rebuke to the highest level. The rich are guilty of judging and putting to death the "righteous." The word "righteous" is singular, referring to a kind of person—the righteous one. This category would include not only Jesus, the ultimate Righteous One, but also all those believers who, like their Lord, endured condemnation and martyrdom for their faith, all at the hands of rich, powerful oppressors. It includes all the righteous people who are treated brutally by wealthy unbelievers.

How does God respond to all this? We saw the human reasons for the rebuke; a look at the divine retribution is chilling. Again, there are four divine responses.

First, *hoarded riches reap miserable dividends* (5:1–3). If you look into the face of the unsaved wealthy today, more often than not you'll see stress, worry, bitterness, and emptiness. Wealthy people finally discover that money can't purchase happiness; on the contrary, it often brings despair.

Second, *riches provide no relief in eternity* (5:3). Proverbs 11:4 says, "Riches do not profit in the day of wrath, but righteousness delivers from death." A day is coming, says James, when the true Accountant will conduct His audit. On that day the unsaved rich will be handed a bill they cannot pay, and all their earthly treasures will be like ashes blowing in the wind. Only God's righteousness — the free gift that comes by faith in Jesus Christ — rescues a person in the day of judgment.

Third, *unjust acts of the unsaved are not forgotten* (5:4). James says that the outcry of those treated unjustly "has reached the ears of the Lord of Sabaoth." The title "Lord of Sabaoth" means "Lord of the armies" or "Lord of hosts." It refers to God as the Judge who wages war against His enemies (Isa. 2:12). James's Jewish audience would have known this title since it came from their native Hebrew language and culture. And they would have caught its allusion to the coming end-times judgment. Just as the voices of the oppressed Hebrews enslaved in Egypt reached God and brought His judgments (Ex. 2:23 – 25), so God today hears the voices of oppressed people.

Finally, *a lack of judgment today does not mean a lack of judgment tomorrow* (5:1 – 6). Throughout this passage James holds the warning of end-times judgment over the pretty heads of the plutocrats. The judgment of believers is behind them — Christ bore the full punishment of death, paying for all of our sins on the cross. But judgment of unbelievers is ahead of them. Those who die rejecting Christ face not only end-times suffering if they are alive during the last days, but also eternal judgment after they are condemned at the great white throne (Rev. 20:11 – 15). Though for a season it may appear that the wicked get away with prospering at the expense of others, in the end their wicked deeds will be remembered.

As we have seen, James uses some sharp words for the wicked, reserving some of his severest warnings for those who are physically wealthy, and at the same time, spiritually poor. Before we shrug our shoulders at this warning and pretend we are exempt, we would be wise to recall a couple of practical principles for all believers to follow.

If James illustrates the extreme examples to avoid, Paul's first letter to Timothy gives us at least two principles to follow. First, God's concern is not with actual wealth, which is neutral, but with our attitudes toward wealth (1 Tim. 6:8 – 10). God urges His people to be content (6:8), rather than longing to be rich. Money itself is not the root of evil. The *love* of money is the root of all kinds of evil (6:10). Second, God is not against the wealthy, but against their misguided priorities (6:17 – 19). The rich have a special obligation to "be rich in good works, to be generous and ready to share" (6:18). God blesses us for the purpose of blessing others, not for the purpose of satisfying our own self-centered pleasures.

If we maintain right attitudes and proper priorities, we won't be led astray by riches and so become spiritual paupers. But this kind of attitude toward riches can come only from a God-given humility in our hearts. The cure for the pride and arrogance of wealth is the work of the Spirit.

In the third major section of his book, James has reminded us that *real faith produces genuine humility* (3:13–5:6). This kind of supernatural other-mindedness looks like a lush oasis on the dry setting of our own natural pride and selfishness. Left to our own natural wisdom, we are infertile and barren; but with the wisdom from above we can produce an abundance of quality fruit (3:13–18). Acting out of self-centered pursuits, conflict ensues; but when we humble ourselves before Him, our relationships are filled with peace (4:1–10). When we boast about our own plans, we fail; but when we surrender to God's sovereignty, we succeed spiritually, regardless of the outcome (4:11–17). Finally, when we trust in our own riches for significance, we will fall; but humility before God will bring spiritual riches regardless of our economic status (5:1–6).

In each case, James encourages the God-enabled humility that flows from genuine faith. For apart from God's grace working in our hearts to produce godly wisdom and good works, we will become as barren and fruitless as the vast Libyan desert.

NOTES:

1. Charles Hodge, *Systematic Theology* (New York: Charles Scribner, 1872; repr., Grand Rapids: Eerdmans, 1940), 3:471.
2. Douglas J. Moo, *The Letter of James*, The Pillar New Testament Commentary, ed. D. A. Carson (Grand Rapids: Eerdmans, 2000), 188.
3. Annie Johnson Flint, "He Giveth More Grace," in *The Hymnal for Worship and Celebration* (Waco, TX: Word Music, 1986), no. 415.
4. William Shakespeare, *Othello*, act 3, scene 3.
5. William Ernest Henley, "Invictus," in *Modern British Poetry*, ed. Louis Untermeyer (New York: Harcourt, Brace, & Company, 1920), 10.
6. Frances Ridley Havergal, "Take My Life and Let It Be," in *The Hymnal for Worship and Celebration*, no. 379.
7. Information adapted, with additional research, from Paul Lee Tan, *Encyclopedia of 7,700 Illustrations* (Rockville, MD: Assurance, 1979), 824; and Walter B. Knight, *Knight's Master Book of New Illustrations* (Grand Rapids: Eerdmans, 1956), 572–73.

REAL FAITH PRODUCES GENUINE PATIENCE (JAMES 5:7–20)

In this short letter to Jewish Christians, James is asking his readers, "If you say you believe like you should, then why do you behave like you shouldn't?" First-century Jewish believers struggled with persevering through hardship, maintaining good works, promoting peace in their churches, and living patiently in anticipation of the Lord's return. They knew Jesus as the Way of life, but they needed a step-by-step guide for walking in that Way.

In the climax of his brief handbook on practical Christianity, James affirms that *real faith produces genuine patience* (5:7–20). Those Jewish Christians, distressed by their faith-challenging circumstances, needed to hear that message repeatedly. James exhorts his readers to be patient in suffering in light of the Lord's coming (5:7–12). He encourages them to seek physical and spiritual wholeness (5:13–18). Finally, he challenges them to steer erring believers back onto the right path (5:19–20). *Patience* in the midst of life's challenges should mark true believers as a sure sign of real faith.

Patience in Suffering (5:7–12)

> [7]Therefore be patient, brethren, until the coming of the Lord. The farmer waits for the precious produce of the soil, being patient about it, until it gets the early and late rains. [8]You too be patient; strengthen your hearts, for the coming of the Lord is near. [9]Do not complain, brethren, against one another, so that you yourselves may not be judged; behold, the Judge is standing right at the door. [10]As an example, brethren, of suffering and patience, take the prophets who spoke in the name of the Lord. [11]We count those blessed who endured. You have heard of the endurance of Job and have seen the outcome of the Lord's dealings, that the Lord is full of compassion and *is* merciful.
>
> [12]But above all, my brethren, do not swear, either by heaven or by earth or with any other oath; but your yes is to be yes, and your no, no, so that you may not fall under judgment.

It can happen when we drive. We accidentally cut somebody off and they drive an extra eighty miles just to return the favor! *It can happen at work.* Somebody makes our job difficult one day and we wait to find an opportunity to "get back

KEY TERMS

μακροθυμέω [*makrothymeō*] (3114) "to persevere, to be patient, to wait long"

This word comes from two Greek words, *makro*, meaning "large," and *thymos*, meaning "intense anger," "burning wrath," or "explosive rage." When joined together, *makrothymeō* refers to the act of holding back one's anger. We might say such a person has a long fuse and can avoid sudden outbursts of rage. It also implies the ability to keep calm and cool for a long time, without exhibiting frustrations with difficult circumstances.

ἐπιστρέφω [*epistrephō*] (1994) "to turn, turn back, turn around, return"

Like the term "repent," *epistrephō* refers to an internal or external turning, or change of path, from one course of thought or action to another. In James's use (5:19–20), the word likely reflects his Jewish wisdom background of "the two ways" — the path of life and the path of death. When a wandering believer is turned back from the wrong path, he or she is restored to the right path of a fruitful Christian life.

at 'em." *It can happen at church.* Somebody offends us and we keep a record of that filed in the back of our minds, ready to crack open when the time is right. *It can happen anywhere.* Somebody wrongs us — either intentionally or accidentally — and the urge to retaliate hits us like an uncontrollable gag reflex. It happens to me . . . and it happens to you.

We've all experienced the hurt of mistreatment and misunderstanding. Such hurts come in a variety of forms — an intolerable working situation, domestic conflicts, overbearing parents, rebellious children, a treacherous friend, a petty parishioner, a gossipy neighbor. Our natural tendency is to retaliate — to return evil for evil, an eye for an eye. Or we bottle it up and allow a slow, grinding ferment. But God has a better idea than either bottling up or bursting out. James reveals this alternative. He tells us not only what to do when we've been wronged, but also how to do it.

— **5:7a** —

James 5:7 simultaneously connects and contrasts with the previous section. James begins with "therefore," indicating that what follows is based on what came before. But he also changes his audience from "you rich" (5:1) to "brethren" (5:7). You will remember that James addressed oppressive wealthy people in verses 1–6, exposing their wrongs and calling for repentant humiliation in light of the coming judgment

From My Journal

Suppressing the Revenge Reflex

Everyday events can sometimes really put your patience to the test. Several years ago I was driving my car into a supermarket parking lot, looking for a good space. Finding a suitable spot, I carefully maneuvered my compact car into a narrow space between two other vehicles. It would be a tight fit, and I'd have trouble squeezing out of my door when I opened it, but it was the only space I could find. My son, who was with me, slipped out his door with no problem. But as carefully as I opened my own door, it still bumped the car beside me.

I frowned and wiped the spot where I had accidentally tapped the car. Nothing. Not a scratch. Was I relieved! Then I glanced up and saw the man in his car. He wasn't smiling. I gestured toward the door and said with a grin, "Sorry about that. But there's no damage." He either didn't believe or me or just didn't like me, because I don't think I could have *chiseled* the frown from his stony face. He stared in silence. I shrugged, closed my door, and headed into the store with my son.

Call it intuition or an unconscious deduction, but something told me to turn around and look. Sure enough, that guy was already opening the back door of his car. SMASH! SMASH! Right into my back fender. Now let me describe what went through my mind in half a second. My first reaction was to storm across the lot and remove his head from his body. With that carnal notion still loitering in my mind, in came a second image—the front page of the local newspaper with the headline, *Pastor Kills Man in Parking Lot*. Then a third thought followed right behind the second: *This guy's bigger than I am!* So the front-page headline changed to the back page containing my obituary.

In the end, I did nothing. My young son had his hand in mine and I thought, *Boy, it would just foul everything up if he saw his dad out there getting smeared all over the parking lot.* Actually, though, I *did* do something. Something remarkable. I applied that rare virtue of patience—the kind of patience that comes only by the work of the Spirit. I didn't shoot him a finger "greeting," didn't phone the police, and didn't shout awful things at him. God's Spirit miraculously suppressed my revenge reflex. As I think back on that day when I walked away from what could have become an ugly scene, I'm grateful I did. But I can't take the credit. It was God's gift of faith producing in me inexplicable patience.

of God. Now, beginning in 5:7, James addresses the victims of their ugliness: "Therefore, *in light of the fact of the ultimate judgment of the wicked rulers oppressing you,* be patient, brethren!"

James continues with the theme of Christ's coming in judgment—"until the coming of the Lord." While persecutors should fear Christ's coming, believers anticipate it through patiently enduring suffering. Don't miss the fact that James has shifted to believers in this section. The man without Christ lives under frustration if he tries to bring patience into persecution, mistreatment, or everyday afflictions. But the believer has the supernatural ability—by the work of the Holy Spirit—to endure under the miseries of life, whether mild or extreme. How valuable is patience!

The exhortation to "be patient" in verse 7 governs the rest of chapter 5. It's the faith-inspired response to a variety of circumstances Christians must endure in this world, from putting up with suffering (5:7–11) to responding to sickness (5:14–15); from the temptation to flippancy (5:12) to the treatment of those who have strayed into sin (5:19–20). James answers a simple question in this section: "How can I do right when I've been done wrong?"

He answers this underlying question with four commands—two positives to embrace and two negatives to avoid.

—5:7b–8a—

Be patient. James illumines the first answer to the question of how we can respond rightly when we've been wronged with an illustration. Just as a farmer learns to wait patiently through the growing season before he can reap the fruit of his labors, so Christians should "be patient" (5:8). The word translated "patience" comes from the Greek word *makrothymeō,* meaning "long-tempered." James says, "When something unjust takes place, have a long fuse. Don't blow your top. Chill."

But let's face it, we would rather take our offenders by the throat. God has a better plan: that we wait on Him. What does that mean? In the ultimate sense, when Christ returns, He will mete out justice on those who have persecuted His people (5:7). But patiently waiting on the Lord also has a here-and-now application. God has a way of working out His purposes and plans on an everyday scale, just as He will work out His grand plan on a cosmic scale. So, being patient in negative circumstances means we deliberately allow God to handle the situation in His own way and in His own time. Like the farmer waiting for a harvest, *be patient.*

— **5:8b** —

Strengthen your hearts. The second command relates to how we should respond when we've been wronged. It refers to our emotional fortitude or inner disposition. The word "strengthen" means to establish, support, or prop up. Under stress and duress, the heart can grow heavy, but the Spirit of God can lighten the load of a heart weighed down with pressures. Psalm 55:22 says, "Cast your burden upon the LORD and He will sustain you; He will never allow the righteous to be shaken." Similarly, 1 Peter 5:6–7 tells us to humble ourselves under God's mighty hand, casting all our anxieties on Him.

Practically speaking, this is where I find the "50–20 principle" helpful. I get the name from Genesis 50:20, the climactic passage on the life of Joseph. Remember the story? Joseph's brothers had sold him into slavery and told their father, Jacob, that he had been killed. As Joseph's tragic life unfolded, he went from imprisoned slave to prime minister of Egypt. Years later, when the same brothers who had sold him down the river show up on the scene again, groveling for mercy, how does Joseph respond? With the "50–20 principle": "As for you, you meant evil against me, but God meant it for good in order to bring about this present result, to preserve many people alive" (Gen. 50:20).

Unless we can see beyond the "someone" who wronged us, we will retaliate. That's the natural (and carnal) response. But God works out all things for our ultimate good (Rom. 8:28). We need to have a big-picture perspective. We don't

EARLY RAINS AND LATTER RAINS

For thousands of years farmers in the Holy Land have experienced an annual cycle of dry and rainy seasons. The dry season, running roughly from June through September, leaves the soil parched. The rainy season, however, quenches the land in two six-week periods in October and November (the "early rains") and then again in April and May (the "latter rains"). The early rains allow seeds to germinate. After a long wait, the latter rains cause the plants to take root and grow. While the land is in its dry season for those five months, farmers eagerly watch the skies for God to send rain and produce a bountiful crop (Jer. 5:24; Joel 2:23; Zech. 10:1).

The Israelites recognized God as their Sustainer and Provider who sent rains of blessing according to His promises (Gen. 1:11–12; 8:22). By contrast, absence of sufficient rain was one of the curses for disobedience under the Old Testament Law (Deut. 11:13–17, 28:12, 23–24). When James likens the farmer's anticipation of the latter rains to the believer's expectation of the Lord's return, he emphasizes the need for patience. Though we are not yet receiving the blessing of final salvation planted in our lives by the seed of faith, our unbreakable new covenant promise of salvation guarantees that one day God will rain His blessings on us through the glorious appearing of His Son.

need "20/20" vision, but "50–20" vision. That shift in perspective from our own limited view to a divine view has helped strengthen my own heart through all kinds of wrongs. Trust me—it can do the same for you.

— **5:9–11** —

Don't complain. The third answer to how believers should respond to suffering concerns our actions toward those around us. When our circumstances try our patience and when we feel discouraged and frustrated by external pressures, we tend to complain. Here, James refers to a phenomenon much more insidious than silently holding a grudge against those who have wronged us. He warns us not to groan, grumble, or complain "against one another" (5:9).

Isn't it odd that when a family, business, or church suffers hardship, the members of that community often internalize their aggression and turn on each other? Or they turn on their leadership. Or they turn on their children, employees, or pets! We vent our frustrations on those around us. On the outside we may appear to have patience in the midst of suffering, but on the inside we've become a tightly wound spring, exploding on those who are nearest to us at the slightest touch.

James already has dealt with the results of this kind of complaining spirit in 4:11–12. The one who speaks against or judges a fellow Christian will be subject to the judgment of God (4:12). Equally serious, those who point fingers and complain against others will be subject to the disciplining hand of God (5:9). We've already seen that God doesn't judge believers with condemnation or hell (Rom. 8:1). He doesn't let our bitterness and bad behavior go without discipline, however, just as a loving father disciplines his children for their good (Heb. 12:5–11).

The ancient Hebrew prophets serve as an example to us for how to suffer with patience (5:10). "Prophets" often refers not merely to those with the prophetic office—people like Isaiah and Daniel—but also to the whole cast of Old Testament figures who spoke and acted on behalf of God (Matt. 5:17; Rom. 1:2). James zooms in on perhaps the greatest example of patient endurance under excruciating suffering—Job. Though Job endured incomprehensible personal, financial, and physical losses, he refused to give in to the revenge reflex, demonstrating his real faith through genuine patience. James reminds us that the suffering of Job was temporary, eventually giving way to an abundance of blessing that reflected the compassion and mercy of God (James 5:11). In the same way, those who patiently endure hardship today without grumbling can rely on God's promise of ultimate reward and blessing, whether in this life or in the life to come. Complaining is one habit worth breaking!

— 5:12 —

Don't swear. This final command relates to how we should respond when we've been wronged refers to our tendency to make rash decisions and promises under duress. The word "swear" doesn't refer primarily to the use of profanity. Rather, it means to "take an oath," to grasp on to something with our words. It's calling God into the circumstance and presenting Him to give validity to our commitments. For example, "I swear by God, I'm not lying!" Or, "Before God, I'll do this." Or, "As God is my witness, this will never happen!"

James got his teaching on oaths from Jesus' Sermon on the Mount:

> But I say to you, make no oath at all, either by heaven, for it is the throne of God, or by the earth, for it is the footstool of His feet, or by Jerusalem, for it is the city of the Great King. Nor shall you make an oath by your head, for you cannot make one hair white or black. But let your statement be, "Yes, yes" or "No, no"; anything beyond these is of evil. (Matt. 5:34–37)

James prohibits swearing with the present tense, suggesting that he wants his readers to stop an action in which they are already involved. We don't know enough about the historical situation to determine exactly why they are taking oaths. We do know, however, that his Jewish Christian readers are caught between Jewish and Gentile persecutors. They live under extreme religious, cultural, and economic pressures to deny Christ in their words or deeds. It may be that James's prohibition of oath-taking relates to going back on their confession of faith in Christ or swearing allegiance to others outside the church. That is, in this context the result of swearing would bring great benefits —

JAMES AND THE COMING JUDGE

James's letter repeatedly mentions the return of Christ, the judgments and rewards of God, and the coming of the kingdom. The following passages underscore the role that the return of Christ plays in James's thinking.

- Blessed is a man who perseveres under trial; for once he has been approved, he will receive the crown of life which the Lord has promised to those who love Him. (1:12)
- Did not God choose the poor of this world to be rich in faith and heirs of the kingdom which He promised to those who love Him? (2:5)
- For judgment will be merciless to one who has shown no mercy. (2:13)
- Let not many of you become teachers, my brethren, knowing that as such we will incur a stricter judgment. (3:1)
- Come now, you rich, weep and howl for your miseries which are coming upon you. (5:1)
- It is in the last days that you have stored up your treasure. (5:3)
- You have fattened your hearts in a day of slaughter. (5:5)
- Be patient, brethren, until the coming of the Lord. (5:7)
- Strengthen your hearts, for the coming of the Lord is near. (5:8)
- Behold, the Judge is standing right at the door. (5:9)
- Your yes is to be yes, and your no, no, so that you may not fall under judgment. (5:12)

a lessening of the suffering, persecution, hardship, or trial. But the cost would be abandoning their Savior.

I see in all this an exhortation to simplicity of speech. Respond to circumstances with a simple "yes" or "no." Answer succinctly and with authenticity. When it comes to the tough circumstances of life, we are wise to avoid long explanations, detailed excuses, and especially pious spiritualizing. This kind of overanalysis leads to stumbling in our words. We will find ourselves bringing God into circumstances to play a role on our terms. We will fall into the trap of making deals with God, promising Him all sorts of extreme things if He'll just lighten the load. In the process, we think we've figured out what's causing the suffering and how we can weasel out of it. Resist this temptation to overspiritualize and overanalyze.

Instead, stay quiet, sit back, and let God work out His purpose.

Have patience.

Application

Doing Right When Done Wrong

In James 5:7–12, James answers a simple question: "How can I do right when I've been done wrong?" His answer comes in the form of four commands: be patient (5:7–8), strengthen your hearts (5:8), don't complain (5:9–11), and don't swear (5:12). In light of these practical exhortations, let me suggest four easy-to-understand applications.

First, don't focus on the situation, or you'll get angry. Instead, be patient! Yes, you've been wronged. Yes, you could express your anger through retaliation. But don't. Resist the revenge reflex and let it go. *Be patient.*

Second, don't focus on yourself, or you'll have self-pity. Instead, be strong! Remember the "50–20 principle" and say, "Lord, I see this person not as an enemy but as a tool. He or she may see themselves as my enemy, inflicting damage on me, but I know You're bigger than that. Thank you for making me the object of Your handiwork. Please make me a vehicle of your grace." Let God get you through it and accomplish His purpose. *Be strong.*

Third, don't focus on someone to blame, or you'll complain. Instead, view others as a means God uses to shape your life. Just as the perpetrators of wrong are tools for your spiritual growth, so those whom God has placed over you, around you, and under you can be tools to teach you patient endurance. Don't redirect your wrath toward them. Don't put them down with your complaining, bitter spirit. Don't shift blame on others. Instead, view others as a means God uses to shape your inner person. *Don't complain.*

Fourth, don't focus on the present. Look to the future for insight. This is a tough principle to apply when you're in the middle of a crisis. So consider memorizing a couple key verses to stitch this idea into the fabric of your heart. Make it a part of how you think.

> For I consider that the sufferings of this present time are not worthy to be compared with the glory that is to be revealed to us. (Rom. 8:18)

> For momentary, light affliction is producing for us an eternal weight of glory far beyond all comparison, while we look not at the things which are seen, but at the things which are not seen; for the things which are seen are temporal, but the things which are not seen are eternal. (2 Cor. 4:17–18)

> In this you greatly rejoice, even though now for a little while, if necessary, you have been distressed by various trials, so that the proof of your faith, being more precious than gold which is perishable, even though tested by fire, may be found to result in praise and glory and honor at the revelation of Jesus Christ. (1 Peter 1:6–7)

I don't know what's in store for you in the next weeks, months, and years. Neither do you. But God knows. It may be a court summons you don't deserve. It may be an unwarranted rebuke from an employer, or an unexpected layoff. It may be a neighbor who causes you prolonged grief over some triviality. It may be a spouse who walks out, a child who rebels, or a parent who treats you like garbage. Whatever comes, the practical advice in James can get you through. Be patient. Prop up your heart. Don't hold a grudge. Don't scheme to get out from under it.

Patience through Prayer (James 5:13–18)

---

[13]Is anyone among you suffering? *Then* he must pray. Is anyone cheerful? He is to sing praises. [14]Is anyone among you sick? *Then* he must call for the elders of the church and they are to pray over him, anointing him with oil in the name of the Lord; [15]and the prayer offered in faith will restore the one who is sick, and the Lord will raise him up, and if he has committed sins, they will be forgiven him. [16]Therefore, confess your sins to one another, and pray for one another so that you may be healed. The effective prayer of a righteous man can accomplish much. [17]Elijah was a man with a nature like ours, and he prayed earnestly that it would not rain, and it did not rain on the earth for three years and six months. [18]Then he prayed again, and the sky poured rain and the earth produced its fruit.

Like a car without fuel, life without prayer grinds to a halt. Like a lamp without electricity, the prayer-starved Christian fails to shine in a dark and desperate world. But show me a man or woman of prevailing prayer, and I'll show you a man or woman with deep faith. Effective, fervent prayer moves the heart of the omnipotent God of the universe. Yet far too many Christians fill their lives with dizzying activities, leaving no time for this crucial ingredient that can transform mere human actions into divine acts of power.

You may recall from the introduction to James's letter that James was well known for his prayer life. He earned the nickname "Camel Knees" because he spent so much time on his knees in prayer that they resembled the calloused knees of a camel. As one would expect from a book written by a man famed for prayer, the theme comes up repeatedly in the letter. In James 1:5, he wrote, "But if any of you lacks wisdom, let him ask of God, who gives to all generously and without reproach, and it will be given to him." And in 4:2, he said, "You do not have because you do not ask." Now, at the climax of his letter, James develops the theme of prayer more fully.

Let me put James's discussion of effective prayer in the context of his argument. In this last major section of the letter, James argues that *real faith produces genuine patience* (5:7–5:20). In 5:7–12, he answered the question of how to respond to suffering through patient endurance. Here, in 5:13–18, we will see James continue to develop the idea of how we are to conduct ourselves with patience as we await the Lord's return. This time, though, true faith exhibited through patience manifests itself differently — namely, in prayer. In the face of every obstacle, whether sickness or sin, the correct response is prayer. Prayer not only reflects an attitude of genuine faith; it also reveals patient endurance as we turn to God to handle life's struggles, in His timing and according to His promises. As such, prayer becomes a quintessential mark of authentic faith.

—5:13—

James begins by referring to two ends on the spectrum of life: suffering and cheerfulness. The one refers to affliction: physical, mental, emotional, or spiritual. It could include disease or discouragement, doubt or anxiety, financial hardships or relationship conflicts. In short, it includes anything that causes trouble or affliction. The response? "He must pray."

People usually don't have a hard time ultimately turning to God in prayer when their lives are unraveling. When pain increases, when worry overcomes them, when events spin out of control, God finally gets His call. But in my experience, people tend to put off prayer as the last option, or they treat it like a time-waster that distracts them from working out a solution to the problem on their own. But James is clear: prayer *is* the solution to the problem. Everything we do must start with prayer. Believers would do well to remind themselves of the words of that nearly forgotten hymn by Thomas Hastings:

> From ev'ry stormy wind that blows,
> From ev'ry swelling tide of woes,
> There is a calm, a sure retreat:
> 'Tis found beneath the mercy seat.

> Ah! wither could we flee for aid,
> When tempted, desolate, dismayed:
> Or how the hosts of hell defeat,
> Had suff'ring saints no mercy seat.[1]

This doesn't mean that God immediately ends the affliction. He never promises to bring instant relief. But He does promise to provide patience and perseverance. Prayer doesn't express faith in God to deliver us *from* trials, but *through* trials. So, when we're afflicted, it's time to pray. And when that affliction is finally lifted, it's time to praise!

This leads us to the opposite of affliction—cheerfulness. The proper response is to sing praises. James sees praise as another form of prayer, lifting our hearts in worship, thanksgiving, and honor to God for who He is and for what He has done. This suggests that in all circumstances—the good and the bad—the right response is to turn to God in prayer and praise. In other words, we are to pray *constantly*.

— **5:14–15** —

James next covers a major area of prayer that most Christians know well. Who hasn't called out to God for healing from sickness, either for themselves or for others? In fact, it seems as if most of the prayer requests in our prayer lists have to do with recovery from illness, surgery, or injuries. So James addresses the issue of the physically ill in verses 14–15.

The word "sick" in verse 14 has the basic meaning of "weak" or "feeble." In the New Testament it often refers to physical sicknesses (Luke 4:40; Acts 9:37). But it also refers figuratively to those who are "weak in faith" (Rom. 4:19; 14:1) or to those who have a "weak conscience" (1 Cor. 8:12). In James 5:14–15, the emphasis is more on the person who is weak from physical illness. James prescribes three things for such a person.

First, he or she must call for the spiritual leaders of the church (5:14). Isn't that interesting? We look at it the other way around nowadays. Sometimes the pastors are the last to know when somebody is sick, hospitalized, or incapacitated. Maybe for serious conditions, those who are sick eventually let the church know. But people seldom go to the leadership of the church first. In fact, some who are sick don't want *anybody* to know it. But James rejects the idea that our physical illnesses are private, personal matters. We're to give the body of Christ the opportunity to minister to us in our weakness, along with the medical community.

Second, James prescribes a specific response by the elders of the church: prayer and anointing. The Greek text combines these two actions, one accompanying the other—"pray, while anointing him with oil." We find two distinct uses of anointing with oil in the Bible. One involves a religious or ceremonial act as a symbol for consecration—as in the anointing of David as king of Israel (1 Sam. 16:13). A second type of anointing was more mundane and common—for medicinal or hygienic purposes. Like the use of lotion for dry skin or the use of ointments for wounds, oils were used to affect the body in specific ways. We see this use when the Samaritan pours wine and oil on the injured man in Luke 10:34. The wine cleansed the wounds while the oil soothed and protected them.

Most likely James has the second use of oil in mind. The idea behind the use of both prayer and anointing is that the church should seek to come to the aid of both the physical and spiritual needs of a sick person. The medicinal use of oil provided physical comfort and promoted the healing process. Note that James sees *no* conflict between prayer and medicine.

The third prescription for the physically ill is to leave the results up to the Lord. Ultimately *God* does the healing—not the oil, not the elders, not the prayer. Praying "in the name of the Lord" means praying according to *His* will. This in turn means accepting His plan and purpose.

Verse 15 sets forth three specific results of the elders' prayer and anointing offered in faith: restoration, raising up, and forgiveness. This suggests that James may have had in mind a particular individual who is suffering illness as a result of sin. The Greek word for "restore," *sōzō*, is the same word for spiritual salvation, but it can also refer to physical healing (Matt. 9:21; John 11:12). Also, James makes it clear that physical ailments can be a result from personal sin. James, however, uses the Greek word *kan* ("and if") in this final phrase, "*and if* he has committed sins, they will be forgiven him." This indicates that not all cases of physical illness are the result of sin. But if the person's illness was caused by his or her own sin, then God's restoration can include both physical and spiritual recovery.

THE FIVE LAWS OF SUFFERING

Does God heal today?

That question sparks an endless debate. Whole denominations have been formed around the belief in God-gifted healers who claim that Christ's death not only bought us forgiveness of our sins and eternal salvation, but also guarantees physical healing in this life. Are they right? Do those who suffer pain, sickness, and hardship lack faith? Are they missing out on some benefits of the Christian life?

Over the years I have developed what I call the "Five Laws of Suffering." These principles will help the hurting and erase their confusion about why we suffer and what God has done (and will do) about it.

Law One: There are two classifications of sin. Original sin is the sinful condition all humans (except Jesus Christ) inherit from Adam, who was the source and "head" of the human race (Rom. 5:12). *Personal sins* are individual acts of wrong we regularly and willfully commit on our own because of our sinful condition (Rom. 3:23). Because of original sin (the root), we commit acts of sin (the fruit).

Law Two: Original sin introduced suffering, illness, and death to the human race (Rom. 5:12). Had original sin never entered the garden of Eden, humanity never would have known sickness or death. In the broadest sense, all sickness and suffering are the result of *original sin*. After Adam and Eve fell, they began to suffer a deathlike existence in a hostile world characterized by suffering, caused by their own departure from God's way (Gen. 3).

Law Three: Sometimes there is a direct relationship between personal sins and sickness. David testified to the relationship between his own personal acts of disobedience and physical ailments in Psalms 32:3 – 5 and 38:3 – 5. Paul also warned that some of the Corinthian believers were "weak and sick" and a number of them had died because of personal sin (1 Cor. 11:27 – 30).

Law Four: Sometimes there is no relationship between personal sins and sickness. Some people

— 5:16 —

Notice the link with the previous verse. James says, "*Therefore*, confess your sins to one another." He shifts from the third person (anyone who is sick) to the second person: "your sins." Verse 16 helps us understand this passage regarding sickness and sin. He is saying, in effect, "Some in your assembly are sick because of sin. The elders are to be called, and they are to pray and wait upon God to bring about restoration. But some of you, right now, need to take care of this matter before sickness sets in. So confess your sins to one another and pray for one another."

At this point we might refer to a similar situation in which sin in the church led to God's discipline of sickness, weakness, and even death. In 1 Corinthians 11:27 – 31, Paul writes,

> Therefore whoever eats the bread or drinks the cup of the Lord in an unworthy manner, shall be guilty of the body and the blood of the Lord. But a man must examine himself, and in so doing he is to eat of the bread and drink of the cup. For he who eats and drinks, eats and drinks judgment to himself if he does not judge the body rightly. For this reason many among you are weak and sick, and a number sleep. But if we judged ourselves rightly, we would not be judged.

This reality of sin that leads to sickness and death stands behind James's exhortation to confess our sins to one another (5:16). What kind of confession is this? James isn't talking about our original confession of faith for salvation. He's not even referring to confession of offenses before God. He's not urging confession to a priest in a dark, small booth. And he certainly doesn't advocate indiscriminately dumping all of your sins and shame in front of everybody in the congregation. The context of James's message suggests making amends with those whom you have wronged and forgiving those who have wronged you.

Perhaps you are ill deep within; your soul is plagued by a gnawing bitterness or guilt. If you allow those thoughts to fester without clearing them out through confession and prayer, they'll consume you. They'll eventually work their way out in the form of unhealthy habits, chronic depression, unmanageable stress, underlying anger, and even physical illness. But it doesn't have to be that way. When believers in Christ confess their sins to those they've wronged, their guilt will be healed. When they pray for those who have harmed them, their bitterness will be cured.

And guess what? When you have released the burdens of guilt and bitterness through confession and prayer, the garbage that has contaminated and diseased your inner life will be cleared away. That condition of righteousness before God and others will result in your ability to pray more effectively. James affirms, "The effective prayer of a righteous man can accomplish

are born with afflictions, suffering before they ever reach the age of committing personal sins (John 9:1–3; Acts 3:1–2). Others, like Job, are living upright lives when suffering comes (Job 1:1–5). Jesus Himself never committed personal sins, yet He often suffered; that is why He can fully sympathize with our plight of suffering in a fallen world (Heb. 4:15; 5:8).

Law Five: It is not God's will that everyone be healed in this life. Some believe God wants every believer to experience complete physical healing in this life. They support their convictions with the words of Isaiah: "By His scourging we are healed" (Isa. 53:5). "Christ's death brought us healing!" they sing and shout. Of course it did! But what kind? Check the context. The whole flow of thought in Isaiah 53 has to do with the *spiritual* needs of humans and Christ's priceless provision for the forgiveness of sin. It's true that Matthew 8:17 quotes Isaiah 53:4 in reference to both physical and spiritual healing, but there Matthew relates it to Christ's personal work of healing as a sign of His true identity as Isaiah's Servant.

By demonstrating His authority to heal sickness and disease, Christ proves His ability to heal spiritual sickness (Matt. 9:4–6). That's why Jesus was wounded and bruised. That's why He died — not primarily to heal sick people in this life, but to give spiritual life to all and to one day raise us from the dead in bodies that will never again suffer sickness and death (Rev. 21:3–4). In fact, Peter himself interprets the verse this same way, connecting its application to the forgiveness of sins and a life of righteousness: "He Himself bore our sins in His body on the cross, so that we might die to sin and live to righteousness; *for by His wounds you were healed*" (1 Peter 2:24). Peter clearly refers to spiritual wholeness, not physical healing.

Still not convinced that physical healing isn't a guarantee for believers? Take Paul as an example. Three times he asked God to remove the thorn of suffering from his flesh. Three times he got a direct

cont.

and unequivocal "no" from God (2 Cor. 12:7–9). Following that traumatic experience he stated that he was "well content with weaknesses" because even without healing, the Lord proved Himself sufficient and strong in the apostle's life (12:10). Physical healing is *not* promised to everybody.

Let me clarify two important points. Am I suggesting God doesn't heal? *Absolutely not!* God can — and does — heal people, sometimes instantly and miraculously, sometimes slowly and gradually. In fact, *every time* healing happens — regardless of the means — God is responsible. *He* is the source of life and health. Most often, healing comes through diagnosis and medical treatment. But sometimes God chooses to heal miraculously — *nothing is too difficult for Him*. His healings are complete and permanent. Therefore, when God heals, there is no way any man or woman can grab the glory or take responsibility.

Am I stating that God uses divine healers today — certain people specially "anointed" by the Spirit of God to lay hands on people and heal them instantly? *Absolutely not!* In the New Testament period, this special sign gift was given to confirm God's new work of revelation in the church, and it was specifically connected with the foundational work during the time of the apostles and prophets (Eph. 2:20; 2 Cor. 12:12; Heb. 2:3–4). Though special healers were present in the first generation of the church, today so-called "divine healers" prey on those who don't know the facts. They blame all sickness on sin or a lack of faith. And when their healing powers don't work, guess whom those charlatans blame — the sick person who didn't have enough faith to be healed. Tragic!

Don't forget these Five Laws of Suffering. Write them in the back of your Bible. Sure as the world, you're going to run into folks who will wonder why they (or their loved ones) are not being healed. Maybe God will use your words to quiet their hearts and remove their confusion.[2]

much" (5:16). This leads us to the fourth area of prayer for the believer.

— 5:17–18 —

When afflicted with trouble, we should pray (5:13). When physically ill, we should pray (5:14–15). When stained with guilt or bitterness, we are to pray (5:16). Now, to conclude this treatise on prayer, James gives us an example of praying for specific requests (5:17–18).

Remember, the context of praying for God to respond to specific requests is the life that has been cleansed from sin through confession and prayer (5:16). If you're bogged down with guilt, bitterness, or a stack of other sins, not only will your prayers be ineffective, but you may not even be in a spiritual state to discern *what* to pray for or *how* to pray. The righteous person has his or her attitude, priorities, and disposition oriented toward God's will. That's what causes the prayer of a righteous person to be effective and unusually powerful. The Greek word for "effective" is *energeō*, from which we get the word "energy." Prayer is the ingredient that turns ordinary utterances into powerful words. The word James uses for the "prayer" of the righteous person refers to asking for a specific need. "Petition" or "entreaty" might be better translations.

Let me offer a few guidelines on how to pray effectively. (1) Know the Scripture and pray in keeping with the Word of God. (2) Be specific; deal directly with particular issues and ask for specific results. (3) Have absolute faith in God's ability, timing, and wisdom, trusting without reservation that His answer to your petition will be right. These things characterize the prayer life of a righteous person. Small wonder that this kind of prayer "accomplishes much!"

James illustrates such prayer with the prophet Elijah. He reminds us that Elijah had a nature just like ours (5:17)—sinful, inconsistent, imperfect, yet forgiven and equipped with gifts from above. Elijah's specific petitions had such an abundance of power that he was able to stop and start the rain.

Before you rush outside and pray for a sudden change in the weather, you need to understand the broad context—the context of James and of Elijah. Elijah, as a righteous man, knew what to pray for and when to pray for it. The Spirit specially enabled him to discern God's will to pray for certain miraculous events to get the attention of the rulers of Israel and drive home his call for repentance (1 Kings 17–18). A righteous believer today also can get in tune with the Spirit's leading and know how, when, and what to pray for. But even when we don't have a clear sense of God's leading in a matter, we can always pray for the things God has explicitly told us to pray for in the Bible (see Romans 8:26).

> **TWELVE SPECIFIC THINGS FOR WHICH BELIEVERS ARE INSTRUCTED TO PRAY**
>
> 1. For those who persecute them (Matt. 5:44)
> 2. For the kingdom of God (Matt. 6:10)
> 3. For daily provision (Matt. 6:11)
> 4. For overcoming temptation (Matt. 6:13)
> 5. For forgiveness (Luke 11:4)
> 6. For all the saints (Eph. 6:18)
> 7. For the gospel's advancement (2 Thess. 3:1)
> 8. For earthly rulers (1 Tim. 2:2)
> 9. For wisdom (James 1:5)
> 10. For suffering (James 5:13)
> 11. For one another (James 5:16)
> 12. For wayward believers (1 John 5:16)

In this brief but pointed passage on prayer (5:13–18), James teaches that true faith exhibited through patience affects how we respond to God. In every circumstance—sickness or health, joy or hardship—we must go to God in prayer. Prayer not only reflects an attitude of genuine faith, but it also reveals patient endurance as we turn to God to handle life's struggles in His timing and according to His promises. As such, prayer becomes a quintessential mark of true faith.

Application

Practical Principles of Prayer

Prayer may be one of the most misunderstood and neglected blessings of the Christian life. The irony is that prayer is one of the simplest concepts to understand and one of the easiest actions to do. Let me share with you four simple and practical lessons I gather from James's profound passage on prayer.

First, *prayer is to be continuous.* If prayer applies to all situations and to every circumstance, then it should be a constant pulse beat in your life. It should represent your inner disposition toward God that creates a rhythm as consistent as your heartbeat or as natural as breathing. I'm not necessarily talking about a scheduled event at three or four specific times during the day, though that's a great discipline worth considering. I'm talking about the need to be in conversation with God throughout the day, responding in prayer and praise to whatever occurs. Believers need to be prayer addicts. We should "suffer" from chronic prayer. Is that you? How much have you prayed since last Sunday when you were asked to bow for prayer in church? Do you speak to your Lord throughout the day—mealtime blessings excluded? Or is prayer an infrequent act?

Second, *prayer is designed for every part of life.* Stop thinking of prayer like a fire extinguisher. It's not to hang around in the back spaces of your mind until a crisis arises or a tragedy strikes. Yes, prayer will normally follow affliction, sickness, sin, fear, and loss. But it also relates to joy, blessing, thankfulness, and intimate conversation with your heavenly Father. Every kind of situation calls for prayer. Do you still act as if you are a member of a volunteer prayer squad—responding in prayer only when needed? Or have you discovered the peace and joy that comes when you respond to the Father in every kind of circumstance?

Third, *prayer is not a substitute for responsibility.* Remember that James says that prayer is supposed to accompany the application of medicine (5:14). Prayer doesn't exclude intelligent action, but includes it. We err when we exclude prayer from our planning and action. But we also err when we exclude action from prayer. Don't pray to be healed without at the same time taking reasonable steps to get healthy. Don't ask God to protect your children if you neglect them yourself. That isn't faith; it's presumption. Prayer and action go hand in hand.

Finally, *prayer is not for the perfect, but for the imperfect.* James used Elijah as an example of the powerful prayer of a man "with a nature like ours" (5:17). You don't need to be a prophet or an apostle to pray effectively. You don't need to wait to be perfect before God will hear your prayers. Cleansing of sin comes through prayer (5:15). Wisdom comes through prayer (1:5–6). Specific needs are met through prayer (4:2–3). Yes, the prayer of a righteous person produces *much* fruit (5:16). But you don't need to be sinless to pray. If that were so, nobody would be able to pray for anything! So, don't wait until you're great. Pray *while* you wait.

Don't forget: God is listening.

Are you praying?

Patience in Correction (5:19–20)

---

¹⁹ My brethren, if any among you strays from the truth and one turns him back, ²⁰let him know that he who turns a sinner from the error of his way will save his soul from death and will cover a multitude of sins.

Lifeguards who have rescued swimmers from drowning know better than most that victims tend to fight their rescuers in the hysteria of that terrifying moment. In an uncontrollable panic, they will even pull their rescuers under the water. Reason should tell them that if the lifeguard goes under, so does their only hope of survival. But when a person is drowning, he isn't thinking reasonably. The same is often true when a believer attempts to rescue those who are floundering spiritually because their faith has suffered shipwreck.

Professor Howard Hendricks of Dallas Seminary, my mentor and lifelong friend, tells the story of a young man who, after straying far from the Lord, was finally brought back by the help of a friend who loved him unconditionally. When he was fully restored, Dr. Hendricks asked him what it felt like when he was straying from God.

The man answered, "It seemed like I was being pulled farther and farther out to sea, into deep water. And all my friends were standing on the shoreline hurling accusations at me about justice, condemnation, and sin." Then he added, "But there was one Christian brother who actually swam out to get me and he wouldn't let me go. I fought him, but he withstood my fighting. He grasped me, put a life jacket around me, and managed to pull me to shore. By the grace of God he was the single reason I was restored—the man refused to let me go."

James doesn't want us to let go of anybody, either. Throughout his letter he stresses the need for a faith that works. He asks, "If you say you believe like you should, then why do you behave like you shouldn't?" Now, at the climactic conclusion of the book, James instructs us on how to actually deal with those who believe like they should, but behave like they shouldn't.

For the last several verses, James has been developing the theme that *real faith produces genuine patience.* But *genuine patience* is different from *passive permissiveness.* Under the excuse of "patiently waiting on the Lord," Christians frequently stand back and "patiently" watch a brother or sister sink deeper into sin. This shouldn't be! When it comes to handling straying saints, the genuine work prompted by real faith calls for more than prayer. It often includes intervention expressed through a patient reliance on God and a patient disposition toward the process of confrontation and restoration.

In these last two verses, James addresses a number of practical questions. Is there ever a time when one Christian ought to intervene and deal with the sin of another? At what point should a Christian's patience run out? Is the correction of straying saints solely a work of the Holy Spirit apart from human involvement, or should we step forward and become part of the solution? If so, how can we do this without appearing legalistic or judgmental? Didn't James condemn this kind of judgmental attitude earlier in his book?

With these questions in mind, let's examine his answer.

— **5:19** —

One summer my older son, Curt, took a metal-working course. One day a tiny particle of metal flew into his eye and became embedded in his cornea. We didn't realize it at the time because it was so small. But his eye was irritated and it became obvious that there was a problem. We took him to an ophthalmologist who quickly discovered the metal speck. So, that physician calmly rested my son's chin on a brace, numbed the cornea, and proceeded to extract the metal particle with care and precision. It was agonizing for me. I could hear the long prong give off a high-pitched *ping . . . ping . . . ping* as he tried to pluck that speck of metal from Curt's eye. (I had to look the other way, since that kind of thing does me in.) Thankfully, the skilled physician removed the speck with delicate care . . . and with great patience.

In Matthew 7:3–5, Jesus gives instructions about removing specks from the eyes of those with sight blurred by sin:

> Why do you look at the speck that is in your brother's eye, but do not notice the log that is in your own eye? Or how can you say to your brother, "Let me take the speck out of your eye," and behold, the log is in your own eye? You hypocrite, first take the log out of your own eye, and then you will see clearly to take the speck out of your brother's eye.

Some people feel called to criticize! Even when their own life is a shambles and their own perspective clouded by sin, they feel it's their duty to point out even the most minor flaws in others. Jesus condemned this kind of hypocritical judgment. Like his older Brother, James also spoke out against those who hypocritically judge, slander, and speak against a brother or sister in Christ (4:11–12). In light of these warnings, we must never hastily rush into the practice of spiritual eye surgery. Only those qualified with clear vision, punctuated by patience and equipped with wisdom and humility, should take on this task (see Gal. 6:1–2).

Given these important warnings and understanding the seriousness of our responsibility for straying saints, we can work through James's principles for handling wayward brethren. Let's follow James's reasonable instruction in verse 19. First, James is addressing the situation of believers who have gone astray. He's not talking about leading unbelievers to salvation, but restoring Christians who have strayed from the truth. The word "strayed" comes from the Greek word *planaō*, from which we get our English word "planet." Unlike stars, which kept their place in relation to other heavenly lights, planets appeared to drift and wander through the night sky. Thus, these individuals have drifted and wandered from the straight path.

Note also that the person James has in mind willfully walks away from the *truth*. That refers to the complete body of Christian truth contained in Scripture. People can stray from the truth in a couple of ways. They can wander *doctrinally*; that is, they can err in their *beliefs*. But they can also stray from the truth *practically*, failing to align their practice with their profession. In either case, the response of healthy believers should be the same: we should turn those who have strayed back to the truth.

The word for "turn back" is *epistrephō*, meaning to turn around and head in the opposite direction — a 180-degree reversal. You may recall that Jewish believers viewed life as heading in one of two trajectories, the path of life or the path of death. Believers growing in faith and good works were on the way of life, but unbelievers were on the way of death. James says that some believers, after making progress along the way of life, can stray, heading in the wrong direction. Such people need firm yet gracious intervention to avoid God's discipline described in 5:15–16.

Not everybody is equipped with the right attitude for turning wayward saints back toward the right way. Earlier I mentioned Galatians 6:1. It gives a clear description of the attitude one must have when approaching straying saints: "Brethren, even if anyone is caught in any trespass, you who are spiritual, restore such a one in a spirit of gentleness; each one looking to yourself, so that you too will not be tempted." Did you catch that? The person who intervenes in the life of a wayward brother or sister in Christ must be spiritual, gentle, wise, and humble. The fleshly, harsh, and arrogant have no business trying to rescue the wandering, though they are often the ones who try to do so.

I'm deeply concerned when we take upon ourselves the practice of digging specks from other people's eyes without first considering whether we're qualified to do so. If a person relishes the idea of confronting a believer, he or she probably shouldn't. Furthermore, if the one who confronts the wandering soul assumes a "holier than thou" attitude, the intervention will do more harm than good. That kind of approach pushes the speck in deeper rather than gently plucking it out.

— **5:20** —

If we succeed at our rescue operation through patience, humility, gentleness, and perseverance, James assures us that we will have restored the person to the right path. He then describes the wholesome and encouraging results of this restoration.

First, *when we turn a sinning Christian from the error of his way, we will "save his soul from death."* Given the Jewish Christian background of this letter, it seems most likely that "death" here refers to the "way of death"—a dark, "deathlike" existence. Recall that in early Christian training, life was viewed as following one of two paths, the path of life or the path of death. The Greek word for "path" or "way" is *hodos*, which refers to a literal road or figuratively to a lifestyle direction. In verse 20, James uses the same word, *hodos*, to describe the wayward Christian's lifestyle as the "error of his way [*hodos*]." So, James has the figurative use of the term in mind—a *lifestyle* characterized by death rather than physical death. We have also seen however, that some unrepentant sin can lead to sickness and physical death (5:14–16), which is viewed as the final destination of those who continue down the "way of death" without turning around through repentance.

Second, *when we turn a sinning Christian from the error of his or her way, we will "cover a multitude of sins."* This has a double application. Not only does a person's confession of sin bring forgiveness for the wayward path he or she took, but it also prevents that person from continuing farther along that dead-end path. The damage that has been done and could be done through the rebellious Christian's personal sins will be covered. Peter uses the same term "cover" when he says that "love covers a multitude of sins" (1 Peter 4:8). The intervention of loving Christians through prayer, patience, and perseverance will save not only that person from accumulating more sin and making a greater mess of this life, but also spare the church from the damage done by a wayward brother or sister.

Although James doesn't fudge on his claim that real faith produces genuine patience, sometimes we must step forward and accompany our prayers for straying saints with deliberate words and actions. In other words, patience is not an excuse for passivity; faith is not an excuse for inaction. If James has taught us anything, He has made it clear that *real faith produces genuine works.*

If you are considering whether to get involved in the life of a straying believer through a word of encouragement, relief, or correction, first check your motives. Make certain you are acting out of genuine love for that person. Be sure you've immersed yourself in prayer. And be ready to apply patience as you endure a long process. Most wayward saints don't suddenly turn around with a tap on the shoulder. It can take a long, long time.

I think it's fitting that James ends his letter with this exhortation to look out for wayward saints. His entire book has been a plea to make sure outward actions accompany inward convictions, that our words match our deeds, that real faith produces genuine works of stability (1:1–27), love (2:1–3:12), humility (3:13–5:6), and patience (5:7–20). He has involved himself in the most intimate areas of his readers' lives, and he has done so with a spirit of conviction and care. James's entire letter exemplifies his own call to restore wayward saints to the path of life. His finale addressed to the original readers could just as easily be addressed to you: "I've come to your rescue in this letter and have invested my time in giving my thoughts to you in these specific areas where you were going astray. Now you do the same."

NOTES:

1. Thomas Hastings, "From Every Stormy Wind That Blows," in *The Hymnal for Worship and Celebration*, no. 432.
2. Adapted from Charles R. Swindoll, "Healing," in *Come Before Winter and Share My Hope* (Grand Rapids: Zondervan, 1985), 313–15.

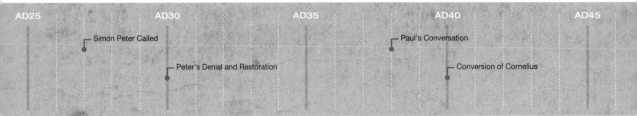

Simon Peter Called

Peter's Denial and Restoration

Paul's Conversation

Conversion of Cornelius

The recipients of 1 and 2 Peter in Asia Minor

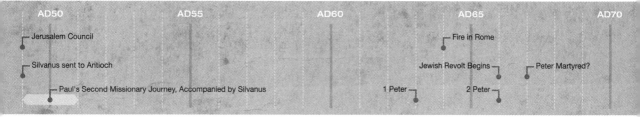

AD50　　　　　　　AD55　　　　　　　AD60　　　　　　　AD65　　　　　　　AD70

Jerusalem Council

Silvanus sent to Antioch

Fire in Rome

Jewish Revolt Begins

Peter Martyred?

Paul's Second Missionary Journey, Accompanied by Silvanus

1 Peter

2 Peter

1 PETER

Introduction

"Even though all may fall away because of You, I will never fall away!" (Matt. 26:33).

Those words of Peter brashly followed Jesus' calm assertion that all of the disciples — without exception — would turn their backs on their Master: "You will all fall away because of Me this night" (Matt. 26:31). Though he should have known better, Peter "piously" rejected Jesus' words and swore absolute allegiance to his Lord. Yet Christ's response to Peter's impetuous devotion only reinforced the fact that Jesus spoke prophetically, not pessimistically: "Truly I say to you that this very night, before a rooster crows, you will deny Me three times" (26:34).

In response to Christ's clear and specific pronouncement, Peter passionately retorted, "Even if I have to die with You, I will not deny You" (26:35). Once spoken, those words lingered, perhaps echoing into the night, replaying in the Master's ears and the other disciples' memories. In any case, Peter seemed to take Jesus' words not as a direct prophecy sealing his fate, but as a personal challenge to prove his worth as the greatest among the disciples. How much he still had to learn!

Just a few hours later the brokenhearted Peter found himself weeping bitterly, having denied his Savior not once, not twice, but three times (Matt. 26:69–75) — just as Jesus had predicted. For many men this scene would have meant the end of a promising ministry. But for Peter the denial became the moment that did more than break his heart; it clarified his absolute weakness before God and prepared him for true God-given greatness in the kingdom of his Lord.

Overview of the Book of 1 Peter

Section	Our Living Hope	Our Strange Life	Our Fiery Ordeal
Themes	**Informing** "May grace and peace be yours . . ." as we claim our hope (1:3–12) as we walk in holiness (1:13–25) as we grow together (2:1–12) Grace to go on. A *living* hope through Christ's resurrection (1:3)	**Exhorting** "Beloved, I urge you . . . " submit! (2:13–3:7) be humble! (3:8–22) arm yourselves! (4:1–6) glorify God! (4:7–11) Grace to stand firm. A *calm* hope through personal submission (3:6)	**Comforting** "Beloved, do not be surprised. . ." Don't be surprised. (4:12) Keep on rejoicing. (4:13) Entrust your soul. (4:19) Cast your anxiety. (5:7) Grace to rejoice. A *firm* hope through faith (4:19)
	Hope . . . Suffering . . . Sobriety		
Key Terms	Imperishable Holy Obedience	Submit Sanctify	Shepherd Humble
Passage	1:1–2:12	2:13–4:11	4:12–5:14

KEY TERMS

ἐλπίς [*elpis*] (1680) "hope, confident expectation"

Hebrews 11:1 says, "Now faith is the assurance of things hoped for, the conviction of things not seen." This parallelism links "things hoped for" with "things not seen," giving us a glimpse of the depth of hope in the Christian life. A Christian's living hope — one of the three prominent Christian virtues (1 Cor. 13:13) — is the future-oriented dimension of faith and love. Hope for a Christian is not abstract but is focused on particular promises, especially the promise of Christ's return and our future resurrection from the dead (1 Peter 1:3, 21; 3:15).

πάσχω [*paschō*] (3958) "to suffer, experience pain, endure hardship"

Either the verb form or its noun counterpart, *pathēma*, or both, appear in every chapter of 1 Peter. Like life itself, Peter's letter is riddled with suffering. This word stands behind our English term "passion," especially as it refers to the sufferings of Christ. In Peter's letter the suffering of believers is closely linked to their continued participation in the ministry of Christ as His body, the church, called not only to eternal glory but also to temporal hardship.

νήφω [*nēphō*] (3525) "to be sober, calm and collected, temperate"

Used three times in 1 Peter (1:13; 4:7; 5:8), the exhortation to "be sober" literally means to avoid drunkenness. But in its six New Testament uses it refers metaphorically to being clearheaded rather than cloudy (1 Thess. 5:6, 8; 2 Tim. 4:5), and having a temperate, discerning spirit, which is the primary meaning in 1 Peter. The term implies the ability to focus fully on what's most important.

It is difficult even to imagine that the same man who spat the denial, "I do not know the man" (Matt. 26:72) later penned the words, "Sanctify Christ as Lord in your hearts, always being ready to make a defense" (1 Peter 3:15). Who is this man? Where did he come from? What transformed his brash audacity into bold confidence?

A REVIEW OF PETER'S MINISTRY

If you are like me, when you get a note, letter, or email, you first observe who sent it. When a total stranger writes me, I can usually understand the words, but I never fully grasp the emotions and motives behind them. But if I know the person, that makes reading and understanding the words much easier. So, before we dive into the New Testament book called 1 Peter, we need to take the time to get acquainted with a man who began life as a rugged, coarse fisherman and ended it as a martyred statesman of the church.

We catch our first glimpse of Peter in Mark 1, when Jesus calls him and his brother, Andrew, as disciples:

> As He was going along by the Sea of Galilee, He saw Simon and Andrew, the brother of Simon, casting a net in the sea; for they were fishermen. And Jesus said to them, "Follow Me, and I will make you become fishers of men." Immediately they left their nets and followed Him. (Mark 1:16–18)

Without hesitation, Simon and Andrew turned their backs on that lucrative fishing business based in the Galilean city of Capernaum and followed Jesus. We could interpret their reaction as either enthusiastic or impulsive. Either way, Simon Peter's immediate response — in fact, the responses of all the Galilean disciples — fits what we know of the character of Galileans in general. The Jewish historian Josephus, a governor in Galilee in the first century, described the Galilean temperament as "ever fond of innovations, and by nature disposed to changes, and delighting in seditions."[1] William Barclay notes, "Quick-tempered, impulsive, emotional, easily roused by an appeal to adventure, loyal to the end — Peter was a typical man of Galilee."[2]

Just think about Simon Peter's response. Most adults I know are fully engaged in their careers. Even if they're bored stiff, they know that making a career change usually means starting over and working up from the lowest rung on the proverbial ladder. So, whether they're just starting out or have been in a job for decades, most would think long and hard before suddenly dropping everything and leaving. But that's just what Simon Peter did. While this may tell us something important about Jesus' compelling personality and preaching, it also gives us a picture of Peter's adventurous abandon.

A casual glance at the biblical record of Peter's role among the disciples reveals that he enjoyed a place of prominence. Matthew refers to Peter as "the first" of the twelve disciples (Matt. 10:2): "Now the names of the twelve apostles are these: The first, Simon, who is called Peter." We see in the account of Peter's calling, however, that he and his brother, Andrew, were called at the same time (Mark 1:16–18). So, in Matthew 10:2, the Greek word *prōtos* means "first in prominence," not "first in order."[3]

Peter quickly became the spokesperson for the disciples. His boldness led him to step forward with questions nobody else would ask (Matt. 15:15; 18:21; 19:27). He acted as Jesus' PR man to those on the outside (17:24). And when they stayed in Capernaum, Jesus used Peter's home as His ministry headquarters (Mark 1:29–32).

Yet the Bible indicates that Peter could be impulsive in his loyalty. He actually argued with Jesus when the Lord (in Matt. 16:21) let the disciples in on His impending death and resurrection. Such a plan didn't fit with Peter's idea of how the Messiah's career should pan out. Matthew writes, "Peter took Him aside and began to rebuke Him, saying, 'God forbid it, Lord! This shall never happen to

Ruins of a Byzantine church built over the likely location of Peter's house in Capernaum (lower right).

You'" (16:22). Peter's loyal but impulsive response drew Jesus' ire: "Get behind Me, Satan! You are a stumbling block to Me; for you are not setting your mind on God's interests, but man's" (16:23).

And, of course, nobody can forget Peter's denial. His great zeal led the man to make promises he couldn't keep. Not because he didn't want to, but because in the power of the flesh—without the enabling Spirit of God—he couldn't. "Even though all may fall away because of You, I will never fall away!" (Matt. 26:33). We've already seen the results—determination, desperation, denial . . . and despair.

When that kind of tragedy occurs, it's tempting to conclude that you're through forever, isn't it? You may never have explicitly denied the Lord. But chances are you know the feeling of having failed to live up to your testimony through a lifestyle that has gotten off track, a failed Christian witness at home, work, or school, or perhaps an unfortunate string of words said in an angry outburst you wish you could retrieve.

The good news is that failure is never final. No failure, no denial, no sin can trump the grace of God that restores the repentant rebel. Peter's life illustrates this beautifully.

Immediately after the resurrection, an angel at the empty tomb instructed the women, "Go, tell His disciples and Peter" (Mark 16:7). I've always loved it that the angel intentionally singled Peter out for the message that Jesus had risen from the dead. With those words, God's plan of restoration began. This rehabilitation of Peter is in keeping with Christ's own promise prior to Peter's denial: "Simon,

POPE PETER THE GREAT?

Was Peter the first in a long succession of popes placed at the head of the universal church by Jesus Himself? By coupling Simon Peter's place of leadership among the disciples with Peter's unique renaming in Matthew 16:18–19, some have concluded that Jesus founded the church upon Peter.

"I also say to you that you are Peter, and upon this rock I will build My church; and the gates of Hades will not overpower it. I will give you the keys of the kingdom of heaven; and whatever you bind on earth shall have been bound in heaven, and whatever you loose on earth shall have been loosed in heaven." (Matt. 16:18–19)

This deserves a closer look. We need to realize that Jesus didn't give special authority to Peter alone or make him the one foundation on which He established the universal church. First, it's true that Jesus renamed Simon the "Rock" (*Petros*) because of his confession about Christ. But when Jesus refers to the foundation of the church He uses the word for "stone," *petra*, which could refer metaphorically to Peter's confession or to Jesus Himself. Second, although the authority of "binding and loosing" is addressed to Peter in the singular in 16:19, it is given to all the disciples in Matthew 18:18 and John 20:23. Finally, Peter Himself uses the same term, *petra*, to refer to Christ as the "rock [*petra*] of offense" (1 Peter 2:8), which he regarded as the cornerstone of the church (2:4–8).

We must remember that although Peter was a great leader in the first-century church, he was never singled out with unique authority over all the other apostles. Nor should he be regarded as the "first pope," the first in a long line of popes in Rome who exert doctrinal authority over the Catholic Church. The earliest church fathers never accepted this notion of the "seat of Peter" having priority over all other Christian churches. In fact, like the Protestant churches, the Eastern Orthodox Church has never accepted the authority of the pope in its nearly two thousand years of history.

Statue of St. Peter on top of St. Peter's Basilica in the Vatican.

Simon, behold, Satan has demanded permission to sift you like wheat; but I have prayed for you, that your faith may not fail; and you, when once you have turned again, strengthen your brothers" (Luke 22:31–32).

We see the climax of this restoration in the gospel of John. After sharing breakfast beside an open fire on the shore of the Sea of Galilee with his disciples, Jesus quietly turns to Simon Peter and says, "Simon, son of John, do you love Me more than these?" (John 21:15). John uses the verb for "unconditional love," *agapaō*, which underscored the kind of superior devotion Peter had claimed when he promised never to abandon the Lord, even if all others did (Matt. 26:33).

Ashamed at his claim to having devotion superior to the other disciples, Peter replies to Jesus' question, "Yes, Lord; You know that I love You" (John 21:15). In this case, John uses the word *phileō*, not *agapaō*, defaulting to a word that means "brotherly love." Peter wasn't about to claim a place of superiority over his fellow disciples. Not again.

This was just the attitude of humility Jesus sought from that broken leader. So he responds to Peter, "Tend my lambs" (John 21:15). And just as Peter had denied his Lord three times, Jesus questioned Peter about his devotion three times (John 21:15–17). But the third time the word *phileō* is used instead of *agapaō*, illustrating how the Master met Peter where he was in his chastened sense of devotion to Christ and reassuring him that he was restored to his position of leadership among the disciples. From that point on, Peter would stand out as a shepherd among Christ's sheep, tending the lambs as a humble servant-leader.

We see this front-and-center leadership play out after Christ's ascension when "Peter stood up in the midst of the brethren" to take the lead in finding a replacement for Judas as the twelfth disciple (Acts 1:15). And Peter didn't hesitate to leap to his feet on the day of Pentecost when the unbelieving Jews questioned the meaning of the miraculous signs of the Spirit: "But Peter, taking his stand with the eleven, raised his voice and declared to them ..." (Acts 2:14). Years later, the apostle Paul regarded Peter as a major pillar in the church, ascribing to him a place of prominence (Gal. 1:18; 2:7–9).

Peter was no stranger to controversy in his growth toward maturity. At Antioch Paul had to publicly rebuke Peter for hypocritically withdrawing himself from the Gentile believers when Jewish believers from Jerusalem arrived. Paul referred to Peter when he reported:

> For prior to the coming of certain men from James, [Peter] used to eat with the Gentiles; but when they came, he began to withdraw and hold himself aloof, fearing the party of the circumcision. The rest of the Jews joined him in hypocrisy, with the result that even Barnabas was carried away by their hypocrisy. (Gal. 2:12–13)

We know Paul's rebuke was effective. Peter learned from it, because at the Jerusalem council he stood up among the apostles and made it clear that the gospel of grace was for the Gentiles apart from works of the Law:

> After there had been much debate, Peter stood up and said to them, "Brethren, you know that in the early days God made a choice among you, that by my mouth the Gentiles would hear the word of the gospel and believe. And God, who knows the heart, testified to them giving them the Holy Spirit, just as He also did to us; and He made no distinction between us and them, cleansing their hearts by faith. Now therefore why do you put God to the test by placing upon the neck of the disciples a yoke which neither our fathers nor we have been able to bear? But we believe that we are saved through the grace of the Lord Jesus, in the same way as they also are." (Act 15:7 – 11)

Clearly, Peter didn't adjust quickly to God's program of bringing the gospel to the Gentiles. God repeated a vision for Peter three times in order to prepare him to preach the gospel to the Roman centurion Cornelius (Acts 10:9 – 48). But once convinced, Peter became a great champion of the Holy Spirit's mission to the Gentiles. He defended the development before Jewish Christians who hadn't yet come around (11:1 – 18).

Truly, Peter had been restored from his great denial. The gruff fisherman turned fisher of men continued to exercise great influence during the foundational years of the infant church. Consider several of the ways Peter left his mark on the first half of the book of Acts.

- Peter took the lead in choosing a twelfth disciple to take Judas's place (Acts 1).
- Peter became the major spokesman for the first outreach of evangelism (Acts 2).
- Peter, with John, healed the lame man at the temple (Acts 3).
- Peter defied the Sanhedrin when he refused to stop preaching Jesus (Acts 4).
- Peter courageously presided over the grim task of dealing with the deception of Ananias and Sapphira (Acts 5).
- Peter confirmed the preaching of the gospel to the Samaritans and dealt with the deceit of Simon the Magician (Acts 8).
- Peter healed the sick and raised the dead in Lydda, Sharon, and Joppa (Acts 9).
- Peter reached out to the Gentiles, accepting God's plan for the universal offer of the gospel (Acts 10).

William Shakespeare wrote, "The evil that men do lives after them, / The good is oft interred with their bones."[4] In grace, Christ gave Peter a second chance at redeeming his legacy. It could easily have ended at dawn that Good Friday morning when the rooster crowed. But God had other plans for Peter.

A PREVIEW OF PETER'S FIRST LETTER

Our brief sketch of the first part of Peter's life should give us enough background to understand the character of the man who penned the words of 1 Peter. (We'll save the latter part of Peter's life for the introduction to 2 Peter.) In light of his life, you'll see some things about the letter that will make better sense. Peter had a heart for the hurting and broken. He had a ministry to the suffering. He did get it. He knew ministry means more than well-crafted messages and gentle pats on the back. Sincerity and truth, encouragement and exhortation—these things go hand in hand. So we shouldn't be surprised that Peter wrote his first letter to hurting people on the brink of hopelessness.

THE WRITER(S) AND RECIPIENTS OF THE LETTER

Though Peter identifies himself as the author of the letter in 1 Peter 1:1, he later mentions, "Through Silvanus . . . I have written to you briefly" (5:12). In the first-century world, this phrase often meant that the named person served as the secretary who either wrote a dictated letter or contributed to the composition of the letter under the direct authority of the primary author. This is likely its meaning here.[5] Peter doesn't say he sent the letter to them by means of Silvanus, but that he actually wrote the letter with his help.

Who was this Silvanus who assisted Peter in composing this great letter of hope? Silvanus, also called "Silas," is first mentioned in Acts 15:22 in the Jerusalem church, where he first met Peter. He was one of the men sent with Paul and Barnabas to Antioch, bearing the results of the Jerusalem Council (15:27). We are told that Silas was himself a "prophet" who encouraged and strengthened the believers in Antioch (15:32). After Paul's abrupt falling out with Barnabas over whether to bring John Mark on the second missionary journey (15:35–39), Paul decided to take Silvanus instead of Barnabas (15:40). Silvanus is then mentioned repeatedly during Paul's second missionary journey. He suffered persecution with Paul, rejoicing through their suffering (16:19, 25). He worked closely with Paul and Timothy in establishing and strengthening the churches throughout Asia Minor, Macedonia, and Greece (Acts 16–18; 2 Cor. 1:19).

It's easy to forget the fact that 1 and 2 Thessalonians are written not by Paul alone, but by "Paul and Silvanus and Timothy" (1 Thess. 1:1; 2 Thess. 1:1). After his ministry with Paul and Timothy, Silas next appears with Peter in Rome, responsible for composing and sending the letter from Peter to the churches in Asia Minor; Silvanus was no doubt personally acquainted with many in these congregations.

So, if Silvanus (Silas) was partly responsible for writing 1 Peter, we have a collaborative writing by both an apostle (Peter) and a prophet (Silvanus).[6] The resultant letter, written in words inspired by the Holy Spirit, bears absolute authority and profound relevance for the church in every age. Although we may be able to discern the influence of Silvanus in this letter through various phrases that connect us to Paul's unique language and imagery, the primary human author responsible for its content is Peter.

The recipients of the letter are "those who reside as aliens, scattered throughout Pontus, Galatia, Cappadocia, Asia, and Bithynia" (1 Peter 1:1). These scattered aliens knew the Lord as citizens of God's kingdom living in exile in the far reaches of the world. From an earthly angle they were refugees, but from a heavenly perspective they were "chosen." Scattered by persecution, victimized by circumstances beyond their control, wandering in the wilderness of despair—these men and women still had reason to rejoice. They were God's chosen!

The believers scattered throughout Asia Minor (modern-day Turkey) included both Jewish and Gentile Christians suffering persecution. Peter, likely writing from Rome, drew from both his Jewish background and his intercultural experience to weave together a message that communicates to both groups. He drew extensively on Old Testament texts and images familiar to Jewish Christians. But he also reminded his Gentile readers that they were no longer ignorant and immoral (1:14), but were now recipients of mercy as the people of God (2:10).

PURPOSE AND PREVIEW OF THE LETTER

Our hope as believers must rise above the treatment we receive from those who dislike and distrust us. It must rely on the Lord and His sure promises. The point of Peter's letter, to put it simply, is that *Christ gives hope in hurtful times.* Who better to know how to keep hope ablaze in the midst of a cold world of dark despair than one who lived his earlier life in physical, mental, emotional, and spiritual gloom?

So, throughout the book of 1 Peter we see reminders of the reality of suffering (1:6–7; 2:18–19; 3:15–16; 4:12–16; 5:8–10). The theme keeps rising to the forefront of Peter's mind. It's the message his readers needed to hear and the message Peter is well-prepared to send. Peter wants to remind the Christians that painful trials are not the end. God will be victorious over His adversaries and bring about a redemptive purpose through these periods of pain. Peter reminds us of what we can so easily forget—Christ gives hope in hurtful times.

Peter develops his encouraging message that Christ gives hope in hurtful times through three movements. First, Peter *informs* his readers regarding their living hope (1:1–2:12). In this section he lets us know that grace and peace can be ours as we claim our hope (1:3–12), as we walk in holiness (1:13–25), and as we grow in Christ (2:1–12). Peter highlights the grace to go on, describing a *living hope* through Christ's resurrection (1:3). Christ becomes the *source* of hope in hurtful times.

Second, Peter *exhorts* his readers to hopeful living despite their strange life (2:13–4:11). He urges his readers to submit to various authorities (2:13–3:7), to be humble in spirit (3:8–22), to be armed with endurance (4:1–6), and to glorify God (4:7–11). These principles become the key to living as Christians in a hostile world. Peter emphasizes grace to stand firm, describing a *calm hope* through personal submission (3:6). Christ becomes the *example* of hope in hurtful times.

Finally, Peter *comforts* his readers in the midst of their fiery ordeal (4:12–5:14). He reminds them not to be surprised at their difficult circumstances (4:12). Instead, they should keep rejoicing (4:13), entrust their lives to God (4:19), and cast their worries on Him (5:7). Peter encourages us with grace to rejoice, turning our attention toward a *firm hope* through faith (4:19). Christ becomes the *foundation* of hope in hurtful times.

Application

Don't Peter Out!

I can't speak for you, but Peter's life and ministry give me hope. When I consider how that rough-hewn Galilean went from failure to faithfulness through God's transforming grace, I can't help but think that God can do the same for you and me. I find at least three key lessons we can learn from Peter's example.

First, *failure in the past does not nullify purpose in the future*. People will try to persuade you (and you'll sometimes convince yourself) that God follows a "one strike and you're out" rule. If you mess things up, He'll check you off and move on to somebody more reliable and faithful. If you're ever tempted to think God has written you off in His plan, think of Peter. After three strikes, he counted himself out — but Christ deliberately restored him, lifting him to a place of leadership among his fellow disciples. I don't believe Peter ever could have led in the infant church had he not come to full terms with Christ's absolute forgiveness of his blatant denials. He received God's forgiveness and in the process forgave himself. He saw himself as God saw him — wiped clean and released from the guilt and shame of his past. Don't think for a moment that failure in your past nullifies God's plans for your future.

Second, *a broken heart is great preparation for healing fractured lives*. Paul said that God "comforts us in all our affliction so that we will be able to comfort those who are in any affliction with the comfort with which we ourselves are comforted by God" (2 Cor. 1:4). Who better than Peter could lead a thriving ministry of reconciliation, proclaiming God's unconditional forgiveness through Jesus Christ? He knew the frailty of humanity, the weak interiors masked by bold veneers, the tendency to fall no matter how hard a person tries to stand. So as he ministers to distressed believers teetering on the brink of their own plunge, he can encourage them from personal experience to pick themselves up and press on. The same is true for you and me. We suffer hardships, survive crises, and recover from failures *for a reason*. God wants to use these experiences from our past to minister to others in similar circumstances. A broken heart is great preparation for healing fractured lives.

Third, *one note of hope brings more encouragement than a thousand thoughts never expressed*. From distant Rome — in the midst of a busy ministry of his own — Peter felt the need to write to beleaguered believers in a region two seas away. He easily could have left them in the care of another. Instead, he took the time to write what he calls a "brief" letter (5:12). That compassionate expression made all the difference in their lives. Perhaps you know of individuals struggling through tough times who could use your encouragement. You've been there. You know what to say (and what *not* to say). Write them. And I don't mean an email or instant message. Give them something real to hold onto, a tangible sign that they are not alone, that somebody out there cares. Take Peter's life as an example and bridge the gap between remote concern and real action. Knowing that one note of hope brings more encouragement than a thousand thoughts never expressed, I urge you to take the next step. Take the time to connect and bring a ray of hope into someone's dark and discouraging world.

NOTES:

1. Flavius Josephus, *The Life of Flavius Josephus*, in *The Complete Works of Josephus*, trans. William Whiston (repr.; Grand Rapids: Kregel, 1981), 5.
2. William Barclay, *The Master's Men* (New York: Abingdon, 1959), 18.
3. Walter Bauer et al., *A Greek-English Lexicon of the New Testament*, 2nd ed. (Chicago: Univ. of Chicago Press, 1979), 726. Using the same Greek word, Paul called himself the "foremost" of sinners (1 Tim. 1:15), and Acts 13:50 refers to the "leading men" of the city with the same term.
4. Antony to Roman citizens in *Julius Caesar*, act 3, scene 2.
5. Peter H. Davids, *The First Epistle of Peter,* The New International Commentary on the New Testament, ed. Gordon D. Fee (Grand Rapids: Eerdmans, 1990), 198.
6. Scholars often point out the difference in Greek style between 1 Peter and 2 Peter, suggesting that one or both of them have no relation to the disciple Peter but were forgeries in his name. But if we acknowledge the assistance of Silvanus, a New Testament prophet and coauthor of other New Testament writings, then the differences in style are easily accounted for. First Peter is from Peter, written through Silvanus, while 2 Peter comes more directly from the pen of Peter himself (2 Peter 1:1).

OUR LIVING HOPE
(1 PETER 1:1 – 2:12)

Bursting into the darkness ahead of his younger companion, who had reached the tomb a few moments earlier, Simon's eyes needed time to adjust to the darkness. It took only a glance for him to confirm Mary's report: *Jesus' body was gone!* But the situation was not as simple as a missing corpse. Instead of a dead body in the tomb, Simon found stained linen wrappings still lying on the slab, with the face-cloth still rolled neatly and set aside (John 20:6–7).

John's voice suddenly broke the silence, echoing off the stone walls. "He's . . . he's risen!"

"Shh!" Peter uttered, still thinking things through. He had made enough rash decisions to last a lifetime. He was not about to make another one. Somebody could have stolen the body. But who? None of the disciples; he knew that for sure. They had been holed up since the crucifixion, fearing that they, too, would be arrested and executed like their Master. And it could not have been the Jewish authorities . . . or the Romans. Of all people, they needed Jesus dead *and buried*. But who else would have snatched the body? And where would they have taken it?

"He's risen!" John insisted. Peter motioned with a hand for him to be silent, then stroked his beard with a trembling hand. Even if somebody *had* taken the body, they had left the burial clothes! And they had even taken the time to fold the face-cloth neatly. How preposterous! You don't just go trudging around Jerusalem with a naked, cold corpse. That wasn't kosher by any standard. Peter closed his eyes as Jesus' words passed through his mind. It was as if the Lord Himself were privately whispering them to him again: "Simon, Simon, behold, Satan has demanded permission to sift you like wheat; but I have prayed for you, that your faith may not fail; and you, when once you have turned again, strengthen your brothers."

Tears welled up, then overflowed as he opened his eyes and visually surveyed the empty tomb. John pressed forward, scanning the burial clothes and turning back to Peter with an expression somewhere between delight and terror: "Simon, listen to me . . . He—has—risen. He—is—alive!"

Nodding his head, Peter leaned against the wall of the tomb and said, "You're right, John. He has risen indeed!" At that moment, Peter felt as if a massive tombstone rolled away from his own heart and stale burial wrappings tore away from his mind.

KEY TERMS

ἄφθαρτος [aphthartos] (862a) "imperishable, not subject to decay, incorruptible"

This word is the negation of the virtually unpronounceable *phthartos* — "corruptible." Whereas everything in this fallen world is subject to decay, including mortal humans (Rom. 1:23) and material rewards (1 Cor. 9:25), Christians look forward with hope to an incorruptible resurrection body (15:53) and an imperishable reward (1 Peter 1:4). Peter further refines this idea by noting that we are imperishable because we have been born by an imperishable seed — the "living and enduring word of God" (1:23).

ἅγιος [hagios] (40) "holy, sacred, set apart; pure, upright"

The concept of holiness plays a major role in Peter's first letter. In its basic sense, "holy" means to be set apart, separated for a special, unique purpose. When used regarding a person, it sometimes means to be consecrated for a particular service (2:5). Other times the moral aspect is emphasized — being morally distinct from the surrounding immoral society (1:15). In either case, the standard for our holiness is God's holiness (1:16), and the means is the calling of the Holy One through the sanctifying work of the Spirit of holiness (1:2, 15).

ὑπακοή [hypakoē] (5218) "obedience, compliance"

This word is related to the verb *hypakouō*, "to hear." In classical Greek it referred to a porter, whose duty was to answer a knock at a door; hence it bears the idea of responding to a call or hearkening to a command. For Christians, absolute obedience is to be rendered to Christ as Lord (1:2, 14, 22). Therefore, we are to listen for His commands; and when He calls, we must immediately respond without reservation.

He knew that everything would soon change ... *everything.*

Almost thirty years later, Peter penned these words of praise: "Blessed be the God and Father of our Lord Jesus Christ, who according to His great mercy has caused us to be born again to a living hope through the resurrection of Jesus Christ from the dead" (1 Peter 1:3).

It is to this *living hope* that Peter points his readers in the first major section of his letter. First he *informs* his readers regarding their hope (1:1 – 2:12). He also broadens his scope as he lets believers of every generation, including us, know that grace and peace can be ours as we claim our hope in the midst of suffering (1:3 – 12), as we walk in holiness in a corrupt world (1:13 – 25), and as we grow together in Christ as His special people (2:1 – 12).

Highlighting the grace that strengthens us to go on in spite of our circumstances, Peter shines the light on the resurrected Christ — not on us or the world —

as the one reliable source of hope in hurtful times. Just as the light of day displaced the darkness in that empty tomb nearly two thousand years ago, so the light of hope can fill all our hearts with joy, driving out the shadows of despair.

Smiling through Suffering (1 Peter 1:1–12)

¹Peter, an apostle of Jesus Christ,

To those who reside as aliens, scattered throughout Pontus, Galatia, Cappadocia, Asia, and Bithynia, who are chosen ²according to the foreknowledge of God the Father, by the sanctifying work of the Spirit, to obey Jesus Christ and be sprinkled with His blood: May grace and peace be yours in the fullest measure.

³Blessed be the God and Father of our Lord Jesus Christ, who according to His great mercy has caused us to be born again to a living hope through the resurrection of Jesus Christ from the dead, ⁴to *obtain* an inheritance *which is* imperishable and undefiled and will not fade away, reserved in heaven for you, ⁵who are protected by the power of God through faith for a salvation ready to be revealed in the last time. ⁶In this you greatly rejoice, even though now for a little while, if necessary, you have been distressed by various trials, ⁷so that the proof of your faith, *being* more precious than gold which is perishable, even though tested by fire, may be found to result in praise and glory and honor at the revelation of Jesus Christ; ⁸and though you have not seen Him, you love Him, and though you do not see Him now, but believe in Him, you greatly rejoice with joy inexpressible and full of glory, ⁹obtaining as the outcome of your faith the salvation of your souls.

¹⁰As to this salvation, the prophets who prophesied of the grace that *would come* to you made careful searches and inquiries, ¹¹seeking to know what person or time the Spirit of Christ within them was indicating as He predicted the sufferings of Christ and the glories to follow. ¹²It was revealed to them that they were not serving themselves, but you, in these things which now have been announced to you through those who preached the gospel to you by the Holy Spirit sent from heaven — things into which angels long to look.

All people, in all places, and at all times have one thing in common: we know what it means to hurt. Whether Jews or Christians, Muslims or Hindus, atheists or idolaters — tears are all the same. Cultures ebb and flow, nations rise and fall, and people groups come and go; but suffering transcends all cultures, invades every nation, and translates its message of pain to each person who has ever lived.

The pervasive problem of pain requires a potent prescription. Peter's first letter dispenses the remedy by telling us how we can endure suffering — not with disciplined determination and clenched teeth, but with a settled sense of peace—yes, even joy. For most, that sounds preposterous. But Peter deserves a fair hearing.

Peter writes to displaced believers, scarred by the flames of persecution. They lived in bleak circumstances, with every earthly reason to give up hope. Many were defecting. But Peter doesn't try to pump them full of positive thinking or offer a pile of empty platitudes. Instead, he came alongside them in their suffering, gently turning their attention heavenward, allowing them to see beyond their circumstances and to find new hope in their celestial calling.

And Peter's words can do the same for us.

— **1:1–2** —

I love modern inventions, technology, and the efficiency and convenience that come with them. But I also like old things: classical music, quaint sayings, leather-bound books. But what I really appreciate is the old style of writing letters, where the person writing puts his name at the beginning. Isn't that convenient? Way back in ancient times, people signed their letters at the beginning, so you knew immediately who put the ink on the parchment or papyrus.

Now imagine yourself as a Christian living in the midst of tremendous pressure from every direction. In your best moments, you grit your teeth and complain about the Lord's delayed return. At your worst, you consider going back to the familiar rituals of the synagogue or even returning to those idol-filled temples. At that disillusioned moment, somebody hands you a letter rolled up and bound. You break the seal, slowly unroll the scroll, and read immediately—"Peter, an apostle of Jesus Christ." Like a cool breeze cutting through sultry summer heat, those opening words blow through your weariness and ignite fresh hope. The chief apostle has written a letter ... *to you*. Suddenly that light roll of papyrus feels heavy in your hands, and you can't wait to gather with your fellow believers and pore over it. Hope has just arrived!

Peter writes to "those who reside as aliens, scattered." They were aliens away from home; their treasured destination was with Christ—in heaven when they died, but ultimately in His kingdom whenever He returns. But *now*? Now they were scattered, displaced throughout the world. The word "scattered" is *diaspora*. James used the same term referring to displaced Jewish believers (James 1:1). Here Peter uses the term in a figurative sense, not referring to literal Jews displaced from their Judean homeland, but to all Christians—Jews and Gentiles—driven by hardship into the wilderness of a harsh and hostile world, persecuted and alienated.

Whether they were living in their own homes or not, these readers had "scattered" lives, fractured spirits, broken hearts. Their pain went to the bone.

When facing persecution, our instincts tell us to flee or fight back. Persevering through suffering and responding with grace is extremely difficult to do. If you've ever had anyone mistreat you, you know the great temptation to defend yourself, to lash back, to get even. Peter writes for the purpose of helping his readers get beyond all that, gain composure, and find hope despite all the unfair treatment.

Because the church first began in Judea among Jews, the Roman Empire initially regarded the church as a "sect" of Judaism. Among all the pagan religions in the Roman world, Judaism was the only legal religion not required to offer sacrifices to the emperor. Instead, they could offer prayers on the emperor's behalf. So long as Christians were viewed as a sect of Judaism, the Romans regarded them as under that umbrella of exemption and protection.

But when the synagogue began expelling Christians and Christianity took on a distinct identity composed of both Gentiles and Jews, it lost its legal protection and became the target of Roman persecution. This is the situation in which the Christians living in Asia Minor (modern-day Turkey) found themselves when they received Peter's letter. The spark of suspicion had lit the flame of persecution, which would eventually engulf the Roman world in a blazing rampage against the infant church, seeking to reduce the movement to ashes. Peter's words are meant not only to comfort these believers in their hot crucible of suffering, but also to prepare them for subsequent waves of persecutions.

Peter begins to encourage his readers by reviewing their position before God. They are "chosen" according to the Father's foreknowledge, made holy and set apart by the Spirit, and consecrated by the blood of Christ, whom they are to serve through obedience (1:1–2). This reminder of God's grace toward them is to bring them peace "in the fullest measure," regardless of the chaos they are enduring in daily life.

— 1:3–9 —

In verses 3 through 9, Peter writes about how we can do more than cope with suffering. We can, in fact, defiantly rejoice in its midst! In this majestic hymn, called a "doxology" ("glorifying words"), Peter praises God for providing at least six reasons we can rejoice through suffering. These verses are the meat on the bones of that "grace and peace" mentioned in verse 2. And if verse 2 asserts our unconditional position before our triune God as His chosen ones, verses 3–9 describe the

THE TRINITY AND SALVATION

If you're not careful, you might zip through 1 Peter 1:2 and miss the Trinity at work in your salvation. Many Christians forget — or at least fail to fully appreciate — the fact that the Father, Son, and Holy Spirit work together in perfect harmony to establish our new identity as children of God. Far too often we imagine that the doctrine of the Trinity is irrelevant to our lives, that it's just so much theory without practical importance. But Peter's opening blessing dismisses that view as shortsighted, at best.

One author writes, "Each person of the Godhead plays a distinct role: the Father chooses, the Son redeems, and the Spirit sanctifies."[1] We must recognize that although each of the three persons in the Trinity affects distinct aspects of our salvation, they do their work in complete unity. At the same time, we must be careful not to confuse the persons of the Trinity in ways that imply that they are the same person, just with different names. For example, Christians who thank God the Father for dying on the cross carelessly attribute the work of the Son to the Father. We need to follow the New

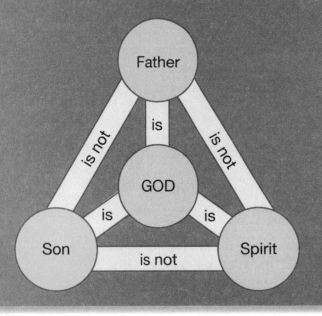

incomparable possessions we have in that abiding relationship with the Father, Son, and Holy Spirit.

A living hope (1:3). First, we can rejoice because we have a "living hope." Believers in Jesus Christ have been "born again" to a living hope because of Christ's resurrection from the dead. When we realize that the ultimate destination on this long, difficult journey is eternity in heaven, it makes the potholes and breakdowns in life worth bearing. To the unsaved, hope is nothing more than wishing upon a star:

- "I hope I win the lottery."
- "I hope my boy shapes up someday."
- "I hope things work out for me in my job."
- "I hope I make it to the next paycheck."

But this kind of wishful thinking differs markedly from a *living hope*. Christian hope is grounded on the reality of Christ and His resurrection. Because He rose from the grave, we, too, will be raised like Him in glorified bodies to dwell in a new heaven and new earth for all eternity (1 Thess. 4:16 – 18; Rev. 21:5).

A permanent inheritance (1:4). Second, we can rejoice in suffering because we have a permanent inheritance. I've had the privilege over my years of ministry to do a lot of traveling, staying in all kinds of motels and hotels around the world. But I freely confess, I get especially irritated when my "guaranteed" room reservation somehow vanishes. You show up at 9:30

p.m., exhausted from a long day of travel, give the guy your name and credit card, wait while he does some voodoo on his computer—and then he stares through you as if you're a ghost. If your name isn't on the little screen, you don't exist! You then give him your confirmation number, but it does no good. In the end, you wind up in a flophouse two blocks down, with nothing but a halfhearted apology because somehow your reservation vanished ... faded away.

Peter offers great news: this will never happen to your reservation in glory! Your heavenly reservations are purchased by the blood of Christ and confirmed by His glorious resurrection. Some celestial receptionist won't look at you and say, "Now, what was your name again?" or "Could I see your credit card just one more time?" No, after your long, painful journey in this life, the living God will welcome you home without an inch of red tape. We can rejoice in times of suffering because our inheritance is sure.

Testament example, understanding that Father, Son, and Holy Spirit — though eternally united and sharing complete deity — have distinct roles.

This working in unity amid distinction reflects the unity and diversity of Father, Son, and Spirit in the Godhead. In contrast to the countless gods of pagan religions, Scripture teaches that there is one true God (Deut. 6:4). In the unity of the Godhead, however, there exist three coeternal persons: Father, Son, and Holy Spirit. The Father is God (John 6:27; Eph. 4:6), the Son is God (John 1:1; Heb. 1:8), and the Holy Spirit is God (Acts 5:3–4). But the Father is not the Son (Luke 23:46; John 20:17), the Father is not the Spirit (Luke 11:13; John 14:26), and the Spirit is not the Son (John 14:16; Acts 2:33). Yet there are not three gods, but one Triune God. This biblical doctrine of the Trinity — "one God in three persons" — is impossible to fully comprehend, but it is foundational to our salvation (1 Peter 1:2).

A divine protection (1:5). Third, we can rejoice in suffering because we "are protected by the power of God." No matter how acute the persecution, you and I will never get lost in the process. God's hand of comfort and strength will remain with us. No matter the calamity, no matter the cause of death, the depth of pain, or the horror of catastrophe—God is in control. And He is all-powerful, all-good, and all-knowing. That means we can trust Him regardless of our circumstances. Death may destroy our bodies, but God has promised to protect our souls—and to raise our bodies immortal and glorious "in the last time." No one can tell us all the reasons why we go through such hard times. Nobody can explain it to our complete satisfaction. But because we know the kind of God we have, we can accept the mystery of suffering and know for sure that God will protect us by His power, from now throughout eternity.

A developing faith (1:6–7). Fourth, we can rejoice in the midst of various trials because they bring about a growing, strengthening faith. Peter acknowledges that his readers have been "distressed by various trials" for some time. He doesn't try to downplay or dismiss the reality of their suffering, but he offers a reason to "greatly rejoice" in spite of—not because of—the testing (1:6). Pain and suffering are not in themselves good; they are the result of a fallen world. We can be certain of this: when God cures this world from its curse, those things will not be present. In spite of the evils of persecution, pain, and hardship, God providentially brings about good results.

Verses 6–7 offer four truths about trials.

- They are necessary to humble us, to turn our attention from self to God.
- They are distressing, painful, and difficult; not good, delightful, or easy.
- They are varied and diverse, and they come in different forms, at different times, and for different durations.
- They prove the genuineness of our faith, just as gold, when refined in fire, is purified and demonstrated to be authentic.

All these things merge to bring about the development of faith as believers endure trials throughout life. Though we don't rejoice over the trial itself, we can rejoice over the result brought about by our God.

An unseen Savior (1:8). Christians can rejoice through times of suffering because we have confidence in the unseen power of Christ. Behind Peter's words may lie an event that happened several years earlier when Jesus revealed Himself alive to Thomas, who had doubted the resurrection. When Thomas finally declared his belief in Jesus as Lord and God (John 20:28), Jesus responded, "Because you have seen Me, have you believed? Blessed are they who did not see, and yet believed" (John 20:29). This is the category in which Peter's readers find themselves; they are especially blessed because though they have not literally seen the Savior, they still believe in Him and love Him as if He were present. We "see" Christ most clearly in times of trial. When suffering comes, it dispels a lot of the fog that clouds our vision. Often, all that remains is the Savior and our trust in Him.

A guaranteed deliverance (1:9). I'll never forget a trip to Canada that lasted eight days. I had clothes with me for two days because my bags ended up in Berlin. The airline delivered them thousands of miles away, across an ocean those bags had no business crossing. That kind of experience will make you think twice about trusting your luggage with the person standing in front of the conveyor belt, ready to send your bags to who-knows-where. I don't blame people who refuse to check bags, because the delivery is never guaranteed. But Christ *can* guarantee delivery. The final reason we can rejoice in suffering is because the salvation of our souls is guaranteed. God has the power to save us physically through trials; but even when our bodies eventually succumb to death, our souls are faithfully delivered, just as promised.

Can we *really* rejoice in the midst of suffering? Peter answers this with a resounding "Yes!" But we do not rejoice because suffering is great. We don't rejoice because we're out of touch with reality, but because we have a living hope, a permanent inheritance, a divine protection, a developing faith, an unseen Savior, and a guaranteed deliverance. Training ourselves to remember all of that helps to soften life's sharp edges.

— **1:10–12** —

What a marvelous salvation! It not only guarantees an inheritance for us in the future, but also provides inexplicable faith, hope, and joy in the present. In light of this glorious truth, Peter shifts gears from the future and present in order to briefly revisit the past; in fact, he goes far back to the distant past.

This slight regression might be regarded as a brief interlude, unpacking something about the "salvation" mentioned in verse 9. He begins, "As to this salvation," and then mentions the Old Testament prophets who prophesied back in their day about the grace that had arrived in Peter's own time. How does this regression fit into Peter's argument that we can have hope in hurtful times? Quite simply, his reflection on how the prophets looked forward to the salvation through Christ increases the value of our current hope. It also affirms that God has a track record of making good on His promises. The prophets looked forward in hope toward Christ — and *Christ came*! In the same way, we look forward to the return of Christ — and *Christ will come*!

Peter says that we have a unique vantage point that the Old Testament prophets lacked. We can look back and see Christ's life and miracles recorded by eyewitnesses. We see His saving death and resurrection, read His words and promises, and see how the church grew and spread throughout the world in spite of persecution. All this gives us confidence that God will work out His current plan in our lives today. But the Old Testament prophets had much less to go on. Their mental images prior to the coming of Christ weren't as clear as our understanding after His coming. In fact, Peter says they "made careful searches and inquiries, seeking to know what person or time the Spirit of Christ within them was indicating as He predicted the sufferings of Christ and the glories to follow" (1:10–11).

Peter says the Old Testament saints saw the high peaks of God's plan — the death and resurrection of Christ and His future kingdom — but they missed the finer points of the space in between. That space, always part of God's plan but kept hidden from the prophets' view, includes the present period of salvation

PROPHETIC TELESCOPING

As they looked into the future, the Old Testament prophets lacked a clear picture of God's full plan. They saw, as it were, two mountain peaks — Mount Golgotha and Mount Olivet. On Golgotha Christ would die in humility and disgrace (Mark 15:22); on Olivet He will return in glory and power (Zech. 14:4). They saw the peaks, but from their vantage point, they couldn't see a great valley that stretched between the two mountains. This valley represents the present age of the church.

The Old Testament believers were also at a disadvantage in that they didn't have the permanent indwelling of the Holy Spirit as we do today. The Spirit of God spoke through the prophets, igniting

Mountain/Cross - PhotoDisc, Crown - © Ivan Ponomarev/www.istockphoto.com

through Christ in the church. The Old Testament prophets may have expected an immediate leap from the sufferings of the cross to the glories of the crown. But between these epochal events we experience the "in-between" events, in which suffering and hope, pain and glory, all mingle.

Those prophets didn't fully grasp what they wrote by the Holy Spirit's revelation. As they obediently wrote, they realized that their words served a future time. Peter reveals that this time came in the person and work of Christ, announced to the believers of Asia Minor by the apostles who preached the good news to them by the empowering work of the same Holy Spirit who inspired the Scriptures (1:12). So profound is the fulfillment of those expectations that even angels long to listen in on our songs of redemption, look over the shoulder of a sinner praying for forgiveness, and linger as believers endure temporary suffering for the sake of eternal glory.

If angels marvel at the hope we have in Christ, shouldn't we?

Application

Making Sense of Your Suffering

In his book *The Problem of Pain*, C. S. Lewis commented on the ramifications of the lofty, creative vision God has for our lives — to make us more like Christ.

We are, not metaphorically but in very truth, a Divine work of art, something that God is making ... Over a sketch made idly to amuse a child, an artist may not take much trouble: he may be content to let it go even though it is not exactly as he meant it to be. But over the great picture of his life — the work which he loves, though in a different fashion, as intensely as a man loves a woman or a mother a child — he will take endless trouble — and would, doubtless, thereby *give* endless trouble to the picture if it were sentient. One can imagine a sentient picture, after being rubbed and scraped and re-commenced for the tenth time, wishing that it were only a thumb-nail sketch whose making was over in a minute. In the same way, it is natural for us to wish that God had designed for us a less glorious and less arduous destiny; but then we are wishing not for more love but for less.[2]

their message, but they had not experienced the spiritual baptism into the body of Christ (1 Cor. 12:12 – 13; Eph. 3:4 – 6). Today the Spirit works to empower us with faith and hope as in no other era. With the cross behind us and the crown of glory before us, we are encouraged to press on.

If you are suffering right now, only Christ's perspective can replace your resentment with rejoicing and your hardness with humility. I have seen it happen in hospital rooms as I prayed with hurting people. I have seen it happen in my study as I counseled hardened hearts. I have seen it happen with individuals lost and wandering in the world as they came to embrace Christ and suddenly realized that Jesus is the central piece of life's puzzle that had been missing all those years. If you fit Him into place, the rest of the puzzle — no matter how enigmatic — begins to make sense.

Are you in the midst of the storm right now? Wondering when, or if, it will ever end? Have you begun to think that maybe you're being punished, that God has abandoned you, or that you need to do whatever it takes to escape all this pain? Stop. When you become a Christian, the storms of life will not suddenly break. Truth be told, they sometimes intensify into hurricanes, at least for a season. But even in the midst of the hurricane, you have the Master of the wind and waves sitting beside you in your tiny boat, manning the helm and keeping you on an even keel.

Staying Clean in a Corrupt Society (1 Peter 1:13 – 21)

[13]Therefore, prepare your minds for action, keep sober *in spirit*, fix your hope completely on the grace to be brought to you at the revelation of Jesus Christ. [14]As obedient children, do not be conformed to the

former lusts *which were yours* in your ignorance, [15]but like the Holy One who called you, be holy yourselves also in all *your* behavior; [16]because it is written, "You shall be holy, for I am holy." [17]If you address as Father the One who impartially judges according to each one's work, conduct yourselves in fear during the time of your stay *on earth*; [18]knowing that you were not redeemed with perishable things like silver or gold from your futile way of life inherited from your forefathers, [19]but with precious blood, as of a lamb unblemished and spotless, *the blood* of Christ. [20]For He was foreknown before the foundation of the world, but has appeared in these last times for the sake of you [21]who through Him are believers in God, who raised Him from the dead and gave Him glory, so that your faith and hope are in God.

In the opening passage, Peter emphasized hope to go on despite suffering. This hope grows stronger as we focus on the relief we'll enjoy in our heavenly home. Still focusing on the believer's life in this fallen world, Peter shifts his emphasis from physical trials to spiritual temptations. If the question in the first section was, "How can I remain joyful in the midst of suffering?" the question in the next is, "How can I stay clean in a corrupt society?"

Throughout history Christians have responded to this question with all sorts of extremes. Some have adopted a hermit mentality, hiding away in caves, living in virtual solitude. Others have modeled a monk mentality, dwelling only with believers in a close-knit community, away from the world's reach. Those with a utopian mentality have attempted to rebuild a perfect society from the ground up—a world without worldliness. Interestingly, each approach falls under the idea of a sanctification by isolation—withdrawing from the world in some way to keep it from rubbing off on them.

Unlike hermits, monks, and utopians, the Bible has a very different approach. Believers have a mission to accomplish in the world, and therefore we can't afford to lock ourselves *outside* the world. The Christian's solution to the problem of holy living in an unholy world is not *isolation*, but *insulation*. This is why 1:13–21 challenges us to be different from our depraved society without fleeing to the caves, cloisters, or communes.

— **1:13–16** —

I can imagine that as Peter dictated the first twelve verses of his letter, he did so in a posture of praise as he paced his room in Rome, where he was staying. Perhaps he stared out the window, directing his prayerful words partly to his secretary, Silvanus, and partly to His heavenly Father as he praised Him for the living hope believers have through Christ. But then, after he spoke the words "things into which angels long to look" in verse 12, I can picture Peter stopping in his tracks, closing his eyes, and taking a deep breath. His tone changes from exultation to exhortation as he says, "Therefore, prepare your minds for action" (1:13). In other words, in light of the great salvation that has been lavishly poured upon us, it's time to get serious. He fires off a series of staccato-like commands, one after the other. If he were writing in today's style, he might have used bullet points:

- Prepare your minds!
- Keep sober!
- Set your hope!
- Don't be conformed!
- Be holy!

Peter wants us to realize that even though we are living in a wicked world filled with thousands of daily trials and dark temptations, our focus must rise beyond present circumstances. This means living by a higher standard than the world around us. That's the meaning of "holiness" Peter is addressing. It means being *different.*

Peter says it starts in the mind — "prepare your minds for action, keep sober" (1:13). But it leads outward, beyond ourselves — "fix your hope completely on the grace to be brought to you at the revelation of Jesus Christ." According to 1 John 3:3, hope and holiness belong together: "And everyone who has this hope fixed on Him purifies himself, just as He is pure." (It sounds as if Peter and John hung out a lot, doesn't it?)

Peter then assumes the obedience of believers in verse 14. It's not an unreasonable assumption if they are obeying the commands of verse 13 — if they've prepared their minds, kept sober and alert with regard to the world around them, and then fixed their hope on the coming of Christ; in that case, obedience will come more easily.

Their obedience takes a specific form: "Do not be conformed to the former lusts which were yours in your ignorance" (1:14). We've already seen how Peter and John used similar language regarding hope and holiness. Now we observe a striking parallel between Peter and Paul. Note Paul's language in Romans 12:2: "And do not be conformed to this world, but be transformed by the renewing of your mind." And take careful note of this: holiness starts in the mind. It includes a departure from ignorance and a renewal of your thought life. And it leads to conforming to Christ's holiness rather than to the lusts of the world.

This leads to Peter's exhortation to holiness: like the Holy One Himself, believers are to be holy in all their behavior (1:15). He reinforces this practical outwork-

From My Journal

Holy Is as Holy Does

When I was eight thousand miles away from my wife in the military, I had nobody around to check up on me in regard to my "holy matrimony." I had only the memory of standing before God and a couple of preachers who said the right words so that Cynthia and I might become husband and wife. I had the memory of being exclusively set apart unto my wife and she exclusively set apart unto me—for the rest of our lives.

We had made a commitment to holiness, setting our lives apart for one another. To go into another life and to be intimate with another partner would be to break that holy relationship, that exclusive oneness that was ours by holy matrimony. But it wasn't enough to have consecrated myself to my wife in that one moment. I had to continue to glance at my wedding band, stare at that photograph, cling to those letters, remember those words. You see, even though I was permanently set apart unto my wife, I still needed to be continually confirmed in that commitment.

What's true in marriage is true in our relationship with God. We were declared "holy" by our gracious God when we were saved and entered into a permanent relationship with Him. But from day to day we must continually remind ourselves of our holy calling, recommit ourselves to it, and live in it.

This is why I begin virtually every morning by saying, "Lord, I set apart my mind for You today. I set apart my passion, my eyes, my ears, my lips. I set apart my motivations, my attitudes, my disciplines. I set apart all these things to You." This kind of simple reminder has kept me moving toward that goal of holiness Peter mentions in verses 15–16. I would urge you to do the same.

ing of their hope and obedience by paraphrasing a famous Old Testament verse, Leviticus 11:44–45. The original verse in context declares, "For I am the LORD your God. Consecrate yourselves therefore, and be holy, for I am holy ... For I am the LORD who brought you up from the land of Egypt to be your God; thus you shall be holy, for I am holy."[3] In Leviticus 20:26, this same mandate is linked to the role of Israel as God's special people: "Thus you are to be holy to Me, for I the LORD am holy; and I have set you apart from the peoples to be Mine."

What does it mean for Christians to be "holy" (*hagios*)? Ask around and you'll get a host of answers—most of them erroneous. The term, in its basic sense, means to be set apart, separated for a special, unique purpose. This is why marriage is sometimes called "holy matrimony"—a husband and wife separate from their former family commitments as they commit themselves to each other in a unique and intimate relationship. We also call the Bible "Holy Scripture" because these writings, inspired by the Holy Spirit, are of such perfection that they have been set apart from all other human writings, however good and helpful others may be. So it is with God's people. Israel in the Old Testament and now Christians in the New Testament era are set apart for the glory of God.

—1:17—

Not only are we to live lives of holiness in light of our hope (1:13–16), we are also to conduct our walk in the fear of the Lord (1:17). I know we are living in a world that doesn't like to talk much about the fear of God. People don't mind talking about the love, grace, mercy, and blessings of God, but to refer to God as Judge, who evaluates our work and who must be feared as our great and holy Father—well, this kind of thinking bothers a lot of people, even Christians. But Peter doesn't hesitate to refer to the great holiness and justice of God, who demands reverence before Him.

The fear of God goes beyond the kind of respect we might show a powerful human figure. Hebrews 12:21 says that the sight of God was so "terrible" that Moses exclaimed, "I am full of fear and trembling." Likewise, our response to God, the "consuming fire," should be one of "reverence and awe" (Heb. 12:28). In fact, Philippians 2:12 says we should live out our salvation "with fear and trembling." We would be wise to conform our attitude to Peter's words rather than to the world's preferences.

When Peter says, "If you address as Father," he has prayer in mind. If we're going to pray to God as "our Father," then we must speak and act as "obedient children" (1:14). We should hold Him in high reverence, knowing that we will one day give account to Him for our time spent on this earth. Hope again fills in the gap, but this is a realization that the hoped-for ascent to our heavenly dwelling will be accompanied by rewards directly related to the quality of our lives. Paul gives us a similar sobering reminder: "So then each one of us will give an account of himself to God" (Rom. 14:12). And in 2 Corinthians 5:10, he writes, "For we must all appear before the judgment seat of Christ, so that each one may be recompensed for his deeds in the body, according to what he has done, whether good or bad."

One day believers will be brought before the judgment seat of Christ. God's people, away from earth, will give account for their lives before God, and He will reward them accordingly. First Corinthians 3:15 makes it clear that the believer who gains no reward will still be saved, but God's judgment will separate the commendable things of his or her life from the wasted time, money, energy, and motives that tainted that believer's holiness.

On this earth Christians applaud other Christians with dynamic ministries, impactful evangelism, and powerful testimonies. And on the surface many appear to be supersaints . . . or at least they have achieved a level of celebrity status in the Christian realm. Regardless of all that adulation and applause, we must never forget that *God* is the Judge. He alone knows the true motivation behind a person's life. In the final analysis, He will be the one to say, "This deserves reward, but *that* does not." He will judge our works and expose our motives without partiality. This is why our hope for heaven must induce us to holiness on earth.

— **1:18–21** —

Peter wants believers to live holy lives (1:13–16) and to conduct their walk in fear (1:17). He also wants them to focus their minds on Christ (1:18–21). We must remain focused on Christ because our primary battlefield is the mind. The enemy has his sights set on our minds. If he can get us to focus on something other than the hope we have in Jesus Christ, he will have won the battle — everything else will be just claiming the spoils of war.

We conduct ourselves with holy lives in fear of the Lord by "knowing that [we] were not redeemed with perishable things . . . but with the precious blood . . . of Christ" (1:18–19). All those who don't know Christ are merchandise in the slave market of sin. They may not realize it, but they are in bondage to desires, impulses, and ignorance — alienated from God, the one source of true freedom. They live in a condition in which they cannot help or change themselves. Spiritually blind and shackled in sin, they get jostled and abused by the uncontrollable flesh, the alluring world, and seducing demons. They continue to dwell in that futile, frustrating lifestyle passed down to them from previous generations. Their only hope is help from the outside.

Christ provided that help at the cross, where His own blood paid the penalty for sin: death. He didn't pay in silver or gold—worthless scrap metal compared to the price of a human soul. No, Christ paid with His blood, breaking the chains, opening the door, and calling the unredeemed to step out of the bondage from which they had been purchased. That's redemption. The only thing keeping any person from receiving this freedom is his or her own reluctance to accept the free offer of eternal life, stepping from the darkness of futility into the light of a joyous, meaningful life.

God, of course, knew our total emptiness—that we are helpless to work or buy ourselves out of sin's slave market. So even before the foundation of the world, He had a plan ready to be implemented (1:20). And that plan meant that His eternal, divine Son would set aside His celestial comforts and privileges, take on full humanity, and voluntarily take on Himself the cross on our behalf so that our faith and hope can rest in God (1:21). There is no other solid basis for hope in hurtful times than the fact that Christ Himself took it all on Himself and rose victorious, ready to lead us, too, to victory.

A stanza from the great hymn of Charles Wesley sums it up brilliantly:

Long my imprisoned spirit lay
Fast bound in sin and nature's night.
Thine eye diffused a quick'ning ray:
I woke—the dungeon flamed with light!
My chains fell off, my heart was free,
I rose, went forth, and followed Thee.
Amazing love! how can it be
That Thou, my God, shouldst die for me![4]

Application

General Orders for Christ's Ambassadors

Christ didn't purchase us with His precious blood to turn us all into hermits, monks, and utopians. We have been redeemed from slavery and called to be His ambassadors—special agents with a mission in the world. This requires us to stay clean in a corrupt society, to be representatives of light in a world of darkness. How can we do this? I have four suggestions that I urge you to remember. Think of them as your four general orders as an agent of Christ sent on a mission into the world.

First, *pay close attention to what you look at.* That takes us back to 1 Peter 1:13: "prepare your minds for action, keep sober in spirit, fix your hope completely on the grace to be brought to you at the revelation of Jesus Christ." Your eyes are the closest connection to your mind. They capture images that are alluring, attractive, sensual, and pleasurable. Take care what you allow to pass through your eye-gate, especially when you're alone! To reinforce this principle, read Job 31:1; Colossians 3:1–2; and 2 Peter 2:13–14.

Second, *give greater thought to the consequences than to the immediate pleasures.* You will notice that one characteristic of the world is that nobody ever mentions the disastrous consequences of pornography, of an affair, or of feeding your greed by neglecting your family. Walk through the consequences of your actions, thinking through the effects, naming the people whose lives will be harmed, and reminding yourself of the high cost of a ruined reputation. Journey through all the consequences of your actions. To help consider the consequences of sin, study Proverbs 7.

Third, *start each day by renewing your sense of reverence for God.* Don't limit that to the church or to a small group. Start each day by spending time with the Lord. Sometimes I simply say, "Lord, I'm here. I'm yours. I give You my day. As inadequate and fragile as I am, I need Your help this day." Reverence Him as the source of your power. Start each day by renewing that Father-child relationship. To remind yourself of your need to fear God daily, read Ecclesiastes 12:13–14 and 2 Corinthians 7:1.

Fourth, *throughout the day, refocus on Christ.* As people, events, and temptations cross your path, you'll begin to drift from that original course. Whatever happens, realign your focus on Christ. Even if it means regularly scheduling short times of prayer or reading your Bible or devotional during breaks or lunch. Take time to focus on Him throughout the day. Take a close look at Hebrews 12:1–2 to consider new ways you can focus fully on Christ.

Reasons for Pulling Together (1 Peter 1:22 – 2:3)

22Since you have in obedience to the truth purified your souls for a sincere love of the brethren, fervently love one another from the heart, 23for you have been born again not of seed which is perishable but imperishable, *that is*, through the living and enduring word of God. 24For,

"All flesh is like grass,
And all its glory like the flower of grass.
The grass withers,
And the flower falls off,
25 But the word of the Lord endures forever."

And this is the word which was preached to you.
²:¹Therefore, putting aside all malice and all deceit and hypocrisy and envy and all slander, ²like newborn babies, long for the pure milk of the word, so that by it you may grow in respect to salvation, ³if you have tasted the kindness of the Lord.

Before Andrew Jackson became the seventh president of the United States, he served as commander of the Tennessee militia. During the War of 1812, his troops reached an all-time low in their morale. A critical spirit grew among them. They argued, bickered, and fought among themselves. Reportedly Jackson called them together on one occasion when tensions reached a breaking point and said, "Gentlemen! Let's remember, the enemy is *over there!*"

What a sobering reminder for the church today!

On the night Christ instituted the Lord's Supper, he told His disciples, "By this all men will know that you are My disciples, if you have love for one another" (John 13:35). To our shame, the world sometimes looks on Bible-believing Christians as self-seeking and factious, even unloving and argumentative. We aren't always known for our love and support for one another. Instead of being loyal and fiercely committed to each other, we tend to look for ways to pick at each other, to put down rather than build up. How strange!

Peter calls his readers to be better than that. Though scattered by persecution and attacked on all fronts, they need to pull together and find strength in each other's company. As a result, their circle refuses to be broken or weakened from within. However, in our day the frequent occurrences of "brother bashing" and "sister smashing" mean that we need to remind ourselves of the reasons for pulling together.

Peter offers some vital thoughts on unity within the body—a unity that can be weakened and even shattered in the midst of suffering and loss of hope. As we have seen, Peter's readers were going through various trials. Some felt tempted to conform, compromise, or give up altogether. They were getting nervous—and getting on each other's nerves! But that wise old apostle, likely having reflected on Jesus' message of unity during the course of his own ministry, prescribes an easily overlooked antidote for the disease of defeat—unity.

—**1:22**—

Scattered, distressed, tested, and tempted—Peter's original readers have experienced all the ingredients of a loss of hope and a fragmenting of community. In this context, Peter begins what we might call his motivational message—taking on the role of a coach or personal trainer, encouraging his team to pull together. Because they are part of the same family, they should be moving in the same direction toward the same goal.

What makes this possible? How do we believers support one another? How do we develop unity and community and avoid loneliness and hopelessness? Peter gives us three answers to this question in the first part of verse 22. (1) It requires "obedience to the truth." We don't follow inner urges, the example of others, or our cultural norms. We obey the truth—God's standard of what it means to be Christians. (2) It requires "purity of soul." This excludes all pride, prejudices, grudges, and bitterness. It means getting rid of—cleansing—those things that stand between brothers and sisters in Christ. (3) It requires a "sincere love." Because of our obedience to the truth and the cleansing of our soul, we are freed to love without hypocrisy. We are given extra measures of grace to overlook the faults of others.

Verse 22 then moves from the conditions that make loving unity possible to the command that makes it real: "Fervently love one another from the heart." On the surface it may look as if Peter is repeating himself—loving each other sincerely, they are to fervently love one another from the heart. Actually, Peter uses two different words for "love" in this single verse. The New Testament primarily uses two Greek words to describe love. One is *philos*, which refers to a brotherly love or the love of a friend. The other is *agapē*, a higher expression of unconditional love (see 1 Cor. 13:4–7). Both types of love are used in 1 Peter 1:22. When Peter spoke of "a sincere love of the brethren," he used the word *philadelphia*: brotherly love. Then, in his exhortation, Peter called his readers to "fervently love one another," using the higher form of love: *agapaō*. This final expression of love, however, is modified by the adverb *ektenōs*, which means "fervently" or "constantly."[5]

In practical terms, Peter's exhortation means we need to support each other. Some people we know are suffering from the devastation of divorce. They need help from others in God's family who have been through this and know how to get through the feelings of rejection, shame, and loneliness. Some have recently lost loved ones and need someone to walk with them through the dark valley of grief. Others are wrestling with an addiction and they need somebody to come alongside them and say, "I've been there. I know what it's like to be one decision away from falling back into the mire. Let me help." In short, we all need—and we can all provide—that refuge of care and encouragement Peter describes as fervently loving one another from the heart.

— **1:23–2:3** —

This kind of selfless love doesn't come naturally. Our old selfish nature kicks against it with all sorts of excuses:

From My Journal

Family Needs

An old Marine buddy became a Christian several years after his discharge from the Corps. When news of his conversion reached me, I felt more than pleasantly surprised; I felt thoroughly shocked! He was one of those guys you'd never picture as having any interest in spiritual things. He cursed loudly, drank heavily, fought hard, chased women, loved weapons, and hated church. He and God weren't on speaking terms when I used to bump around with him.

Then one day, years later, we ran into each other. As the conversation turned to his salvation, he frowned, put his hand on my shoulder, and admitted: "Chuck, the only thing I miss is that old fellowship all the guys in our outfit used to have down at the slop shoot [base tavern]. Man, we'd sit around, laugh, tell stories, drink a few beers, and really let our hair down. It was great! I just haven't found anything to take the place of that great time we used to enjoy. I ain't got nobody to admit my faults to ... to have 'em put their arms around me and tell me I'm still okay."

My stomach churned. Not because his words shocked me, but because I could only agree. The man needed a refuge—someone to hear him out. He needed the *family of God*—not a rehearsed, staged, impersonal production that too often passes for "church." He needed the body of Christ, brothers and sisters of faith who will laugh with him, cry with him, understand and accept him, struggle with him, and suffer with him. When God's family forgets its call to authentic living and genuine love for each other, it fails to live up even to the camaraderie of a local bar!

In my earliest years growing up in the Swindoll family, my dad would remind us about the need for sticking together as a family. "We may have a few differences inside these walls, but kids, remember, if your brother or sister needs you, you take care of 'em. You love 'em. You pull for 'em." This is a pep talk we brothers and sisters in Christ could use today.

- "Those aren't my gifts."
- "Other people have more experience in that."
- "I have my own problems."
- "I wish I had time!"

But Peter preempts all our excuses when he dives into four essential reminders of why we are to care for and support each another in the family of God.

First, *we are all children of the same heavenly Father.* Note the logical connection between verses 22 and 23. We "fervently love one another from the heart" (1:22). But why, Peter? "*For* you have been born again" (1:23). The verb form relating the idea of "for" in the Greek text suggests this rendering: "*because* you all have been born again." The implication is that all of us have the same Father. While the specific circumstances that led up to our conversions to Christ are unique, we believers have all been reborn spiritually the same way—"through the living and enduring word of God" (1:23). We are all members of a permanent family—brothers and sisters in Christ. Peter's point? Because you are all born into the same family of God, *live like it*!

Second, we need to pull together as a family because *we take our instruction from the same source.* The living and abiding "word of God" endures forever. Peter's reference to the Word of God as "the seed" by which we are reborn may reach back to Jesus' parable of the sower and the seed in Matthew 13:1–23. For that seed to take root and bear fruit in our lives, it must be well-planted and watered. It always amazes me when the same Scripture, read, taught, or preached to the same group of people, leads to such radically different results with different people. That's because the Word needs to be understood, embraced, and applied, not merely heard.

Note how Peter quotes Isaiah 40:6–8, intentionally contrasting the frailty of the human flesh with the power of God's Word. Peter might even have had in the back of his mind Jesus' own words of rebuke when He asked Peter, James, and John to pray with Him on the Mount of Olives. As they kept dozing off instead of supporting Christ in prayer, Jesus said, "The spirit is willing, but the flesh is weak" (Matt. 26:41). How true this is! Even though the Word of God is powerful, effective, and imperishable, we are quite the opposite: weak, defective, and perishable. So, to pull together as God's family, we need to receive the instruction from God's Word and diligently implant it in our minds, our hearts, and our lives.

Third, we need to pull together because *we have our struggles in the same realm.* Peter begins chapter 2 with "therefore," continuing to build on the implications of our relationship as brothers and sisters in the family of God and our common tutelage under the Word. In light of this, we should put aside five things with which we all struggle. Like a soiled shirt, we are to strip off malice, deceit, hypocrisy, envy, and slander. (For definitions of these sins, see the sidebar on "Sins That Push Us Apart.") Notice that all of these have potentially disastrous effects on our relationships with others, and each one of them flies in the face of Peter's call for both brotherly love (*philadelphia*) and unconditional love (*agapē*). Peter narrows in on areas in which every believer will continue to struggle for the rest of his or her life.

The fourth reason we ought to pull together as the family of God is because *we focus our attention on the same objective* (2:2–3). For over three years Peter followed Jesus closely, listening to His words, tracking with His actions, and witnessing His mighty deeds. He had personally tasted the kindness of the Lord as Jesus showed Peter patience beyond measure and forgiveness beyond what he deserved. And because of his growth in Christlikeness, Peter could encourage his own disciples to follow the same path. As newborn babies, believers must feed on the milk of the Word and grow in their understanding and application of their salvation. If the goal of the Christian life is spiritual maturity, then the nourishment comes from God's Word, and the model is God's Son.

Jesus Christ is the sure hope in hurtful times. But tragically far too often, the family of God is the source of the hurt! It was the same in Peter's day. We must all strive to set aside our petty differences, embrace our common salvation, and live as reflections of hope for the sake of our brothers and sisters in Christ. That sounds simple and easy, but it is a full-time task!

> **SINS THAT PUSH US APART**
>
> *Malice.* The Greek word *kakia* is a general word for evil.[6] In this passage it characterizes those entrenched in the world system.
>
> *Deceit.* The Greek word *dolos* means "cunning" or "treachery."[7] It involves more than just lying to a person's face. It includes acting in disingenuous or two-faced ways.
>
> *Hypocrisy.* The underlying word, *hypokrisis*, refers to one who acts a part, "being one thing inside and another thing outside."[8]
>
> *Envy.* Commenting on Peter's use of this word, Edward Selwyn describes envy as "a constant plague of all voluntary organizations, not least religious organizations, and to which even the Twelve themselves were subject at the very crises of our Lord's ministry."[9] Envy remains one of the "favorite indoor sports" among fellow believers.
>
> *Slander.* Literally the word means "evil speech."[10] It is especially prevalent when a rumor is passed around. This disparaging gossip destroys our confidence in an individual and can weaken that person's reputation.

Application

Four Steps to Unity

Strangely, in churches where biblical teaching and theological knowledge are strong points, love and unity are often weak. Christians must strive for both maturity in knowledge and unity in love. We should keep the important objective of Christian growth at the forefront, treat each other with humility and respect, and help each other along the path as we seek to become like Christ. Jesus set the example; His disciples ultimately showed that it could be done. Only the remnants of our old natures keep us from doing the same. It's time we put off the old and pull together around the new!

Let's take a few minutes to probe our own hearts and habits in light of Peter's lesson on the need for unity, particularly the four reminders regarding the need for unity. Ask yourself these questions.

First, *are you treating your fellow believers as children of the same heavenly Father* (1:23)? Disunity in churches is often indicated by practices such as gossiping about other believers, complaining about leadership, grumbling about decisions, criticizing others' shortcomings, and developing cliques. Take a few moments to examine your own church social life and note any of these or other indications of disunity that you might be exhibiting. Especially consider specific people toward whom you have exhibited unloving attitudes or actions.

Second, *are you actively seeking to implant the seed of God's Word in your heart* (1:23–25)? When it comes to relationships with others, it's easy to become merely a hearer of the Word rather than a doer. Take time now to set out specific actions you will take to submit yourself more intentionally to the instruction of God's Word. Do you faithfully hear it and regularly read it? Do you ponder its meaning and significance for you personally? Do you plan specific actions to respond to that Word? Applying God's truth isn't automatic; it calls for the discipline of personal follow-through.

Third, *what common struggles affect you the most in your relationships with others* (2:1)? Do you struggle most with malice (evil thoughts, intentions, or actions)? Deceit (lies, half-truths)? Hypocrisy (putting on a show, hiding real intentions, covering motives)? Envy (spite, jealous feelings, ambitious actions that harm others)? Or slander (gossip, unrestrained criticism, cynical comments, exaggerated sarcasm)? Be painfully honest, now. How have these things specifically hurt others?

Finally, *is Christlike spiritual maturity your primary ambition* (2:2–3)? Stop and think before you answer. What is your top priority in life? Toward what are you directing most of your time, energy, and money? If a video crew were to follow you around for a week or if an accountant were to flip through your checkbook, would any of them conclude that your growth as a Christian is the most important thing in your life? Support your answer with real examples.

These questions can help you get to the root of the issues, but until you make a decision to do what's necessary to come together and provide love and hope for your fellow believers, nothing will change. Take time in prayer to ask God to conform you to the image of Christ. Ask for help in "putting aside" old habits that produce disharmony and hurt and in putting on the new habits that promote harmony and hope. If you've surfaced broken relationships that need healing, swallow your pride and take the difficult steps needed for reconciliation. Write a note, make a call, or go for coffee. Don't let bad relationships fester.

Becoming Living Stones (1 Peter 2:4–12)

⁴ And coming to Him as to a living stone which has been rejected by men, but is choice and precious in the sight of God, ⁵you also, as living stones, are being built up as a spiritual house for a holy priesthood, to offer up spiritual sacrifices acceptable to God through Jesus Christ. ⁶For *this* is contained in Scripture:

"Behold, I lay in Zion a choice stone, a precious corner *stone*,
And he who believes in Him will not be disappointed."

⁷This precious value, then, is for you who believe; but for those who disbelieve,

"The stone which the builders rejected,
this became the very corner *stone*,"
⁸ and,
"A stone of stumbling and a rock of offense";

for they stumble because they are disobedient to the word, and to this *doom* they were also appointed. ⁹But you are a chosen race, a royal priesthood, a holy nation, a people for *God's* own possession, so that you may proclaim the excellencies of Him who has called you out of darkness into His marvelous light; ¹⁰for you once were not a people, but now you are the people of God; you had not received mercy, but now you have received mercy.

¹¹Beloved, I urge you as aliens and strangers to abstain from fleshly lusts which wage war against the soul. ¹²Keep your behavior excellent among the Gentiles, so that in the thing in which they slander you as evildoers, they may because of your good deeds, as they observe *them*, glorify God in the day of visitation.

Far too many Christians picture God with His jaws clenched, brows furled, and arms folded, constantly disapproving of everything we think, say, or do. Clucking His tongue at our mess-ups and shaking His head at our errors, He's always frowning, ready to pounce on us with severe discipline the moment we inevitably go astray.

Amazingly, we Christians tend to forget our kind, loving Father who held us in His arms, protected us, taught us how to walk and talk, and fed us just what we needed to grow. Most new believers feel free and open with their heavenly Father, asking Him anything, sharing everything with Him. But as they advance in biblical and theological knowledge, an erosion begins to occur. Many drift away from the original childlike intimacy with God and before long, that caring Father seems distant, uninterested in our everyday problems, even a bit irritated by our constant mistakes and nagging requests.

Peter's first letter addresses those whose hope has waned. Displaced by persecution and stripped of their earthly comforts and conveniences, they were enduring times of undeserved suffering and persecution. Having nearly forgotten their identity as God's beloved children, they felt tempted to return to a lifestyle less offensive to their pagan neighbors. If nothing else, it seemed a safer way to live. Through Peter's words, God gave Spirit-inspired instruction and encouragement to remind believers that in hurtful times we can embrace the hope that comes through knowing who we are in God's eyes. For those who have come to view themselves as troublesome schoolchildren suffering under the sour stare of a divine schoolmaster, the reality of God's positive estimation of us can truly liberate.

— **2:4-8** —

"And coming to Him . . ." With the opening words of verse 4, we face two immediate questions. To whom is Peter referring when he says "Him"? And what does it mean to come to Him? The context answers the first question. Verse 3 ends with, "if you have tasted the kindness of the Lord." Verse 4 refers to the One "rejected by men," verses 6 and 7 refer to the "precious corner stone" and "the stone which the builders rejected." The first comes from a paraphrase of Isaiah 28:16:

> Therefore thus says the Lord GOD,
> "Behold, I am laying in Zion a stone, a tested stone,
> A costly cornerstone for the foundation, firmly placed.
> He who believes in it will not be disturbed. (Isa. 28:16)

Peter says that salvation by faith in the Cornerstone relieves disappointment (1 Peter 2:6), which brings "precious value" to the life of the believer (2:7). That's good news for those who have come to the living Stone! But for those who have failed to notice that firm Foundation, that same Stone can become the very thing that trips them up. Peter strings together images from Psalm 118:22 and Isaiah 8:14, referring to the stone rejected by the builders that has become a "stone of stumbling and a rock of offense" (1 Peter 2:8). Given the context of the passage in Isaiah, Peter probably has in mind his fellow Jews who rejected Jesus as their Messiah (Isa. 8:14). And because they disobeyed the word, they were appointed to stumble. Yet this text also applies to anybody who refuses to come to Christ, the one "rejected by men" (1 Peter 2:4). Clearly, Peter refers here to Jesus Christ.

To answer the second question, "coming to Him" refers not to our initial conversion, but to our drawing nearer to God through our spiritual growth in fellowship with God and others. The Greek verb "coming" is a present participle connected to the main verb of the sentence in verse 5 — "you . . . are being built up." So, Peter declares that by drawing nearer to Christ, we get built up. Notice that this verb is in the passive, not the active, voice. That means God is the One ultimately responsible for all of this. We participate, yes, and we do so obediently, voluntarily, and actively (see 1:14–15, 22; 2:1–2). But we should never let it enter our minds that we are ultimately responsible for our own spiritual growth. As Paul said in another context, "I planted, Apollos watered, but God was causing the growth" (1 Cor. 3:6). We play our parts in our own and in others' growth toward maturity, but God is the Master Gardener who brings about the effects by His own grace.

We know that Christ is the living Stone, a precious Cornerstone, and that those who reject Him are bound to trip and fall. But what about those who believe in Him? Peter uses a special metaphor for believers. He calls them "living stones" who "are being built up as a spiritual house" (2:5). Where did Peter get this illustration of the people of God as a building? Back in the events recorded in Matthew 16, Peter confessed, "You are the Christ, the Son of the living God" (Matt. 16:16), to which Jesus famously responded, "You are Peter, and upon this rock I will build My church" (16:18).

A continuing construction project is going on. Christ is in the process of building up His church, those dead stones quarried from the pit of sin, brought to life as "living stones," then fit into His glorious structure called the church. Each time someone trusts Christ as Savior, another stone gets placed into that living, growing church. Please understand, becoming a stone in a building of countless stones doesn't detract from your significance. In fact, it enhances it! You represent a vital part in the outworking of God's plan. Without you, something would be missing. The wall would be weakened. Never underestimate your important part in the larger community of Christ.

In these verses Peter draws out another analogy. Not only are we living stones in God's spiritual house, but we are "a holy priesthood" called "to offer up spiritual sacrifices acceptable to God through Jesus Christ" (2:5). Peter repeats this description in verse 9—"a royal priesthood." Here we find a twofold implication of our call into the new royal and holy priesthood of all believers. First, we have unmediated access to the throne of God. Because of our relationship with Christ—our High Priest—we can "draw near with confidence to the throne of grace" (Heb. 4:16). We need no animal sacrifice to cleanse us, no earthly priest to serve as a middleman, no ritual or ceremony to give us access to the door to heaven. We have direct access to God. We can simply pray, "Our Father."

LIVING STONES IN THE BUILDING OF GOD

First-century building practices often included cutting new stones from fresh quarries, then fitting the fresh-cut stones perfectly in place. But a faster and less expensive way of gathering building materials was to use stones from old or toppled buildings, chiseling them to the appropriate shape and fitting them into new buildings. In fact, archaeologists often unearth buildings that had incorporated many stones from earlier centuries. And some of these recycled blocks may even have traces of old inscriptions, revealing the original identities of those earlier stones.

The early church saw in these construction practices a great metaphor for God's work in building His church with "living stones." Whether the stones come from new quarries (Gentile believers) or from old buildings (Jewish believers), they both require some cutting, chiseling, and shaping to fit them into a unified and stable structure. Paul uses this image of God's building His temple in his letters to Corinth (1 Cor. 3:16–17; 2 Cor. 6:16), and the picture is well-developed in his letter to Ephesus (Eph. 2:20–22). Even after the time of the apostles, leading pastors of the ancient church continued to use metaphors of buildings, towers, and temples in reference to the church.[11]

Ignatius, a pastor of Antioch martyred early in the second century for his unwavering faith in Christ, wrote to the Ephesian church around AD 110: "You are stones of a temple, prepared beforehand for the building of God the Father, hoisted up to the heights by the crane of Jesus Christ, which is the cross, using as a rope the Holy Spirit" (Ignatius, *To the Ephesians* 9). Temples were common in the ancient world, the centers of worship and meeting places for encounters with the divine. By using the temple as a metaphor for the church, with its individual stones as members, Peter emphasized the unity of the body of Christ and the supernatural presence of the Holy Spirit as believers gathered for worship and communion with God.

© Robert C. Magis/National Geographic Stock

Second, we have the privilege—and the responsibility—of serving as priests on behalf of each other. We're admonished over and over again in the New Testament to intercede for each other through prayer and even to confess our sins to one another. James 5:16 says, "Confess your sins to one another, and pray for one another so that you may be healed."

Not every believer is gifted and called to be a career pastor, preacher, teacher, missionary, or evangelist. But we are all called to be full-time priests. At minimum we're to "offer up spiritual sacrifices" (2:5). But what does that look like? The book of Hebrews gives us a clear indication of what kinds of sacrifices are appropriate for New Testament believers:

> Through Him then, let us continually offer up a sacrifice of praise to God, that is, the fruit of lips that give thanks to His name. And do not neglect doing good and sharing, for with such sacrifices God is pleased. (Heb. 13:15–16)

Praising God ... thanking Him ... doing good ... sharing. These kinds of sacrifices please God. Clearly, all of us can serve as priests in that "holy" and "royal" order (2:5, 9).

—2:9–10—

Besides being living stones in God's building and priests in His temple, we are also members of a "chosen race," citizens of a "holy nation" (2:9), a new people of God "for God's own possession" (2:9–10), and the benefactors of God's "mercy" (2:10). For these designations Peter borrows language and imagery from the book of Deuteronomy, drawing an analogy between the nation of Israel as a specially chosen people of the Old Testament and the church as the special people of the New.

> For you are a holy people to the LORD your God; the LORD your God has chosen you to be a people for His own possession out of all the peoples who are on the face of the earth. The LORD did not set His love on you nor choose you because you were more in number than any of the peoples, for you were the fewest of all peoples, but because the LORD loved you and kept the oath which He swore to your forefathers, the LORD brought you out by a mighty hand and redeemed you from the house of slavery, from the hand of Pharaoh king of Egypt. (Deut. 7:6–8)

Just as God called the people of Israel to be a unique nation with a special purpose among the pagan kingdoms, the church has also been called to be a unique witness of Jesus Christ in the midst of a wicked world. Our heads might swell

DID THE CHURCH REPLACE ISRAEL AS GOD'S PEOPLE?

When Peter snatches Old Testament language addressed to the nation of Israel and applies it to the New Testament church, is he implying that Israel has been completely rejected and replaced by the church? Many Christians today believe that God's plan for the Jewish people has come to an end, that the promises of a glorious nation and ultimate blessing in the land have been abolished. Some say the promises have been fulfilled in a spiritual sense by Christians. Others propose that God has divorced Israel so He could take to Himself a new bride, the church.

The New Testament, however, tells us that God does not plan to reinterpret or abolish His Old Testament promises to Israel, but to fulfill them through Jesus Christ. Although most of ethnic Israel has remained in a state of unbelief since the time of Jesus, God will one day bring a remnant to faith in Christ and restore them in the land promised to their forefathers (Gen. 13:15). Jesus Himself promised the apostles, "In the regeneration when the Son of Man will sit on His glorious throne, you also shall sit upon twelve thrones, judging the twelve tribes of Israel" (Matt. 19:28).

Years later, Paul addressed the problem of the present unbelief of most Jews by declaring that this rebellion will one day be reversed: "A partial hardening has happened to Israel until the fullness of the Gentiles has come in; and so all Israel will be saved" (Rom. 11:25–26). In other words, when God has accomplished His purposes through the church, He will again turn His attention to the nation of Israel and bring them to faith in Christ. God will not forget His people or His promises.

So, when Peter refers to Israel as those "builders" who rejected the Cornerstone, Jesus Christ (2:7), we must understand this in light of Paul's teaching: "I say then, they did not stumble so as to fall, did they? May it never be!" (Rom. 11:11). And

at the notion that we're chosen by God, unless we realize that this wasn't an election for which we campaigned. It wasn't something we earned or deserved. Just as the Hebrew people were not chosen based on any merit of their own (Deut. 7:7), so Christians have not been chosen because of their superior intellect, beauty, influence, or morality.

When He chose us, He made us into a "holy nation." As we learned earlier, holiness means being set apart. As a "nation" among the nations, we are called for special purposes — "so that you may proclaim the excellencies of Him who has called you out of darkness into His marvelous light" (2:9). As such we are "a people for God's own possession." Think about how much the value of something ordinary increases when it has been owned by someone extraordinary. An old dictionary becomes more valuable if it was Abraham Lincoln's dictionary. A desk suddenly becomes more expensive and interesting if Winston Churchill wrote his famous speeches hunched over its worn surface. And, yes, a normal man or woman takes on a different kind of significance if she or he is the personal possession of God Almighty (2:10).

The fact that we are not our own makes a difference in how we live and for whom we live; that's the whole point of Peter's summary in 2:11–12. Renewing our relationship with God involves remembering our position in Him and responding to Him with hope, regardless of our circumstances.

— **2:11–12** —

In light of our new, unique, "called-out" position before God, Peter instantly turns the theological into the practical. Their position as "aliens and strangers" in this world means they should live in such a way that sets them apart from the attitudes and actions of their culture. In these two short verses, I find at least four simple, yet urgent exhortations.

when Peter applies passages from the Old Testament Scripture to the New Testament church, we must not assume the chosen people of the Old have been utterly divorced and replaced by the new people. Rather, the Old Testament serves as an example with application to us, though the primary meaning of the passage remains unmoved. As Paul writes with reference to Old Testament Scripture: "Now these things happened to them as an example, and they were written for our instruction, upon whom the ends of the ages have come" (1 Cor. 10:11).

First, *God's royal priesthood must live exemplary lives* (2:11–12). For unbelievers, the world is a playground of passions. But for believers it's a battleground of opposition and temptation. We must shout "No!" to fleshly lusts.

Second, *God's chosen race must leave no room for slander* (2:12). The most compelling defense against false accusations by unbelievers is unimpeachable integrity. Denying false charges is easy. But there must be more. Our lives must make those charges sound ridiculous to those who know us best.

Third, *God's holy nation must do good deeds among unbelievers* (2:12). When we see somebody in need, our first question is not, "Can I see your Christian I.D.?" but "What can I do to help?" This might mean crossing the sometimes well-guarded borders of our Christian communities and hanging around with those outside our circles. Or it might mean inviting "aliens" into our midst. Only then will they see our good deeds, as Jesus said: "Let your light shine before men in such a way that they may see your good works, and glorify your Father who is in heaven" (Matt. 5:16).

Finally, *God's own people should never forget they are being watched* (2:12). Peter says "as they observe" our good deeds, unbelievers will glorify God. Whether we like it or not, we are being observed. The world is watching. If they don't see us reflecting the unwavering love and hope they're longing for, they won't think much of our salvation ... or our Savior.

Warren Wiersbe illustrated these points with the following story:

> In the summer of 1805, a number of Indian chiefs and warriors met in council at Buffalo Creek, New York, to hear a presentation of the Christian message by a Mr. Cram from the Boston Missionary Society. After the sermon, a response was given by Red Jacket, one of the leading chiefs. Among other things, the chief said:

"Brother, we are told that you have been preaching to the white people in this place. These people are our neighbors. We are acquainted with them. We will wait a little while and see what effect your preaching has upon them. If we find it does them good, makes them honest and less disposed to cheat Indians, we will then consider again of what you have said."[12]

NOTES:

1. J. Carl Laney Jr., "God: Who He Is, What He Does, How to Know Him Better," in *Understanding Christian Theology*, ed. Charles R. Swindoll and Roy B. Zuck (Nashville: Nelson, 2003), 206.
2. C. S. Lewis, *The Problem of Pain* (New York: Macmillan, 1962), 42–43.
3. Peter may also be alluding to Leviticus 20:7, 26 or 21:8, which reiterate the exhortation in Leviticus 11:44–45.
4. Charles Wesley, "And Can It Be?" in *The Hymnal for Worship and Celebration*, no. 203.
5. Bauer et al., *A Greek-English Lexicon*, 245.
6. Ibid., 397.
7. Ibid., 203.
8. Stuart Briscoe, *1 Peter: Holy Living in a Hostile World*, rev. ed., Understanding the Book Series (Wheaton, IL: Harold Shaw, 1992), 73.
9. Edward Gordon Selwyn, *The First Epistle of St. Peter*, 2nd ed. (New York: St. Martin's, 1961), 153.
10. Bauer et al., *A Greek-English Lexicon*, 412.
11. See William R. Schoedel, *Ignatius of Antioch: A Commentary on the Letters of Ignatius of Antioch*, ed. Helmut Koester, Hermeneia (Philadelphia: Fortress, 1985), 66.
12. Warren W. Wiersbe, *Be Hopeful* (Wheaton, IL: Victor, 1982), 57.

OUR STRANGE LIFE
(1 PETER 2:13 – 4:11)

I love the story of an American missionary couple who returned to the United States by ship after several decades of faithful service in Africa. On board with them was an important diplomat who received V.I.P. treatment during the voyage while the missionary couple simply stood back and watched the fanfare. Upon arrival in New York City, a crowd and a band had gathered to receive the politician. And when he walked down the gangplank, music and loud applause erupted as his motorcade whisked him away.

Then, quietly, with no fanfare, no attention, and no music, the missionary couple walked arm in arm down the gangplank, taking their first steps on American soil in over thirty years. After some silence, the husband turned to his wife and said, "Honey, it doesn't seem right after all these years that we would have nobody to greet us while that man got such a grand reception."

The wife put her arms around her husband and gently reminded him, "But, honey, we're not home yet."

> By faith he lived as an alien in the land of promise, as in a foreign land, dwelling in tents with Isaac and Jacob, fellow heirs of the same promise; for he was looking for the city which has foundations, whose architect and builder is God. (Heb. 11:9 – 10)

Because of his hope, driven by faith, Abraham, like countless Old Testament saints, lived in this world like a foreigner. Noah, having been a preacher of righteousness and recipient of God's grace, didn't fit in his world of constant wickedness (Heb. 11:7; 2 Peter 2:5). Moses, too, lived the life of a sojourner and wanderer, never feeling at home in Egypt, in the land of Midian, or in the wilderness of Sinai. In fact, Moses named his first son "Gershom," which means "foreigner"—a constant reminder that he was "a stranger in a strange land" (Ex. 2:22 KJV). Like Noah and Abraham before him, Moses knew all too well that as a servant of God, his ultimate citizenship was not in any earthly kingdom, but in the kingdom of God.

You and I live as Christians away from home. Although we're temporary residents of particular nations here on earth, we're actually eternal citizens of another land. Let me put this plainly. We live in the midst of a *pagan* culture surrounded by *pagan* people who embrace a *pagan* philosophy, a *pagan* way of life, and a *pagan*

KEY TERMS

ὑποτάσσω [*hypotassō*] (5293) "to place under, subject, submit, rank under"

From the preposition *hypo* ("under") and Greek word *taxis* ("order"), this term literally means to "order under" another. The word was used a Greek military term describing voluntary deference to the commands of another. It implies a conscious, willing subjection to another person's authority. This theme of submission runs throughout Peter's letter. All must submit to human governments (2:13–14), servants to employers (2:18), wives to husbands (3:1), and young men to their elders (5:5). In other words, every aspect of life is to be conducted with order, not disarray.

ἁγιάζω [*hagiazō*] (37) "to make holy, consecrate, set apart"

Related to the adjective *hagios* ("holy"), this verb form refers to the process that sets something or someone apart. Usually the word refers to God's work in making believers more holy (Eph. 5:26; 1 Thess. 5:23). But Peter's single use is unique in that believers are called to "sanctify" Christ (1 Peter 3:15). When we consciously "set Christ apart," we are regarding Him as holy, placing Him in the unique place as Lord and Master over our lives.

attitude toward believers. But God has planted us here to be the ambassadors of a different kingdom and to lead others to that better city whose architect and builder is God.

In this second major section of 1 Peter — the longest of the three — Peter *exhorts* his readers to hopeful living despite their lives as strangers in a strange land (2:13 – 4:11). He urges his readers to submit to various secular authorities (2:13 – 3:7), to be humble in spirit (3:8 – 22), to be armed like soldiers stationed in foreign territory (4:1 – 6), and to glorify God in light of Christ's coming to take them to their real home (4:7 – 11). These principles become the key to living as Christians in a hostile world. Throughout this section Peter emphasizes grace to stand firm, describing a *calm hope* through personal submission (3:6). And the Lord Jesus becomes the *example* of unjust suffering in light of untold glory — the model of hope in hurtful times.

Pressing On Even Though Ripped Off (1 Peter 2:13 – 25)

> [13]Submit yourselves for the Lord's sake to every human institution, whether to a king as the one in authority, [14]or to governors as sent by him for the punishment of evildoers and the praise of those who do right. [15]For

such is the will of God that by doing right you may silence the ignorance of foolish men. ¹⁶*Act* as free men, and do not use your freedom as a covering for evil, but *use it* as bondslaves of God. ¹⁷Honor all people, love the brotherhood, fear God, honor the king.

¹⁸Servants, be submissive to your masters with all respect, not only to those who are good and gentle, but also to those who are unreasonable. ¹⁹For this *finds* favor, if for the sake of conscience toward God a person bears up under sorrows when suffering unjustly. ²⁰For what credit is there if, when you sin and are harshly treated, you endure it with patience? But if when you do what is right and suffer *for it* you patiently endure it, this *finds* favor with God.

²¹For you have been called for this purpose, since Christ also suffered for you, leaving you an example for you to follow in His steps, ²²who committed no sin, nor was any deceit found in His mouth; ²³and while being reviled, He did not revile in return; while suffering, He uttered no threats, but kept entrusting *Himself* to Him who judges righteously; ²⁴and He Himself bore our sins in His body on the cross, so that we might die to sin and live to righteousness; for by His wounds you were healed. ²⁵For you were continually straying like sheep, but now you have returned to the Shepherd and Guardian of your souls.

Ever bought a used car and realized a few weeks later that you got a lemon? Ever drop ten bucks on a movie that made last summer's home video of your family vacation look like *The Sound of Music*? Who hasn't been hoodwinked by a smooth-talking salesman in a striped suit with styled hair and patent leather shoes? And who hasn't been burned by a glitzy political campaign that promised much more than it delivered?

Common rip-offs like these occur relatively often and are easy to recover from. It's much more difficult to endure when the suffering gets personal. If you've ever been the brunt of a raw deal, then you're in good company. David was done wrong by Saul; Esau was cheated by Jacob; Joseph was brutalized by his brothers; and Job got a raw deal in body and soul, visible and invisible! Of course, being numbered among the ranks of David, Esau, Joseph, and Job isn't all that great when it means being treated unjustly.

When someone slanders our reputation, gossips behind our back, or threatens our livelihood, things can get pretty nasty. In my experience, our knee-jerk reactions to unfair treatment generally fall into one of three categories. First, we may adopt the aggressive pattern of blaming others, focusing on the person who did us wrong and doing whatever it takes to exact revenge. Second, we may embrace a passive pattern of feeling sorry for ourselves, becoming absorbed in self-pity and whining constantly about our plight. Third, we may slip into a holding pattern of postponing feelings, placing our emotions on the back burner, and seething beneath a calm surface.

All these natural reactions make sense from a human standpoint, don't they? But that's all they are—*natural and human*. The apostle Peter offers a supernatural and divine alternative to these typical human responses. Let me warn you, though. Peter's stout examples of unjust treatment probably outweigh most of our relatively petty grievances, stripping us of any excuse to default to the three typical knee-jerk reactions.

— 2:13–17 —

Remember that Peter wrote this letter to point his readers in Asia Minor to Jesus Christ as the true source of hope in hurtful times. And what hurtful times they were! Those Christians were scattered and mistreated, imprisoned, and enslaved. They were rejected by family members, singled out by employers, and attacked by law-enforcement officials who were supposed to protect them. Besides these instances of day-to-day trials, all of them—throughout the empire—were living under an emperor growing increasingly insane and anti-Christian: Nero.

So, when Peter begins his God-honoring response to the unfair treatment with "Submit yourselves for the Lord's sake to every human institution," that doesn't sound strange; it sounds *radical*! The word "submit" comes from the Greek word *hypotassō*, a military term describing voluntary deference to the wishes of another. It means a conscious, willing subjection to another person's authority.

Photo by Mary Harrsch

Nero Caesar, reigning from AD 54 to 68, was known for his tyranny, brutality, and brief but horrific persecution of Christians in Rome.

Submitting to human government requires that we "render to Caesar" our civil obedience (Matt. 22:21). It involves sincere prayer for rulers in authority over us (1 Tim. 2:1–2), regardless of whether we agree with their politics and policies. And it means we live honorably and peacefully in their realm (Rom. 13:1–7). Believers are to be model citizens, not social rebels and misfits. So Peter urges his readers to recognize both local authorities ("governors") and higher authorities ("kings"). Regardless of their corruption and idolatry, the existing authorities were to be respected and supported. But why?

Peter gives the reason for this radical submission in verse 15: "For such is the will of God that by doing right you may silence the ignorance of foolish men." The word for "silence" literally means "to muzzle," as in, "You shall not muzzle the ox while he is threshing" (1 Tim. 5:18). But more often the New Testament uses the term in its metaphorical sense: to render somebody speechless, unable to answer because of exposure of guilt (Matt. 22:12), defeat in debate (22:34), or even submission to higher authority (Luke 4:35). This is the kind of "muzzling" of Christianity's foolish opponents Peter has in mind.

You see, baseless charges and rumors were flying around about Christians in those days. "They're loyal to a different king." "They're a rebellious sect." "They want to overthrow the government." "They're subversives!" By submitting voluntarily, by doing right before God and other people, they would muzzle the mouths of those spreading such vicious and erroneous rumors.

Behind Peter's command to submit (2:13–14) and his reason for submission (2:15) stands an important principle about our attitude in submission (2:16–17). In today's context, we submit to the president even if we didn't vote for him or his party. And we submit to the decisions of lawmakers even though we think their laws are sometimes senseless and excessive. In short, we submit not because we're blind nationalists, but because we're "bondslaves of God." And as such, our obligation is to serve Him, and to do so we need to live in such a way as to bring honor to His reputation in the public square.

With this principle come four brief commands, like a barrage of gunfire in rapid succession: "Honor all people, love the brotherhood, fear God, honor the king" (2:17). These eleven words are easy to write, but together they create a tough balancing act, don't they? We are to honor and respect *all* people, regardless of their faith in Christ, their godless lifestyles, or their attitudes toward Christians. At the same time, we must love the brotherhood of believers unconditionally. The word is *agapē*—unconditional, Christlike love. God must always have our reverence, and we must treat His will as supreme. But we must also honor the king, who may in fact hate us, hate his own people, and hate God!

Let's be realistic. The Bible never suggests that rulers will be perfect, and our civil submission is not conditioned by our government's modeling Christian virtue or reflecting Christian morality. Remember, in Peter's day the empire wasn't a benevolent, pro-Christian monarchy. A percentage of the taxes Christians paid supported the construction of pagan temples and funded unjust wars. Moreover, the insane dictator, Nero, was notoriously cruel toward Christians. This combination posed a dilemma for Peter and his readers: How does one honor all people, love the brothers and sister in the faith, fear God, *and* honor that particular king? Shouldn't they refuse to pay taxes that support such an oppressive regime? Or maybe take up arms and resist a government with such a leader? Peter said no. Nowhere does Scripture promote revolt and anarchy.

But Peter's call to submit to established government as a system for maintaining order doesn't mean that God endorses every particular ruler. Nor does He approve of particular laws that stand in defiance of His will. Believers are not obligated to follow laws that conflict with His clearly revealed will (see Dan. 6; Acts 5:29). The Bible does not instruct God's people to keep silent in the face of obvious social and political injustices (see Mark 6:17 – 18). In cases where God has given His people a command — like preaching the gospel and shunning idolatry — believers must obey God rather than human leaders. But in so doing, they must also be ready to suffer the legal consequences for that disobedience and outspoken criticism.[1]

Clearly, we must wisely and prayerfully approach our responsibility to submit to human government. We also need to consider carefully our responses to the injustice and evils of that same government. The answer is not to follow the unholy agenda of a tyrant while waving our flags of patriotism. That would dishonor God, the church, and the world. We are not to barricade ourselves in a barbed-wire compound and wage war against corrupt government officials who come knocking with a tax bill or a search warrant. That would dishonor the king and bring reproach on Christ. Between these two extremes, we live in the uncomfortable, constant tension of Peter's seemingly impossible commands: "Honor all people, love the brotherhood, fear God, honor the king." Only God-given wisdom can help us live appropriately in this tension.

— **2:18 – 25** —

Leaving the larger issue of submission to government authority, Peter zooms in on a particular example of submission that was common in the first century: slavery.

In a twenty-first-century world that rightly shudders at the sound of slavery,

Peter's words seem shocking. To some, they will sound downright offensive! But the institution of slavery in Peter's day was much different than the disgusting racist system in modern history, or even the deplorable underworld slave-trafficking in our own days. Nevertheless, slavery in the ancient world could still be miserable, even deadly—especially if a master didn't appreciate his slave's newfound faith in Christ!

Many people have drawn an analogy between first-century slavery and today's employer-employee relationship, suggesting they have enough similarities to warrant applying this passage to our modern-day work situation. In some ways this is appropriate, but in many fundamental ways the analogy breaks down. While the

SLAVERY IN THE ROMAN EMPIRE

We would be wrong to understand slavery in Peter's day as similar to slavery in the modern world. We should regard slaves in the ancient world as a social class. Historians believe the total percentage of slaves in Roman society may have constituted between 25 percent and 40 percent of the population.[2] Prior to the time of Peter, the Romans acquired most of their slaves as the spoils of war. Over time, however, men and women could become slaves in a number of ways. Children of slaves automatically became the property of their masters. Abandoned children could be brought up as slaves. People could even sell themselves into slavery to fulfill debts or other obligations. As such, slavery in the Roman world was based more on social, economic, and political status than on race or ethnicity.

The daily tasks of slaves varied depending on their skills, the status of their masters, and the city or region in which they lived. Duties could be as menial as cleaning or as brutal as mining. Other slaves could be prized cooks, teachers, or even physicians. And the treatment of slaves depended on the temperament of their masters or mistresses.

Masters could set their slaves free at their leisure, at which time the slave took his master's name and was typically granted the same social status as his master.[3] Since Roman law allowed for the possibility of granting rights to such slaves, the composition of the slave population began to change over time, especially in regard to an increase in ethnic diversity. Whereas at one time only non-Roman peoples were slaves, by the time of Peter, the population of slaves had become diverse, made up of both Romans and non-Romans.[4]

Werner Forman/Art Resource, NY

Relief showing a Roman woman and her servant.

realm of our employment is the place to start, we must never forget that the vast majority of employment situations in the world today are voluntary, not compulsory.

Some radical Christians throughout history have interpreted the freedom they have in Christ as warranting a social and political freedom from authority and oppression. During the Reformation, Martin Luther's emphasis on "the freedom of the Christian" from spiritual bondage at the hands of the Catholic Church was taken to an extreme by enthusiastic peasants who took up arms against the German overlords. Today many advocates of "liberation theology" have interpreted the message of the cross in socialistic or communistic ways, pushing for the overthrow of oppressive social systems and for economic equality for all.

The apostles and the early church leaders, however, knew the dangers of pushing for social and political upheaval apart from a true conversion of hearts and minds within society. It is true that where the gospel of Jesus Christ penetrates people's hearts on a wide scale, that culture is transformed and evils like poverty, slavery, and oppression radically diminish. But these social changes are the result, not the goal, of God's ultimate priority — transforming hearts and minds (Rom. 12:1 – 2; 1 Cor. 7:20 – 24).

Knowing the human tendency to rebel against unfair treatment, Peter urges Christian servants to submit to their masters — even to those who are rough and unreasonable. Admittedly, that's a hard load to bear. But Peter's exhortation for submission makes sense when we connect it to our calling to shine as reflections of Christ's character in a dark, godless world. Peter makes this point clear when he brings it back to Christ's own unjust suffering: "For you have been called for this purpose, since Christ also suffered for you, leaving you an example for you to follow in His steps, who committed no sin, nor was any deceit found in His mouth" (2:21 – 22). When we suffer unjustly at the hands of a cruel dictator or an unfair and overbearing boss, we participate in Christ's own ministry of unjust suffering on behalf of others. Christ suffered on our behalf. We suffer on behalf of unbelievers who need to see the gospel lived out in everyday lives.

Nobody suffered as unjustly as Christ. The only perfect Man who ever lived was misunderstood by listeners, maligned by enemies, forsaken by family, betrayed by friends, abandoned by disciples, tortured by law enforcers, and executed by politicians. The only One in history with every right to lodge a complaint remained silent. The only Man who could have called on God to judge His enemies quietly endured undeserved judgment (2:23). And He did all of this not for Himself, but for us (2:24). Dying in our place on the cross — the just for the unjust — He healed our souls so that we can live a new life of righteousness (2:24).

Peter calls his readers — including us — to submit willingly to authority, even if those with power behave unjustly. But he doesn't make this call simply to keep the peace or to uphold a world system. Rather, he points us to Jesus Christ as the epochal example. Christ entrusted Himself to "Him who judges righteously" and could therefore endure injustice with hope. Similarly, believers can entrust their souls to the Shepherd and Guardian of their souls (see 2:25). In short, by following the example of Christ, we can secure an unshakable hope in hurtful times.

Application

Benefits of Bearing the Brunt

Peter's approach to facing unjust treatment from both government authorities and those who dominate us in our work appears radical. In fact, outright rebellion and overt revenge seem *less* revolutionary than patiently enduring unjust suffering for the cause of Christ.

Not many of us currently suffer persecution at the hands of civil government, but as Christians in an increasingly pluralistic society that is growing less tolerant toward Christianity, we face challenges from political and social institutions involving unfair treatment. With the rapid deterioration of Christian values, we are more likely to suffer mistreatment in our employment because of our commitment to Christ. In both cases, our initial response will likely be to speak out radically. But Peter offers an *even more radical way*.

Our world bombards us with messages that urge us to stand up for our personal rights. We are quick to defend ourselves when we feel somebody steps on our toes, crosses the line, ignores boundaries, or intrudes on our personal domain. We can find a lawyer's phone number quicker than we can a passage of Scripture calling us to endure hardship. Stop and think! When did you last take it on the chin for the cause of Christ? When did you last surrender your rights for the deliberate purpose of following Christ's example? How rare that is, especially in our fight-back, get-even culture!

Peter's message to that fledgling first-century church can feel to the twenty-first-century church like a punch in the stomach. We simply can't downplay the significance of his call to patiently endure the intolerance, prejudice, and unjust treatment that comes with being a follower of Christ. And because this kind of attitude doesn't flow from us naturally, take some time to work through your own approach to unfair treatment by answering some of the following questions.

First, consider which "natural" reactions to unfair treatment generally characterize your own. Do you instantly strike back? Look for opportunities for revenge?

In your experience, what have been the negative effects of these responses? How might unbelievers perceive Christians and Christianity because of your reactions?

Second, reflecting on Jesus' words in Matthew 5:38–42, how does Christ's teaching apply to everyday situations in your life? How might unbelievers perceive Christians and Christianity if you lived this radical response to harsh treatment?

We might enjoy a rush of personal gratification when we stand up for ourselves or exact revenge against those in authority over us, but Christ calls us to a better way. Instead of meeting the world's slap in the face with a punch in the gut, Christ tells us to turn the other cheek. We must never let the world's sense of right and wrong dictate our own. We submit to the lordship of a perfect Leader who has set an example of surrendering personal rights for a greater glory.

The Give-and-Take of Domestic Harmony (1 Peter 3:1–7)

---

¹In the same way, you wives, be submissive to your own husbands so that even if any *of them* are disobedient to the word, they may be won without a word by the behavior of their wives, ²as they observe your chaste and respectful behavior. ³Your adornment must not be *merely* external — braiding the hair, and wearing gold jewelry, or putting on dresses; ⁴but *let it be* the hidden person of the heart, with the imperishable quality of a gentle and quiet spirit, which is precious in the sight of God. ⁵For in this way in former times the holy women also, who hoped in God, used to adorn themselves, being submissive to their own husbands; ⁶just as Sarah obeyed Abraham, calling him lord, and you have become her children if you do what is right without being frightened by any fear.

⁷You husbands in the same way, live with *your wives* in an understanding way, as with someone weaker, since she is a woman; and show her honor as a fellow heir of the grace of life, so that your prayers will not be hindered.

With a twinkle in his eye, a young groom helps his beautiful bride onto the coach and then hops on as well. He takes the reins of the one-horse carriage and with a word he begins a leisurely trot. The crisp, clear night is perfect for the ride. Romance is in the air; the newlyweds sit close, staring more at each other than at the beauty of their moonlit surroundings. After a few miles, however, things begin to change. The husband now gets distracted from steering the horse. The carriage swerves. The wife tries to take control, and conflict breaks out. As the two play a game of fierce tug-of-war with the leather reins, the horse breaks into a gallop and darts into the woods. A once smooth tour under a star-studded night quickly deteriorates into a bumpy and dangerous ordeal that worsens by the second. When the carriage finally topples, the couples' internal wounds hurt more than their external bumps and bruises.

This imaginative picture illustrates an important fact: *a wedding is one thing; a marriage is something completely different.* Having been married to Cynthia for well over fifty years, I've become a realist — not an idealist — with respect to marriage. Our decades of marriage have been years of learning and growth, difficulty, delight, discovery, heartaches, tragedies, hurtful times, and ecstatic moments together. These experiences have made our marriage stronger. The apostle Peter, too, spoke about marriage, but not from some remote prophet's cave or from a scholar's proverbial ivory tower. No, Peter was a married man. In fact, his wife accompanied him on many of his travels (1 Cor. 9:5). So Peter knew firsthand the struggles that all married couples endure.

Like a diamond nestled in a platinum setting, Peter's focus on Christian marriage is set in the midst of his discussion of our strange life as believers living in a hopeless and hostile world. Throughout this letter Peter has turned the spotlight on Jesus Christ, through whom we can have hope in hurtful times. In the immediate context of this passage, remember, Peter began discussing the issue of submission, calling on believers to submit for the sake of Christ to human institutions as well as to human masters (2:13–25) — even those who treat them harshly. We *must* submit because it will bring honor to God and keep those on the outside from having a basis for slander against Christianity. And we *can* submit because Christ serves as an example of patient endurance of undeserved suffering for a greater purpose and with an eye toward the hope of glory that follows.

So, the context of 1 Peter 3:1–7, dealing with marital harmony, has to do with the ability to live in an unfair and even unbearable situation. Most marriages I know aren't exactly "unbearable." Tough, challenging, and frustrating? Yes. But usually not so excruciating that they can't be tolerated or so dangerous that they're borderline deadly. That's not the common marriage. I also know that almost all marriages go through days, weeks, maybe even recurring periods that are difficult to bear, in which one partner drives the other to the brink of exhaustion or even despair. Peter addresses this kind of marital struggle, offering hope through following the example of Jesus Christ.

— 3:1-6 —

Peter begins with the phrase "In the same way," or "likewise." This connective immediately sends us back to Peter's previous discussion, since it prompts us to ask, "In the same way as *what*?" A more appropriate question should be, "In the same way as *whom*?" It shouldn't surprise us that the immediate context is the example of Christ's faithfulness to the plan and purpose of God. But stepping out of this call to imitate Christ, we see the theme of faithful citizenship (2:13) and faithful service (2:18). In other words, just as we are called to be faithful to the institutions of government and servanthood, so we should also be faithful to the institution of marriage.

We should not be surprised, then, when Peter reiterates the same command he has given to citizens and servants: "Wives, be submissive." It's the same verb, *hypotassō*, meaning to subject oneself voluntarily to another, with the implication of following the other's lead in obedience. I am acutely aware of how sensitive the issue of submission in marriage can be, especially in a world where women have too often been the object of physical and emotional abuse at the hands of thug-like husbands who display nothing of the love of Christ. Note that Peter addresses husbands later in verse 7.

I don't believe Peter has any intention of forcing a person to endure the abuse of that kind of relationship, in which a wife, husband, or child risks health or life to stay faithful to the marriage. That's not submission; that's intolerable surrender. Nevertheless, some have interpreted this passage on marital roles as a product of Peter's cultural context, irrelevant in today's world. So it becomes a mere option — and an outdated one at that. But wouldn't that mean that submitting to human government is also optional? Or that insubordination at work is now acceptable for Christians? Though popular, that kind of relativistic approach to the principles of Scripture doesn't work. So, conscious of the two ditches on either side of this narrow path, we should let Peter's own words explain this wise counsel to husbands and wives.

In the first six verses, I find four implied imperatives woven into the fabric of Peter's general principle of a wife's call to submit to the leadership of her husband:

- Analyze your actions (3:1 – 2).
- Watch your adornment (3:3).
- Check your attitude (3:4).
- Evaluate your attention (3:5 – 6).

Let's look more closely at each of these.

First, *Peter urges wives to analyze their actions* (3:1 – 2). Peter first addresses a common response to the principle of submission: "Turnabouts are fair play; I'll be the kind of wife God wants me to be ... when George is the kind of *husband* God wants him to be!" But verse 1 explicitly portrays a husband who is *not* living up to biblical ideals. Peter says wives should exhibit a submissive spirit toward their husbands "even if any of them are disobedient to the word." The phrase "disobedient to the word" at least means those who are not living by biblical principles, but it could also include those who have not personally submitted to the lordship of Christ.

Peter isn't writing this to "put wives in their place." Submission has a greater purpose than simply domestic order: "so that ... they may be won without a word by the behavior of their wives." Here's the point: when a Christian wife lives a Christ-like life in her attitudes and actions, it can attract husbands who might otherwise be hard-hearted toward biblical truth. In fact, Peter says such a husband may be drawn to Christ because he will observe her "chaste and respectful behavior" (3:2). The term "observe" implies a careful observation, not a casual glance. One "good deed" of remarkable and gracious submission is not sufficient. Peter has in mind a consistently virtuous character. This chaste and respectful submission is not a cringing, spineless cowering. It's the commitment of a wife to chastity, purity, and devotion to her husband. It requires a calm spirit of unselfish cooperation rather than flashes of stubborn opposition. A wife like that cannot (and will not) be ignored.

Second, *Peter urges wives to watch their adornment* (3:3). The Greek word translated "adornment" is the word *kosmos*, from which we get the term "cosmetics." It refers to anything used to beautify or decorate. Luke uses the verb form of this word when describing the temple in Jerusalem as "adorned with beautiful stones" (Luke 21:5). It's the same Greek word used for the ordered world — the physical world of ordered creation (Acts 17:24), the world of humanity in general (John 3:16), or the human system oriented in opposition to God (1 John 5:19).

Please note that Peter does not forbid the appropriate use of cosmetics, jewelry, or hairstyling. Some have taken this out of its context and opted for a "plain Jane" approach, resulting in an unkempt, even sloppy appearance that draws attention to the externals just as much as an exaggerated, flamboyant adornment does. That approach misses Peter's point. Wives who use cosmetics appropriately and in good taste are not "worldly." Those who substitute an emphasis on their external appearance for the lack of cultivating their internal character, however, have chosen the wrong priority.

Third, *Peter urges wives to check their attitudes* (3:4). Verse 4 begins with a contrasting conjunction, "but." Peter points his readers to the internal attitudes of the heart rather than to the external adornments of the body. The word "heart" is *kardia*, which is the source of one's true character. Though the source of this adornment is invisible, it manifests itself in external words and actions. So, in verses 3 and 4, Peter contrasts *kosmos* with *kardia*, the external with the internal, the superficial decking of one's body with the superior displaying of one's virtue. It may take only a few hours to prepare for an elegant evening, but it takes a lifetime to build an elegant character. Mothers should pay close attention to this warning because young daughters especially take their cues about priorities from Mom. You can teach your little girls how to fret over hair, makeup, jewelry, and clothing—all the while missing the important virtues of modesty, gentleness, and peace.

This kind of emphasis isn't popular today. Western culture values the showy, the fashionable, the trendy. Media bombards us with one message: "Look your best at all costs!" The world lavishes its treasures on those considered the most physically beautiful. But God turns the tables on the world's agenda. The internal adornment of virtue never goes out of style; *it's imperishable*. While the quality of a gentle and quiet spirit may not impress the red-carpet crowd at the Academy Awards, *it's precious in God's sight*.

Finally, *Peter urges wives to evaluate their attention* (3:5 – 6). To illustrate the principle of biblical submission, Peter turns to Old Testament heroines, whom he calls "holy women" who "hoped in God." We should take careful note of Peter's connection between holiness and hope—a theme he has developed and will continue to develop throughout the letter. By hoping in God—looking to Him as the source of strength, holiness, provision, and protection—the saints of old were able to conduct themselves in humility, gentleness, and submission. Apart from this divine hope, such a divine disposition is impossible to maintain.

Also note how Peter uses the word "adorn" for the inner attitudes that manifest themselves in both words and deeds. Sarah, the wife of Abraham, becomes the model of this kind of hopeful and holy submission to her husband. She showed him respect in her words and in her works—which she did without fear. She didn't rebel, lash out, or abandon Abraham so she could do her own thing. She gave him the attention and honor due him as her husband.

I realize some reading this may be tempted to cross their arms and respond, "Okay, but Sarah was married to Abraham—the father of faith! If my husband were a saint like Abraham, I'd gladly follow him wherever he goes!" But let's not forget the hard life Sarah had to endure as the wife of Abraham. Think about the following things from Sarah's limited perspective.

- Her husband claimed to have had visions from God instructing him to move (when they were quite old) into a strange land (Gen. 12:1 – 5).
- Her husband convinced Sarah to pretend to be his sister while they were in Egypt, where the Pharaoh temporarily took Sarah as his wife (Gen. 12:10 – 20).
- She followed her husband's lead when Abraham surrendered the best grazing land to his nephew, Lot (Gen. 13:1 – 11).

- A second time Abraham tried to pass Sarah off as his sister, this time attracting the attention of Abimelech, king of Gerar, who wanted Sarah as his wife (Gen. 20:1–18).
- She endured the near sacrifice of her only son, Isaac, at the hands of Abraham, who claimed God had instructed him to offer Isaac (Gen. 22:1–19).

From Sarah's perspective, Abraham may have appeared unpredictable, devious, foolish, rash, and irresponsible. In some cases, her estimation of the man would have been quite accurate! Yet Peter tells us in 1 Peter 3:6, "Sarah obeyed Abraham, calling him lord." Not because of her secure and perfect marriage, but because of her insecure and imperfect marriage, Sarah becomes a paragon of submission for all believers.

At this point it would be appropriate for wives to ask themselves some probing questions.

- Am I looking to saints like Sarah as role models, or to daytime soaps and nighttime drama?
- Is my husband at the top of my prayer list?
- Do I put my husband first in my planning?
- Do I look for ways to honor him?
- Do I make his life easier or more difficult?

These kinds of questions are appropriate in light of Peter's exhortation to hopeful and holy living as a godly wife.

— **3:7** —

Peter doesn't drop a heavy weight on the side of wives and leave husbands scot-free. In fact, though he addresses husbands in only one verse, that single verse contains three strong imperatives, either explicit or implied: *live with your wife*; *know your wife*, and *honor your wife*. Before we jump into those commands, please note how he begins his address to husbands: "You husbands *in the same way*" (3:7). This language parallels Peter's opening line to the wives:

> *In the same way*, you wives ... (3:1)
> You husbands *in the same way* ... (3:7)

The Greek word is *homoiōs*, an adverb meaning "similarly," "in like manner," or simply, "likewise." Remember the broader context of this section? Because of the hope we have in Christ, we can have security in Him to submit ourselves for

His sake to others in every context of life—government, employment, and marriage. Just as Christian wives have certain responsibilities in marriage, so Christian husbands have equally important roles to play.

First, *husbands are to live with their wives.* The phrase means more than "putting up with" or "surviving." It means dwelling together in close relationship—physically, emotionally, mentally, and spiritually. Husbands too easily substitute making a good living and providing physical needs for sharing their time, their words, and their feelings. But this kind of close relationship is necessary to truly *live with* their wives.

Second, *husbands are to know their wives.* The Greek text literally states that husbands are to dwell together with their wives "according to knowledge." This has nothing to do with superficial knowledge, like her favorite colors or least favorite foods. Nor does it pertain to psychological knowledge about the needs of women in general. No, Peter means a deep understanding and appreciation of one's wife. It includes perceiving her most intimate desires and personal needs. It involves discerning her unspoken concerns and worries. And it includes assisting her in working through issues in a careful, caring manner. It's directly related to "living together," so it means a constant, moment-by-moment understanding of one's wife.

Along with this understanding, Peter urges husbands to treat their wives as they would treat, literally, a "weaker vessel." We might paraphrase this as "delicate vase."[5] The idea is that the husband's tendency may be to act like a bull in a china shop, handling situations in a masculine manner as he would with his male friends or colleagues. Instead, he is to treat his wife as a fine piece of china—tenderly, carefully, with gentleness. While one might toss around a football, nobody would play catch with an expensive Etruscan vase!

Peter's description here of the "weaker vessel" isn't meant to demean a woman or regard her with less value. In fact, just the opposite! This can't mean that women are morally or intellectually weaker than men. And I've been close to enough women who have endured the trials of pregnancy, childbirth, and motherhood, to know it can't refer to a weakness in stamina! Rather, most commentators believe this phrase refers to general physical strength of women as compared to men.[6]

It is true that *on average* men are physiologically built to have greater muscle mass than women. This means that in a game of tug-of-war, if we had a hundred average men on one side of a rope and a hundred average women on the other, the men would win. So, when Peter calls on husbands to understand their wives, treating them as one would treat a delicate vessel, he has in mind a woman's need for physical care and protection. This is still true today, but it was especially relevant in the ancient world, where a woman could easily fall victim to crime or be taken

From My Journal

Hands Off!

In the early years of my pastoral ministry, I married a man and woman I should have known were headed for trouble. In hindsight, I probably ought to have refused to conduct the ceremony; but even though I tried my best to put it off, they wouldn't hear of it. Blinded by love or driven by passion, they were determined to get married ... *now*!

I remember bluntly telling the wife-to-be when we were alone that I thought the groom was "a little weird." I couldn't say exactly what it was that struck me as strange, but something about him just didn't seem right. To my surprise, she agreed with me. But like so many men and women viewing their premarital world through pink, heart-shaped glasses, she responded, "I know. But I think we can work it out." She thought she could put up with his odd behavior, or that she could help him change it.

Several months after the wedding, that couple passed through the door of my study again. He sheepishly walked in and took a seat; the tension in the air grew thick. Finally she opened her mouth and asked, "Is it normal for a husband to take all the doors off the house after you get married?"

"Well," I answered, "I've never heard of that before, but ..."

"Because several days after we got home from our honeymoon, he took every door off the hinges so there wouldn't be any secrets between us!"

That man distrusted his wife so much that he had to be able to watch her every move—*while they were at home!* Talk about creepy! But that kind of thing is all too common. Distrust and suspicion turn to jealousy. Jealousy leads to rage. And rage results in violence. I can't think of a more despicable man than the one who abuses his wife, physically, emotionally, or verbally. If a husband can't control himself enough to keep from pummeling his wife with his words or his hands, he needs to get help *immediately*. And just because your *hands* are clean doesn't mean you're guilt-free. Oppression, manipulation, obsession, neglect—yes, and removing all the doors to keep a watchful eye on her—these are all ways to flat-out *disobey* Peter's exhortation for men to live with their wives in an understanding way.

advantage of legally without a husband's protection. But another implication is that Peter calls on husbands to reject all verbal and physical abuse of their wives. Behind Peter's words looms a sharp rebuke: "What kind of sick man, built twice the size of his wife, would even *consider* lifting a hand against her?"

Third, *husbands are to honor their wives*. At this point Peter makes it clear that he views women as honorable and equal partners in the marriage. Husbands are to assign their wives a place of honor. A man's wife should be his top priority, occupying the greatest place not only in his heart and mind but also in his schedule, with his words, and through his actions. And she deserves this kind of honor because she is *not* inferior. She is "a fellow heir of the grace of life." Husband and wife share a common relationship with their Lord Jesus Christ. In the spiritual realm, they are unquestionably equal.

Finally, Peter points out a great purpose for maintaining domestic harmony: "so that your prayers will not be hindered." Have you ever tried to pray after having an argument with your wife? How easy is it to hold your husband's hands in prayer after butting heads in conflict? When a husband and wife don't keep their married life intact, they'll have trouble keeping their spiritual life on track. Why? Because there's a direct relationship between the love of God and the love of our fellow believers (1 John 4:20). Marriage, then, functions like a barometer, measuring our spiritual lives through an everyday relationship. Think about it. If Jesus Christ is in the midst of two people gathered in His name (Matt. 18:20), then just imagine how powerful the prayers of a unified husband and wife can be—which more than any human analogy pictures the union between Christ and His church (Eph. 5:31–32)!

Application

Beyond Crotchety Husbands and Ornery Wives

Let's be honest. Many husbands have a real problem understanding and honoring their wives. They tend to crowd their schedules with things that advance their careers or satisfy their interests or inflate their egos, rather than things that build a closeness with their wives. At the same time, many wives have a problem respecting and following the lead of their husbands. They openly complain about their husbands or belittle them in front of friends. Some wives engage in either active or passive manipulation to get their way.

Both husbands and wives are wise to remind themselves of their marital roles and responsibilities. The principles of 1 Peter 3:1–7 can take a number of practical forms, but let me suggest a few projects to get you going right away.

First, over the next week, spend some time together as a couple and write down four qualities you appreciate most about your spouse. Speak of them. Let your spouse know how you desire to honor him or her as persons.

Second, using 1 Peter 3:1–7 as a guide, admit one thing you would like to change about *yourself* as it relates to the treatment of your spouse. Don't get it backward! Don't mention four things you want to change about *your spouse*. Stick with the section of this Scripture that applies to you. Having done this, admit to your spouse that you've failed to live up to this and you want to work on it. Then do it with prayer and patience.

Third, if you struggle with your role as a husband or wife, consider finding a role model to help you grow in your relationship with your spouse (Titus 2:3–5). Contact somebody you look up to as a good example of a harmonious marriage and ask him or her to meet with you to discuss their own approach to marital harmony. Or, if you have been through the ups and downs of marriage and have some wisdom to share with a couple just starting out, consider seeking out somebody you might mentor through this season of their marriage.

Above all, remember that real domestic harmony doesn't come easy. Sometimes it feels downright impossible. Crotchety husbands set in their ways or ornery wives unwilling to budge can be real obstacles to the application of Peter's principles in this passage. But don't give up! With hope in God even through hurtful times, you can press on until you see the fruit of your faithfulness in the life of your spouse.

Righteous Life and Ready Defense (1 Peter 3:8–17)

8To sum up, all of you be harmonious, sympathetic, brotherly, kind-hearted, and humble in spirit; 9not returning evil for evil or insult for insult, but giving a blessing instead; for you were called for the very purpose that you might inherit a blessing. 10For,

> "The one who desires life, to love and see good days,
> Must keep his tongue from evil and his lips from speaking deceit.
> 11 He must turn away from evil and do good;
> He must seek peace and pursue it.
> 12 For the eyes of the Lord are toward the righteous,
> And His ears attend to their prayer,
> But the face of the Lord is against those who do evil."

13Who is there to harm you if you prove zealous for what is good? 14But even if you should suffer for the sake of righteousness, you are blessed.

And do not fear their intimidation, and do not be troubled, [15]but sanctify Christ as Lord in your hearts, always *being* ready to make a defense to everyone who asks you to give an account for the hope that is in you, yet with gentleness and reverence; [16]and keep a good conscience so that in the thing in which you are slandered, those who revile your good behavior in Christ will be put to shame. [17]For it is better, if God should will it so, that you suffer for doing what is right rather than for doing what is wrong.

Without a doubt, the process of spiritual growth is a long and often painful one. En route to maturity, we all spill our milk, say things we shouldn't, and fail to act our age. Sometimes we throw temper tantrums like toddlers, or pout like preschoolers, or argue and complain like teens. All the while we should be conducting ourselves as mature believers, setting an example to those younger in the faith. We may have the knowledge, but we don't have the will to do what's right. Even the spiritually mature have days when they take a return trip to the "terrible twos."

Human parents rejoice as their children grow from infancy through childhood, up through adolescence and into adulthood. In the same way, our heavenly Father wants all His children to grow in their faith. Sadly, too many Christian *grow old* without *growing up*! There's a difference. A lot of people can say, "I've been a child of God for thirty years." Sometimes I want to say, "Then quit acting like a three-year-old saint!"

In 3:8 – 12, the apostle Peter sums up what he sees as the kind of lifestyle that epitomizes Christian maturity. As such, these virtues provide believers with a sort of measuring rod for spiritual growth. As a tangible, objective set of checkpoints, we can use them to measure the level of our own maturity in different areas of life. In only five verses, he summarizes his comments in the form of nine marks of maturity.

Remember that Peter's purpose in this section of the letter is to describe with accuracy the *strange life* we live in relation to the world. This list of Christian virtues certainly flies in the face of prevailing cultural norms, setting believers apart as God's holy people in an unholy world. Again and again, though, Peter ties this lifestyle of holiness to the life of hope—consistent anticipation of the reward that will come at the appearing of Jesus Christ. Mature, holy living can come only as we embrace Christ as our hope in hurtful times.

— **3:8–12** —

Peter begins this checklist of maturity with the phrase "to sum up." The Greek *to telos* literally means "the end" or "the conclusion." Peter isn't concluding the letter, but he is summing up the purpose of his previous teaching concerning attitudes and actions.[7] The preceding context instructed believers to live as "aliens and strangers" in their personal conflict against fleshly desires (2:11–12). This conflict plays out in the battlefields of unjust treatment by human government (2:13–17), unfair behavior of masters (2:18–25), and the struggles of married life (3:1–7). When Peter sums up the virtues of the ideal "resident alien" living in this world, he touches on a number of things he has already covered—and anticipates several themes he will address in the rest of the letter.

The maturity checkpoints include unity, mutual interest, friendship, affection, compassion, humility, forgiveness, a controlled tongue, a pure life, and a peaceful disposition.

A like-minded unity—"harmonious" (3:8a). The Greek word is *homophrōn*, literally "having the same mind."[8] This implies oneness of heart, similarity of purpose, and agreement on major points of doctrine. Unity isn't the same as *uniformity*—where everybody looks and acts exactly the same. Nor is it the same as *unanimity*—when everybody agrees 100 percent on everything. Peter isn't calling us to sing together in *unison*, but in *harmony*—which means we all contribute our unique notes in a beautiful chorus that far surpasses any single note.

A mutual interest—"sympathetic" (3:8b). The original Greek word *sympathēs* lies behind our English "sympathy." It means, literally, "to feel with" someone. When we are in as close a fellowship with fellow believers as Peter has in mind, we will naturally affect each other emotionally, rejoicing when others rejoice, weeping when others weep. We will have a mutual interest in each other.

A true companionship—"brotherly" (3:8c). The Greek word *philadelphos* is the adjective form of the same word Peter used for "brotherly love" in 1:22. It refers to an affectionate friendship or the love of a sibling. This affectionate companionship is much deeper than the often superficial activities that pass for "fellowship" in many churches. *Philadelphos* indicates a sense of loyalty just as strong as one's natural family relationships.

A heartfelt compassion—"kindhearted" (3:8d). Paul uses this term in Ephesians 4:32—"Be kind to one another, tender-hearted, forgiving each other, just as God in Christ also has forgiven you." This heartfelt compassion, closely associated with forgiveness, emphasizes the actions taken to reach out to the hurting.

A spirit of humility—"humble in spirit" (3:8e). This means to be lowly and bowed down in mind. It might be easy to appear humble, to act with false modesty. But Peter has in mind a deep-down humility where nobody can see—in our thought life. In our me-first world, it's hard to swallow the "last shall be first" principle. People blessed with exceptional talents or skills fight a great temptation to promote themselves and crave the limelight. A true spirit of humility curbs from within the ego's insatiable appetite.

The first five virtues of a mature Christian have related to how we think (like-minded and humble in spirit) and how we feel (sympathetic, brotherly, compassionate). The last four characteristics relate to what we do and say—the outward actions as they directly affect people. None of these, of course, is mutually exclusive. A person won't be able to feel compassion, affection, and sympathy if she is proud and contentious. And a believer won't manifest virtuous words and deeds if his thoughts and emotions are those of a novice Christian. Rather, mind, emotion, and will all must grow together into a well-rounded, balanced believer. This will lead to the kind of lifestyle befitting a Christian and attractive to unbelievers.

A forgiving nature—"not returning evil for evil" (3:9). Refusing to exact revenge when we've been injured in some way is one thing. Replying with a blessing—either in word or in deed—is something quite different. But because we have been called to inherit a blessing and because Christ has secured this hope, we can endure evil and insults with patience and grace.

A controlled tongue—"the one who desires life ... must keep his tongue from evil" (3:10). Peter quotes Psalm 34:12–13, grounding the call for the controlled tongue firmly in the Old Testament. This quote immediately follows the warning against lashing out in vengeance (3:9), so the thought is that our words are more likely to get away from us when we feel tempted to strike back. The mature believer tames his or her tongue, avoiding gossip, slander, crude language, deception, exaggeration, and all kinds of wickedness and folly. This reminds me of another psalm: "Set a guard, O LORD, over my mouth; Keep watch over the door of my lips" (Ps. 141:3). Those lines are worth praying every morning before a single stray word slips from our tongues.

A life of purity—"He must turn away from evil and do good" (3:11). Continuing his quote from Psalm 34:14, Peter recasts his repeated exhortation to holy living. Purity from wickedness means turning away from evil inclinations, temptations, and even the sins that once beset us in our past. Instead, we are to replace these bad thoughts and habits with pure, positive ideas.

A peaceful disposition—"He must seek peace and pursue it" (3:11). We love to argue and fight. We jump to our feet when wronged, dig in our heels when challenged, and clench our fists when crossed. Whether it's over minor doctrinal differences or carpet color, Christians can quickly rob each other of peace. Instead of seeking and pursuing peace, more often we pursue controversy or engage in open conflict. Instead, shouldn't the servants of the Prince of Peace (Isa. 9:6) reflect something of that peace—both in their churches and in the world?

Behind Peter's list of Christian virtues stands an important assumption: believers *can* grow in spiritual maturity to a point where they walk consistently in light of God's Word. Note that I didn't say we will walk *perfectly* without stumbling, but consistently. A consistent life of unity, mutual interest, friendship, affection, compassion, humility, forgiveness, self-control, purity, and peace doesn't mean we will never fail. It means that when we do fail, we acknowledge it and allow God's grace to restore and strengthen us.

While these ten virtues of spiritual maturity are general enough to encompass all areas of our lives, they also are specific enough to hit us where it hurts. When properly understood, Peter's rapid-fire arrows point out the weakest spots in our spiritual armor, convicting us that we are all still soldiers in training. As we examine the chinks in our own armor, however, we can easily lose sight of Peter's bigger perspective. He has in mind a greater purpose for the holiness and hope we should have in an unholy and hopeless world.

— 3:13–17 —

Peter makes it clear that the spiritually mature men and women described in 3:8–12 will get responses from the world around them. But don't be surprised when these responses aren't always positive! Many in the world live lifestyles of conflict instead of peace, sin instead of purity, pride instead of humility, or hatred instead of compassion. Some will view believers as speed bumps on their super-highways of self-gratification. Others may simply wonder what would motivate somebody to live such a strange life of holiness and hope.

So Peter asks his readers to consider an important question: "Who is there to harm you if you prove zealous for what is good?" (3:13). He has already defined what it looks like to be zealous for "good" with the nine virtues in 3:8–12. For the most part, living this way—though strange in the world's eyes—will generally keep believers out of trouble. Why? Because "the eyes of the Lord are toward the righteous, and His ears attend to their prayer" (3:12). Just think about it. If you pay your debts, normally you'll stay financially sound. When you stay sexually pure, usually you'll avoid disappointment and jealousy. If you behave with humility and peace, most often you'll keep from making enemies. And when you maintain close relationships with other believers, you'll always have people to help you through tough times. So in general, Peter's advice for wise living will bring good—not harm—from others.

Though the principle may be generally true most of the time and in most situations, Peter knows that exceptions exist. In fact, at certain times in history and at certain places in the world, the smoldering cinders of opposition can burst into outright persecution. And the lifestyle that keeps believers safe may actually endanger them! Peter says that we may actually "suffer for the sake of righteousness" (3:14).[9] In Peter's discussion of the possibility of unfair treatment, I find five pieces of advice on how to respond as Christians who have centered their hope on Jesus Christ.

First, *consider yourself blessed by God* (3:14a) when you receive unfair treatment. This isn't the response we might expect. When we experience unfair treatment, we might think, *What have I done wrong?* or *Hasn't God seen my good works? Why is He allowing this?* Instead, Peter takes an approach similar to James 1:2 — "Consider it all joy, my brethren, when you encounter various trials."

How can believers count themselves blessed by God in light of unfair treatment? First, they are blessed because God uses this kind of unfair treatment as part of His plan to strengthen us and to make us more like Christ (see 2:21 – 3:9). Rather than marking us as outside God's will, unfair treatment for righteousness indicates that we are *in* God's will and plan. Second, we are blessed because we can look forward to a future reward for enduring such trials. Jesus said, "Blessed are those who have been persecuted for the sake of righteousness, for theirs is the kingdom of heaven" (Matt. 5:10). Peter likely has these words of his Lord in mind when writing this letter.

The second response to poor treatment for righteous living is to *refrain from panic and worry* (3:14b). This directs attention toward the perpetrators; there's no reason to fear their methods of intimidation or be troubled. The Greek verb for "fear" is *phobeō*, from which we get our word "phobia." It implies fleeing or avoiding something.[10] The word "trouble" refers to stirring up, unsettling, or intimidating somebody.[11] Jesus uses it in John 14:1, when He tells the disciples, "Do not let your heart be troubled; believe in God, believe also in Me." The background of Peter's call to avoid panic and worry lies in Isaiah 8:12 – 13, where the Lord called on His people, Israel, to turn away from fear and dread of the pagan nations threatening to undo them. Instead of fearing and trembling before the nations, they are to rely on God's promises and tremble before Him alone.

In fact, Isaiah's call to regard the Lord as holy leads us to Peter's third response to mistreatment: to *acknowledge Christ as Lord* (3:15a). The phrase "sanctify Christ as Lord in your hearts" is contrasted with fearing the intimidation of persecutors. The language and imagery tracks closely with Isaiah's own exhortation in Isaiah 8:13 – 14, as seen in the comparison on the next page. Peter uses similar Greek terms as in the Greek version of Isaiah found in Peter's day.

Isaiah 8:12–13	1 Peter 3:14–15
[12]And you are *not to fear* what they fear or *be in dread* of it.	[14]And *do not fear* their intimidation, and *do not be troubled*,
[13]It is **the LORD of hosts** whom you should *regard as holy*.	[15]but *sanctify* Christ **as Lord** in your hearts.

We should not quickly pass over this allusion to Isaiah 8:13 without noticing that the Hebrew Old Testament text to which Peter refers uses the personal name of God — Yahweh — for "LORD." Therefore, Peter is making clear and direct claims about Jesus' deity, equating Him with the Lord God of the Old Testament and declaring that we should "sanctify" or "regard as holy" Jesus Christ as the Lord over our lives. When Christ is Lord and God over all aspects of our lives, we need not fear the opposition of enemies.

The fourth response to unjust treatment is to *be ready to give a defense* (3:15b). The term "defense" is the Greek word *apologia*, which means "to give an account" or to provide legal testimony. Our English word "apologetics" is derived from this term. Peter tells his readers that they should be ready to give a reason for the hope that they have in Christ. Note that this explanation for their hope comes only when they have considered themselves blessed, refused to panic and worry, and acknowledged Christ as Lord over their unfair treatment. When that happens, people on the outside will see their behavior and marvel: "How can you put up with this kind of treatment? I would have snapped by now!" Here Peter's overarching theme of Christ as the source of hope in hurtful times rises again to the fore. Jesus alone provides a solid basis for hope in the midst of suffering.

Finally, Peter urges believers to respond to the world's unfair treatment by *keeping a good conscience* (3:16). Not only do we set Christ apart as Lord over every event of our lives, but we must maintain a good conscience. Peter began this section by cataloguing Christian virtues that mark us out as God's holy and hopeful people (3:8–12). Then he pointed out that although living in this way generally brings good, it can sometimes draw the ire of wicked people (3:13). But when this happens, Peter writes, we should endure the unjust treatment of others, unwavering in our integrity. This maintenance of a good conscience even in the midst of persecution will draw attention from the pagan crowd and will silence even slanderers. In other words, Peter argues that a life of consistent integrity is a quiet defense of the Christian life, opening the opportunity for testimony regarding the lordship of Jesus Christ.

Peter brings this section to a close by echoing a principle he stated earlier in 2:20. Though we may suffer unjust treatment for living a virtuous Christian life, we must be careful that we are not incurring deserved punishment for doing wrong. Only when we suffer unjustly on behalf of Christ and as a testimony to others can we claim to be truly walking after the pattern of our Lord, who suffered and died for our sakes (3:18).

Application

Apologetics 101

Back in my seminary days, I learned about the great "apologists" of the Christian faith—those great minds who provided a well-reasoned defense of the Christian faith in response to unreasonable philosophical objections and unfounded charges of lawlessness. Throughout the past two thousand years of church history, every generation has had its Christian scholars who stood strong for the faith—sometimes against overwhelming opposition. Even today the field of Christian apologetics is filled with PhDs who can argue atheists and unbelievers into silence. I thank God for such men and women trained in both the philosophies of the world and the true wisdom of the Word.

But sometimes the rest of us may think we're off the hook because we can't explain arguments for the existence of God, or we can't fire off three responses to the theory of evolution, or we can't explain where Cain got his wife! We leave those questions to qualified scholars as we tell ourselves that we're not meant to be involved in apologetics.

But the truth is, according to Peter, *every believer is called to be an apologist*. We are to be always ready to make a defense for the hope we have in Christ. Yet presupposing this explanation, Peter describes a particular kind of consistent lifestyle of virtue that draws the attention of unbelievers. So, Apologetics 101 begins not with having the right answers to others' skeptical challenges, but with having the right lifestyle to raise the right questions!

To be faithful to Peter's exhortation, then, we need to examine our own lives to see if we're measuring up to his standards of spiritual maturity, described in 3:8–12. It wouldn't hurt to assign yourself a maturity level for each area. If you're really brave, have a close friend (or your spouse) rate you, too! Once you've discovered the areas of your life that seem most susceptible to the charge of immaturity, you can see where your own lifestyle apologetics needs to be strengthened. Use the chart on the next page to grade your level of maturity as infant, toddler, youth, teen, and adult. You may need to go back in the text to review the description of each of these areas.

Now select one area in which you need the most growth. Commit this area to prayer. Focus on submitting this area to Christ's lordship as described in 3:15,

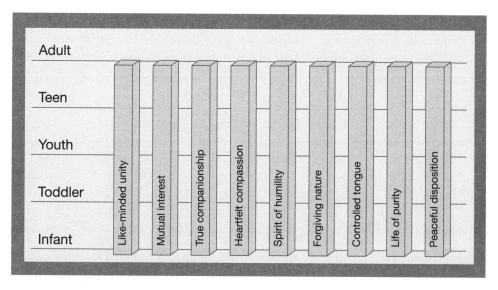

aiming for keeping a "good conscience" toward God (3:16). Because we're called to grow together in the body of Christ, consider sharing your desire to grow in this area with a close friend, pastor, or teacher who can hold you accountable and pray for your growth (see Eph. 4:15–16). Also, make this area of growth a focal point in your Bible reading, study, and devotional life, growing from infancy by feeding on "the pure milk of the word" (1 Peter 2:2).

Focusing Fully on Jesus Christ (1 Peter 3:18–22)

[18]For Christ also died for sins once for all, *the* just for *the* unjust, so that He might bring us to God, having been put to death in the flesh, but made alive in the spirit; [19]in which also He went and made proclamation to the spirits *now* in prison, [20]who once were disobedient, when the patience of God kept waiting in the days of Noah, during the construction of the ark, in which a few, that is, eight persons, were brought safely through *the* water. [21]Corresponding to that, baptism now saves you — not the removal of dirt from the flesh, but an appeal to God for a good conscience — through the resurrection of Jesus Christ, [22]who is at the right hand of God, having gone into heaven, after angels and authorities and powers had been subjected to Him.

The year is AD 200. The place is Rome. After fasting for several days and preparing his heart for a rite of initiation and dedication to the triune God, the moment had finally arrived. With all the excitement and anticipation of a wedding celebration, the small group of believers gathered together with their pastor, elders, and deacons, and the young convert to the Christian faith stepped into the water as the congregation awaited the proclamation of his "vows"—the confession of faith. Though the exact form varied from region to region and from church to church, they all told the same story; they all pointed to the same essential truths:

> I believe in God the Father Almighty, maker of heaven and earth;
>
> And in Jesus Christ His only Son, our Lord; who was conceived by the Holy Spirit, born of the Virgin Mary, suffered under Pontius Pilate, was crucified, dead, and buried; He descended into Hades; the third day He rose again from the dead; He ascended into heaven, and sitteth on the right hand of God, the Father Almighty; from thence He shall come to judge the quick and the dead.
>
> I believe in the Holy Spirit, the holy Christian church, the communion of saints, the forgiveness of sins, the resurrection of the body, and the life everlasting. Amen.[12]

When that new believer affirmed this creed and the church accepted his confession of faith, he was baptized in the name of the Father, the Son, and the Holy Spirit, rising up from the water as a full member of the church, validated by the rite of baptism.

Fast-forward many centuries. As a lad, my family and I attended a church where the congregation recited the Apostles' Creed every Sunday. Within months I had it memorized. Reciting wasn't the same as understanding, and the pastor of that church never made a point of explaining it. I didn't have the luxury of a three-year training period, as the second-century believers had, in order to clarify the rich theology of the creed. So when we got to the part that said, "He descended into Hades," I wasn't at all sure what that meant. Some forms of the creed even translated the phrase, "He descended into Hell." I recall putting it out of my mind, and I didn't recall it again until years later when I sat in a seminary classroom and we studied the Greek text of 1 Peter. Finally, some light was shed on the dim corners of that creed—the activity of Jesus during the hours between His death and His miraculous, bodily resurrection.

While 3:18–22 may have explained one aspect of the Apostles' Creed, it brought up several new questions and controversies. In fact, 3:20–21 are some of the most difficult verses not only to translate but also to interpret. Let's take a closer look at this passage, focusing closely on its context to help us better grasp its content.

— 3:18 —

This section begins in the middle of a paragraph—a larger unit of Peter's thought and argument. In the previous section, Peter referred to the believer's appropriate response to unjust suffering (3:14–17). Believers who conduct their lives virtuously (3:8–12) *sometimes* incur unjust treatment as a result (3:14). Peter makes his point clear in verse 17: "For it is better, if God should will it so, that you suffer for doing what is right rather than for doing what is wrong." At this point in the paragraph, Peter turns our attention to Christ, who exemplified unjust punishment. Now in verses 18–22, Christ alone is the focus of our attention.

Peter outlines in summary fashion the major movements of Christ, from His suffering and death on our behalf (3:18) to His resurrection and exaltation to the right hand of God (3:21–22). Sandwiched between the familiar recounting of Christ's death and resurrection, we find a few brief statements about what Christ did in the midst of His descent (3:19–20) and how we as believers publicly associate ourselves with Christ's death and resurrection through our conversion and baptism (3:21).

But before we follow Christ's ultimate descent in verses 19–20, look closely at how His own suffering is described. Here we have a clear and concise statement of the gospel.

- Christ died for sins.
- Christ died once for all.
- Christ died in place of sinners, "the just for the unjust."
- Christ died to bring us to God.

Here we have the need (our sins), the complete payment (Christ's death in our place), the all-sufficiency of that payment (once for all), and the outcome (our access to God). It doesn't get any clearer than this. These are the facts of the gospel—the message of good news for lost sinners. Peter already mentioned this salvation in chapter 1 when he noted that God's mercy "caused us to be born again to a living hope through the resurrection of Jesus Christ from the dead" (1:3). Through faith we are saved by God's power (1:5). Those verses emphasize the divine work of salvation—*God's provision*. In 3:18 and 21, we see the work of the cross and resurrection that secured our salvation—*Christ's payment*. And in 3:21, Peter focuses on the believer's inward and outward responses to the gospel—*our profession*.

So, the central theme of the passage is Christ's unjust (but saving!) suffering, death, resurrection, and ascension. This V-shaped work of Christ is meant to give us hope. We live and suffer as followers of Christ and as strangers in a strange world. We also have been spiritually united to Christ's death and resurrection on our behalf, and we have physically identified with that spiritual reality through baptism. As such, we can look forward with absolute hope that—like Christ—we will be resurrected and glorified when this life ends.

Most of the time when the New Testament addresses this good news of Christ's death and resurrection, the focus remains on Good Friday and Resurrection Sunday. Peter could have followed suit, and his explanation would have made perfect sense. Instead, the Spirit moved him to discuss briefly the work of Jesus on Saturday between His death and His resurrection.

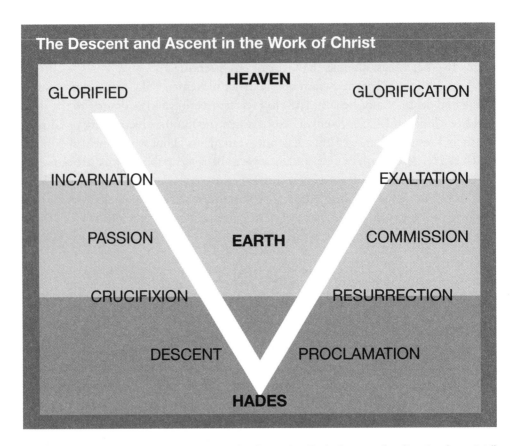

The Descent and Ascent in the Work of Christ

HEAVEN

GLORIFIED   GLORIFICATION

INCARNATION   EXALTATION

PASSION   EARTH   COMMISSION

CRUCIFIXION   RESURRECTION

DESCENT   PROCLAMATION

HADES

Peter says that Christ was "put to death in the flesh, but made alive in the spirit" (3:18). In Greek the words "in the flesh" (*sarki*) and "in the spirit" (*pneumati*) could mean any number of things. It could mean that after Christ died on the cross, the Holy Spirit made Him alive at His resurrection. But this wouldn't explain why Peter focuses on "the spirits now in prison" in 3:19. Something in his thinking about Christ's being made alive "in the spirit" brought to mind the current condition of wicked spirits in spiritual prison. So, it seems better to view Peter's discussion of what Christ's human spirit did on the Saturday between the death of His flesh on the cross and the resurrection of His flesh on Sunday. In my view, "in the flesh" refers to Christ's physical death and dying in this physical, earthly world, and "in the spirit" refers to His continued existence as a disembodied spirit being alive in the spirit world.[13]

— 3:19–20 —

What, then, did Jesus do on the Saturday between His death and resurrection? Peter tells us that when Jesus was made alive in the spirit realm, He "made proclamation to the spirits now in prison" (3:19). Who are the "spirits" he mentions? Peter says these were the spirits of those who were once disobedient in the days of Noah (3:20). In fact, Peter's language and narrative reflect a common understanding among Jews and early Christians, based on a normal reading of Genesis 6:1–4. According to that account, prior to the flood of Noah, fallen angels (demons) sinned gravely by cohabiting with human women. Though not a part of the inspired biblical writings, the ancient book of *1 Enoch* paraphrases the events of Genesis 6:1–4, giving us a clear example of the view prevalent in Peter's time:

> It happened after the sons of men had multiplied in those days, that daughters were born to them, elegant and beautiful. And when the angels, the sons of heaven, beheld them, they became enamored of them, saying to each other, Come, let us select for ourselves wives from the progeny of men, and let us beget children. (*1 Enoch* 6)

But is there any way we can be sure Peter had this common historical interpretation of Genesis 6 in mind when he wrote 1 Peter 3:19–20? When we compare parallel passages in Jude and 2 Peter with language from *1 Enoch's* traditional understanding, we see that this is, in fact, in both Peter's and Jude's minds. Note the similarities in language and imagery as we compare these passages.

1 Peter 3:19–20	He went and made proclamation to the spirits now in prison, who once were disobedient, when the patience of God kept waiting in the days of Noah, during the construction of the ark.
2 Peter 2:4	For if God did not spare angels when they sinned, but cast them into hell and committed them to pits of darkness, reserved for judgment.
Jude 6	And angels who did not keep their own domain, but abandoned their proper abode, He has kept in eternal bonds under darkness for the judgment of the great day.
1 Enoch 10:4; 12:4	"Bind Azaz'el [one of the wicked angels] hand and foot [and] throw him into the darkness … that he may be sent into the fire on the great day of judgment … [The angels] have abandoned the high heaven, the holy eternal place."

IMMORAL IMMORTALS?

For centuries — even millennia — students of Scripture have wrestled with various interpretations of the "sons of God" and their sin described in Genesis 6:1–4. Some say this refers to the righteous line of Seth ("sons of God") turning away from God and marrying daughters of the unrighteous descendents of Cain ("daughters of men"). Others say the "sons of God" were powerful human rulers — possessed by demons — who turned the world into an arena of polygamy, immorality, and bloodshed. In both of these interpretations, the sinfulness of the world reached such a height of severity that God judged the earth with a flood.

The most ancient understanding of Genesis 6:1–5, however, takes the "sons of God" in its normal sense as a reference to angelic beings (see Job 1:6; 2:1; 38:7).[14] In this interpretation, these angelic beings produced inhuman offspring (called Nephilim or "giants" in Gen. 6:4). These demons apparently attempted to corrupt the entire human race in order to thwart God's promise to send a Savior who was an offspring of Eve (Gen. 3:15).

But is it possible for angelic beings to procreate with humans? Many point to Matthew 22:30 as a text that rules out such a possibility — "For in the resurrection they neither marry nor are given in marriage, but are like angels in heaven." This text, however, specifically limits the unmarried angelic beings to those "in heaven," not necessarily to those who left their heavenly abode and fell into sin. Also, we don't know how demonic beings might have been responsible for producing offspring by human women; it may have been a case of some sort of supernatural genetic manipulation rather than natural reproduction. We simply don't know how such a thing might have happened, and it's wise to cease speculating on the point.

Nevertheless, as bizarre and distasteful as it may sound, it seems the most probable interpretation of Genesis 6:1–4 is that the "sons of God" are demons who somehow impregnated human women.

So, Peter referred to a general tradition — likely passed down from the ancient Old Testament prophets — that because of the nature of their rebellion, these demons have been kept in a special place of imprisonment in the spirit realm, even to this day. There they await future judgment, when they will be cast into the lake of fire, the place originally created for the devil and his angels (Matt. 25:41).

If this expression refers to these fallen angels, what kind of "proclamation" did Jesus make when He passed into this spirit realm? The Greek verb *kēryssō* refers to an official pronouncement of an edict.[15] It most likely refers to Christ's proclamation of victory over death, sin, and the power of Satan. Though the imprisoned angels once tried to wipe out the human race by genetic pollution, the Promised Offspring still arrived, the "Seed of the woman" (Gen. 3:15). And though Satan and his wicked spirits tried to destroy, through crucifixion, the Offspring destined to crush the serpent's head, Christ's proclamation on Saturday revealed their efforts as vain and that *victory* — not defeat — was achieved through that crucifixion (see 1 Cor. 2:8; Col. 2:13–14). In 1 Peter 3:22, Peter even makes mention of this subjection of the spiritual realm to Christ's victory: Christ went into heaven "after angels and authorities and powers had been subjected to Him."

With his mind on the preflood era when the spirits of wickedness committed their abominable sin, Peter focuses further on the contrast with the one beacon of righteousness in that age: Noah. Like Peter's own readers, Noah and his family lived in a strange and hostile world filled with wicked spirits and wicked men who persecuted them because of their righteousness. In the end, though, it was Noah and his family who were saved when the judgment swept through the world in the form of a flood. All of those unjust persecutors, alone with their own world of unbridled sin, were washed away, cleansing the earth and making way for a new world.

Peter then makes a clever analogy between the cleansing water of the days of Noah and the water used in baptism in Peter's own day. The same waters that buried the earth in judgment and death also lifted the eight humans (and animals) to safety. This is why the early church often viewed the ark of Noah as a symbol or picture of salvation. Membership in the ark and association with Noah could be compared with membership in the universal body and union with the victorious Christ.

To complete the analogy, Peter points his readers to their own act of association with Christ: water baptism.

— 3:21–22 —

Peter begins his compact statement concerning Christian baptism by tying it directly to the analogy of Noah's family brought safely "through the water" (3:20). He says baptism "corresponds" to the flood of Noah, using the Greek term *antitypos*—an "antitype." At this point it's important to understand the biblical concept of "type" and "antitype." After Christ came and revealed God's plan hidden to past ages (Eph. 3:9), the apostles began to see foreshadowing patterns in the Old Testament that vividly illustrated New Testament truths. The Old Testament image is called the "type," while the New Testament correspondence is called the "antitype." For example, Paul said the things in the Old Testament "happened as examples [types] for us" (1 Cor. 10:6), and specifically Adam serves as a "type" of Christ—the type (Adam) was the source and head of the old humanity that fell into sin, while the antitype (Christ) is the source and head of the new, redeemed humanity (Rom. 5:14).

How, then, does the water of the flood in Noah's day correspond to the way baptism "saves" believers in the New Testament? The waters of the flood were the means of judging a sinful human race, allowing Noah and his family to escape from that wicked world to begin a new life after the floodwaters receded. In the same way, the water of baptism represents a break from the old, sinful lifestyle and a new beginning as a believer in Christ. In the Bible, water baptism provides a vivid picture of our response to the gospel and the salvation it brings. The water of baptism, like the floodwaters, portrays death, the penalty for sin. It is a magnificent object lesson—a sermon without words. The believer's descent into the water represents death and burial with Christ. The believer's ascent from the water illustrates the resurrection into a new kind of life (see Rom. 6:1–4).

The parenthetical explanation of baptism in 1 Peter 3:21 is especially difficult to translate. We know the first part attempts to remove the focus from the physical act of cleansing. That is, baptism is not merely bathing a soiled body; it's "not the removal of dirt from the flesh." But Peter's explanation of how water baptism functions is a little more difficult to translate. Consider a few examples of the diversity of interpretations:

NASB	... but an appeal to God for a good conscience
NKJV	... but the answer of a good conscience toward God
Young's Literal Translation	... but the question of a good conscience in regard to God
NLT	... but as a response to God from a clean conscience
NET	... but the pledge of a good conscience to God

The understanding of this phrase that makes most sense in light of the Bible's whole teaching about the function of baptism seems to be "the pledge to God from a good conscience." That is, Peter views baptism as an outward ceremony—much like a wedding ceremony—that includes a public confession and commitment to live the new life redeemed from sin. The water of baptism does not cause a person to have new life or a good conscience, but it is the response to God based on a conscience that already has been purified by the Holy Spirit through faith. This "good conscience" comes with new life because of the resurrection of Jesus Christ from the dead (3:21).

So, just as Jesus Christ proclaimed His triumph over sin and death through His own suffering and death on the cross, believers proclaim their triumph over sin and death through water baptism. The water of baptism itself does not save a person or cleanse the conscience. These are the works of the Holy Spirit, who baptizes and saves a believer by faith apart from water baptism, a distinction confirmed clearly in Acts 10:44–48. Peter himself was present and saw with his own eyes that water baptism could not be viewed as the necessary cause of a person's salvation:

> While Peter was still speaking these words, the Holy Spirit fell upon all those who were listening to the message. All the circumcised believers who came with Peter were amazed, because the gift of the Holy Spirit had been poured out on the

Gentiles also.... Then Peter answered, "Surely no one can refuse the water for these to be baptized who have received the Holy Spirit just as we did, can he?" And he ordered them to be baptized in the name of Jesus Christ. (Acts 10:44–48)

When sinners believe the gospel of Christ's person and work, they express their faith by reenacting their association with Christ through baptism. The death and resurrection are vividly portrayed in that ancient rite. And when we come up out of the water, we are committed to serving not the philosophy or teachings of a dead sage or legendary teacher. No, our Savior ascended to heaven and is seated at the right hand of God (1 Peter 3:22). That living Lord, who has authority over all powers in heaven, earth, and Hades, provides His followers a living hope in hurtful times.

Application

Bringing Baptism to Life

Peter's words in 1 Peter 3:21 echo the practice in the early church that closely associated a person's conversion to Christ by faith in His death as payment for their sins with the practice of baptism as an outward profession of that inner faith. So closely was baptism associated with a person's genuine conversion to the Christian faith that Peter could even say "baptism now saves" believers from their former lives of sinfulness, just as the floodwaters in the days of Noah saved God's people from the world of wickedness in which they lived.

Though water baptism itself doesn't save, some Christians have gone to the extreme of neglecting or delaying water baptism for years ... or even decades. Yet in light of the importance associated with baptism as the appointed means of public confession of faith, it would be a deviation from Scripture for believers to abandon or neglect baptism unnecessarily. To use a modern analogy, becoming a Christian without submitting to water baptism would be like getting married without a wedding! Yes, I know that men and women can elope or have common-law marriages today. But when they do, they deprive family and friends from participating in an important public ceremony. And they avoid a meaningful opportunity to express their covenant commitment to each other. For the rest of their lives, married couples look back on their wedding day as the official mark of their lives together.

In the same way, baptism can serve to remind us that we have died to the old lives we once lived before faith in our Lord Jesus Christ. Paul wrote:

How shall we who died to sin still live in it? Or do you not know that all of us who have been baptized into Christ Jesus have been baptized into His death?

Therefore we have been buried with Him through baptism into death, so that as Christ was raised from the dead through the glory of the Father, so we too might walk in newness of life. (Rom. 6:2–4)

Water baptism reminds us that the Holy Spirit has made us alive with Christ, uniting us to Him and freeing us from the power of sin. So Paul can urge us, "Consider yourselves to be dead to sin, but alive to God in Christ Jesus" (Rom. 6:11). A husband struggling with faithfulness in his marriage can look back on his wedding vows to renew his commitment. In the same way, believers can look back on their baptism as the visible mark of spiritual death to their old lives and resurrection to a brand-new life.

If you are a believer in Jesus Christ and haven't yet submitted to water baptism, why are you waiting? In most Third World cultures, it is a person's public baptism that announces to all, "I am a devoted follower of Jesus Christ!" And it is at that point that persecution against that believer begins.

Let that ancient and meaningful celebration of your new life mark a firm commitment to follow Christ. If you are a baptized believer, remind yourself of the confession and commitment to new life exemplified in that significant celebration. Don't let the sin that once sullied your old life compromise your new life. Publicly testify of your faith in Christ! Return daily to the reality that baptism represents—the cleansing power of the Holy Spirit, who is also the source of power for victorious living.

Admittedly, your conversion to Christ is a private matter between you and your Lord. But once you have come by faith alone to Christ alone, don't hide your relationship with Him. Water baptism is your way of saying to the world, "I am a devoted follower of Jesus Christ!" It will make an amazing difference in your public witness and your personal journey toward maturity.

How to Shock the Pagan Crowd (1 Peter 4:1–6)

[1]Therefore, since Christ has suffered in the flesh, arm yourselves also with the same purpose, because he who has suffered in the flesh has ceased from sin, [2]so as to live the rest of the time in the flesh no longer for the lusts of men, but for the will of God. [3]For the time already past is sufficient *for you* to have carried out the desire of the Gentiles, having pursued a course of sensuality, lusts, drunkenness, carousing, drinking parties and abominable idolatries. [4]In *all* this, they are surprised that you do not run with *them* into the same excesses of dissipation, and they malign *you*; [5]but they will give account to Him who is ready to judge the living and the dead.

⁶For the gospel has for this purpose been preached even to those who are dead, that though they are judged in the flesh as men, they may live in the spirit according to *the will of* God.

Throughout the New Testament we read of the changed life that follows genuine conversion. When God freely and fully forgives the sins of our former life—when the righteousness of Christ is credited to our account and the Spirit of God takes up residence in our hearts—the old things pass away and all things become new (2 Cor. 5:17). The lifelong process of transformation begins. This radical series of changes results in an alteration of our attitudes, inner motives, habits, and pursuits, as well as our choice of close friends.

As far back as the first century, Peter wrote of all these things. Though almost two thousand years separate us from Peter's original audience, many a Christian today can identify with the apostle's words. Written for a particular time, his words are nevertheless timeless. They speak with incredible relevance today—especially his comments regarding the reaction of those who do not know the Lord.

In this section, Peter reminds us that because our citizenship is in heaven, the world in which we dwell isn't our true home. We are representatives of a different kingdom. And like foreign tourists from an exotic land visiting another country, we may be the only way people get a picture of what God's kingdom is really like. As a result, unbelievers today will either be attracted or repelled by our heavenly home.

— **4:1–3** —

With the logical conjunction "therefore," Peter is saying in shorthand, "Now in light of everything I have just written about Christ, I'm going to present you with some practical conclusions." In the previous section, Peter has discussed Christ's suffering and death to pay for our sins and His resurrection to give us new life. But Peter's discussion also included the reality that those who have responded to this message in faith have put to death the old life and have begun anew—a private transformation marked by public baptism.

In light of our relationship to Christ's saving work, Peter urges us: "Arm yourselves also with the same purpose" of dying to the old and living for the new. The Greek word *hoplizō* ("arm yourselves") is a military term that refers to a soldier taking up weapons in preparation for battle. Paul uses the related noun, *hoplon*, to refer to the "armor" of light (Rom. 13:12), "weapons" of righteousness (2 Cor. 6:7), and "weapons" of spiritual warfare (2 Cor. 10:4). The word picture of the Christian as a soldier is common in the New Testament, reinforcing the truth that

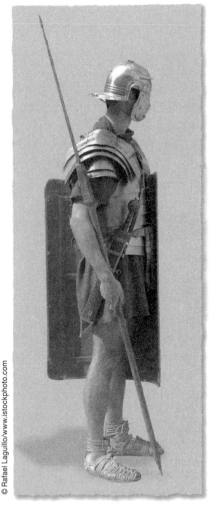

© Rafael Laguillo/www.istockphoto.com

Roman soldier armed for battle.

we are soldiers in a spiritual battle.[16] Commentator Kenneth Wuest writes, "The noun of the same root was used of a heavy-armed foot soldier who carried a pike and a large shield ... The Christian needs the heaviest armor he can get, to withstand the attacks of the enemy of his soul."[17]

Peter's point is clear. Christ has not sent us into the world as vacationers on a self-guided tour of a playground, but as soldiers on a tour of duty in a battlefield. We are not called to kick back, relax, take in the scenery, and wait for our Guide to take us home. Rather, we are engaged in a fierce conflict on foreign soil. We need to arm ourselves with spiritual armor to withstand the temptations of this world (cf. Eph. 6:10 – 18). Peter says if you have been conformed to Christ's death and resurrection, then the power of sin has been broken (1 Peter 4:1). Because the old person you used to be has died, as it were, with Christ, you are now free to live with Christ.

Let me point out in verses 1 – 3 four reminders of our new condition that will help us arm ourselves with the righteousness necessary to fight well against temptation and sin during our tour of duty in this hostile world.

- We no longer serve sin as our master (4:1).
- We don't spend our days overwhelmed by desires (4:2a).
- We have opened the door to the will of God (4:2b).
- We have closed the door on godless living (4:3).

Don't overlook the strong contrast between the "will of God" (v. 2) and the "desire of the Gentiles" (v. 3). Peter says, "The time already past is sufficient for you to have carried out the desire of the Gentiles." In a certain sense, all believers have in their lives a BC and an AD—before Christ and after Christ. Peter saw "year one" as the moment of conversion, officially marked by baptism (3:21).

Before this spiritual birthday, the old person lived out the old course of life—"sensuality, lusts, drunkenness, carousing, drinking parties and abominable idolatries" (4:3). Peter's list isn't exhaustive, but it paints an ugly picture of many believers' "BC" years. When we consider that most people in the world still live in this "BC" period, it shouldn't surprise us that they expect everybody to speak their foul language, follow their distorted mind-set and customs, and uphold their corrupt cultural values. When we don't conform, they notice. When we allow our transformation to play out on the stage of life, we will stand out from the rest of the crowd by the fact that we don't participate in their self-indulgent escapades.

— **4:4–5** —

Maybe you've heard some of these reactions to your new and different way of life in Christ.

- "What do you mean, you don't do that?"
- "C'mon! You mean God doesn't want you to have fun?"
- "So, you think you're some kind of saint?"
- "You think you're better than we are?"
- "What's *wrong* with you?!"

When we close the book on the old chapter of our lives and open up the new, our former friends and/or current colleagues usually respond with surprise, sometimes even shock. Often, their astonishment at your new life will result in their abandoning or ignoring you. You soon discover that you no longer get invited to their parties, they won't ask you over for dinner, or you may even lose their companionship.

In many cases, the world will respond with disdain. Peter says they will "malign" you. The Greek word is *blasphemeō*, from which we get our word "blasphemy." It refers to a harsh, slanderous outburst against sacred things. In this context, the sacred thing they malign is the believer—the person set apart for holy living in an unholy world (3:15). By blaspheming the ambassadors, however, they're also blaspheming the kingdom and its King—the great Lord and Judge. Your very presence in the world, taking a stand for what's true and good, becomes a standard of righteousness against which unbelievers don't measure up. They are reminded that God has a righteous standard and they will one day be called to account for their lives (4:5). That kind of reminder will make any fast-living pagan despise believers as "speed bumps" of life.

— **4:6** —

I would love to say that in every case those who get turned off by the new lives of believers will ultimately surrender their lives to the Lord. Peter himself presents this as a possibility and even a goal for sustaining our Christian testimony in the midst of persecution (2:15; 3:1, 15 – 16). Yet running parallel to that thread of hope is the threat of reprisal (2:18 – 19; 3:14, 17). The history of the church provides numerous examples of believers whose new lives in Christ led to harsh treatment, threats, persecution, imprisonment, and sometimes death.

FACING FURY WITH FEARLESS HOPE

All believers would benefit from reading both historical and modern accounts of Christians who have suffered for their faith. Foxe's *Book of Martyrs*, for example, traces the martyrdom of Christians throughout the centuries and demonstrates how darkly the world can act to extinguish the light of Christlike character. We see one famous account in the second-century martyrdom of Polycarp, pastor of the church in Smyrna, who had known and learned from the apostle John himself. Polycarp faced the fury of the proconsul of Smyrna with fearless hope.

Therefore, when he was brought before him, the proconsul asked if he were Polycarp. And when he confessed that he was, the proconsul tried to persuade him to recant, saying, "Have respect for your age," and other such things as they are accustomed to say: "Swear by the Genius of Caesar; repent; say, 'Away with the atheists!'" So Polycarp solemnly looked at the whole crowd of lawless heathen who were in the stadium, motioned toward them with his hand, and then (groaning as he looked up to heaven) said, "Away with the atheists!" But when the magistrate persisted and said, "Swear the oath, and I will release you; revile Christ," Polycarp replied, "For eighty-six years I have been his servant, and he has done me no wrong. How can I blaspheme my King who saved me?"

But as he continued to insist, saying, "Swear by the Genius of Caesar," he answered: "If you vainly suppose that I will swear by the Genius of Caesar, as you request, and pretend not to know who I am, listen carefully: I am a Christian …"

So the proconsul said: "I have wild beasts; I will throw you to them, unless you change your mind." But he said: "Call for them! For the repentance from better to worse is a change impossible for us; but it is a noble thing to change from that which is evil to righteousness." Then he said to him again: "I will have you consumed by fire, since you despise the wild beasts, unless you change your mind." But Polycarp said: "You threaten with a fire that burns only briefly and after just a little while is extinguished, for you are ignorant of the fire of the coming judgment and eternal punishment, which is reserved for the ungodly. But why do you delay? Come, do what you wish."

As he spoke these and many other words, he was inspired with courage and joy, and his face was filled with grace, so that not only did he not collapse in fright at the things which were said to him, but on the contrary the proconsul was astonished, and sent his own herald into the midst of the stadium to proclaim three times: "Polycarp has confessed that he is a Christian."[18]

Verse 6 addresses the reality of those believers—known to Peter's readers—who had given their lives for the gospel. Remember that this second major section of Peter's letter answers the question of how believers are to live as strangers in a hostile world, where they can expect to be treated unfairly for their faith in Christ. Peter refers to those who heard the gospel of Christ but were judged (literally) "according to men" in the flesh—that is, declared "guilty" by human standards and put to death. Similarly, Christ had been put to death "in the flesh" as a result of human judgment (3:18; 4:1). Yet He also was made alive "in the spirit" and resurrected to new life (3:21–22). In the same way, believers who suffer the ultimate expression of rejection, persecution, and judgment in this life will "live in the spirit according to the will of God" (4:6) and, like their Lord, will one day be resurrected to eternal life.

Most Christians throughout history have never had to face martyrdom, though all have been the object of various levels of ridicule and rejection (John 15:18–20; 1 John 3:13). As we face anger from friends and family, we should never forget that even though we are judged "according to men" in the flesh, God has judged us "not guilty" by His grace. So now we can live in the spirit regardless of what people may do to us.

Application

Standing Out in the Crowd

Everything in 1 Peter 4:1–6—both the warnings and the rewards—presupposes that something in your character marks you as a Christian. I'm not referring to wearing a cross around your neck, sticking a fish symbol on your bumper, or driving to church on Sunday mornings. No, I mean something that really makes you stand out in the crowd. It's easy to appear to be a Christian at certain times and in certain places. But to live a life of integrity in which your internal attitudes match your external actions everywhere and at all times—*that's* something different.

This is the kind of radical discipleship described in the heart of 1 Peter. You recall Peter mentioned "the time already past" in which believers lived in the flesh before converting to Christ (4:3). He gave a few ideas of what that old life looked like, in case his readers forgot the kinds of things from which they were saved. This is an ideal moment to personally reflect on some specific things from which you were delivered. In the boxes on the next page, list some of the inner and outer characteristics that marked you in your "BC" days (negatives). Then, note in the "AD" box the observable changes in your attitudes and actions (positives). Think before you write.

Rather than quickly moving past this exercise, return to the first box ("BC") and note the elements of the old lifestyle that somehow keep jumping over the cross and

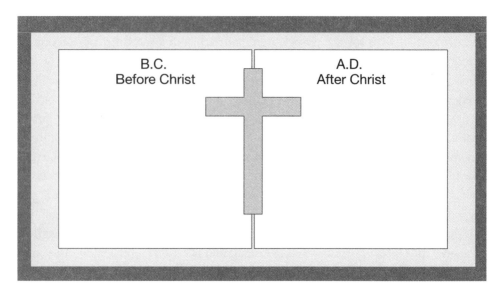

back into your new life. Circle these lingering habits of your old character. Mark them as exposed parts of your character over which the armor of God needs to be strengthened. As you take up Peter's challenge to "arm yourselves," focus Christ's transforming power on these issues, surrendering them to Him through prayer. Ask God to strengthen you in those specific areas by His Holy Spirit. Then, trusting that His power is working in you and with you, take the first step to strengthen these areas in your life. It may not come easily. It will definitely take time. In some cases, it may take help from others. But the outcome will make you a stronger soldier of Christ.

Like brave soldiers of the faith throughout history, do you want to stand out as an ambassador for the kingdom of light in the midst of an empire of darkness? Of course you do! You don't need to arm yourself with fanaticism. You won't want to cultivate a judgmental attitude or wag a condemning finger. All you have to do is put on a lifestyle impervious to unreasonable assaults. Many will give you the cold shoulder. Others will strike out with slander. You may live in a danger zone where others may even try to harm you physically. But a few people will see the noble character reflected in your changed life and inquire about your King.

Marching Orders for Soldiers of the Cross (1 Peter 4:7–11)

⁷The end of all things is near; therefore, be of sound judgment and sober *spirit* for the purpose of prayer. ⁸Above all, keep fervent in your love for one another, because love covers a multitude of sins. ⁹Be hospitable to

one another without complaint. ¹⁰As each one has received a *special* gift, employ it in serving one another as good stewards of the manifold grace of God. ¹¹Whoever speaks, *is to do so* as one who is speaking the utterances of God; whoever serves *is to do so* as one who is serving by the strength which God supplies; so that in all things God may be glorified through Jesus Christ, to whom belongs the glory and dominion forever and ever. Amen.

The name "Peter" and "practical" go hand in hand. Being married helped. So did his career as a fisherman. Prior to following Christ, Peter's life consisted of tangible, practical things: boats, nets, fish, sweat, hard work, family — the nitty-gritty of real life. We shouldn't be surprised, then, to discover that both his rugged personality and to-the-point prose flow through his writing.

Being neither scholarly nor sophisticated, Peter had little interest in theoretical discussions. Truth was meant to be lived, not simply talked about and then ignored. If there was a cause worth fighting for, fight, don't philosophize! If urgency required action, the man rolled up his sleeves and dug in. When Peter took up his pen to write a letter to suffering saints, he didn't beat around the fig tree. He cut through the fluff and got down to basics. Urgency led to simplicity.

In the midst of his discussion of how to face suffering with hope in Christ, Peter couldn't avoid the practical effects of living in light of Christ's return. He didn't get bogged down speculating about the hows, whens, and wheres of the end times, but he focused instead on the question, "So what?" He answered this bottom-line question in 4:7 – 11. In five short verses, we will see four urgent commands to obey, followed by one simple goal to remember.

— **4:7** —

When we know time is short, two otherwise neglected operating principles suddenly kick in: urgency and simplicity. When people discover that they don't have long to live, for example, their relationships with loved ones take center stage and their schedules become simplified. Or think about what happens when people hear that a hurricane or tornado is imminent. They don't pull out a croquet game or start landscaping the backyard. Instead, they grab the essentials and head for cover — immediately! Being short on time requires urgency and simplicity.

Scripture treats the end times in the same way. Over and over again it reminds us that the time is short or that the end is near.[19] Beginning in verse 7, Peter switches into this mode of end-times urgency and simplicity in this passage with a somewhat puzzling phrase: "The end of all things is near." I say "puzzling" because nearly two thousand years later the end of all things—so far as I can tell—hasn't happened yet. Was Peter wrong? No! The key to understanding Peter's language comes from understanding the Christian doctrine of imminence.

The Greek phrase translated "is near" is the verb *engizō*. The opening line literally says, "The goal of all things has come near." Peter pictures Christ in heaven at the right hand of the Father, awaiting one word from the throne—"Go!" So, when the Bible speaks of the end as "near" or "coming quickly," it refers to the suddenness and unexpectedness of the return of Christ. That is, Christ could come at any moment.

In light of this "any moment" view of Christ's return and the unfolding of end-times judgments, Peter says we should respond with certain specific actions. The first command is found in verse 7, following an important "therefore." In light of Christ's imminent return, *use good judgment and stay calm with a spirit of prayer.* Having sound judgment and a sober spirit means you don't panic when a natural disaster hits, or when an official is elected that you don't like, or if the nightly news seems packed with increasingly bad news. Don't worry! Don't jump off a tall building! This also means you don't quit your job because Jesus just might come back today. Rather, you keep your nose to the grindstone and continue your work with an ongoing sense of purpose and urgency. You live as if Christ may come today but plan for the possibility that it could be long after you've passed away. That's a reasonable, balanced approach to life in light of the unknown hour of Christ's coming. The motto of the Revolutionary War minutemen comes to mind: "Trust in God ... but keep your powder dry!"

The secret to maintaining this kind of balance and calmness is prayer. When something alarms you, pray. When current events confuse you, pray. If the world looks like it's spinning out of control, pray. Prayer sharpens our awareness so that we are able to be more discerning. It gives us genuine hope and confidence in Christ in the midst of confusion. When you're panicking, you're not praying. When you're reacting, you're not trusting in your sovereign God.

—**4:8**—

The second command to follow in light of Christ's imminent return is to *stay fervent in love for one another.* The word "fervent" comes from the Greek word *ektenēs*, meaning "strained."[20] It speaks of intensity and determination, like an athlete stretching to reach the finish line at the end of the final lap. Peter sat at Jesus' feet and heard Him describe the end times with the phrase, "Most people's love will grow cold" (Matt. 24:12). And Paul reminded Timothy that in the last days people will be "lovers of self" (2 Tim. 3:2). Peter completely reverses this frigid self-love; in sharp contrast, believers are to have *fervent* love directed *toward one another.*

From My Journal

Commence Prayer

It happened in 1968 on an airplane headed for New York—a routine and normally boring flight. But this time it proved otherwise. As the plane was on its descent pattern, the pilot realized that the landing gear was not engaging. He messed around with the controls, trying again and again to get the gear to lock into place ... without success. He then asked ground control for instruction. As the plane circled the landing field, the emergency crew coated the runway with foam as fire trucks and other emergency vehicles moved into position.

Meanwhile, the passengers were told of each maneuver in that calm, unemotional voice pilots do so well. Flight attendants glided about the cabin with an air of cool reserve. Passengers were told to place their heads between their knees and grab their ankles just before impact. There were tears and a few cries of despair. It was one of those "I can't believe this is happening to me" experiences.

Then, with the landing only minutes away, the pilot suddenly announced over the intercom: "We are beginning our final descent. At this moment, in accordance with International Aviation Codes established at Geneva, it is my obligation to inform you that if you believe in God, you should commence prayer." Scout's honor—that's exactly what he said!

I'm happy to report that the belly landing occurred without a hitch. No one was injured and, aside from some extensive damage to the plane, the airline hardly remembered the incident. In fact, a relative of one passenger called the airline the very next day and asked about that prayer rule the pilot quoted. The answer was a cool, reserved, "No comment."

Amazing. The only thing that brought into the open a deep-down "secret rule" was crisis. Pushed to the brink, back to the wall, right up to the wire, all escape routes closed, only then does our society crack open a hint of recognition that God may be there and—"if you believe, you should commence prayer."

This reminds me of a dialogue I heard on television shortly after Mount St. Helens erupted back in 1980. The guy being interviewed was a reporter who had "come back alive" from the volcano with pictures and sound track of his own personal nightmare. He was up near the mouth of that mountain when she blew her top, and he literally ran for his life—with camera rolling and the mike on. The pictures were blurred and dark, but his voice was recorded.

It was eerie, almost too personal to be disclosed. He breathed deeply, sobbed, panted, and spoke directly to God. No formality, no clichés—just the despairing cry of a creature in crisis.

cont.

Things like, "Oh, God, oh, my God … help! Help!" More sobbing, more rapid breathing, spitting, gagging, coughing, panting. "It's so hot, so dark … help me, God! Please, please, please, please …"

There's nothing like crisis to expose the otherwise hidden truth of the soul. Any soul.

We may mask it, ignore it, pass it off with cool sophistication and intellectual denial; but if you take away the cushion of comfort, remove the shield of safety, inject the threat of death without the presence of people to take the panic out of the moment, it's fairly certain most in the ranks of humanity "commence prayer."

Crisis crushes. And in its crushing, it also refines and purifies. I've stood beside too many of the dying, ministered to too many victims of calamity, listened to too many of the broken and bruised to believe otherwise.

Unfortunately, it usually takes such brutal blows of affliction to soften and penetrate hard hearts.[21]

This has immediate application to our own day. In the midst of unjust treatment, persecution, and confusion in the present world, nothing helps strengthen and encourage believers more than mutual love and care for each other. Peter quotes a line from Proverbs 10:12 to demonstrate the practical manifestation of this love: "Hatred stirs up strife, but love covers all transgressions." Nothing more quickly turns unbelievers off of Christ than witnessing His church viciously fighting with each other rather than loving each other fervently.

— **4:9** —

The third command Peter issues in light of Christ's imminent return is to *be hospitable toward one another*. I think most of us are fine with the idea of hospitality, so long as we get to define what that looks like. We invite people we like into our homes and make appropriate adjustments as willing hosts—within limits, of course. But Peter refers to "one another" in the broadest sense of that term. He used it in 4:8 with reference to fervently loving even those who need our forgiveness—that is, those who have wronged us. And he uses "one another" in 4:10 to refer to the larger body of Christ, whom we are to serve with our spiritual gifts. So, picking and choosing whom you will invite into your lives isn't at all what Peter had in mind.

Peter tacks on another phrase that makes this command even more convicting: "without complaint." Being truly hospitable can cost money. It definitely takes time. It can become inconvenient and occasionally frustrating. Peter urges believers to have a positive attitude toward hospitality—one that flows from the fervent love and prayerful hope described in 4:7–8.

Nevertheless, Christians shouldn't take advantage of hospitality. Having discernment and love doesn't mean we enable people to leach off of us while they sit back and fulfill their lazy, parasitic cravings. Some Christians in Peter's day were living unbalanced lives in response to the teaching about the imminent return of Christ. They thought, *If Christ is coming soon, why bother working? Why not just sell everything and live off others?* Paul specifically addressed this problem in 2 Thessalonians 3:6–15 and Peter indirectly addresses the other side of true, self-sacrificial hospitality in verses 10–11—the mutual contribution of *all* believers in the body of Christ.

— **4:10–11** —

The fourth and final command Peter issues in light of Christ's any-moment return is to *keep serving one another*. Peter makes it clear in just a few words that each believer has a spiritual gift. He says (lit.), "Just as each one received a gift." He takes it for granted that if you're a believer, God has graced you with a gift. But this isn't a gifting to make you feel better about yourself, to boost your ego, or to serve your own interests. Rather, these are investments God has made in various members of His the body, and He expects a return on that investment.

In other words, we are to be "good stewards of the manifold grace of God." The term "manifold" is the Greek word *poikilos*, meaning "many-colored." The term implies a great variety of giftedness within the Christian community. Though Peter doesn't list all these gifts, his fellow apostle, Paul, gives us a good idea of the diversity of the gifts in several places in his writings. (See the comparative chart on this page.)

Peter encourages his readers to responsibly use the unique gifts God has given each of them. Peter gives two specific examples by selecting two representative gifts from the broad variety of gifts—a speaking gift and a serving gift (4:11). He insists that we should treat our giftedness as a unique responsibility and honor—relying on God's strength and never forgetting that the message we proclaim is *His* message, not ours. Moreover, the purpose is not to serve ourselves but to serve "one another" (4:10).

SPIRITUAL GIFTS LISTED IN SCRIPTURE

Peter mentions only two "spiritual gifts" in 1 Peter 4:11, but the apostle Paul mentions several more that supplement Peter's representative gifts of speaking and serving.

Romans 12:6–8	1 Corinthians 12:4–11	Ephesians 4:11	1 Peter 4:10–11
Prophecy	Word of knowledge	Apostles	Speaking
Service	Faith		Serving
Teaching	Healing	Evangelists	
Exhorting	Miracles	Pastors	
Giving	Prophecy	Teachers	
Leading	Distinguishing spirits		
Mercy	Speaking in languages		
	Interpreting languages		

So, in summary, our hopeful expectation of the Lord's return should motivate us to *use good judgment and stay calm with a spirit of prayer* (4:7). We should *stay fervent in love for one another* (4:8). We must remember to *be hospitable toward on another* (4:9). And we should never neglect to *serve one another* through the use of our spiritual gifts. These four commands answer Peter's question, "What should we be doing in light of the any-moment return of Christ?"

Yet Peter doesn't leave this discussion merely with four marching orders for spiritual soldiers. He reminds us of our ultimate mission—the purpose for which we have been called, equipped, and sent. Every army's general has an ultimate military objective, and God is no exception. We find it at the end of verse 11 in the form of a "doxology"—a brief, lively hymn of praise to God. We are to do all these things, live this way as strangers in a strange world, put up with unfair treatment by others, and abide with one another in loving unity "so that in all things God may be glorified through Jesus Christ, to whom belongs the glory and dominion forever and ever. Amen."

When we keep this ultimate objective at the forefront of our minds, little else in life matters. It all falls into place. I didn't say it will make sense! I didn't say it will make everything easy! But we will be able to step back and confess with confidence that God alone will get the glory through each event and in every circumstance. When we give Him the glory, we'll leave the results of our labors to Him and we'll also trust Him for the strength we need. Seeking God's glory in all things is a difficult assignment in the spiritual battlefield of this present world. But when we look forward to the specific hope of Christ's return—when the battle will be decisively won—we will embrace a specific hope to help us persevere through hurtful times.

NOTES:

1. See Robertson McQuilkin, *An Introduction to Biblical Ethics*, rev. ed. (Wheaton, IL: Tyndale, 1995), 483–86.
2. Sam Tsang, *From Slaves to Sons: A New Rhetoric Analysis on Paul's Slave Metaphors in His Letter to the Galatians* (New York: Peter Lang, 2005), 22.
3. Mark Hassall, "Romans and Non-Romans," in *The Roman World,* John Wacher ed. (London: Routledge, 2002), 2:685–700.
4. Tsang, *From Slaves to Sons*, 39.
5. See Barclay M. Newman Jr., *A Concise Greek-English Dictionary of the New Testament* (Stuttgart: German Bible Society, 1993), 27; Bauer et al., *A Greek-English Lexicon*, 115–16.
6. J. Ramsey Michaels, *1 Peter*, Word Biblical Commentary, vol. 49, ed. David A. Hubbard, Glenn W. Barker, and Ralph P. Martin (Waco, TX: Word, 2988), 169.
7. Ibid., 175–76.
8. Bauer et al., *A Greek-English Lexicon*, 569.
9. In the Greek language, writers can express four different types of "conditional" phrases. That is, the "if... then" construction can imply different types of circumstances, each with varying degrees of likelihood depending on the words and grammatical forms used. A first class condition assumes the "if" part of the phrase is true. For example, Satan said to Jesus, "If you are the Son of God, command that these stones become bread" (Matt. 4:3). A second class condition assumes the "if" is *not* true—"If I were still trying to please men, I would not be a bond-servant of Christ" (Gal. 1:10). The third class condition regards the "if" statement to be uncertain—only when the "if" statement occurs does the "then" statement prove true. This is the form used in 1 Peter 3:13. Peter is saying, "If you prove zealous for what is good, *then* who is there to harm you?" He emphasizes the unlikelihood of harsh treatment as long as we are living as we should. But then, in verse 14, Peter follows up the third class condition with a fourth "if... then" construction. The fourth class condition describes an unlikely "if" that results in an unlikely "then." "But even if you should suffer for the sake of righteousness [which is not common], then ..."

10. Bauer et al., *A Greek-English Lexicon*, 863.

11. Ibid., 805.

12. "The Apostles' Creed," in *The Hymnal for Worship and Celebration*, no. 716.

13. Paul sometimes uses the terms "flesh" and "spirit" to contrast the physical body that dies and the spiritual part of a person that continues on (1 Cor. 5:5). Peter uses the same contrast in 1 Peter 4:6. It is also noteworthy that the apostle John uses the term "in the spirit" to refer to a translation to the "spirit realm," where he is able to perceive things unseen in the physical world (Rev. 4:2).

14. For alternative views on this passage, see Allen P. Ross, "Genesis," in *The Bible Knowledge Commentary: Old Testament*, ed. John F. Walvoord and Roy B Zuck (Wheaton, IL: Victor, 1985), 36–37.

15. Bauer et al., *A Greek-English Lexicon*, 431.

16. See Ephesians 6:11–13; Philippians 2:25; 2 Timothy 2:3–4; Philemon 2.

17. Kenneth Wuest, *Wuest's Word Studies from the Greek New Testament for the English Reader* (Grand Rapids: Eerdmans, 1973), 2:110.

18. *Martyrdom of Polycarp* 9.1–10.1; 11.1–12.1. Translation from Michael W. Holmes, *The Apostolic Fathers: Greek Texts and English Translations*, 2nd ed. (Grand Rapids: Baker, 1999), 233–37.

19. See, e.g., Romans 13:11; James 5:3; 1 John 2:18; Revelation 1:3.

20. Bauer et al., *A Greek-English Lexicon*, 622–23.

21. Adapted from Charles R. Swindoll, "Commence Prayer," in *The Finishing Touch: Becoming God's Masterpiece* (Dallas: Word, 1994), 550–52.

OUR FIERY ORDEAL
(1 PETER 4:12 – 5:14)

Like life itself, the book of 1 Peter presents constant reminders of the reality of suffering. The consummate realist, Peter has made no attempt to sugarcoat the bitter truth that believers should expect to face—not escape—various trials in their lifelong journey. But Peter is no cynic. In the midst of his down-to-earth portrayal of suffering saints, he consistently directs us toward the hope that God will bring about His redemptive plan through periods of pain. Peter reminds us of what we can so easily forget—*Christ gives hope in hurtful times.*

Like a symphony composed in both minor and major keys, Peter develops his encouraging message through three movements. At this point in the letter we have already experienced the first two. First, Peter *informed* his readers regarding their living hope (1:1 – 2:12). He let us know that grace and peace can be ours as we claim our hope (1:3 – 12), walk in holiness (1:13 – 25), and grow in Christ (2:1 – 12). Peter highlighted the grace to go on, describing a *living hope* through Christ's resurrection (1:3). In mostly upbeat and exuberant notes, the first movement of Peter's symphony reveals Christ as the *source* of hope in hurtful times.

In the second movement, we notice a change of key. In deeper, somber, and even darker tones, Peter *exhorted* his readers to hopeful living in spite of the reality of their strange life of suffering (2:13 – 4:11). Peter urged us to submit to various authorities (2:13 – 3:7), to be humble in spirit (3:8 – 22), to be armed with endurance (4:1 – 6), and to glorify God in everything (4:7 – 11). These principles became the key to living as Christians in a hostile world. Peter emphasized *grace* to stand firm, describing a *calm hope* through personal submission (3:6). Through this second movement, we perceived Christ as the *example* of hope in hurtful times. This second movement concluded with a doxology of praise, reminding us that everything we say, do, think, or experience should be to the glory of God through Jesus Christ.

It is time for us to move on to the third and final movement. Here, Peter revisits the motifs of hope and struggle—two competing themes working together toward an awe-inspiring climax. In this section, Peter will comfort his readers in the midst of their fiery ordeal (4:12 – 5:14). He will remind them not to be surprised at their difficult circumstances (4:12). Instead, they are exhorted to keep rejoicing (4:13), entrust their lives to God (4:19), and cast their worries on Him (5:7). Peter also will encourage all of us, his readers, to focus on God's grace—to rejoice, turning our attention toward a *firm hope* through faith (4:19). So, in this grand finale of Peter's

KEY TERMS

ποιμαίνω [*poimainō*] (4165) "to shepherd, watch over a flock"

Literally, "to shepherd" meant to tend sheep or keep watch over a flock. It's related to the noun for "shepherd" (*poimēn*) as well as the word for "flock" (*poimnē*). *Poimēn* soon became a common term for the leader of a congregation of believers, translated "pastor" (Eph. 4:11). In Peter the verb "to shepherd" is a command to elders of a church, whose task it is to oversee the spiritual life and personal growth of the congregation (1 Peter 5:2).

ταπεινόω [*tapeinoō*] (5013) "to humble, lower, make low"

Peter uses this word only once in his letter, in a way that makes it appear he was familiar with James's similar exhortation to "humble yourselves" (James 4:10; 1 Peter 5:6). The concept of humility is woven through the fabric of Peter's letter, forming the basis for themes such as obedience, submission, and perseverance. In Peter, as in James, the result of humbling oneself before God is a future exaltation in God's own timing.

great symphony of hope, we see Christ Himself as the Composer and Conductor of our lives — our sure *foundation* of hope in hurtful times.

A Firm Foundation through Fiery Trials (1 Peter 4:12–19)

¹²Beloved, do not be surprised at the fiery ordeal among you, which comes upon you for your testing, as though some strange thing were happening to you; ¹³but to the degree that you share the sufferings of Christ, keep on rejoicing, so that also at the revelation of His glory you may rejoice with exultation. ¹⁴If you are reviled for the name of Christ, you are blessed, because the Spirit of glory and of God rests on you. ¹⁵Make sure that none of you suffers as a murderer, or thief, or evildoer, or a troublesome meddler; ¹⁶but if *anyone suffers* as a Christian, he is not to be ashamed, but is to glorify God in this name. ¹⁷For *it is* time for judgment to begin with the household of God; and if *it begins* with us first, what *will be* the outcome for those who do not obey the gospel of God? ¹⁸And if it is with difficulty that the righteous is saved, what will become of the godless man and the sinner? ¹⁹Therefore, those also who suffer according to the will of God shall entrust their souls to a faithful Creator in doing what is right.

Pause for a moment and replay these words in your mind. Take your time. Ponder each line.

When through fiery trials thy pathway shall lie,
My grace all sufficient shall be thy supply;
The flame shall not hurt thee; I only design
Thy dross to consume, and thy gold to refine.[1]

These timeless lyrics from a classic hymn have been sung with boldness and confidence for generations. But they are quickly forgotten when the things we hold dear suddenly ignite in the incinerator of earthly trials. When the flames of the furnace begin to singe our lives and livelihoods, those timeworn lyrics can seem strangely remote ... even unreal.

In his classic book *The Problem of Pain*, C. S. Lewis wrote this about the impact of fiery trials:

> I am progressing along the path of life in my ordinary contentedly fallen and godless condition, absorbed in a merry meeting with my friends for the morrow or a bit of work that tickles my vanity to-day, a holiday or a new book, when suddenly a stab of abdominal pain that threatens serious disease, or a headline in the newspapers that threatens us all with destruction, sends this whole pack of cards tumbling down. At first I am overwhelmed, and all my little happinesses look like broken toys. Then, slowly and reluctantly, bit by bit, I try to bring myself into the frame of mind that I should be in at all times. I remind myself that all these toys were never intended to possess my heart, that my true good is in another world and my only real treasure is Christ. And perhaps, by God's grace, I succeed, and for a day or two become a creature consciously dependent on God and drawing its strength from the right sources. But the moment the threat is withdrawn, my whole nature leaps back to the toys.[2]

Such is human nature. We so easily forget the promises that accompany the trials of life. We forget the hymns, Scriptures, sermons, and lessons that taught us the purpose of testing and the outcome of suffering. And when trials subside, it isn't long before we return to patterns of thinking and living that set us up for yet another surprise attack when the inevitable fires return. Two numbers illustrate this perfectly: 9/11.

Peter wrote his letter to Christians who faced desperate circumstances—undeserved suffering, unfair treatment, unexpected calamities. Peter cycles back to this major theme of hope in hurtful times in his concluding counsel, giving us practical insights to help us not merely survive the flames but thrive in their midst.

— **4:12–13** —

Peter's term for "fiery ordeal" is a single Greek word, *pyrōsis*. It refers to an agonizing experience of burning with fire (Rev. 18:9, 18). The definite article, "the," indicates that Peter has in mind a particular circumstance his readers are enduring together. We know this trial related to unjust treatment at the hands of first-century despisers of Christianity. That excruciating trial grew severe enough for Peter to write a letter reminding them of their source of hope in such times. We don't know the precise details of that trial. Occasionally trials are slight and brief, quickly forgotten. At other times they linger and lean hard on us, leaving us exhausted and dispirited. Sometimes they even put us out of commission for an extended period of time.

Peter gives us two appropriate responses to these agonizing trials. First, we must "not be surprised" (4:12). We are not to think it strange that such things are happening to us. Peter doesn't open this section with "beloved" for nothing; this is an address to faithful believers, not disobedient saints or phony frauds. He also describes the "fiery ordeal" as occurring "among you," "upon you," and "to you." This isn't something that accidentally swept them up, like innocent victims caught up in a mob stampede by being in the wrong place at the wrong time. Make no mistake: the fiery ordeal came upon them because of their faith in Christ.

Ironically, a lot of Christians believe they should be fireproof. Their first reaction is just the thing Peter rejects — surprise! Too often I hear objections like, "I can't believe this is happening *to me*!" or "Why doesn't God protect me from these things?" or "Why is God allowing this to happen now?" But Peter responds to this normal reaction of surprise with an important reminder: the fiery ordeal comes on believers for their testing. Like refining fire that tests and purifies gold, separating the precious metal from its impure contaminants, the fire of trials test and purify us deep within.

It might help to view our present life as a schoolroom, with God as our Instructor. We would never be surprised when our human teachers give surprise quizzes and tough exams. Tests are normal when we're involved in the pursuit of intellectual growth or development of skills. Why should it alarm us if the Master Teacher tests us as we follow His instruction in the curriculum of Christlikeness?

This should logically lead to the second reaction to our fiery ordeal: rejoicing (4:13). Peter is not alone in promoting the paradox of joy in the midst of suffering. James writes, "Consider it all joy … when you encounter various trials" (James 1:2). Paul declares that trials draw us into more intimate fellowship with Christ (Phil. 3:10). Yet Peter takes the believers' present suffering in this world and directs them backward to the sufferings of Christ as its source and then sends all of it forward to the return of Christ as its goal. In suffering unjustly, we participate to a limited degree in the kind of suffering Christ experienced on our behalf. If our Master suffered, so will His disciples. At the same time we are urged to rejoice, knowing that at Christ's return He will bring with Him relief and rewards for those who suffered faithfully in this life. Our firm hope for the future can reflect backward into the present, allowing us to rejoice even in the midst of the fiery ordeal. James 1:12 puts it this way: "Blessed is a man who perseveres under trial; for once he has been approved, he will receive the crown of life which the Lord has promised to those who love Him."

That, too, is worth our pausing … and pondering.

—— **4:14–18** ——

Having instructed believers on how to react during fiery trials, Peter then describes five truths to remember. As the flames intensify:

1. Trials provide an opportunity to draw upon divine power (4:14).
2. Sometimes our suffering is deserved (4:15).
3. Most suffering should not cause us to feel shame (4:16).
4. Suffering is usually timely and necessary (4:17a).
5. What believers suffer now cannot be compared to what the unrighteous will suffer later (4:17b–18).

First, *trials provide an opportunity to draw upon divine power* (4:14). When faced with excruciating trials, we easily come to the end of ourselves. At that desperate point, we can quickly become mentally confused, emotionally drained, physically exhausted, and spiritually spent. From a purely human perspective, we often think this is the worst possible situation to be in. But from a divine perspective, this is the precise condition necessary to draw believers closer to God. We are never more dependent on the Holy Spirit's strength than when we've come to the absolute end of ourselves. As long as we operate under the illusion that we can handle things ourselves, we will wallow in spiritual weakness. But when we finally admit that apart from Christ we can do nothing (John 15:5), we can begin to draw upon divine power. When we're reviled for our faith in Christ, God promises to provide strength by His Spirit. In this way we are "blessed" even in the midst of the unfair treatment.

Second, we should keep in mind that although spiritual blessing and strength are given to those who suffer for the cause of Christ, *some suffering is actually deserved* (4:15). Peter chooses several examples of things believers could do to incur the wrath and reviling of civil authorities and unbelieving observers.

The first two offenses—murder and thievery—are extreme and obvious legal infractions that bring the wrath of governmental authorities. That kind of punishment is just and deserved. It is appropriate for believers and unbelievers both to be punished for such crimes. They should not expect blessing from God in the suffering that results, but rather His discipline.

The second two offenses—committing evil and meddling—seem to refer not to lawbreaking, but to moral and social offenses. Believers can sometimes conduct themselves hypocritically, becoming instruments of wickedness instead of being conduits of righteousness. And they can also needlessly align themselves with causes and activities that annoy and irritate unbelievers. The term "troublesome meddler" (4:15) refers to somebody who interferes in things that are unrelated to his or her calling. It is easy for Christians to drift off into political involvements or social causes that have little to do with the gospel of Jesus Christ. Peter advises us to make sure we don't engage in activities that would not only get us off target and bring a reproach on the name of Christ, but also cause us to miss God's blessing and lose our reward when Christ returns.

Third, if we suffer as Christians because of our righteousness, this suffering *should in no way cause us to feel shame* (4:16). Though we use the word commonly today, the name "Christian" appears only three times in the New Testament, and its original meaning gives us some insight into Peter's use of the name here. Acts 11:26 says that "the disciples were first called Christians in Antioch." In fact, "Christian" originally may have been a derogatory word used by opponents of Christianity to "label" these disciples. Simply naming Christ's followers distinguished the Christian beliefs and practices from all others, making them easily identifiable. So, Peter says if a Christian suffers because he or she bears the name of "Christ" in word and deed, there is no reason for shame. In fact, such suffering is to be viewed as an honor.

Fourth, Peter reminds us that *suffering is usually timely and necessary* (4:17a). Though always difficult to endure and often impossible to comprehend at the time, believers need hurtful times to be purified. God uses suffering as a tool to sanctify, cleanse, and refine His people. The "household of God" not only needs daily dusting and sweeping, but also periodic spring cleaning. Proverbs 3:12 provides an important parallel to Peter's thoughts here: "For whom the LORD loves He reproves, / Even as a father corrects the son in whom he delights."

The reality is that we endure purifying discipline *because* we are God's children, not in spite of it. And as parents know, discipline can be both positive and negative—discipline to correct bad behavior, but also discipline to promote good behavior. Hebrews 12:11 describes negative discipline, while 1 Timothy 4:7 describes its positive counterpart. The fact that God allows us to endure fiery trials for the purpose of discipline should not surprise or disillusion us. Quite the contrary! It should encourage us to know that God cares enough about His children to reprove and discipline us in order to bring us to maturity in our walk with Him.

Finally, Peter reminds us that even though the church suffers a little while for her own benefit, with blessings and rewards to follow, those who afflict us will not get away scot-free. Essentially, we need to keep in mind that *what believers suffer now cannot be compared to what the unrighteous will suffer later* (4:17b–18). Peter reasons that if God's own children, whom He loves and cares for, cannot escape His discipline, then we can't begin to imagine what kind of punishment is in store for unbelievers who shake their fists at God! Peter paraphrases the idea behind Proverbs 11:31, "If the righteous receive their due on earth, how much more the ungodly and the sinner" (NIV). When Peter refers to being "saved" with difficulty, he refers to the life of difficulty, hardship, and struggle that accompanies salvation, not to earning salvation because of our suffering.

The word "difficulty" refers to the quality of the spiritual journey. Luke used the word to recount the difficult voyage he and others experienced as they sailed toward Crete: "we had sailed slowly for a good many days, and with difficulty had arrived off Cnidus" (Acts 27:7). Similarly, believers encounter many difficulties throughout their spiritual journey, from their initial launch at conversion to their ultimate destination of glory in the heavenly harbor. John Bunyan's classic work, *The Pilgrim's Progress*, illustrates this beautifully.

— **4:19** —

During this difficult journey of the spiritual life, in which believers suffer "according to the will of God" for the purpose of godliness, we could lose heart if we didn't have absolute confidence in both the goodness and the power of God. Because God is all powerful, we know that no trial can ever be so far out of control that God's ultimate purposes are thwarted. We can also be sure that God is able to accomplish His plan through these painful circumstances. And because God is all-good, we know that those purposes are to mature us, not destroy us. This is why Peter reminds us that God is a "faithful Creator" — all-powerful and all-good! As we continue to do what is right in the midst of unjust suffering, we can entrust our lives to Him with hope even in hurtful times.

Application

Rest in Him

The tests and trials we endure as Christians are never wasted or mistaken. God never says, "Woops, made a mistake! That was meant for Frank. Sorry, Bob." He doesn't indiscriminately toss trials into the lives of a hundred believers, hoping to affect a few. God has designed a specific curriculum for each of us — a particular course of study designed to bring out the virtuous character of Christ deep within us. These uniquely designed and tailor-made trials provide the needed stimulus to drive us to the Lord and produce measurable spiritual growth.

The common response is to resist. Such reactions are only human. Sometimes the tests are so grueling that we want to drop out of God's training school entirely. But we all need to come to grips with the fact that God's tailored trials are not simply *elective* courses in the Christian life. They are, in fact, *prerequisites* for Christlikeness. But let me give you a couple suggestions, both tied to 1 Peter 4:19, that have helped me face trials without dashing for the nearest exit.

First, when trials come, remember that God is faithful. Contrary to what your circumstances may seem to tell you, God hasn't abandoned you. Forget about what cynics tell you. God hasn't forgotten you. God is faithful. We can trust that He's working out His purposes for our ultimate good (Rom. 8:28). When you doubt whether God has kept His promise never to desert you or forsake you (Heb. 13:5), remember that He's the "faithful Creator" (1 Peter 4:19). This means He can never lie (Heb. 6:18). But it also means that everything He created was "very good" (Gen. 1:31) ... everything He is making is good in time (Eccl. 3:11) ... and everything will be ultimately restored to perfection (Rev. 21:5).

This truth about God's faithfulness leads to a specific action: *rest in Him*. The key word in 1 Peter 4:19 is *entrust*. The Greek word *paratithēmi* means to place something in the care of another, making a deposit for safekeeping.[3] This is the same word used in Luke 23:46 when Jesus says, "Father, into your hands I commit My Spirit." Because He is faithful and powerful, we can entrust our entire life to Him.

When the X-ray doesn't look good, remember God is faithful. Rest in Him. When you read a note from your spouse that you never thought you'd receive, remember God is faithful. Rest in Him. When you get news about one of your children that no parent wants to believe, remember God is faithful. Rest in Him. When you get that dreaded pink slip at work and you realize the axe just fell, remember God is faithful. Rest in Him.

How do you remember that God is faithful? By His Word. I've mentioned several passages above. But you have only to read a few pages in the Bible to see the absolute faithfulness of God demonstrated in the lives of His people in spite of their faithless rebellion against Him. Begin by reminding yourself of God's faithfulness through His Word.

But how do we fully entrust ourselves to God? How do we finally rest in Him? We mentally deposit ourselves into God's safekeeping. What a wise deposit! It yields peace and joy in this life, but also eternal dividends in the next. The concept of entrusting our souls to God during trials includes turning our situation over to God in prayer. It also means revealing our struggles to members of the body of Christ, the church, who can help us through our trials. And it means continuing to do this, moment by moment, as the fiery trial continues to burn.

When trials come—and they will come—be confident that God is faithful. Rest in Him.

A Job Description for Shepherds (1 Peter 5:1–4)

[1]Therefore, I exhort the elders among you, as *your* fellow elder and witness of the sufferings of Christ, and a partaker also of the glory that is to be revealed, [2]shepherd the flock of God among you, exercising oversight not under compulsion, but voluntarily, according to *the will of* God; and not for sordid gain, but with eagerness; [3]nor yet as lording it over those allotted to your charge, but proving to be examples to the flock. [4]And when the Chief Shepherd appears, you will receive the unfading crown of glory.

Charles Haddon Spurgeon (1834–1892) was one of England's best-known preachers. At the age of twenty he was called to the pastorate at New Park Street Chapel in London. Soon after he took the pulpit, his sermons drew crowds that overflowed capacity, necessitating the construction of the famous Metropolitan Tabernacle six years later. During his thirty-eight years as a pastor, Spurgeon led a congregation that swelled to over fourteen thousand members on the roster.[4]

Though he lived over a century ago, his prolific pen still flows with relevance. Some of Spurgeon's eloquence is preserved for us in his classic volume, *Lectures to My Students*. His shepherd's heart beats loudly through his words.

> Every workman knows the necessity of keeping his tools in a good state of repair … If the workman lose the edge … he knows that there will be a greater draught upon his energies, or his work will be badly done.
> … It will be in vain for me to stock my library, or organise societies, or project schemes, if I neglect the culture of myself; for books, and agencies, and systems are only remotely the instruments of my holy calling; my own spirit, soul, and body are my nearest machinery for sacred service; my spiritual faculties, and my inner life, are my battle axe and weapons of war.[5]

Spurgeon's poignant principles are part of a centuries-old tradition of seasoned pastoral advice to younger ministers. The shepherding of shepherds' hearts goes far back, to Jesus Himself, who spent three years preparing His own disciples to carry on

From My Journal

Curb Your Expectations

As I look back on a lifetime of pastoral ministry, a couple personal insights come to mind regarding expectations, which can happen on both sides of the pulpit. A young minister comes to a church and has a boatload of unrealistic expectations for the flock. On the other side, the flock calls a man to pastor the church—and they have such an array of expectations, nobody could live up to them!

So, one of the secrets to a long-term pastorate is clear-thinking realism for both the pastor and the congregation. Not every church will experience phenomenal growth. Most preachers won't be eloquent or in great demand. These are illusions of the ultimate. Both pastor and congregation need to banish from their minds the expectations of grandeur and popularity.

Another principle that has kept me going is the importance of two-way tolerance. A pastor needs to be tolerant of the people he is serving. And the flock is to be tolerant of the minister who serves as their undershepherd. We need to have attitudes of grace, providing a lot of wiggle room. Give each other the freedom to try and fail, to be imperfect, to be oneself. Grace, mercy, forgiveness, and unwavering love are key ingredients to the acceptance, patience, and tolerance needed to thrive in ministry.

I should add that the path to a large and effective ministry is never without its disappointing dips and unexpected turns. I've encountered church members who have accused me of wrong motives, criticized my candor, questioned my sincerity, and walked out in anger. I've made my share of mistakes and miscalculations, too, failing to live up to the qualifications set forth in 1 Timothy 3:1–7. That's ministry in the raw. Imperfect shepherds leading imperfect sheep in the service of a perfect God who has a perfect plan.

His work after His departure. The tried-and-tested Paul encouraged the young ministers Timothy and Titus to stay hard at the work of the ministry after he was gone.

At this point in his letter, Peter turns from a general readership to those responsible for spiritual leadership in the churches. He now fine-tunes his words to the shepherds, or "pastors," of those churches, lest they "neglect the culture" or themselves.

This discussion of pastoral leadership appears in the context of how Christians can endure the fiery ordeal of unjust treatment, trials, and tribulations in this life as they look with hope toward the next. Peter argues that strong, spiritual leadership is essential to thriving in this world. When leaders model holiness and hope to those sheep within their charge, the whole church will be able to look to the Chief Shepherd, who provides hope in hurtful times.

— **5:1–2a** —

Peter begins his address with "therefore." It may appear that suddenly shifting into low gear in order to plow through issues of church leadership seems a little out of place in his fast-paced treatment of the practical Christian life. But in Peter's mind, how believers live in a hostile and unholy world is closely tied to the function of leaders who serve as shepherds to guide their flocks.

I see in these first couple of verses two effective principles for those called to leadership in ministry. The first is that *pride of position must be absent*. Notice how the apostle Peter refers to himself. Although he was an eyewitness of Christ's suffering, death, and resurrection, he calls himself a "fellow elder" (5:1). He is also a "partaker," or partner, in the coming glory that will be revealed when Christ returns. He shares the readers' destiny, and he serves with them on the same ministry team. They're in this together.

Ministry can lead to a proud life for several reasons:

- Ministers speak and serve on behalf of God.
- They regularly address large groups of people.
- People make major life decisions based on their teaching.
- They are trusted by most and are held accountable by few.

All these things can easily lead to pride, arrogance, and a terrible fall. This is what make's Peter's humble identification with other church leaders so insightful. If Peter, one of the original twelve disciples and the earliest spokesman for the church, identifies himself as a "fellow elder," all of us in ministry ought to follow suit with humility of position.

The second effective principle is that *the heart of a shepherd must be present* (5:2a). The first imperative in this passage is "shepherd." The verb finds its root in the Greek term *poimainō*, which means "to tend a flock." The word is used figuratively in ancient literature and in the New Testament for any kind of general leadership role or special position.[6] Besides the figurative use of this term, many analogies in Scripture compare God's relationship to His people with that of a shepherd to His flock.[7] The noun form of this word, *poimēn*, is the basis for our English word "pastor." It is used of church pastors in Ephesians 4:11.

Verse 2 doesn't tell the pastor-elders to "shepherd your own flock," but to "shepherd the flock of God." Throughout this passage the flock is seen as those *entrusted* to the care of the pastors—not as their own followers. The ultimate Shepherd is God. But pastors and teachers should serve as faithful undershepherds, looking to the Chief Shepherd as their inspiration and model. Peter uses the image of a shepherd intentionally. The role of a shepherd certainly includes teaching, but it's not the same as being only a teacher. It includes administration, but it's more than being an organizer. It includes having a heart for evangelism, but it involves more than preaching the gospel. Peter addresses some of the specific attitudes and responsibilities required of shepherds of God's flock in 5:2b–3.

Peter also refers to the responsibility of shepherding—or "pastoring"—as "exercising oversight." The Greek word here is *episkopeō*. The noun form, *episkopos* ("overseer" or, traditionally, "bishop") is used synonymously with "elder" (*presbyteros*) in Philippians 1:1 and in the qualifications for the office of overseer in 1 Timothy 3:2 and Titus 1:7. Back when the original apostles exercised direct oversight in the churches, the office of elder, pastor, and overseer were synonymous. After the apostles departed, the office of a senior overseeing elder developed to help stabilize church authority, and it is this position that in later centuries developed into the "episcopacy" of a single bishop over a number of churches.

In the New Testament period, however, elder, pastor, and overseer were all one calling with the same responsibility to shepherd the flock. All three of these terms—"elders," "pastors," and "overseers"—are used together in Acts 20:17, 28. Paul called the "elders" (*presbyteros*) of the church of Ephesus to meet him in Miletus, then instructed them: "Be on guard for yourselves and for all the flock, among which the Holy Spirit has made you overseers [*episkopos*], to shepherd [*poimainō*] the church of God which He purchased with His own blood" (Acts 20:28).

— 5:2b–3 —

After exhorting the leaders of the churches, Peter gives three practical attitudes with which earthly shepherds are to exercise oversight. He structures each of these in the same form, including both a negative quality and its corresponding positive attitude. A simple chart highlights the contrasts:

Not	But
- under compulsion	- voluntarily
- for sordid gain	- with eagerness
- lording over the flock	- being examples to the flock

The first attitude is one of willingness: "not under compulsion, but voluntarily" (5:2b). Compulsion implies doing something by force. Peter knows that it can become a chore for pastors to motivate themselves to maintain the high-energy requirements of ministry.

Let me illustrate the negative side of this admonition with an amusing story. A young man fell sound asleep one Sunday morning when his mother burst in and said, "Wake up, son. You need to get out of bed *right now*!"

With his face buried in his pillow, he responded with a muffled voice, "Give me three good reasons why I should get out of this bed."

Engaging in a tug-of-war with his bedsheet, she said, "One: because it's Sunday and as Christians we always go to church on Sundays."

The man moaned.

"Two: because we have only forty minutes until church starts and you haven't even showered!"

The man tried to ignore his mother.

"Three: because you're the pastor and you need to be there!"

That's ministry under compulsion! While most pastors don't need their mothers to pull them out of bed on Sunday mornings, pulpits are often filled with preachers at the verge of ministry burnout, who can barely keep going. Maybe they went to Bible college and/or seminary and acquired the degree and skills for ministry, but their heart is no longer in it. Maybe they've been in ministry for so long that to make a career change now would mean starting their lives over. Maybe they've been corralled into a particular ministry position that doesn't match their gifts or training, and they can't find a way to switch to something more appropriate. Whatever the case, involuntary ministry leads to lack of enthusiasm, lack of motivation, mediocrity, and even depression. If this is the case, Peter's words imply that a change needs to be made — either fix the problem leading to compulsion or find a way to step down for a while until the joy of ministry returns.

The second attitude for shepherds is eagerness — "not for sordid gain, but with eagerness" (5:2c). Peter contrasts true excitement for ministry with financial motivation. The term "sordid gain" implies a motivation of greed. It means focusing on what the flock can do for them rather than what they can do for the flock. Titus

1:10–11 illustrates the same idea with a concrete example: "For there are many rebellious men, empty talkers and deceivers, especially those of the circumcision, who must be silenced because they are upsetting whole families, teaching things they should not teach for the sake of sordid gain" (Titus 1:11). This is why one qualification for elders is that they be free from the love of money (1 Tim. 3:3; 6:10).

God's shepherds should have an attitude of self-sacrificial zeal—not merely a willingness to serve, but an authentic enthusiasm that springs from the heart. This principle flies in the face of the excessive professionalism common in the ministry today. Degrees, résumés, popularity, and references don't qualify a person for ministry. Rather, an eagerness to serve—occasionally at great personal cost—is a vital ingredient found in a well-rounded shepherd and well-grounded ministry.

The third attitude for successful ministry is meekness—"nor yet as lording it over those allotted to your charge, but proving to be examples to the flock" (5:3). With the phrase "lording it over," Peter echoes Jesus' own warning against a domineering leadership attitude:

> You know that the rulers of the Gentiles lord it over them, and their great men exercise authority over them. It is not this way among you, but whoever wishes to become great among you shall be your servant, and whoever wishes to be first among you shall be your slave; just as the Son of Man did not come to be served, but to serve, and to give His life a ransom for many. (Matt. 20:25–28)

The idea of "servant leadership" finds its basis in warning against "lording leadership." Admittedly, "servant leadership" is an overworked expression that's often misunderstood. It does, however, summarize Jesus' teaching on the importance of resisting authoritarian approaches to shepherding. Jesus didn't exhibit that attitude, nor should we. We are to be *team leaders*—fellow learners, sharers, and partners in the same work. We can be "examples to the flock" only when we're engaged in the same kind of service we expect from others serving with us. Shepherds who lead like Christ exemplify servanthood.

— **5:4** —

With regard to the role of leaders in the church, Peter has pointed out two effective principles: *pride of position must be absent* (5:1), and *the heart of a shepherd must be present* (5:2a). He then illustrated the shepherd's heart with three essential attitudes: *willingness* (5:2b), *eagerness* (5:2c), and *meekness* (5:3). Granted, shepherding the flock of God can involve hard work! This is why Peter ends his address to the elder-pastors of the churches with a reminder of their eternal reward. If Christ's shepherds faithfully discharge their duties with the proper attitudes, they will receive "the unfading crown of glory" from Christ at His return. As the "Chief Shepherd," Jesus serves as the model of how His earthly shepherds are to serve. As such, Christ Himself is the perfect model of ministry.

As he has done throughout this letter, Peter wraps up his discussion on leadership by pointing to Christ as the source of true hope in hurtful times. When the going gets tough in ministry—and times come when it is borderline *unbearable*—we can find the motivation to go on. Christ Himself continued on in His ministry in spite of horrendous obstacles and hostile reactions, but the result of His sacrificial service was magnificent. We, too, can be assured of our future reward for faithful service at the judgment seat of Christ (1 Cor. 3:10–14).

Application

Some Advice for Shepherds

As Peter did nearly two thousand years ago, I would like to address those involved in vocational Christian ministry—shepherd to shepherd, elder to elder.

First, if you teach, remain a good student. Stay teachable. Read. Listen. Learn. Observe. Admitting when you're wrong is just as important as standing firm when you're right. Share the things you learn with those you teach. Not one of us in ministry is a know-it-all, so don't set yourself up as one. Few things are worse than an arrogant teacher of the Bible!

Second, if you lead, follow well. Think about what it would be like to listen to yourself. Exaggerating your leadership role is as dangerous as underestimating your gift and service. Leading well includes delegating well. No, others won't do things exactly as you would. No, it won't always result in the quality of work you expect from yourself. But learn to let things go. If you don't, you'll model a horrible form of "lording leadership" through your example, and this will result in the kind of leadership husbands will take home with them, bosses will implement in the office, and other pastors will reflect in their own ministries.

Third, don't take yourself too seriously. Laugh often—especially laugh at yourself. Make yourself the brunt of your humor. Point out your own foibles and fumbles. Remind others and yourself that you're only human, and that the Almighty God, through the Good Shepherd, Jesus Christ, is working out His perfect plan through imperfect people empowered by the Holy Spirit.

Finally, get some rest. Back off. Loosen up. Recharge your batteries. Refresh your personal life. Keep yourself from running at full throttle day after day. Back in seminary a lot of us thought that to minister ourselves to death was the modern-day equivalent of martyrdom. We repeated stupid statements like, "I'd rather burn out than rust out!" And our fat calendars and flat family lives reflected it. Looking back, I realize how stupid that statement really was. Either way, you're *out*. Don't go there.

Finally, take your day off—I mean, a *real* day off—once a week. And *take your vacations*. A burnt-out, exhausted, depressed, and unmotivated pastor is not a healthy, wholesome shepherd.

A Formula That Brings Relief (1 Peter 5:5–7)

⁵You younger men, likewise, be subject to *your* elders; and all of you, clothe yourselves with humility toward one another, for God is opposed to the proud, but gives grace to the humble. ⁶Therefore humble yourselves under the mighty hand of God, that He may exalt you at the proper time, ⁷casting all your anxiety on Him, because He cares for you.

Our society has gorged itself on the pursuit of success. Upward mobility, getting ahead, snagging that promotion—only one direction will do: up ... *up* ... *UP*! We've stuffed ourselves with moneymaking schemes and binged on books and seminars teaching us how to make ourselves great. In fact, not long ago our gluttony for financial success inflated an economy until it exploded. But not to worry! We'll just pick up the pieces and start all over again.

The world tells us that to be satisfied we need *fortune*: make a lot of money—in fact, make a *boatload* of money! Society persuades us that to be significant we need *fame*: be well known and well connected. The culture tries to convince us that to have true success we need *influence*: wield power, be in control, and don't take orders—*give them*! And if this "big three" of success doesn't do it, then the real secret lies in *indulgence*: fulfilling your wants, desires, and pleasures. The world's methods of achieving these things aren't difficult. *Work hard*, or at least harder than everybody else. *Push ahead*, even if it means stepping on others. *Remove all obstacles* such as friends, family, and faith. And *promote yourself* even if it means exaggerating a bit or trashing somebody else!

The great irony of all this is that the more success we have, the more we want. History, experience, religion, psychology, and sociology all have taught us that such purposeless pursuits can never ultimately quench our thirst for true meaning or relieve our hunger for true happiness. Instead of fulfillment, we experience the bloated nausea of disappointment. In the end, the all-you-can-eat lifestyle leaves us weighed down in our spirit, nauseated with worry, and let down by life.

In an age like ours, the countercultural message of humility is neither popular nor appreciated. At a time when looking good is considered more important than being good, and when superficial impression makes a bigger splash than solid integrity, who has time for things like submission, dependence, and trust? In our dog-eat-dog, cut-in-line lifestyle, deferring to others looks stupid and sounds silly.

In contrast to the world's narcissistic plan for success, Peter outlines in 5:5–7 the essential ingredients for *relief*.

— **5:5** —

In 5:1–4, Peter addressed pastor-elders in authority as overseers of the flock. They had been given special responsibilities necessary for effective ministry. Those principles of leadership went against the typical human tendency of "lording it over" those under authority. So, when Peter turns to the younger men, who were under the authority of those older saints, we can anticipate that he will again confound our cultural expectations.

In fact, in the Greek he begins with the adverb "likewise." Just as the older leaders are to conduct themselves in a Christlike, countercultural manner, so the younger must do so as well. Though the positions may differ, our calling to live in conformity with Christ never changes.

Who is Peter addressing in verse 5? The term *neōteros* ("younger man") can mean several things. Our English prefix "*neo*" borrows from this term, which means "new" or "young." Its most common use in the New Testament is the most general — something new as opposed to old.[8] It can also refer to a person of physically youthful age in contrast to somebody more mature.[9] It's used once in reference to the "new" identity we have in Christ after salvation (Col. 3:10). It may also generally refer to those under the authority of leaders — that is, servants, disciples, or assistants (Acts 5:6).

How does Peter use the term *neoteros* in 5:5? I think a key to understanding this use comes from Jesus' own words, no doubt recalled by Peter in this context. In the previous section on leaders, we saw the echoes of Jesus' warning about the Gentile method of leadership: "The kings of the Gentiles lord it over them … But it is not this way with you" (Luke 22:25–26a). This corresponds to Peter's call for leaders to reject "lording leadership" and to instead set an example of submissive servanthood (1 Peter 5:3). Similarly, Jesus continued: "But the one who is the greatest among you must become like the youngest [*neōteros*], and the leader like the servant" (Luke 22:26b). Thus, according to Jesus, the "greatest" in rank contrasted with the "youngest" in the same way a leader contrasts with a servant. Peter likely picks up on this contrast. Having called on leaders to serve in 1 Peter 5:1–4, he then gives directions to those who are under their leadership — the "newer" believers in verses 5–7.

This brings us to Peter's exhortation to those under the elders' authority. Simply put, they are to submit to the elders' authority. What a novel idea in this era that promotes an entrepreneurial, independent spirit necessary for personal success! But Peter doesn't stop there. With another possible allusion to the words and work of Jesus prior to His crucifixion, he instructs believers to "clothe" themselves with humility (5:5). It may be that Peter was recalling the last meal in the upper room, when Jesus — the greatest leader of all — girded Himself with a towel and washed the disciples' feet (John 13:4 – 17). The Master served the servants. The spiritually older stooped down and washed the feet of the spiritually younger.

The word Peter used for "clothe yourselves" literally means to "put or tie something on oneself."[10] Wuest notes that this word "speaks of the act of tying or tucking up the long outer garments … around the waist as a roll or band or girth … The word in its noun form referred to a slave's apron under which the loose outer garments were gathered."[11] Jesus even *looked* like their servant. What humility!

Peter's main exhortation in verse 5 is to *submit to those who are wise*. He calls the younger believers under the authority of the elders to listen to their counsel. Be open to their reproofs. Watch their lives and follow their good examples. Accept their decisions without second-guessing and challenging them. Respect their years of experience and honor their seasoned lives. All of this is included in the call for the younger believers to "be subject to" the elders.

To support his call for humility and submission, Peter paraphrases a favorite saying found in various forms throughout the Old and New Testaments.

Psalm 138:6	For though the LORD is exalted, Yet He regards the lowly, But the haughty He knows from afar.
Proverbs 3:34	He mocks proud mockers but gives grace to the humble. (NIV)
Matthew 23:12	Whoever exalts himself shall be humbled; and whoever humbles himself shall be exalted.
James 4:6	God is opposed to the proud, but gives grace to the humble.
1 Peter 5:5	God is opposed to the proud, but gives grace to the humble.

God has demonstrated His ability to humble the proud, but He also has a penchant for promoting the humble. We see this clearly in the lives of both Joseph and Daniel — two men who suffered unjustly at the hands of family members and friends. But God used their humble status to raise them up through the ranks to accomplish His purposes. All the same, God also reduces to nothing those world leaders puffed up with pride (Isa. 14:4–21; Ezek. 28:1–10; Dan. 4:28–37). This prominent theme is woven through the fabric of the Old and New Testaments.

So, the first strong word of counsel for those who want to find genuine satisfaction and true success comes from a whole parade of passages in Holy Scripture — submit yourself to those who are wise instead of flaunting your own authority. To those who genuinely submit with humility, God will provide a greater measure of grace.

— **5:6** —

The second in Peter's series of three commands has to do with our attitude. To experience true success in life, we must *humble ourselves under God's mighty hand* (5:6). God's "hand" in the Old Testament represented two things: discipline (see Ex. 3:20; Job 30:21; Ps. 32:4) and deliverance (Deut. 9:26; Ezek. 20:34). So, humbling ourselves means we accept whatever comes from Him. We follow our sovereign Lord along the smooth highways as well as the bumpy back roads. We don't manipulate events or people. We don't hurry things to conform to our own timetable. Instead, we allow our God to orchestrate things at His own tempo. Only in this way will the promise of 1 Peter 5:6 be fulfilled in us: "that He may exalt you at the proper time."

Let me illustrate. Let's say you write music and you're fairly talented. But you're a young upstart and unknown except in your small church and circle of Christian friends. But you love the Lord and want to serve Him with the talents He's given you. So you have a quandary. Do you push hard at being discovered? How hard? After all, your gifts are good only if you use them, right? What would it mean to humble yourself under God's mighty hand in this situation? We're not left to wonder.

King David serves as a good biblical example. Back in 1 Samuel 16 you find a young homegrown musician who kept his father's sheep. He had never heard the applause of the public. His world was limited to bleating sheep. But he kept playing his music and writing his songs, and all the while he had no idea that one day his original compositions would find their way into the book of Psalms. David didn't pursue fortune and glory with his music. He didn't rent a carriage to take his songs on the road. Nevertheless, more than any other collection of "hits," David's inspirational psalms have brought glory to God. In His timing, God found young David. His attitude of humility exalted him and his work to a place he never could have reached on his own. In fact, look at what Psalm 78 says about David:

He also chose David His servant
And took him from the sheepfolds;
From the care of the ewes with suckling lambs He brought him
To shepherd Jacob His people,
And Israel His inheritance.
So he shepherded them according to the integrity of his heart,
And guided them with his skillful hands. (Ps. 78:70–72)

When David humbled himself under God's mighty hand, God exalted Him at the proper time.

— **5:7** —

I've never been one to jump out of airplanes with a parachute on my back or to leap off high bridges strapped to a giant rubber band. But I suppose the feeling of freefall one experiences by skydiving or bungee jumping is similar to the way we feel when we've totally submitted to the authority of others and humbled ourselves before God. The feeling of absolute surrender and powerlessness could cause us to panic. But when we realize that our lives do not depend on a parachute or bungee cord, *but on the living God*, we'll realize that we've traded insecurity for true security. We'll discover that we'd been depending on our own man-made devices rather than trusting in God's supernatural strength.

This leads to Paul's third strategy for true success: *throw yourself on the mercy and care of God* (5:7). The original meaning of the term "cast" is literally "to throw upon."[12] It represents a decisive action on our part, neither passive nor partial. When Peter tells us to cast all our anxiety on Him, this is the means by which we humble ourselves under His mighty hand in verse 6. We surrender all those anxieties, questions, and concerns. Psalm 55:22 reflects the same thought: "Cast your burden upon the LORD and He will sustain you; He will never allow the righteous to be shaken." Similarly, Peter accompanies his exhortation of radical surrender with a reminder of the character of God. We can cast everything on Him because He cares for us.

Do you want a simple formula that will enable you not only to handle whatever success God may bring your way, but also to provide you with the relief you need? Peter gives us just such a formula in 5:5–7. It's not popular and it certainly doesn't conform to the world's advice. I should warn you that when you try to put it into practice, your natural instinct will be to resist it. But it's the raw material of a life lived in hope:

Submission to others + *Humility* before God – *Worry* of the world = *Genuine Relief*

Application

True Success

In order for us to get a grasp on what true success is and how to obtain it, we need to tune out the world's seductive messages and tune in to the instructive messages from God's Word. We need to look to Christ as the model of humility and turn away from Satan as the example of hubris. The way I see it, our great need for this reorientation involves three dimensions: direction, discipline, and discernment.

First, we need *direction* so we can know to whom we should submit. We aren't called to submit to everybody indiscriminately. But neither are we to follow our own ways in our own wisdom. Peter identifies the ones to whom we must submit: our "elders." But how do you know they're trustworthy? One way is to make sure they're pointing to Christ, not themselves. Paul wrote, "Be imitators of me, just as I also am of Christ" (1 Cor. 11:1). We should also follow those who guide us by the light of God's Word, not their own suggestions and opinions. Psalm 119:105 describes the Word as "a lamp to my feet and a light to my path." Finally, we should follow those whom God has placed in authority over us in official leadership in our churches. Hebrews 13:17 says, "Obey your leaders and submit to them, for they keep watch over your souls as those who will give an account."

Second, we need *discipline* to restrain our hellish pride. Pride will keep rearing its ugly head. The more successful you are, the more temptation you'll have to chuck God's plan for the world's. You'll start out just dabbling in the world's ways, but before you know it, you'll find yourself on the wrong road, heading in the wrong direction. First Timothy 4:7–8 offers a good perspective here: "But have nothing to do with worldly fables. On the other hand, discipline yourself for the purpose of godliness; for bodily discipline is only of little profit, but godliness is profitable for all things, since it holds promise for the present life and also for the life to come." Paul sets up a contrast between "worldly fables" and "bodily discipline" on the one hand and godliness and future-oriented hope on the other. Our pride will never sit down and stay quiet. It needs strong discipline to keep it in its place.

Third, we need *discernment* so we can spot the beginnings of anxiety. If we don't pounce on our fears the moment they begin to creep in, they'll soon latch on to our hearts and minds, choking out our joy and peace. Ever have some little worry start to nag you? You can't get it out of your head. Like a poison, it starts to eat away at your insides, and soon you're paralyzed with fear. It takes discernment to spot that kind of anxiety before it gets out of control.

Do you find yourself caught up in the success syndrome, hopelessly running on the treadmill of discontent? Are you still convinced that the world's path to success is the best? Do you find yourself manipulating people and pulling strings to get ahead? Stop! That kind of success never satisfies. Only God's formula for success brings real relief. Through submission to mature believers, humility toward God, and turning our anxieties over to Him, we can experience lasting relief. Direction, discipline, and discernment are essential components to our having enduring hope in hurtful times.

Standing Nose to Nose with the Adversary (1 Peter 5:8–14)

[8]Be of sober *spirit*, be on the alert. Your adversary, the devil, prowls around like a roaring lion, seeking someone to devour. [9]But resist him, firm in *your* faith, knowing that the same experiences of suffering are being accomplished by your brethren who are in the world. [10]After you have suffered for a little while, the God of all grace, who called you to His eternal glory in Christ, will Himself perfect, confirm, strengthen *and* establish you. [11]To Him *be* dominion forever and ever. Amen.

[12]Through Silvanus, our faithful brother (for so I regard *him*), I have written to you briefly, exhorting and testifying that this is the true grace of God. Stand firm in it! [13]She who is in Babylon, chosen together with you, sends you greetings, and *so does* my son, Mark.

[14]Greet one another with a kiss of love.

Peace be to you all who are in Christ.

With this section we arrive at the end of Peter's powerful message of hope in hurtful times. The dramatic climax of his letter reads like a general rallying his troops before leading them into battle. Peter began by reminding his readers of the fiery ordeal that will test and strengthen their faith (4:12–19). He then turned to the appointed commanders—elders of the churches—and exhorted them to lead their battalions as noble examples of Christlike leadership (5:1–4). Peter then addressed those who are younger in the faith, urging them to submit to their commanders' authority and leadership. They must follow their examples with humility, entrusting themselves to the great Commander in Chief, in whose service the battle can never be lost (5:5–7).

Finally, in this final section, Peter sounds the alarm for battle. He does so by drawing the army's attention to their spiritual opponent who plans the evil strategy behind their fiery trials (5:8). Peter informs the soldiers of Christ how to defeat the adversary (5:9). He reminds us that the fierce conflict will soon be over and that we will one day emerge as victors (5:10). Ultimately, he points to Christ, who will triumph and exercise dominion over all (5:11).

— 5:8 —

Whoever lives under the impression that Satan doesn't exist is living in a dreamworld. In clear, unmistakable terms, Peter identifies and describes the devil in verse 8.

Satan goes by several names in the Bible. The term *diabolos*, "devil," is used. This title refers to his slander of God's people.[13] The Greek word *Satanas*, "Satan," comes from a Hebrew word for "adversary."[14] In Revelation 9:11, he is called *Abbadon* and *Apollyon*, meaning "Destroyer," names that refer to his destructiveness.[15] Together these and other labels for the adversary describe him as a dangerous, destructive deceiver who slanders and accuses us at every opportunity. Revelation 12:9–10 describe Satan's future and final fall from the heavens in vivid terms that reveal both his nature and his activity:

> And the great dragon was thrown down, the serpent of old who is called the devil and Satan, who deceives the whole world; he was thrown down to the earth, and his angels were thrown down with him. Then I heard a loud voice in heaven, saying, "Now the salvation, and the power, and the kingdom of our God and the authority of His Christ have come, for the accuser of our brethren has been thrown down, he who accuses them before our God day and night."

I take Satan very seriously. No, I'm not intimidated by him. I'm not afraid of him. But I don't underestimate his power to inflict great harm on people through temptation, deception, and destruction. Satan is the source of all kinds of pain and suffering in the world — even in the lives of believers. His activities may come in subtle forms of temptation and discouragement. Or he may unleash fury, tragedy, and destruction. We can't ignore the potential damage he can do to our physical and spiritual lives. We would be wise to remember that Jesus called Satan a "murderer from the beginning" (John 8:44).

However, there is no reason to overestimate Satan's power. Too many Christians do this. They believe that anything bad that happens to them comes directly from the devil or his demons. But this is as much a mistake as underestimating his power. Satan isn't the immediate cause of all suffering and sin. Fallen, depraved human beings can do enough damage to themselves and others without the devil's prodding. Furthermore, the world system offers its own evil allurements that can take a vicious toll on the believer's walk.

Acting on these two extremes — attributing too much power or too little power to Satan — leads to either overreaction or a lack of preparation. So an awareness of some of Satan's tactics is necessary for believers. One writer notes:

> No military commander could expect to be victorious in battle unless he understood his enemy. Should he prepare for an attack by land and ignore the pos-

sibility that the enemy might approach by air or by sea, he would open the way to defeat. Or should he prepare for a land and sea attack and ignore the possibility of an attack through air, he would certainly jeopardize the campaign.

No individual can be victorious against the adversary of our souls unless he understands that adversary; unless he understands his philosophy, his methods of operation, his methods of temptation.[16]

Peter calls Satan our "adversary, the devil" (5:8). And because he's on the prowl like a lion hunting for prey, we must be "of sober spirit"; we must remain "on the alert." In each of the three major sections of 1 Peter, we are exhorted to be "sober" in spirit:

The first call to spiritual sobriety comes as a response to the assurance of our faith and the hope we have in Christ: "Therefore [in light of the promises made sure], prepare your minds for action, *keep sober in spirit*, fix your hope completely on the grace to be brought to you at the revelation of Jesus Christ" (1:13, italics mine).

The second call to sober up is found in the context of the imminent return of Christ and the need for prayerful diligence: "The end of all things is near;

GOD VERSUS SATAN?

People often think that Satan is the opposite of God — that he is God's mortal enemy and that the forces of good and evil have battled each other for eons. But this picture is not accurate, according to the biblical view of God and Satan.

The ancient Zoroastrians believed in a dualistic concept of God — that two equally powerful gods, one good and one evil, stood in opposition to each other. Similar to the Eastern concept of the yin and yang, light and dark, positive and negative, these two gods are engaged in immortal combat with each other over the obedience of humans.[17]

This ancient dualistic image of the spiritual realm has influenced many pagan religions and has even worked its way into popular art and culture. Various ancient heresies advanced a dualistic view of the world that split divinity into balancing forces of good and evil. Numerous superstitious Christians of the medieval period viewed God as the good and Satan as the evil influencers in the world. And even today films have popularized the idea of a "force" with a light and a dark side.[18]

But the Bible teaches that Satan is an angelic creature of God (Ezek. 28:12–16) who can do nothing apart from God's control or permission (Job 1:1–12; Luke 22:31). He is not an "equal but opposite" counterpart of God, but rather of the archangel Michael (Jude 9; Rev. 12:7). Yet he is also the enemy and accuser of humans (Zech. 3:1–2; 1 Peter 5:8). While we must not deny that Satan has power to attack and ensnare us (Eph. 4:27; 6:11; 1 Tim. 3:7), we also must guard against attributing to Satan more power than he actually has.

therefore, be of sound judgment and *sober spirit* for the purpose of prayer"
(4:7, italics mine).

This third and final call to stay sober and alert combines the need for firm-
ness of faith and patient endurance in the face of satanic attack as we look
forward to our eternal reward with Christ (5:8 – 10).

Like wanderers in the wild savannahs of Africa, we must always be aware that
someone is hunting us. The lion lurks quietly in tall grass, stalking our every step,
waiting for a moment to catch us off guard. If we stray from the group, put down
our weapons, or doze in the sun, he'll strike. Satan knows our weaknesses and our
strengths. He's had thousands of years to observe humankind and has become an
expert on human nature. In fact, Satan knows the depths of your depravity far
better than you do. We must never forget that we are his prey and that this roaring
lion is ravenous with hunger.

Satan prowls and pounces when we least expect it, which explains our need to
remain alert and sober. His one purpose is to destroy us — our testimonies, our
hope, our holiness, and, if possible, our lives. Therefore, we must be aware of his
tactics and have a respect for his power. In the same way as a Pacific islander might
respect the power of the volcano or a sailor must respect the devastating might of
a hurricane at sea, we must never allow ourselves to underestimate the adversary's
ability to outwit, deceive, and attack us.

— **5:9** —

What are we to do when standing nose to nose with the adversary? Panic? Run?
Surrender? No! Peter says, "Resist him, firm in your faith" (5:9). The word "resist"
means to "stand against, oppose." But this command is met with a vital qualification. We don't resist Satan with confidence in our own power or ability. Any time
we do that, we're overmatched. We are to be firm in our faith. Peter certainly isn't
speaking of faith in self, in other humans, or in some sort of method or mantra or
gimmick. Rather, we stand with unshakable faith in our all-powerful God, relying
on His defense to stand against the wicked works of the devil.

James affirms the need to stand confidently against Satan in the shadow of
God's mighty presence: "Submit therefore to God. Resist the devil and he will flee
from you. Draw near to God and He will draw near to you" (James 4:7 – 8). And
in his letter to the Ephesians, the apostle Paul expresses the same wise counsel:
"Finally, be strong in the Lord and in the strength of His might. Put on the full
armor of God, so that you will be able to stand firm against the schemes of the

devil" (Eph. 6:10 – 11). Peter, James, and Paul all knew that believers can win a decisive victory over Satan. They knew, though, that we have insufficient strength in and of ourselves. But when we turn to our Lord and draw on His limitless power through faith, we can stand against the adversary.

Peter adds another source of strength: the confidence that comes from knowing that we do not fight alone (5:9). A great army of saints, stretching throughout history right up to present-day believers, is joined in the relentless battle. Our hope gains strength when we remember that believers stand shoulder to shoulder with each other across the globe in the same spiritual battle, enduring the same kinds of suffering, facing the same kinds of obstacles, experiencing the same kind of victory. The strength that comes from God's caring and praying community cannot be appreciated enough. Support groups and prayer chains are popular for a reason — they work! God has designed the body of Christ to function in this way. Remember, we are not Lone Rangers doing hand-to-hand combat with a superior foe. Rather, we are a platoon of vigilant soldiers watching each other's backs, with a victory assured by the power of God.

— **5:10 – 11** —

Though victory is certain, Peter reminds us that suffering and pain will accompany the battle. No one who has endured enemy attack emerges without some measure of pain. The battle will shake us, shock us, and often leave ugly scars. But what happens when the dust settles? Peter lists the benefits that come with God's heavenly version of the "Purple Heart":

- He will perfect us.
- He will confirm us.
- He will strengthen us.
- He will establish us.

Peter paints the picture of a well-grounded, seasoned warrior who comes through the battle with maturity and stability that couldn't have been developed any other way. But even as we go through the necessary fiery ordeal that God allows to refine, strengthen, and grow us, we can continue to have hope because of four unforgettable truths. Every believer should inscribe these truths in his or her mind. The suffering is only "for a little while" (5:10a). It is accompanied by God's grace and calling (5:10b). It has a holy purpose that reverses and spites Satan's pursuits (5:10c). And through it all, thankfully, God remains in control (5:11).

In light of these truths, let's not confuse confidence in Christ with cockiness in the flesh. Never attempt to stand on your own, that is, to wage war against the flesh, the world, and the devil by your own means or with your own methods. As Proverbs 21:31 says, "The horse is prepared for the day of battle, / But victory belongs to the LORD." Always remember that suffering is temporary, but God's rewards are eternal. Paul expresses our hope with eloquence: "For I consider that the sufferings of this present time are not worthy to be compared with the glory that is to be revealed to us" (Rom. 8:18).

— 5:12–14 —

If you had been a member of the original Greek-speaking recipients of this letter, you would have noticed a sudden change in 1 Peter 5:12. The style of writing suddenly shifts from the elegant, flowing handwriting of a cultured composer, to the large, deliberate script of a rugged fisherman. The grammar, syntax, and vocabulary immediately change. At this point it becomes obvious that Peter's secretary, Silas, has handed the pen to the aged apostle, who personally concludes his letter with his own calloused hand.

Peter reaffirms the overall exhortation of his letter. Because we hold to the true faith in a trustworthy God, we are to stand firm in God's grace. In the midst of all oppression, mistreatment, temptation, or trials, we can endure with hope because of the sustaining power of God (5:12). In short, through Christ we can have unwavering hope.

The last few lines end with cryptic statements that continue to puzzle interpreters: the lady, the city, and the son. The first involves the personal greeting Peter passes on from an unnamed female described as "chosen together with you" (5:13). Some say that Peter refers figuratively to the church in Rome as the "bride of Christ." Others take this literally, referring perhaps to his own wife (see Mark 1:30; 1 Cor. 9:5).[19] Unfortunately, we don't have enough information to make a definite identification. Either interpretation is possible. But one thing is clear: believers in the early church had a great sense of kinship with fellow believers and churches throughout the world. This kind of concern for other Christian churches besides our own is an important lesson to remember today.

The second mystery relates to Peter's mention of "Babylon," where the woman dwells. Is this the same Babylon of the Old Testament, located in modern-day Iraq? Or is this a figure of speech, referring symbolically to another city? Or does it signify the "Babylon-like" world system? According to our earliest Christian sources outside the New Testament, Peter's ministry never extended to the literal city of Babylon in Mesopotamia. His later ministry centered in Rome. Furthermore, the literal city of Babylon had dwindled in size and significance by the first century, so it had a very small Jewish community at the time 1 Peter was written. Peter would not have had a thriving ministry in the ancient city of Babylon, especially with Silas at his side.

Most likely, then, "Babylon" in 5:13 refers to the city of Rome. This name was code language for Rome in both Jewish and Christian circles in the first and second centuries AD. The use of symbolic city names with negative or positive connotations is also used elsewhere in the New Testament (see Gal. 4:24 – 26; Rev. 11:8).[20]

Finally, who is the "Mark" mentioned at the end of verse 13? Peter calls him his "son," though this need not be taken literally, as the term is often used with reference to a close assistant or even convert in the faith (1 Tim. 1:2; Titus 1:4). We can't, however, rule out the possibility that Peter refers to a literal son named Mark. But most likely this is the same person as "John Mark" (Acts 12:12, 25; 15:37). Remember him? In the book of Acts Mark was a figure of contention between Barnabas and Paul. Barnabas wanted to bring John Mark with them on their second missionary journey; Paul opposed the idea (15:37 – 38). As a result, Barnabas took Mark with him, alone, to Cyprus while Paul took Silas and traveled with him (15:39 – 40).

> ## A FINAL SUMMARY
>
> When we step back and look at Peter's letter as a whole, we see these final themes of love, unity, peace, faith, grace, and hope running throughout the letter. He has certainly taken us on a sobering — but encouraging — journey. We first visited the theme of the *living hope* in 1:1 – 2:12. We can all claim this hope by focusing on the Lord and trusting in His Word.
>
> Peter then explored the ups and downs of our *strange life* as aliens living in a world that is not our ultimate home (2:13 – 4:11). We live as pilgrims through submission to authorities even in the midst of unjust treatment, keeping our testimony of holiness strong in the midst of an unholy world.
>
> Finally, Peter led us home through our *fiery ordeal* to land safely in the arms of the Savior for whom we are called to suffer and serve (4:12 – 5:14). We endure these trials not in isolation, but as a flock tended by faithful shepherds in the face of a dreaded but defeated foe. Through mutual love and concern and absolute reliance on the power of God, the fires sent by our enemies to consume us will serve only to purify and strengthen us.
>
> In short, Peter's magnificent letter accomplishes the vital purpose of providing essential hope in hurtful times.

It is interesting to see that both Silas and Mark are found together—working closely with Peter—some fifteen years later. This illustrates the essential unity of the apostles' ministries, despite strong disagreement along the way. Early Christian history tells us that this same Mark is responsible for the gospel that bears his name. This gospel always has been regarded as Mark's record of Peter's firsthand account. Likely it was written while Mark was with Peter in Rome, close to the writing of 1 Peter.

Peter ends this remarkable letter of hope by reemphasizing love and peace. Believers are to "greet one another with a kiss of love" (5:14). This formal kiss was a sign of peace among early Christians, demonstrating their brotherly affection, commitment, and unity (1 Cor. 16:20). The outward kiss reflected the inward peace between believers. This is why Peter can write, "Peace be to you all who are in Christ."

NOTES:

1. "How Firm a Foundation," in *The Hymnal for Worship and Celebration,* no. 275.
2. C. S. Lewis, *The Problem of Pain* (New York: Macmillan, 1962), 106.
3. Bauer et al., *A Greek-English Lexicon,* 622–23.
4. See J. E. Johnson, "Spurgeon, Charles Haddon," in *The Concise Evangelical Dictionary of Theology,* ed. Walter A. Elwell (Grand Rapids: Baker, 1991), 488.
5. Charles Haddon Spurgeon, *Lectures to My Students* (Grand Rapids: Zondervan, 1954), 7–8.
6. Bauer et al., *A Greek-English Lexicon,* 683.
7. See Genesis 48:15; Psalm 23; 100:3; Isaiah 53:6–7; Luke 15:3–7; John 10:1–16.
8. See Matthew 9:17; Mark 2:22; Luke 5:37–39; 1 Corinthians 5:7; Hebrews 12:24.
9. See Luke 15:12–13; John 21:18; 1 Timothy 5:1–2, 11, 14; Titus 2:4, 6.
10. Bauer et al., *A Greek-English Lexicon,* 216.
11. Wuest, *Wuest's Word Studies,* 2:127.
12. Bauer et al., *A Greek-English Lexicon,* 298.
13. Ibid., 182.
14. Ibid., 744–45.
15. Ibid., 1.
16. J. Dwight Pentecost, *Your Adversary, the Devil* (Grand Rapids: Zondervan, 1969), introduction.
17. See Edwin M. Yamauchi, "Religions of the Biblical World: Persia," in *The International Standard Bible Encyclopedia*, ed. Geoffrey W. Bromiley et al. (Grand Rapids: Eerdmans, 1988), 4:123–129.
18. See Robert P. Lightner, "Angels, Satan, and Demons: Invisible Beings that Inhabit the Spiritual World," in *Understanding Christian Theology*, ed. Charles R. Swindoll and Roy B. Zuck (Nashville: Nelson, 2003), 572–73.
19. See Roger M. Raymer, "1 Peter," in *The Bible Knowledge Commentary: New Testament*, ed. John F. Walvoord and Roy B. Zuck (Wheaton, IL: Victor, 1983), 857.
20. For discussions on the identification of "Babylon" in 1 Peter 5:13, see Edwin A. Blum, "1 Peter," in *The Expositor's Bible Commentary*, ed. Frank E. Gaebelein (Grand Rapids: Zondervan, 1981), 12:253–54; Loenhard Goppelt, *A Commentary on 1 Peter*, ed. Ferdinand Hahn, trans. John E. Alsup (Grand Rapids: Eerdmans, 1993), 373–75; and R. C. H. Lenski, *The Interpretation of the Epistles of St. John, St. John, and St. Jude* (Minneapolis: Augsburg, 1966), 231–32.

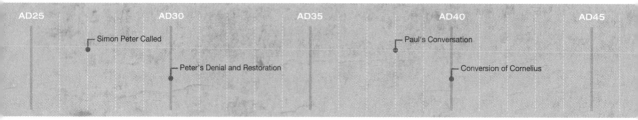

The recipients of 1 and 2 Peter in Asia Minor

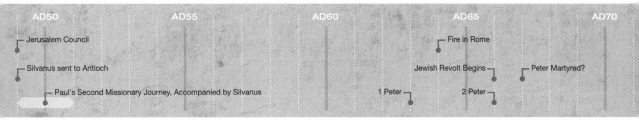

AD50   AD55   AD60   AD65   AD70

Jerusalem Council

Silvanus sent to Antioch

Paul's Second Missionary Journey, Accompanied by Silvanus

Fire in Rome

Jewish Revolt Begins

Peter Martyred?

1 Peter

2 Peter

2 PETER

Introduction

Though we sing choruses like "Turn Your Eyes upon Jesus" and "Open My Eyes, Lord, I Want to See Jesus," these are prayerful pleas for spiritual illumination, not physical encounters with the risen Christ. In fact, even in the first century, the majority of Christians never met Jesus Christ *personally*. They met Him in the same way we meet Jesus—through the preaching of apostolic eyewitnesses like Peter, James, John, Andrew, Thomas, and the rest.

The story of Christianity begins with the birth, life, death, and resurrection of Jesus Christ—events experienced by numerous witnesses (1 John 1:1–3). But the story of Christianity continues with Christ's ascension to heaven, His exaltation at the right hand of the Father, and the sending of the Spirit upon that small band of believers at Pentecost, as well as upon those witnesses of the resurrection—perhaps around five hundred men and women in all.

This continuing saga of God's explosive work of redemption in the world is the reason Luke the physician wrote a sequel to his gospel, known today as the Acts of the Apostles. That action-packed account follows the work of the Holy Spirit that spread the good news of Jesus Christ from Jerusalem, to Judea and Samaria, and far beyond that to the ends of the earth (Acts 1:8). The leading men in that adventure, without question, were the apostles Peter and Paul.

Overview of the Book of 2 Peter

Section	Exhortation to Spiritual Maturity	Denunciation of False Teachers	Anticipation of Christ's Return
Themes	**Moral Corruption** QUESTION: How can I grow in grace and escape defilement? Warning: Be pure! (1:2–4) Reminder: (1:12–14) Promise: You will never stumble (1:10) Perspective: Looking within	**Doctrinal Compromise** QUESTION: What should I expect from false teachers? Warning: Be aware! (2:1–3) Reminder: (2:21–22) Promise: The Lord will rescue you (2:9) Perspective: Looking back	**Prophetic Questions** QUESTION: What sort of people ought we to be in light of Christ's coming? Warning: Be diligent! (3:14) Reminder: (3:1–2) Promise: Look for a new heavens and earth (3:13) Perspective: Looking ahead
	Knowledge . . . Diligence . . . Remember . . . Corruption		
Key Terms	Faith Prophetic Word	Heresy Judgement Destruction	Persevere Day of the Lord Promise
Passage	1:1–21	2:1–22	3:1–18

KEY TERMS

ἐπίγνωσις [*epignōsis*] (1922) "knowledge, insight, recognition"

Similar to the more general term for knowledge, *gnōsis*, this term refers to "true" or "precise" knowledge (2 Peter 1:3, 8). This deeper knowledge refers not to mere intellectual awareness or theoretical knowledge, but to "heart knowledge." Believers do not know only *about* God; they have an intimate, personal knowledge *of* God, a knowledge that can deepen through spiritual growth (1:2; cf. 3:18).

σπουδάζω [*spoudazō*] (4704) "give diligence, make haste, exert oneself"

Christianity is not meant to be a passive faith. It calls for active participation. Peter uses a Greek word that implies hard work that results in observable change, demonstrating the authenticity of our calling (2 Peter 1:10; 3:14). To the basic foundation of faith, therefore, believers are to build Christian virtue, "applying all diligence" (1:5).

ὑπομιμνῄσκω [*hypomimnēskō*] (5279) "cause to remember, remind, recall"

This term refers to reviewing something already learned. The New Testament uses the word several times to describe the strengthening of areas of vital Christian knowledge that have been forgotten or neglected (2 Tim. 2:14; Titus 3:1). For Peter, bringing to remembrance important truths is a major purpose for his letter (2 Peter 1:12). In fact, he calls his letter a "reminder" of things his readers already know (1:13; 3:1).

φθορά [*phthora*] (5356) "destruction, corruption, decay, ruin"

This word, often translated "corruption," can have both a nonmoral and moral sense. In a neutral, nonmoral sense, it refers simply to the decay of perishable things (1 Cor. 15:50). In a moral sense, "corruption" means to engage in unnatural or unclean activities that lead to discipline or judgment (2 Peter 1:4; 2:19). It also can refer to the destruction that will come in the future judgment (2:12), so those who practice corruption will receive corruption as the outcome for their actions.

THE MINISTRY OF PETER

In fact, the book of Acts can be roughly divided between its focii on the distinct ministries of those two apostles. In the beginning of the disciples' ministry of proclaiming the resurrection of Jesus Christ, Peter often stands as the chief spokesperson.[1] Then we encounter the dramatic conversion of the hostile and passionate opponent of Christianity, Saul of Tarsus. His startling transformation into the apostle Paul marks a sudden turning point for the New Testament church (Acts 9), especially with regard to the preaching of the gospel to the Gentiles. But it's actually the apostle Peter—not Paul—who is personally involved in the first Gentile conversion to Christ: the salvation of Cornelius, the Roman centurion (Acts 10).

The next two chapters in Acts continue to follow the ministry of Peter, but in Acts 13 the point of view changes to the first missionary journey of the apostle Paul, who is called by God to bring the gospel to the Gentiles. In fact, Peter's name appears only once after chapter 13; Paul's ministry dominates Luke's account from chapter 13 to 28. (See the chart below for a comparison of the treatment each apostle receives in the book of Acts.)

The fact that Peter drops completely out of the narrative of the book of Acts could lead us to believe that Peter's ministry became irrelevant—or at least less significant—compared to Paul's daring exploits. But this would be far from the truth. Though we don't have a blow-by-blow account of Peter's ministry between about AD 45 and the end of his life around AD 67, we shouldn't interpret this to mean Peter retired from ministry, went back to his fishing business, or withdrew to a remote island away from the spotlight. Peter continued to travel widely, ministering to both Jewish and Gentile believers. What we know of the last twenty years of Peter's life comes to us from hints in the New Testament as well as accounts from early church historians.

Peter traveled from Jerusalem throughout the northern Mediterranean, likely teaching and preaching in Antioch (Gal. 2:11), Corinth (1 Cor. 1:12), and Rome (1 Peter 5:13). His believing wife accompanied him in his travels (1 Cor. 9:5). Though Peter and Paul experienced minor conflict over practical issues related to applying the truth of the gospel to a different cultural context (Gal. 2), they

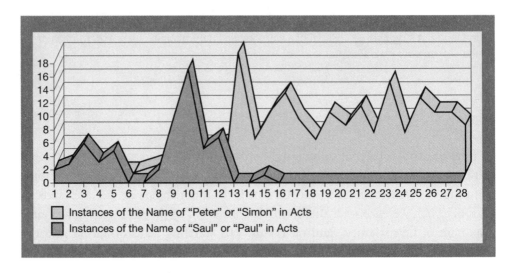

☐ Instances of the Name of "Peter" or "Simon" in Acts
☐ Instances of the Name of "Saul" or "Paul" in Acts

regarded each other's ministries as complementary and united, not conflicting and divided (Gal. 2:9; 2 Peter 3:15). In fact, their ministries overlapped, though Peter focused primarily on Jewish evangelism while Paul emphasized his Gentile mission (Gal. 2:7–8).

Toward the end of his life, Peter settled in Rome, where he ministered with Paul's early associate, Silvanus (also known as "Silas"). Silvanus assisted Peter in writing his first letter to churches in Asia Minor (1 Peter 1:1; 5:12). John Mark also was with him (5:13), and early Christian tradition informs us that Mark wrote his gospel by using Peter as his primary eyewitness source.[2]

The earliest mention of Peter after his death comes from Clement, the pastor of the church in Rome around AD 98, who may have been the same Clement mentioned by Paul in Philippians 4:3. Clement wrote in a letter to the church at Corinth, "Peter, through unrighteous envy, endured not one or two, but numerous labors, and when he had at length suffered martyrdom, departed to the place of glory due to him" (*1 Clement* 5.4). So we know that Peter became famous for his suffering, trials, and death. In fact, around AD 200 Tertullian of Carthage recalled that Peter had been crucified like Christ in Rome,[3] and the earliest accounts of the details of his death suggest that the Romans crucified him upside down, for he was unwilling to suffer in the exact manner as his Lord.

Peter suffered that final fate under the reign of Nero. The most likely location of his crucifixion was the "Circus" of Nero, an arena where numerous Christians were tortured and killed in the first and second centuries. Not long after Peter's death, a shrine was built to mark his grave. Later centuries saw a series of churches built upon the site, and today the great St. Peter's Basilica (at the Vatican) rests on the location where Peter likely was martyred and buried. Incidentally, in the 1950s, excavations beneath St. Peter's Basilica in Rome unearthed the first-century remains of a sixty- to seventy-year-old male near the traditional location of Peter's burial, and these may very well be the bones of the apostle Peter himself.

Peter wrote his second letter around AD 66, approximately one year before the aging apostle's execution. Peter knew his time on this earth was nearing its end and that he would die before the Lord returned (2 Peter 1:14). Brief but powerful, 2 Peter serves as his last written words to the churches and a permanent testament of Peter's practical teachings.

After the apostle Peter wrote the letter, churches scattered throughout five Roman provinces in Asia Minor received their second letter from him. Unlike the first letter, which pointed to Christ as the source of hope in hurtful times, Peter writes his second letter, as we would say today, to rattle some cages. He knows his time on earth is nearly up. Peter wants to leave an unfailing written record of his

The present-day plaza before St. Peter's Basilica in Vatican City. The arrow marks the approximate location where Peter probably was crucified, while his mortal remains likely are entombed deep beneath the altar under the dome.

teaching, in addition to the fading echoes of his oral preaching that soon will be forgotten. Understandably, Peter picks his battles wisely. He doesn't have time or patience for incidental matters. Instead, he treats essential themes that matter not only to his original readers, but to us as well.

TWO INITIAL OBSERVATIONS

Let me make two introductory observations about Peter's last words to the church before jumping into an overview of the letter.

First, Peter's second letter is more difficult to interpret than the first. His few short chapters are dense and sometimes difficult to interpret and understand. It will be important for us to return again and again to the overall purpose of the letter—to warn against false doctrine and moral compromise in the last days.

Second, the concern in this second letter differs from Peter's first letter. That first one focused on external sources of hardship, such as persecution by civil authorities, unfair treatment by slave owners, and an increasingly hostile pagan society. By contrast, 2 Peter addresses the problem of false teachers—people who claimed to be Christians but were not. In fact, Peter clearly states the purpose for writing this second letter: "This is now, beloved, the second letter I am writing to you in which I am stirring up your sincere mind by way of reminder, that you should remember the words spoken beforehand by the holy prophets and the commandment of the Lord and Savior spoken by your apostles" (3:1–2).

To combat the problem of heresy, Peter reaffirms the foundation of Holy Scripture—both of the Old Testament and the early writings of the apostles and prophets, which eventually would be collected to form the New Testament. Peter writes: "Therefore, I will always be ready to remind you of these things, even though you already know them, and have been established in the truth which is present with

WHO WROTE SECOND PETER?

Even though the first two words of the letter say "Simon Peter" (2 Peter 1:1), many liberal scholars doubt that the apostle wrote the book. They believe someone wrote the book long after Peter's death. The theory suggests that second-generation Christians wanted to address their own problems with the same authority as Peter. The critical scholars' complaints against the letter involve three major areas: (1) the drastic difference in style between 1 Peter and 2 Peter; (2) the limited use of the letter in the early church; and (3) its concern with issues such as Paul's writings and the delay of Christ's return that would have concerned only later generations.

First, everybody acknowledges that the two letters have different styles, vocabulary, and uses of Greek grammar. One of the main reasons for this is that the first letter was written "through Silvanus" (1 Peter 5:12). This likely meant that Silvanus assisted in writing the letter, serving, perhaps, as Peter's translator and/or secretary. The language of 1 Peter is noticeably more polished and precise.[4] We have no indication that Peter had that same level of help writing his second letter. Peter's name alone is mentioned as the author (2 Peter 1:1), though he could have used a different, unnamed assistant to help write the second letter.[5]

Second, it is true that 2 Peter didn't have as wide a popularity as 1 Peter. It isn't quoted as often by later Christians in their writings and doesn't appear in the earliest list of New Testament books. But the process of copying and collecting the inspired writings of the New Testament apostles and prophets took time, and the historical situation in which the letter was written could have limited the ability of communities in Asia Minor to pass it around to other churches. In fact, as early Christians around the Roman Empire got hold of 2 Peter, they soon identified it as inspired Scripture from the apostle Peter.[6]

Third, with the rise of false teachers in the 60s and the arrest and martyrdom of many original disciples, questions regarding the use of Paul's writings and the delayed return of Christ were bound to come up. As the authoritative apostles and prophets were dying, where would the churches turn for authoritative teaching? Peter answers by pointing not only to the Old Testament (1:19–21), but also to the teachings of Jesus and all the apostles (1:16–18; 3:1, 15–16). And as the original apostles passed off the scene, many scratched their heads and wondered why Christ hadn't come back during that first generation. Peter addresses this issue as well, confirming that the delay of the end affords more opportunities for repentance, but that the return of Christ will come suddenly.

In short, no compelling reason exists to doubt that the apostle Peter wrote 2 Peter toward the very end of his life to address issues he knew — by the wisdom of the Holy Spirit — would concern Christians long after his departure.

you. I consider it right, as long as I am in this earthly dwelling, to stir you up by way of reminder" (1:12–13). Because of his inevitable passing and the imminent threat of false teachers, Peter wants to stir up their memories of sound teaching, spur them on to diligence in the faith, and shore up the biblical foundations of their beliefs and practice.

OVERVIEW OF THE BOOK

Like the feathers, shaft, and head of an arrow, Peter develops three themes that guide his letter to a particular point. We might name the three feathers *warnings*—"watch out, beware"; *reminders*—"Remember, don't forget"; and *promises*—"It will happen, count on this." Peter doesn't use these feathers to tickle the ears of his readers. Instead, they help guide the diligent application of these truths; thus, the label on the shaft of our imaginary arrow that he shoots in chapter 1 is *diligence*—diligence in fostering within oneself Christian moral behavior. The basic question Peter faces is: "How can I grow in grace and escape the defilement of the world?" If Peter's readers diligently heed his warnings, consider the reminders, and embrace the promises, the arrow will reach its intended target: *hope*.

Chapter 2 shifts from a context of moral corruption to the second major issue: doctrinal compromise. Peter addresses the critical question, "What should I expect from false prophets?" Firing his second arrow, he first gives a *warning* that false prophets are coming (2:1–3). He then provides a *reminder* that false teaching brings judgment (2:21–22). And he also shares a *promise*—God will rescue the righteous from wrath (2:9). This second arrow calls for *diligence* in avoiding false teachers and their apostate teachings (2:1–3). It also aims for a *hope* that comes from God's promise to preserve His people (2:10).

Finally, chapter 3 presents Peter's prophetic concerns. He advances the question, "How will all this end?" That is, he addresses issues related to the coming of Christ and the end times. This third arrow serves as a final *warning*—avoid worldly corruption and false teachers (3:11, 17–18). It also functions as a last *reminder* that the biblical testimony is trustworthy (3:1–2). And here Peter proclaims a glorious *promise*—a new creation is coming in which righteousness dwells (3:13). This final arrow calls for *diligence* to be found spotless (3:14). And it finds its target in an unwavering hope—both now and forever (3:12, 18).

Beware! Be ready! Those two commands could succinctly summarize the theme of Peter's second letter. Peter addresses moral corruption (chap. 1), doctrinal compromise (chap. 2), and prophetic concerns (chap. 3). Having matured in his own faith and having reached the end of his life, Peter wants to leave a written legacy for some of the most pressing concerns facing the young church. Like a last will and testament to believers of every generation, Peter writes this rapid-fire, urgent reminder to warn against false doctrine and moral compromise in the last days. And because the Holy Spirit inspired his writing, his final words remain as timely for us as they were for believers in the first century.

Application

Living HOPE in Second Peter

Using each of the letters of the word "HOPE," let me share four important tips on how we can maintain the diligent, alert spirit Peters urges believers of every generation to pursue.

H — *Heed what you already know* (1:12 – 13; 3:1 – 2). Many of us have learned enough truth in our lives to hold us strong and keep us faithful. For most of us, the problem isn't a lack of biblical knowledge, but of personal application. We can get so caught up in learning more biblical truth that we forget to heed the truth we already know. Because we so easily forget the basics, we must often return to the foundation of our Christian beliefs and practices. If you've gotten into the rut of acquiring biblical, theological, and historical knowledge without a lifestyle that reflects it, take a step back and give attention to the basic disciplines of the faith — prayer, confession, fellowship, and worship. Heed what you already know.

O — *Open your eyes and ears* (2:1 – 3; 3:17). Discernment is a developed skill. New Christians sometimes soak up ideas and habits that have nothing to do with authentic Christian belief and practice. Part of the growing process involves developing a better ability to filter these things through a more mature grid. Pay attention to your sources of knowledge. Give further attention not only to what teachers say, but to what they don't say. Study the lives of preachers who claim to teach the Word of God. Are they living it? Do they affirm the authority of Scripture, or do they push their own or somebody else's authority above the Bible? Aids to help us interpret and apply Scripture are one thing, but replacing Scripture with a competing source of truth and motivation is something else. Open your eyes and ears and keep them open.

P — *Pursue a godly lifestyle* (1:5 – 8; 3:11, 14). Throughout the New Testament, whenever the subject of Christ's return or end times surfaces, almost without exception the Scriptures emphasize living a pure life. The Bible doesn't waste words on theory without practice. It doesn't indulge in ideas without action. So when we approach 2 Peter, we must be eager to put its words into action. We must eagerly pursue a godly lifestyle.

E — *Expect Christ's return* (3:12). Live in light of the end. Begin the day with a recurring reminder that He could come today. Don't join ranks with the scoffers and skeptics who throw Christ's past and present works into doubt because He hasn't yet carried out His promise. Instead, embrace the truth that He is coming when we least expect Him. It will make a major difference. It will affect your priorities, purpose, and pursuits. It will change your attitudes and actions. It will transform your outlook and worldview. Expect Christ's return. Live on tiptoe.

NOTES:

1. See Acts 1:15–22; 2:14–40; 3:1–26; 4:8–12; 5:1–11.
2. Papias of Hierapolis, *Fragments of Papias* 6.1.
3. Tertullian, *Prescription against the Heretics* 36.
4. See introduction to 1 Peter for a discussion of Silvanus's involvement in the writing of the letter.
5. See Kenneth O. Gangel, "2 Peter," in Walvoord and Zuck, *The Bible Knowledge Commentary*: *New Testament*, 860.
6. See Edwin A. Blum, "2 Peter," in Gaebelein, *The Expositor's Bible Commentary,* 12:257–61.

EXHORTATION TO SPIRITUAL MATURITY (2 PETER 1:1–21)

Staring out of the second-story window from his secret dwelling in Rome, the gray-haired Simon Peter looked west across the Tiber River toward the distant hill of Mount Vaticanus. If he squinted, he could trace the outline of the arena of Caligula, where Nero had been making sport of Christians—torturing them, burning them, hanging them, crucifying them, even feeding them to wild animals. So far the Lord had prevented Peter's capture, but he knew it was only a matter of time. Though he wasn't yet sure when, where, or how it would happen, the Lord had revealed to him that he would soon depart this life. At any moment he would hear the door downstairs burst open, the clank of Roman armor, outbursts of coarse Latin slang, and the drawing of swords. Bound like a dangerous criminal, he would be dragged away for a sham trial and condemned to a tortuous sentence that far outweighed his alleged "crimes."

He closed his eyes and recalled the quiet but somber words of his Lord, "Truly, truly, I say to you, when you were younger, you used to gird yourself and walk wherever you wished; but when you grow old, you will stretch out your hands and someone else will gird you, and bring you where you do not wish to go" (John 21:18). The Lord, of course, had it right. Though Peter had grown old, he didn't want to go. Not because he didn't want to see His Lord again and to be reunited in glory with those who had already died for their faith—he did! But as he looked around, he saw so much work left to be done.

With persecution under the now insane Nero accelerating in frequency and severity, many believers already had grown silent or even fallen away. Others, overburdened with worry and fear, bottomed out in their spiritual progress, like a fishing boat weighed down in shallow water. They needed a nudge into deeper waters to dislodge their lives and a fresh gust of the Spirit's breath to push them along their original course. The question haunted Peter: *Who will provide that nudge when I am gone?*

Also in recent years a few false teachers had weaseled their way into the Christian community. Some were easy to spot—like that scoundrel of Samaria, Simon the Magician, now claiming to be a god. In fact, he had snared so many followers by his devil-inspired magical arts that some Romans had erected a statue in his honor on the Tiber that read, "SIMONI DEO SANCTO"—"To Simon, the holy god."[1] Peter knew that Simon's form of "knowledge" was but the first trickles of a

KEY TERMS

πίστις [*pistis*] (4102) "faith, trust, the [Christian] faith"

Though "faith" in the New Testament most often refers to assent, belief, and trust in Christ as the means of salvation, sometimes it refers to the whole *content* of Christian belief — "the Christian faith." This is the likely meaning in 2 Peter 1:1. It is also the foundation on which every other virtue of the Christian life is built (1:5).

προφητικὸς λόγος [*prophētikos logos*] (4397 + 3056) "prophetic word, message of the prophets"

The key phrase "prophetic word" appears only once in the New Testament (2 Peter 1:19), where it is parallel to "prophecy of Scripture" (1:20). Therefore, the phrase "prophetic word" refers to the written Word of God — the Bible. The word "prophecy" does not necessarily mean foretelling the future. It most often refers to divine revelation given through prophets (Rom. 12:6; 1 Cor. 13:2). So, the "prophetic word" is the message of accurate and reliable revelation from the prophets as recorded in Scripture.

flood of heresy about to burst from the abyss. Again, the question: *Who will protect the flock from such wolves when I am gone?*

Peter sighed as he pulled out his scroll and stylus. Years ago the resurrected Lord had instructed him, "Simon, tend My lambs. Shepherd My sheep" (see John 21:15–17). With his departure near and the ravenous wolves and roaring lions on the prowl, Peter knew the fledgling flock would be in danger of deception after his departure. With pen in hand, he began to write his last words to the sheep: "Simon Peter, a bond-servant and apostle of Jesus Christ, to those who have received a faith of the same kind as ours ..."

In the first major section of 2 Peter, the aging author addresses the coming moral corruption of the last days (1:4–21) — a condition he already perceives from his vantage point in the persecuted church in Rome. He answers the urgent question his readers would surely ask: "How can I avoid defilement?" He warns them to avoid the corruption of the world (1:4). Then he reminds them of the provision of power supplied to them, as well as their need for active participation, resulting in usefulness and fruitfulness in the Christian life (1:5–13). Peter also extends the promise that holy living brings stability, the ability to stand against temptation and false teaching by the power of God (1:10). With these themes guiding his apostle's pen, Peter begins to exhort the scattered flocks to endure with diligence and to persevere with hope (1:19). Soon he will be taken from them ... but, he prays, his words will remain long after his body lies cold in the ground.

A Fruitful Faith (2 Peter 1:1–11)

> [1] Simon Peter, a bond-servant and apostle of Jesus Christ,
>
> To those who have received a faith of the same kind as ours, by the righteousness of our God and Savior, Jesus Christ: [2] Grace and peace be multiplied to you in the knowledge of God and of Jesus our Lord; [3] seeing that His divine power has granted to us everything pertaining to life and godliness, through the true knowledge of Him who called us by His own glory and excellence. [4] For by these He has granted to us His precious and magnificent promises, so that by them you may become partakers of *the* divine nature, having escaped the corruption that is in the world by lust. [5] Now for this very reason also, applying all diligence, in your faith supply moral excellence, and in *your* moral excellence, knowledge, [6] and in *your* knowledge, self-control, and in *your* self-control, perseverance, and in *your* perseverance, godliness, [7] and in *your* godliness, brotherly kindness, and in *your* brotherly kindness, love. [8] For if these *qualities* are yours and are increasing, they render you neither useless nor unfruitful in the true knowledge of our Lord Jesus Christ. [9] For he who lacks these *qualities* is blind *or* short-sighted, having forgotten *his* purification from his former sins. [10] Therefore, brethren, be all the more diligent to make certain about His calling and choosing you; for as long as you practice these things, you will never stumble; [11] for in this way the entrance into the eternal kingdom of our Lord and Savior Jesus Christ will be abundantly supplied to you.

Just about every person I know wants the same two things in life. We all want our lives to *matter to others* and we want our lives to *make a contribution*. To put it another way, everybody feels the need to be significant, to have some kind of unique purpose to fulfill in this life rather than to take up space with a purposeless existence. They also want to leave behind a legacy when they're gone, to bestow meaningful results of their labors on future generations. Once in a while I stumble on a few exceptions to this general principle. Some who are, for some reason, incessantly wicked or excessively depressed have completely lost their way. But as a general rule, most people want to be *useful* and *fruitful*.

Like a nagging hunger or lingering thirst, people crave purpose and meaning. Physical needs can be met while spiritual needs go completely neglected. The disastrous result plays havoc with a person's mental and emotional states. Perhaps this is why chronic illness is so difficult to bear. Lying in bed can result in empty feelings of uselessness as our bodies atrophy and our spirits wither. Or take elderly shut-ins who rarely, if ever, make it out of their homes. After just a short stint of feeling unproductive, they often feel like prisoners of their own inactivity, which can lead to regret, sadness, and bitterness.

IF JESUS IS "GOD," WHO'S THE FATHER?

Don't miss the fact that Peter refers to Jesus as "our God and Savior" (1:1). This is one from among a handful of places in the New Testament where Jesus is explicitly referred to as "God." But to avoid the error that Peter might be replacing the God of the Old Testament with Jesus, he makes a distinction between "God" and "Jesus Christ" in his opening blessing, where he refers to the grace and peace that come from the knowledge "of God and of Jesus our Lord" (1:2).

The apostle John makes the same distinction when he says that Jesus (the "Word") was both "with God" and "was God" (John 1:1), and that no one has ever seen God, but that "the only begotten God" has revealed Him (1:18). Paul, too, describes the Lord as "our great God and Savior, Christ Jesus" (Titus 2:13), but also makes the distinction between "God the Father" and "Christ Jesus our Savior" (1:4). The author of Hebrews applies the Old Testament name, Yahweh ("Lord"), to Jesus when he quotes Psalm 102:25 — "You, Lord, in the beginning laid the foundation of the earth" (Heb. 1:10), but makes it a point to clarify that the divine Son of God is the one "through whom" God made the world (1:1–2).

The solution to this string of apparent double-talk lies at the heart of the biblical doctrine of the Trinity. The Son of God — who took on true humanity in the incarnation — is fully God, equal to God the Father, as is God the Holy Spirit. But this doesn't mean that the Father, Son, and Holy Spirit are the same *person* with three different names. Rather, the Father, Son, and Holy Spirit are three distinct (not separate) divine Persons who have eternally existed in union with one another. Therefore, all three divine Persons are properly called "God," "Lord," "Savior," and "Creator," though God the Father, God the Son, and God the Holy Spirit are distinct in their roles and activities in the history of creation and salvation.

The German poet Johann Goethe once said, "A useless life is only an early death" — but this kind of living death isn't limited to those who are physically incapable of making a contribution to the lives of others. The bored student, the burnt-out CEO, and the bone-weary mother may all slip into feelings of uselessness and fruitlessness. It happens to unbelievers who have embraced the empty philosophies of the world system, but it can also happen to believers who have lost track of their diligence in pursuing God's meaning and purpose for their lives.

The first section of Peter's letter provides clear counsel on how to keep from feeling useless and unfruitful. Written to people just like you and me, this letter begins by focusing on the kind of lifestyle that will keep us from slipping into irrelevance. Pay close attention to Peter's words. Nobody wants to look back over their years with regret, concluding that they have lived useless and fruitless lives.

— **1:1–3** —

Peter begins his letter with a simple identification: "Simon Peter, a bond-servant and apostle of Jesus Christ" (1:1). Peter doesn't merely emphasize his apostleship in this second letter, he also identifies with his fellow Christians — bond-servants of Christ. Interestingly, he combines his birth name, Simon, with the name Christ gave him upon his confession of Jesus as the Messiah (Matt.

16:16–18), Peter. Behind this simple statement the old fisherman-turned-apostle demonstrates that he does not hesitate to point out the God-given new identity and significance he has through Christ, though this identity is accompanied by a humble calling.

In keeping with his humble introduction, Peter counts himself among the readers as having "a faith of the same kind" as theirs. That is, both Peter as a believing Jew and his readers as believing Jews and Gentiles have been equally called, saved, and equipped to live the Christian life because of the righteousness of Christ. Together they are "fellow heirs," "fellow members," and "fellow partakers" of the same grace and peace that unites them in Jesus Christ (see Eph. 3:1–6).

Christians experience ever-increasing grace and peace "in the knowledge" of God and Christ (1:2). The word for "knowledge" here (*epignōsis*) refers not to mere intellectual awareness, or to theoretical knowledge, but to "heart knowledge." Peter and his fellow believers do not merely know *about* God and Jesus; rather, they share an intimate relationship with their God—they literally *know* God through Jesus Christ. The point is that when intimate "heart knowledge" of God through Christ increases, our grace and peace increase as we become more like Christ.

Peter continues his thought of growing in grace, peace, and knowledge of God in verse 3 as he emphasizes that God's divine power—not our own effort at self-reformation—gives us everything we need for "life and godliness." When our lives are immersed in this God-given power, two things happen: our relationships with others become more useful and fruitful and our relationship with God abounds in godliness. That adds up to "everything" we need!

But note that God doesn't merely provide a spiritual seed that we ourselves need to water and cultivate by our own strength in order to develop it into a fruitful Christian life. No, God provides *everything* we need—from the seed to the sunlight, from the hoe to the harvesting tools. Through the indwelling person of the Holy Spirit, all believers are fully equipped with the power of God when they first believe (see Eph. 3:16). Wonderful thought!

This magnificent truth provides no excuse for passivity but is an invitation for participation. While God provides everything necessary for us, still we must act. The fact that we must use the power God has given us in no way negates the fact that God is completely responsible for the cause and the effects. Paul illustrates this important point about our spiritual growth when he writes, "I planted, Apollos watered, but God was causing the growth. So then neither the one who plants nor the one who waters is anything, but God who causes the growth" (1 Cor. 3:6–7). Did you catch that? Paul and Apollos were active, not passive. They were doing real work, and had they not participated in the work of the ministry, growth would not have occurred. Yet at the same time, Paul acknowledged that through the process, God Himself was causing the growth.

Along with our initial salvation, God has equipped us—by the indwelling Spirit—with an introductory packet that includes everything we need. We have access to resources that, when utilized, will result in usefulness and fruitfulness both horizontally (our relationships with others) and vertically (our relationship with God). But having the right equipment is no guarantee that we will benefit from it. We must use that equipment properly. This leads directly into the thoughts Peter develops in verses 4 through 9.

—1:4–9—

In light of God's powerful provision (1:3) and His precious "promises" (1:4), Peter calls us to step out in diligent participation (1:5–9). God has given us—at conversion—"precious and magnificent promises" (1:4). These promises become ours when we are spiritually united with Christ by the invisible yet dynamic work of the Holy Spirit. Becoming partakers of Christ, we inherit all the promises that go along with our union with Him. Paul wrote, "For as many as are the promises of God, in Him they are yes; therefore also through Him is our Amen to the glory of God through us. Now He who establishes us with you in Christ and anointed us is God, who also sealed us and gave us the Spirit in our hearts as a pledge" (2 Cor. 1:20–22). What are some of these promises?

- forgiveness of all our sins—past, present, and future
- spiritual adoption by God the Father
- spiritual strength by the Holy Spirit
- comfort through suffering and hardship
- provision of our needs
- hope of heaven when we die
- bodily resurrection when He returns
- reigning with Him in His kingdom

The list of promises could go on and on. But this sampling gives us a handful of examples to help us understand how Peter can say that "by them" we can achieve two things: (1) we "become partakers of the divine nature," and (2) we "escape the corruption that is in the world." These two are the positive and negative aspects of putting to use the provision God has given us, relying on the promises that accompany salvation. That is, as we put away the lust that causes corruption, we increasingly partake of the divine nature. We become, quite literally, more and more like Christ in both our inner beings and our outward actions. What has been once-for-all declared by grace through faith — our righteousness before God — becomes progressively manifest in our everyday lives — our righteous behavior before God and others. The former is called "justification" (when we are declared righteous); the other is called "sanctification" (when we are made increasingly more righteous).

How does this righteousness become a part of our lives? Peter answers this question in verse 5. Because God has given us power and promises, our participation takes the form of "applying all diligence" (1:5). The phrase is an idiom that literally means "to bring every effort to" some task. It implies haste, eagerness, and determination. It means to apply ourselves as much as possible.[2]

With this kind of diligence Peter tells his readers to "supply" a number of things "in your faith." Note that faith already is present. Faith is the foundation, the taproot of the Christian life. It means relying on what Peter has described as the provision and promises for spiritual growth. It means abandoning ourselves to our God — His will, His strength, His wisdom. Upon this foundation of faith — focused on Christ and established by the Holy Spirit — we are to build. So, to "supply" to this foundation means to add to it, to advance it toward an objective. Peter then lists seven qualities to be added to this foundation of faith.

Moral excellence (1:5). Synonymous with "virtue," this implies moral fortitude, courage, the ability (based on internal motivators) to do what's right and to stand alone, if necessary. Here it emphasizes the inner disposition of moral correctness more than specific observable activities, which will come later in Peter's list.

Knowledge (1:5). This refers to practical knowledge — knowledge learned by keen observation and experience. Peter used the same word, *gnōsis*, in 1 Peter 3:7, encouraging a husband to live with his wife (lit.) "according to *knowledge*," meaning to know a wife personally and intimately. It's the same word used with reference to personal knowledge of Jesus Christ through an intimate relationship (Phil. 3:8).

Self-control (1:6). As believers building on faith with moral excellence and knowledge, we must never allow anything or anyone to control us except the Master. Not money, sex, power, food, drink, drugs, habits, work, or personal goals. Self-control means maintaining a balanced life, even when the world encourages indulgence. It means saying "No" to the second helping . . . or the second glance.

Perseverance (1:6). Believers must keep on the narrow path even when everything around us tries to push us off. Remain steadfast, stable, clearheaded in the midst of distress or disaster. The word means to "remain under" whatever may come. It requires a firm footing on the foundation of faith, a clear focus on the pursuit of hope, and an unparalleled patience.

Godliness (1:6). The Greek word *eusebeia* means authentic piety, and it runs in two directions. First, it refers to one who has the right perspective and attitude toward God, showing the proper reverence and worship due the Almighty. Second, it reflects itself in a right view toward others—a genuine servant's heart, giving others their proper honor and respect.

Brotherly kindness (1:7). The word *philadelphia* refers to treating others as if they were members of our own family. It includes living in such close relationship with others that we bear one another's burdens, feel each other's joys and pains. We make room for others' opinions, feelings, ideas, and suggestions. Brotherly love is the key to living in true and harmonious community.

Love (1:7). The whole seven-step ladder from the foundation of "faith" leads to love—*agapē*. This kind of love seeks the highest good for others, putting their needs above self; it means unconditional devotion. God demonstrated this kind of love by sending Jesus Christ (Rom. 5:8). Paul, like Peter, marks this kind of love as the highest Christian virtue (1 Cor. 13:13).

What a list! If Peter hadn't prefaced these steps from faith to love with a reminder of the divine provision of power (1:3), these seven tiers built on the foundation of faith might appear as insurmountable as Mount Everest. But accompanied by God's promises and presence through the Spirit, we can take Peter's instruction seriously and begin to apply diligence, having a firm hope that God will work in us and with us as we grow more like Christ.

Peter then reveals the purpose of cultivating these virtues. We don't engage in these things to earn salvation—that's already ours by grace through faith plus nothing! In fact, we wouldn't even have the necessary power available to us if we weren't already saved. Rather, Peter says that if these things are present in our lives and increasing through diligence, we will be *useful* and *fruitful* in our Christian lives (1:8).

Peter acknowledges that not everybody will maintain the diligence that leads to maturity. Some blind believers fail to look back on their conversion, when God purified them from their sins. Shortsighted believers cannot look far enough ahead to see the coming of Christ and His reward to the faithful. So, those focusing on the present life and living for themselves will lack these qualities and squander the provision of power God has given them (1:9).

— **1:10–11** —

Peter caps his exhortation to spiritual maturity with another appeal for diligence. He tells us to "make certain about His calling and choosing" (1:10). This doesn't mean that we must do these things to secure our salvation or to guarantee our places in heaven. Rather, this is an urgent and passionate appeal to live out our calling, to demonstrate the reality of our salvation. The entire context supports the fact that Peter already regarded his readers as "brethren" who had been called and provided everything necessary for godly living. He appeals to them to subjectively live out that objective calling through spiritual growth. One commentator writes, "One's godly behavior is a warranty deed for himself that Jesus Christ has cleansed him from his past sins and therefore that he was in fact called and elected by God."[3] The result of diligence is not salvation but stability, usefulness, and fruitfulness. With these things comes eternal reward upon Christ's return.

In fact, verse 11 speaks of God abundantly supplying us with a grand entrance into the kingdom of Jesus Christ. This target of hope at Christ's return should encourage us to press on, unwavering in diligence. If we do so, we will receive great reward. But if we fail to grow in our faith, we will lose reward at the judgment seat of Christ, as Paul sternly warns: "If any man's work which he has built on it remains, he will receive a reward. If any man's work is burned up, he will suffer loss; but he himself will be saved, yet so as through fire" (1 Cor. 3:14–15).

We don't want to face the Lord Jesus Christ ashamed of uselessly and fruitlessly squandering the powerful provision and precious promises He bestowed on us at our salvation. Rather, we must heed Peter's warnings, reminders, and promises, and through diligence in spiritual growth, aim for the target of hope in Christ's return.

Application

A Secure Investment

In the world of financial investments, nothing is guaranteed. Even the lowest risk investment strategies can potentially result in loss—or in such a small gain that it hardly seems worth the effort. The same can be true in pursuing education. Although most of the time the hard work of achieving an advanced degree pays off, sometimes graduates at every level will have a difficult time finding a job that makes the long years in the classroom seem worthwhile. Our careers can play the same trick on us. We can put in long hours, give 100 percent, and do everything in the playbook to get ahead, but we can still fail to see a return on the investment of our time and energy as we keep hitting our head against a glass ceiling of opportunity.

By contrast, none of this is true about investing our time, energies, and resources into spiritual growth. God has given us irrevocable promises that what we invest in our spiritual lives, He will duly reward. We never have to wonder or worry about whether our godliness, perseverance, and love are worth it. First Timothy 4:8 reminds us that "godliness is profitable for all things, since it holds promise for the present life and also for the life to come." Likewise, Hebrews 6:10–12 describes this beautifully:

For God is not unjust so as to forget your work and the love which you have shown toward His name, in having ministered and in still ministering to the saints. And we desire that each one of you show the same diligence so as to realize the full assurance of hope until the end, so that you will not be sluggish, but imitators of those who through faith and patience inherit the promises.

How should we respond to this great promise of a guaranteed return on our investment of diligence? Clearly, Peter urges us to build a pyramid of Christian virtues on the foundation of faith. Take a moment to review Peter's list of virtues, checking off those you feel are most developed in your life. Then circle any that you believe need cultivation.

Every one of us is unique. How we nurture each of these qualities will vary depending on our backgrounds, temperaments, personalities, and experiences. But take time to reflect on how you can strengthen the qualities you lack. For everyone this must begin with prayer, especially a prayer of thanksgiving to God for providing us everything we need to live in a way that pleases Him. Then petition Him to make that power evident in your life, based on His promises to do so. Finally, participate! Take specific steps to put away behavior that does not build from faith toward love.

Will this take time? Yes! Will it take energy! Of course! But you can rest assured that your investment will be eternally secure . . . and your return on investment will be incredibly gratifying!

Be Sure of Your Source (2 Peter 1:12–21)

---

¹²Therefore, I will always be ready to remind you of these things, even though you *already* know *them*, and have been established in the truth which is present with *you*. ¹³I consider it right, as long as I am in this *earthly* dwelling, to stir you up by way of reminder, ¹⁴knowing that the laying aside of my *earthly* dwelling is imminent, as also our Lord Jesus Christ has made clear to me. ¹⁵And I will also be diligent that at any time after my departure you will be able to call these things to mind.

¹⁶For we did not follow cleverly devised tales when we made known to you the power and coming of our Lord Jesus Christ, but we were eyewitnesses of His majesty. ¹⁷For when He received honor and glory from God the Father, such an utterance as this was made to Him by the Majestic Glory, "This is My beloved Son with whom I am well-pleased" — ¹⁸and we ourselves heard this utterance made from heaven when we were with Him on the holy mountain.

¹⁹*So* we have the prophetic word *made* more sure, to which you do well to pay attention as to a lamp shining in a dark place, until the day dawns and the morning star arises in your hearts. ²⁰But know this first of all, that no prophecy of Scripture is *a matter* of one's own interpretation, ²¹for no

prophecy was ever made by an act of human will, but men moved by the Holy Spirit spoke from God.

I hear it often. Christians freely toss out phrases like "God told me" or "the Lord spoke to me." Those who give such testimony don't like to be cross-examined on exactly *how* God spoke to them. Why? Because when you look at the sources of their messages from the Lord, quite frankly, they usually lack biblical justification. In fact, sometimes they flat out contradict God's written Word!

Now, I'm not talking about people who sense God's leading through the orchestration of prayer, meditation on God's Word, guiding circumstances, and godly counsel. Often when people say "God led me" or "God showed me," that's what they mean. But sometimes when they claim God spoke to them or revealed something to them, they're making much bolder claims. They believe they've received a bona fide message directly from the Almighty! Occasionally I will ask if His voice is baritone or bass. (Folks don't like that question.)

During my lifetime I've seen all kinds of methods come and go, all claiming to be sure sources of revelation from God ... or at least from the supernatural world. The kaleidoscope of claims is maddening — the zodiac, crystals, cards, beads, dreams, visions, voices from the dead, signs and symbols, inner feelings, aliens, angelic beings, cloud formations, and personal conversations with the Holy Spirit Himself! Not only do these sources of "truth" contradict each other; more often than not they contradict what Scripture declares.

But how do we know the Bible can be trusted? Why is God's Word set apart from all other claims of divine revelation? Why does it stand above all other standards of divine truth? In 1:12–21, Peter reminds us of the only reliable source of truth — the Holy Scriptures — and tells us why God's sacred Word can, and *must*, be trusted as the sure standard for our beliefs and actions.

This is a vital topic in a letter written to stir up believers' memories regarding sound teaching, to spur them on to diligence in the faith, and to shore up the biblical foundations of their beliefs and practices. In verses 12–18, Peter reminds us what the truth *is* and *isn't*. Then, in verses 19–21, he gives us a rare description of the process by which God communicated his Word through human authors in the Holy Scriptures and why we can be sure of our source.

— 1:12–14 —

In light of present benefits and future rewards, Peter has exhorted his readers to diligently develop Christian virtues in the upward journey from foundational faith to unconditional love (1:1–11). Peter then says that he will continue to remind them of these things so long as he remains in his earthly dwelling—that is, as long as he is physically alive (1:12–13). The fact that he "reminds" them means that Peter is not writing about new revelations or radical principles they have never heard. Instead, Peter clearly states they already know these things and have been "established in the truth" (1:12). So important are these things that Peter makes sure to reinforce them one last time, knowing by special revelation from the Lord (divine communication was not uncommon among apostles) that he will soon be suffering martyrdom (1:14).

So, basic Christian truth is something in which God's people are to be "established" and of which they are to be reminded (1:12). Truth isn't a cosmic guessing game we stumble upon if we're lucky, nor is it or a mysterious riddle waiting to be solved by clever people. And it's not vague, uncertain, or indefinite; it doesn't change with the winds of culture or the whims of experience. The fact that Peter reminds them of the truth in which they were *previously* established underscores that it doesn't change.

Peter also says that truth is objective. It can be expressed in words that can be called to mind (1:15). Truth establishes believers in the faith, regards God's own person and will, and reveals the reality of human life—past, present, and future.

— **1:16–18** —

Having touched on what truth *is* (1:12–15), Peter then describes what truth is *not* (1:16–18). Drawing on his own experience as a chosen apostle of Jesus Christ, he answers the doubts of some who may not view Christian claims as reflecting dependable truth.

Truth is not myth. Peter's word "tales" comes from the Greek word *mythos*, which gives us our English word *myth*. Myths are speculations, fables, or fictions dreamed up by people to illustrate life, compare analogies to spiritual truths, or simply entertain people by drawing them into a moving story. Peter was surrounded by ancient religions of the Romans, Greeks, Persians, and Egyptians, who concocted all sorts of myths regarding the exploits of their gods.

Fictional movies and novels would be the modern equivalent of myths. *Star Wars* may entertain, delight, move, and excite us, but nobody in his right mind would believe these characters really existed somewhere in a galaxy far, far away! And though some epic stories like J. R. R. Tolkein's *Lord of the Rings* or C. S. Lewis's *Chronicles of Narnia* contain intentional parallels to Christian truths, nobody believes in the existence of Middle Earth or that a parallel universe exists in a spare closet! Such fantastic stories are easily discerned as mythological fictions.

Peter makes it perfectly clear that the foundational Christian claims about the coming of Christ, His death, and His resurrection do *not* fall into the genre category of "myth." How could Peter make such a claim with certainty? Because he was an eyewitness! He and other disciples had seen the majesty of Christ with their own eyes (1:16). And Peter declares that he communicated the truth to his readers without any mixture of legend, myth, or fiction. Edwin A. Blum writes:

> The [New Testament] always uses *mythos* in a negative sense and in contrast to the truth of the gospel (1 Tim. 1:4; 4:7; 2 Tim. 4:4) ... It is likely that the false teachers claimed that the Incarnation, Resurrection, and coming kingdom the apostles spoke about were only stories![4]

Whereas false religions and false teachers in Peter's day rested their beliefs and practices on fabricated stories presented as historical truth, everything Peter taught concerning Christ came from authentic, personal experience. Peter selects one such event that he, James, and John had witnessed—the transfiguration on the "holy

GLORY ON THE MOUNT

Toward the end of His earthly ministry, Jesus began teaching his puzzled disciples that He was going to Jerusalem to suffer, die, and be raised to life (Matt. 16:21). Peter took Jesus aside and rebuked Him for even suggesting such things, unbecoming of the Messiah (16:22). Six days after revealing this hidden plan, Christ brought three disciples with Him to a "high mountain" (17:1). Peter simply calls this the "holy mountain" (2 Peter 1:18), and no further identification is made in Scripture.

Though church tradition identifies it as Mt. Tabor west of the Sea of Galilee in the direction of Nazareth, many scholars believe it was actually Mt. Hermon, north of Galilee in the direction of Caesarea Philippi. This makes sense, as Jesus already was in the far north when Peter uttered his Spirit-enabled confession of Jesus as "the Christ, the Son of the living God" (Matt. 16:16). Mt. Hermon lies only about fifteen miles from Caesarea Philippi, whereas Mt. Tabor was about a fifty-mile journey.

Mount Hermon, the likely location of Christ's transfiguration.

mountain," likely Mt. Hermon to the far north of Galilee. We can read the gospel accounts of this event in Matthew 17:1–8; Mark 9:2–8; and Luke 9:28–36.

Peter chooses this account primarily because he personally heard the voice of God testifying about Jesus from the cloud of glory, declaring, "This is My beloved Son with whom I am well-pleased" (2 Peter 1:17). Peter can legitimately say that God Himself has validated the words and works of Jesus as something other than merely human (1:18). And besides hearing those divine words with his own ears, Peter saw with his own eyes Jesus' brilliance shining forth during a brief moment of transformation. So, with his eyes and ears, Peter both saw and heard a confirmation of the truth of Jesus' person and work.

Peter insists that while the Lord God spoke in written form on Mt. Sinai as He gave Moses the Ten Commandments, here on Mt. Hermon, God spoke audibly, pointing to Jesus, the Word made flesh (John 1:14). And when Moses and Elijah appeared (Matt. 17:3)—the Old Testament representatives of the Law and the Prophets—Peter understands that in Jesus the Old Testament finds its fulfillment (Luke 24:44; John 1:45). With such a stunning validation of Jesus' ministry, nobody could doubt that in Him we see truth itself personified.

Of course, not everybody has the privilege of standing on Mr. Hermon to see the spirits of departed saints and to hear God Himself confirm the truth of the Christian message. This is why Peter transitions from the reliability of the message of the apostles to the reliability of the enduring written Word of God—the Holy Scriptures.

— 1:19–21 —

Peter begins his discussion of Scripture by saying that through his personal witness of Christ's glory and the voice of God, we have "the prophetic word made more sure" (1:19a). *The prophetic word* here refers to all Scripture, not just the books of prophecy. Peter himself clarifies this definition in verse 20 when he refers to "prophecy of Scripture." In Scripture we have God's truth stated in written form—able to be read, studied, pondered, and applied by the guidance and power of the Holy Spirit. Its truth never changes. It never goes out of date. Though Old Testament saints relied on their Scriptures as infallible witnesses, its trustworthiness was made even more sure when Peter saw prophecies written regarding the Messiah actually come to pass. It is to this sure foundation of truth that Peter directs his readers.

Peter says that we would do well to pay attention to this prophetic word of Holy Scripture (1:19b). To "pay attention" means to focus our concern, care, and commitment on something (see Heb. 2:1). That is, we must cultivate more than a casual familiarity with Old Testament characters or a superficial understanding of its stories. In practical terms it means we must study, not merely read, the text. We ponder it: we don't simply scan it. We memorize Scripture we don't simply mutter it. We apply it to our lives, not frame it and hang those words on our walls.

In this way, we will handle the sure and authoritative written Word of God as it was meant to be handled: as "a lamp shining in a dark place" (1:19). Here, "dark" literally means "murky." Peter describes the world we live in as a barren, squalled, dimly lit place. It may be that he had in mind a tomb or dungeon from which there was little hope of escape. While we as believers live in this condition, where even our own human wisdom and understanding are untrustworthy guides, we must rely on the sure guidance of God's Word to light our path. The psalmist said in Psalm 119:105, "Your word is a lamp to my feet and a light to my path." If we don't follow the penetrating light of God's Word, it's easy to go astray and find ourselves neck-deep in the mire of the world's murky swamp.

In keeping with his pattern, Peter injects a bright ray of hope in the midst of this desperate situation. He reminds his readers that a day will come when God's glory through Christ will shine, replacing the darkness of this world with the light of a new dawn. Jesus Christ, the Morning Star and the Light of the world, will return and raise us up with Him to share in His glory (John 8:12; Rev. 22:16). Until then we must adjust our eyes to the sure source of light in the darkness.

When Peter begins verse 20 with the phrase "know this first of all," we should perk up and give the following statement our full attention; what he's about to say is of utmost importance. The truth he wants all of us to know is this: "no prophecy of Scripture is a matter of one's own interpretation." The word "interpretation" is the Greek term *epilysis*. The normal Greek words for interpreting the meaning of a biblical text are *dianoigō* (Luke 24: 32) and *diermēneuō* (Luke 24:27). So, "one's own interpretation" does not mean that individual believers can't interpret Scripture through humble dependence on the Holy Spirit and diligent study of the biblical text.[5]

Then what does Peter mean by "one's own interpretation"? Perhaps Peter is declaring that no passage of Scripture is meant to stand on its own — that is, that no prophet speaks or writes a word contrary to what already has been revealed. The implication is twofold: (1) one passage of Scripture will never contradict another passage, even when written by a different author; and (2) every individual passage must be understood in light of the whole of Scripture and in light of parallel or related passages.

A third view, which ties in best with the following verse, means that all prophecies of Scripture come ultimately from God as the source of Scripture; they do not reflect merely a prophet's personal interpretation and human explanation of God's revelation. Peter explains the process in verse 21: "for no prophecy was ever made by an act of human will, but men moved by the Holy Spirit spoke from God." If we allow this verse to interpret what Peter means by "one's own interpretation," then this third view makes the best sense. Scripture is not a record of fallible human ideas and interpretations of God's revelation. It is God's actual inerrant and authoritative Word, written through human authors who were prevented from error as they wrote their original documents by the providential work of the Holy Spirit. By the way, if this third view is correct, the second view—that Scripture does not contradict itself and must be read as a whole—is also true, because one divine Author stands behind both the Old and New Testaments.

Verse 21 is one of the most significant verses in the Bible related to the inspiration and inerrancy of Scripture. Peter clearly says that Scripture is not ultimately a result of human ideas or human will. Yes, humans clearly are involved in the process, but the product—Holy Scripture—has a character and quality that surpasses what any mere human being could compose. Unlike all those "cleverly devised tales" of the world's myths, the Word of God has come about from God's direct involvement.

Peter describes this truth through the use of a vivid word picture. Human authors were "moved by the Holy Spirit." In Greek the word "Spirit" is *pneuma*, which is also the word for "wind." And the term "moved" is *pherō*, meaning to "bear" or "carry along," apart from one's own ability or power. Luke used the term in a nautical sense in Acts 27:15, 17 of his storm-tossed ship being "driven along." In the same way, Scripture is God-breathed because in the process of writing, the authors remained under the unique control of the Holy Spirit. This means they were consciously involved in the process.

The inspiration of Scripture doesn't mean God audibly dictated the words the human authors wrote, nor does it mean that the human authors went into some kind of hypnotic trance. Most likely they did not know that the Holy Spirit was moving them to compose and record God's inspired words, without error. Nevertheless, the result of the process is an inspired, inerrant text of Scripture.

When New Testament writers referred to "Scripture," they had in mind primarily the Old Testament writings, which the Jews and early Christians accepted as God's inspired Word. We'll see, however, that Peter already knew the writings of the New Testament apostles and prophets had the same quality as those of the Old Testament and should be treated with the same kind of respect and obedience (3:16).

How does Peter's technical description of the inspiration of Scripture fit with his overall purpose in writing this letter? Peter wrote to stir up his readers' memo-

From My Journal

The Pastor and the Scholar

Near the beginning of my ministry I took a pastorate in Waltham, Massachusetts. I followed a man who had served as the interim pastor for several months. His name is Dr. Bruce Waltke, renowned Hebrew scholar and biblical teacher. Over the years we became good friends.

When Dr. Waltke led me down to the basement of the house where he lived, it looked like a library had exploded. Old Bibles in Hebrew, Greek, Aramaic, and Latin were strewn about, various editions and versions of the Bible covered long tables, and pages of notes lay everywhere.

"Bruce, what in the world is all this?" I asked, trying to figure out what kind of work he was doing. If this represented his sermon preparation, I probably would have developed a lifelong inferiority complex!

"Well," he said, "I'm helping in the cross-referencing of a new Bible that's coming out. It will be known as the New American Standard Bible."

I looked at all those books again. Remember, this was before Bible software or online search engines. If you wanted to cross-reference, you did the work by hand—agonizing, tedious, painstaking work. Only somebody like Bruce Waltke could do this sort of thing . . . and enjoy it. But the words that came from his mouth next had a profound impact on me, demonstrating that the common division between the pastor and the scholar can be overcome.

"Oh, Chuck," he said with a smile, "this has been absolutely life-changing. I've read every verse in the Bible at least five times."

Now, that's passion for God's Word! In my years of ministry, I've come across Bible students and scholars who treat Scripture like a textbook . . . and that's about all. They read it for head knowledge without letting its truth seep into their hearts. Some scan it simply to find a sermon text. Only rarely do I come across people like Bruce Waltke. I can't imagine anything more grueling (and potentially boring!) than cross-referencing every Bible verse. But in the midst of that kind of detailed, in-depth scholarship, Bruce never forgot that God gave us His inspired words for a reason—to point us to Christ and to change lives by the power of His Holy Spirit. What a model of careful, devoted scholarship he is!

ries regarding sound teaching, to spur them on to diligence in the faith, and to shore up the biblical foundations of their beliefs and practices. In all these areas, an understanding of Scripture's authority is essential. When the apostles departed this life, as Peter soon would, Scripture was to guide the church in sound teaching. His readers were to turn to Scripture to reaffirm their biblical foundations, not only for what they believed, but also for how they lived. Only by centering their faith on God's Word would they be able to discern false doctrine and defeat the deceitful claims of heretics. Paul describes the importance of Scripture in this way: "All Scripture is inspired by God and profitable for teaching, for reproof, for correction, for training in righteousness; so that the man of God may be adequate, equipped for every good work" (2 Tim. 3:16–17).

Peter's message to first-century believers is just as relevant to us. His words are meant to turn our minds to two important truths. First, remember that when you turn to God's Word, you are consulting the most reliable of all sources. The world is filled with truth claims, alternate sources of revelation, and competing philosophies. The Bible alone contains God's Word written, an objective and unchanging standard of truth.

Second, remember that when you make other sources—experiences, dreams, feelings, supernatural phenomena, or opinions—equal to or more reliable than the Scriptures, you'll fall into error. Nothing can be exalted above God's Word, as Psalm 138:2 says: "For You have magnified Your word according to all Your name." Peter knows this all too well. He fills his entire letter with warnings against those who have placed a different source of knowledge above God's Word. As we will see later in this letter, the results are disastrous.

NOTES:

1. See Justin Martyr, *1 Apology* 26.
2. Johannes E. Louw and Eugene A. Nida, eds., *Greek-English Lexicon of the New Testament Based on Semantic Domains,* vol. 1, *Introduction and Domains,* 2nd ed. (New York: United Bible Societies, 1988), § 68.64.
3. Gangel, "2 Peter," 867.
4. Blum, "2 Peter," 273.
5. See examples where individuals study and interpret Scripture in Deuteronomy 17:19; Daniel 9:2; Luke 10:26. This does not mean, however, that believers should avoid studying Scripture with trained and gifted teachers or in community, a practice also prevalent in the Bible (see Neh. 8:8; Acts 17:10–12; 1 Thess. 5:27).

DENUNCIATION OF FALSE TEACHERS (2 PETER 2:1–22)

Chances are that a con artist has victimized all of us at some time. Perhaps more than once! Maybe it's been years ... or only yesterday. It could be as harmless as losing your spare change playing a rigged game at a carnival. Or it may be as disastrous as losing your retirement in an investment scam. It's possible that the deception nearly cost you your sanity, as it did Christopher Edwards. In the preface to his book *Crazy for God,* he describes his nightmare of deception.

> My story began innocently enough when I was lured into a "fun weekend" in June of 1975 on a farm owned by a front group for Sun Myung Moon's Unification Church....
>
> I was transformed from an intelligent, independent human being into a completely subservient disciple of my new Messiah—terrified of questioning, dependent on my leaders for my every move, ready and willing to die or even kill to restore the world under the absolute rule of Reverend Moon.[1]

Of all the cons to which we might fall prey in this world, the most damaging is the deception of religious phonies. Swindlers of this kind deal in counterfeit truth, an imitation meant to fool the unsuspecting. Everyday peddlers of falsehood receive nodding approval on television, in bookstores, on the silver screen—and, yes, behind pulpits. Counterfeit truth is big business. Today whole ministries have formed to counter the counterfeits and challenge the charlatans. Books that catalogue and refute cults are often massive and can treat their false teachings only in a summary manner.

In 2 Peter 2, that rugged apostle candidly describes false teachers who traffic in religious things but who lack authentic faith. Appearing to be resourceful and real, they are empty and deceitful. Claiming to offer answers and hope, they bring lies and despair. Pretending to proclaim reliable information, they use the same words as believers but use a different dictionary. And acting like those who have embraced Christian freedom, they are enslaved by corruption and seek to enslave others. They may look as though they are succeeding, and it may seem that the score for heretics far outweighs that of the saints. But in reality, they are merely heaping up judgment for themselves in the coming day of wrath.

In his previous message to the church, Peter exhorted Christians, "Beware! Be ready!" He wrote this letter to remind believers of sound teaching, to encourage diligence in the faith, and to strengthen biblical foundations of beliefs and practices. Now in chapter 2, he explores the kinds of people who forget sound doctrine,

KEY TERMS

αἵρεσις [*hairesis*] (139) "choice, different opinion, false doctrine"

This word originally was a neutral term that described various branches or "schools" of philosophy or theology — a "choice" among various "sects" (Acts 5:17; 15:5). New Testament writers, however, used the term "heresy" to refer to the incorrect choices or deviant sects outside the bounds of apostolic teachings (1 Cor. 11:19). Peter is the first to use the term in a more technical sense of "false Christian teaching" (2 Peter 2:1), a meaning that will become common in the second century.

κρίσις [*krisis*] (2920) "decision, judgment, condemnation"

As a legal term for rendering a decision in a court of law, its secular usage could be either positive or negative — innocent or guilty, good or bad (2 Cor. 5:10). In Peter, the word *krisis* carries an almost technical sense, pointing to the final end-times sentence carried out against the wicked, including condemnation and destruction (2 Peter 2:4, 9).

ἀπώλεια [*apōleia*] (684) "perishing, ruin, loss, destruction"

Closely associated with *krisis*, "judgment," this term emphasizes the sentence — destruction — as opposed to the verdict. Peter uses the term in reference to the judgment of heretics (2:1, 3), which will come in the form of fire (3:7). Similarly, the book of Revelation describes the ultimate fate of the beast in the lake of fire as "destruction" (Rev. 17:8, 17). It does not necessitate total annihilation, but absolute ruin.

turn away from the faith, and deviate from biblical belief and practice. As such, this sometimes gloomy but always truthful and ever-relevant section serves as a warning to us all.

An Exposé of Counterfeit Communicators (2 Peter 2:1–3)

¹But false prophets also arose among the people, just as there will also be false teachers among you, who will secretly introduce destructive heresies, even denying the Master who bought them, bringing swift destruction upon themselves. ²Many will follow their sensuality, and because of them the way of the truth will be maligned; ³and in *their* greed they will exploit you with false words; their judgment from long ago is not idle, and their destruction is not asleep.

In 2 Corinthians 11:3, Paul writes about the world's first con artist: "But I am afraid that, as the serpent deceived Eve by his craftiness, your minds will be led astray from the simplicity and purity of devotion to Christ." A little later Paul describes the deceiver's disciples: "For such men are false apostles, deceitful workers, disguising themselves as apostles of Christ. No wonder, for even Satan disguises himself as an angel of light" (11:13–14). Don't miss the description of Satan's methods in these verses. He deceives, leads minds astray, clouds the simplicity of Christian devotion, disguises himself as good and glorious, and enrolls others in his mass deception.

False teachers often appear doctrinally sound, personally attractive, sincere, and logically compelling. But they are deceivers, mind-benders, truth-twisters. Second Peter 2:1–3 warns us to be aware of their wicked schemes.

— 2:1 —

In the preceding paragraph, Peter pointed to the Holy Scriptures and the testimony of the apostles and godly prophets as the trustworthy source of truth. We can believe Scripture because true prophets, moved by the Holy Spirit, spoke from God (2 Peter 1:21). But false prophets had been among the true prophets of God, peddling their cheap imitations of the truth. Peter says that in the same way, his fellow believers should expect false prophets among preachers of the truth in their own day. Just as God sent true apostles and prophets of Jesus Christ by the power of the Holy Spirit, so Satan will send his own false apostles and prophets. Implied in the phrase "but false prophets" is a black-and-white contrast between the words of true prophets and false prophets.

True Prophets	False Prophets
Words are faithful, firsthand accounts.	Words are cleverly devised myths.
Words must be heeded.	Words must be rejected.
Words are light to shine in darkness.	Words are darkness to be driven out.
Words are inspired by the Holy Spirit	Words are inspired by human or wicked spirits.

In light of this contrast, Peter presents at least four characteristics of false teachers in 2:1–3.

- They deceitfully present heresy (2:1a).
- They openly deny the truth (2:1b).
- They unashamedly model sensuality (2:2).
- They selfishly represent greed (2:3).

First, the false prophets among Christians will "secretly introduce destructive heresies" (2:1a). The term "heresy" comes directly from the Greek word *hairesis*, which conveys the idea of "making a choice."[2] With stealth and cleverness, the "heretics" offer up alluring alternatives to the truth. Often they do this by rejecting aspects of the truth that seem difficult to accept either intellectually or emotionally. They create something much more appealing and seducing, urging others to "make a choice" as they consider an alternative way of thinking. This isn't always an offensive or obvious affront to the truth. Rather, they "secretly introduce" their doctrines, camouflaging them in something that looks like the truth in form but which in substance denies it. Warren Wiersbe puts it well: "The false teachers use our vocabulary, but they do not use our dictionary."[3]

The false teachers talk about "sin," "salvation," "inspiration," "God," "Jesus Christ," and "resurrection"—but they don't mean what the Bible means by these terms. *Sin* may simply be the failure to actualize our human potential. *Salvation* might mean self-actualization or psychological well-being. To false teachers today, Scripture is *inspired* in the same way great poetry or literature is "inspired." *God* is often seen as our personal Higher Power—a projection of our need for a belief in a transcendent reality beyond ourselves. *Jesus Christ* is viewed as a great moral teacher with a high degree of God-consciousness—or He's a cosmic symbol for the highest in human potential. And *resurrection* can be taken as a metaphor for keeping "Jesus" alive through observing His teachings and following His ethics. False teachers rethink and redefine terms as they encourage us to question long-standing doctrines. They hate the "conservative" form of Christianity, preferring a "progressive" form that constantly updates and modifies fundamental truths.

The second characteristic of false teachers is that *they openly deny the truth* (2:1b). They will be known for what they deny about Jesus Christ's person and work even more than what they embrace. This is because they intentionally set themselves up against the true prophets, the Scriptures, and the church. They reject many—if not all—of the orthodox truths of historical Christianity set forth in the Bible and reaffirmed over and over again throughout church history. Christians from the earliest days of church history to the present day have held certain biblical doctrines of the faith as central, defining marks of orthodoxy. Those who have strayed from this center of orthodoxy have been regarded as outside the true Christian faith. Some of those core truths include:

- the inspiration and inerrancy of Scripture
- one eternal, triune God in three persons: Father, Son, and Holy Spirit
- the undiminished deity and true humanity of Jesus Christ
- Christ's virgin birth, sinless life, substitutionary death for sin, miraculous bodily resurrection, and literal future return
- the special creation and fall of humanity
- salvation by grace through faith
- the eternal life of believers and condemnation of unbelievers

Are such false teachers saved? According to what Peter writes in this chapter, we can conclude that those guilty of teaching doctrines at extreme odds with classic

HISTORIC HERESIES

Jesus and the apostles predicted the coming of false prophets and teachers who would try to deceive Christians and snatch the truth from unbelievers (Matt. 24:11; 2 Peter 2:1). Although they differed from one another in many ways, they all rejected central truths of the Christian faith. Here are a few false teachers whose doctrines may have been around at the time of Peter or in the years immediately following.

Simon the Samaritan. Acts 8:9–24 mentions this man as having a false faith worthy of Peter's rebuke. Early Christian history tells us that he began claiming he was the great God come down from heaven and that his accompanying prostitute, Helena, was his first creation.[4] Simon the Samaritan lived in Rome during the reign of Claudius Caesar, the emperor preceding Nero. The great infamy of Simon may explain why Luke chose to include his false conversion when he wrote the book of Acts in the 60s. Peter would have been aware of Simon's false teachings and may have had him and his followers partly in mind when he wrote against counterfeit communicators in 2 Peter.

Cerinthus. Toward the end of the first century in Asia Minor, Cerinthus denied the true incarnation of Christ, teaching that Christ was a heavenly spiritual being who descended and adopted the body of the purely human man, Jesus.[5] The apostle John may have written the fourth gospel partly to refute Cerinthus's heresy. John made it clear that the divine Son of God did not merely adopt or take possession of a human body, but that "the Word became flesh, and dwelt among us" (John 1:14).

Gnostics. The diverse sects commonly labeled "Gnostic" find their roots in the syncretistic and esoteric teachings of Simon the Magician's followers, like Menander and Saturninus, in the late first century. The Gnostics generally taught that Christ was only one of many spirit beings that sprang forth from the unknown God to bring salvation by special knowledge (*gnōsis*) to the spiritually elite through initiation and enlightenment. Many of these either wrote their own false scriptures to replace Holy Scripture, or they reinterpreted Scripture in a highly allegorical and spiritual sense to support their strange theologies.[6]

orthodoxy are not, in fact, Spirit-regenerated believers. Peter says they have denied the Master who bought them—rejecting Jesus Christ's payment for their sins. Christ paid a price for the sins of the world by dying in place of wicked humanity—taking their deserved punishment on Himself as an undeserving substitute. Though Christ's death is sufficient payment for everybody's sins (1 John 2:1–2), only those who believe in Him receive the benefit of this salvation (John 3:16–18). The false teachers are in a particularly acute predicament, because although they have heard the preaching about Christ's salvation, they reject it, replacing it with false teachings about the Master. Because of this rejection, clearly, they are lost.

Peter also says these counterfeit communicators face a "swift destruction" (2:1). The Greek word for "swift," *tachinos*, refers to the suddenness of the destruction. That is, for false teachers, judgment comes when they least expect it. While they believe and live as though there will be no consequences, destruction will interrupt their lives like a rude intrusion.

What kind of destruction does Peter have in mind? In the rest of the New Testament, the term for destruction, *apōleia*, often refers to the judgment and damnation of the unsaved (Matt. 7:13; Phil. 1:28; Heb. 10:39). More importantly, Peter himself uses the term exclusively for the judgment of the unsaved (2 Peter 2:3; 3:7, 16). True believers—those who have been saved by faith in Jesus Christ and are forever sealed by the Holy Spirit—may doubt, be deceived, and sin. But they can never utterly fall away and lose their salvation. Never! God, in His powerful grace, keeps them forever in His hand (John 10:29; Rom. 8:38–39; Jude 24).

We must therefore conclude that those who appear to us to "fall away" from the faith, denying the essential truths of Christianity, were never truly saved, as the apostle John says regarding some counterfeit communicators in his own day: "They went out from us, *but they were not really of us*; for if they had been of us, they would have remained with us; but they went out, so that it would be shown that they all are not of us" (1 John 2:19, italics mine).

—**2:2**—

The third characteristic of many false teachers is that *they unashamedly model sensuality*. The term for "sensuality" is a vivid Greek word for blatant immorality. Commentator William Barclay says it "describes the attitude of a man who is lost to shame; he is past the stage of wishing to conceal his sin and of being ashamed of it."[7] Here Peter gives us an insight into the underlying motivation for tampering with the truth. In order to be free to indulge their carnal appetites without restraint, they must redefine the standard of righteousness.

Let's face it. Religions that say, "Do what thou wilt," are much more appealing to our sinful desires than the one that teaches, "Thou shalt not." Therefore, many follow the lure of sensuality, unbridled moral freedom, and licentious behavior masked by a twisted doctrine of "grace." You see, "grace" to these deceivers means freedom to do as they wish—when and where and with whom they wish. In contrast, biblical grace for the believer is freedom from the punishment of sin and the God-given power to freely love and serve Christ apart from legalistic dos and don'ts.

If you want to build a big following, just develop a religion that removes the restraints on people's sinful behavior and that also appeals to their base urges—pleasure, greed, selfishness. Instant popularity will result. But at the same time, those teachers and followers will bring reproach on the name of Christ. Because such teachers refuse to abandon the name "Christian," their devious and deviant behaviors get associated with Christianity. The cause of Christ is damaged and the Great Commission impeded.

— **2:3** —

Finally, counterfeit communicators *selfishly represent greed.* The word "exploit" is a marketing term meaning to traffic or trade. How true it is that most often false teachers are motivated by unrestrained greed for money. In order to fill their coffers, they become masters of what Peter calls "false words." The word "false" comes from the Greek word *plastos*, from which we get our modern word *plastic.*[8] By replacing the truth with a cheap—but convincing—imitation, false teachers make it easy for followers to adopt falsehood instead of the truth.

Our heresy meters should buzz loudly when we see an overwhelming emphasis on money. When the preacher's whole theology presents miraculous ways of acquiring financial blessing, alarms should go off in our minds. If the application of virtually every message is to sow a financial seed or reap a material harvest, *run.* If the primary texts such teachers quote have to do with satisfying self-serving desires, *leave skid marks.*

A true minister of the gospel preaches the whole counsel of God—even the uncomfortable, unappreciated, and unpopular parts. He may make a living preaching the gospel (1 Cor. 9:14), but he shouldn't make a killing. He serves others, not himself. He lives in a house, not an amusement park. He drives a car, not a limousine. He is accountable, not unaccountable. He is transparent with his finances, doesn't flatter or sell out, refuses to cater to the wealthy, and exhibits none of the attributes of unbridled greed. His private life is an open book, not a series of secrets.

Peter concludes his description of false teachers with a reminder of their fate. In case anybody might feel tempted to trade in the truth for unhindered immorality and unlimited greed, Peter reminds us that the judgment of false teachers is imminent (2:3). It may appear for the time being that false prophets are getting away with their wicked deceptions, but God's judgment has been simmering for centuries. It's not idle—merely waiting. It's not asleep, but prepared to pounce at the proper time. His judgments grind slowly, yet exceedingly fine.

Peter has written this letter to remind believers of sound teaching, to encourage diligence in the faith, and to strengthen biblical foundations of beliefs and practices. In Peter's day, counterfeit communicators represented a clear and present danger that threatened to undo orthodoxy, weaken faith, and lure people away from holy living. The same dark menace threatens the church today. Beware!

Application

Spotting the Spurious

Not to downplay the threat of false teachers in Peter's day, but with the advent of radio, television, and the Internet, the early trickles of trickery in the first century have become a hurricane of heresy in the twenty-first. How can we avoid being swept away by the high-velocity winds and torrential rains of satanic deception? Let me give you three practical tips that can protect us from the acid rain of deception: *stop, look,* and *listen.*

Stop! Refuse to plunge into a certain person's teaching just because it appears harmless on the surface. You could find yourself in a deep abyss of deception. It's never enough that others have been entertained, persuaded, inspired, or blessed by a charming person, church, or ministry. Put the breaks on long enough to compare the views being taught with the clear teaching of Holy Scripture and the central doctrines of the orthodox faith. Don't be afraid to turn and run if things don't feel right deep within your spirit.

Look! Observe the life of the main spokespersons for any particular ministry or movement. Do they model Christlike values and virtues? Do they point to Christ or to themselves? Do you see accountability and transparency? Do they exhibit true humility? Authenticity? Love? Do they submit themselves to the authority of God's Word? What do their followers look like? Never be swayed by somebody's apparent sincerity, intelligence, or charisma.

Listen! Pay close attention to the words teachers use. Listen not only to *what* they say, but *how* they say it. Also note what's *not* being said. Don't fall into the trap of judging something to be true because it makes you feel good. Often the real truth will feel like a slap in the face or a punch in the stomach. Real truth almost always brings conviction and an obligation to change. But lies are often crafted to provide false security, freedom to sin, and emotional excitement. Listen closely. Think critically.

We all need to be more aware of the false teachings prevalent in our world. We need to identify errors, motives, and dangers. Why not begin to sharpen your discernment by keeping your eyes open over the next few days for various forms of falsehood. Stop, look, and listen — then seek to determine where these false teachers have gone wrong. By sharpening your skills in spotting deception on your own turf, you'll be better prepared when deceivers spring at you from unexpected corners.

The God of Wrath and Rescue (2 Peter 2:4–11)

> [4]For if God did not spare angels when they sinned, but cast them into hell and committed them to pits of darkness, reserved for judgment; [5]and did not spare the ancient world, but preserved Noah, a preacher of righteousness, with seven others, when He brought a flood upon the world of the ungodly; [6]and *if* He condemned the cities of Sodom and Gomorrah to destruction by reducing *them* to ashes, having made them an example to those who would live ungodly *lives* thereafter; [7]and *if* He rescued righteous Lot, oppressed by the sensual conduct of unprincipled men [8](for by what he saw and heard *that* righteous man, while living among them, felt *his* righteous soul tormented day after day by *their* lawless deeds), [9]*then* the Lord knows how to rescue the godly from temptation, and to keep the unrighteous under punishment for the day of judgment, [10]and especially those who indulge the flesh in *its* corrupt desires and despise authority.
>
> Daring, self-willed, they do not tremble when they revile angelic majesties, [11]whereas angels who are greater in might and power do not bring a reviling judgment against them before the Lord.

Since we're still on the subject of heretics, let me introduce you to one of the greatest. Marcion arrived in Rome about eighty years after Peter wrote his words of warning regarding the coming false teachers. Marcion had traveled from his native Pontus on the north side of Asia Minor along the Black Sea. Tradition tells us he was the son of the bishop of Pontus, so he likely knew his Christian doctrines and Scriptures well. He could no doubt quote verses from memory. He read the Bible closely — very closely. In the course of his study, he decided that the strict, law-giving, wrathful, judgmental God of the Old Testament looked nothing like the loving, compassionate, gracious God who sent Jesus Christ to save us. He also concluded that this physical universe was so full of imperfection and corruption that the good, holy, and spiritual God never could have conceived of such a place. So, Marcion reasoned that the Old Testament God — Yahweh — was a different god from the God of the New Testament, the Father of Jesus.

But what about all the clear New Testament connections between the God of Israel and the Father of Jesus Christ? To solve this problem, Marcion simply rejected the Old Testament Scriptures, then selected and edited his own New Testament to accommodate his theology. He rejected all the gospels except a pared-down gospel of Luke. He then edited a handful of Paul's letters and rewrote them to emphasize the disjunction between law and grace. The result? The Old Testament God of justice and judgment was a totally different God from the New Testament God of grace and salvation.

Though the early church reacted quickly and decisively against Marcion's madness in the second century, the "problem" of the two sides of God's character still puzzles believers. Scripture does seem to present two sides of the same God — the attributes of justice, judgment, and wrath on the one side, and the attributes of mercy, salvation, and blessing on the other. These two "sides" of God are reflected well in Exodus 34:6–7.

Exodus 34:6–7a	The LORD, the LORD God, compassionate and gracious, slow to anger, and abounding in lovingkindness and truth; who keeps lovingkindness for thousands, who forgives iniquity, transgression and sin ...
Exodus 34:7b	... yet He will by no means leave the guilty unpunished, visiting the iniquity of fathers on the children and on the grandchildren to the third and fourth generations.

The first part of this description is the kind of picture we all want to frame and hang over the mantle — the loving Father who sends forth kindness, who forgives our sins, who overflows in blessing. But the second part of this verse reminds us of the sobering reality that God refuses to wink at sin. In fact, His judgment sometimes is so severe that its waves ripple forward three or four generations!

The truth is, whether God appears as a kind, loving Father or a vengeful, wrathful Judge depends on our relationship with Him. Paul said, "Behold then the kindness and severity of God; to those who fell, severity, but to you, God's kindness" (Rom. 11:22). In fact, Paul says the message of the gospel itself can appear either sweet or sour, depending on whether a person believes or disbelieves: "For we are a fragrance of Christ to God among those who are being saved and among those who are perishing; to the one an aroma from death to death, to the other an aroma from life to life" (2 Cor. 2:15–16).

These same two sides of God—His compassion and His judgment—come together in 2 Peter 2:4–11. For the false teachers, judgment is coming. But for the saved, God will provide rescue from wrath. In this passage, Peter shares a warning, a promise, and a hope—calling believers to persevere in sound doctrine.

By the way, 2:4–10a is one long sentence in Greek. Structurally, though, it's quite simple. It follows a basic "if . . . then" pattern in which Peter says: "*If* God has historically established a pattern of reserving judgment of the wicked for the proper time while rescuing His righteous people, *then* we can be confident that He will do the same in the future—rescue us from the coming wrath and leave the wicked, false teachers behind for judgment."

Recognizing the basic argument, let's look at how Peter builds his case in verses 4–10.

—2:4–8—

We can divide the "if" side of Peter's "if . . . then" statement in 2:4–10 into two historical episodes—the judgment of the world in the days of Noah, and the judgment of Sodom and Gomorrah in the days of Lot. The first episode included not only the judgment of wicked angels (2:4), but also the judgment of wicked men and women (2:5).

Who are the angels that sinned (2:4)? We have three options. First, some have held that Peter is referring to the original fall of angelic beings that coincided with the fall of Satan (Ezek. 28:11–19). In our 2 Peter passage, however, we read that all of these sinning angels were cast into pits of darkness and reserved for judgment. By contrast, Satan and his angels are free and active in the world (Matt. 12:27–28; 1 Peter 5:8).

As a second option, some have considered this to be a second fall of good angels that took place sometime after the first fall of Satan and his demons. But we have no record of such a second fall, and it seems likely that those angels who did not fall with Satan were afterward sealed in their state of righteousness. Paul refers to "chosen angels" (1 Tim. 5:21), and this has often been understood to refer to angels who passed the test of Satan's fall and were sealed in their state of tested perfection, never able to fall.

The most likely option, then, seems to be that the wicked angels noted in 2 Peter 2:4 were a part of the original group who fell with Satan, but who then committed some subsequent sin—a sin so heinous that it necessitated a more severe judgment than what already had befallen them. Peter does not tell us what sin the wicked angels committed. It seems his readers already know to what event Peter is referring. In fact, Peter does help clarify his meaning in this text when he talks about their judgment.

Peter says that God "cast them into hell and committed them to pits of darkness," reserving them for future judgment (2:4). He uses a unique word for "hell" that is different from the typical New Testament terms *hadēs* (Matt. 11:23) or *gehenna* (Matt. 5:22). Peter says that God cast the angels who sinned into *Tartarus*. In the Greek world, this was regarded as a place of torment and punishment beyond Hades. We might call it the "hellhole of hell." Not only does Peter draw on Greek imagery to reinforce the severity of this judgment, but he also refers to a book popular among Jews and Christians in the first century called *1 Enoch*. The writers of that book creatively recast the biblical account of the flood (Gen. 6), describing the sins of the angelic beings who cohabited with human women. For this heinous and unnatural crime, they were cast into the place of deepest darkness and reserved for the day of judgment. On that future day, the spirits of wickedness will be cast into fire (*1 Enoch* 10.6–9).[9]

In this light, it seems that what Peter calls "Tartarus" is the same as the "abyss" mentioned several times in the New Testament. During His earthly ministry, demons implored Jesus not to send them into the "abyss" (Luke 8:31). Satan himself will be cast into the "abyss" for a thousand years after the return of Christ (Rev. 20:3) before he is finally consigned to the "lake of fire" (20:10). This seems to be a deep, dark holding place for wicked spirits that prevents them from having any contact with or influence on the world. Like a cross between solitary confinement and death row, Tartarus is the place where the most wicked spirits await judgment. This interpretation fits Peter's argument best.

In verse 5, Peter connects the timing of this sin of fallen angels to the period of time leading up to the flood (Gen. 6–8). All humanity had reached such a degree of wickedness that "every intent of the thoughts of his heart was only evil continually" (Gen. 6:5). Because of the depths of evil, God did not spare the ancient world but brought a flood upon the earth to destroy the ungodly (2 Peter 2:5).

Yet in the midst of this judgment, God preserved eight people—Noah, "a preacher of righteousness," his wife, three sons, and their wives. This salvation of the righteous in the midst of the judgment of wicked angels and humans serves as an example for Peter. In the coming judgment, God will preserve Christians who preach righteousness in their own day and who condemn the wicked false teachers.

The second historical episode Peter chooses to use as an illustration is the judgment of Sodom and Gomorrah (Gen. 19). God did not overlook the wickedness of the inhabitants of those cities. Instead, they became examples of just how serious God is about judging sin. These cities had not been given the Law, but God nevertheless held them accountable for their extreme wickedness and violence. Genesis 13:13 says "the men of Sodom were wicked exceedingly and sinners against the LORD," and in Genesis 18:20, God told Abraham, "The outcry of Sodom and Gomorrah is indeed great, and their sin is exceedingly grave." Because of this, God condemned them to destruction.

Yet Abraham inquired, "Will You indeed sweep away the righteous with the wicked?" (Gen. 18:23). God's answer gives us an important picture of His mercy in the midst of His judgment and wrath. God will not destroy righteous inhabitants of the city together with the wicked (18:25). In fact, God promised that if there were even ten righteous in the city, He would stay His hand of judgment (18:32). Because God is just and will not pour out His wrath on the righteous, He sent two angels into Sodom to retrieve Lot and his wife before judgment fell.

This is the aspect of the illustration Peter emphasizes. God "rescued righteous Lot" (2 Peter 2:7) by removing him and his family from the presence of the wicked in order to pour out His judgment on them. In many ways Peter's original readers could relate to Peter's description of Lot, who lived among the wicked men of Sodom; their sensual conduct oppressed him, and his soul felt constantly in anguish over their lawless deeds (2:7–8).

Peter uses this illustration of the salvation of the righteous in the midst of the judgment of the wicked as an example for Christian hope. In the coming judgment, God will preserve Christians who live righteous lives in the midst of the day-to-day immorality and lawlessness of the pagan world. And He will condemn the wickedness of unprincipled pagans in the judgments that precede the coming of Christ.

— **2:9** —

Having illustrated the "if" side of his "if … then" argument with two well-known examples of God's pattern of rescuing the righteous before sending judgment, Peter presents the important "then" side of his statement: "The Lord knows how to rescue the godly from temptation, and to keep the unrighteous under punishment for the day of judgment" (2:9). Peter insists that God's coming judgment will not sweep up the righteous with the wicked. Because God is just, He will spare the righteous believers in Christ, rescuing them from coming judgment. But the wicked stand condemned, awaiting future wrath.

The word translated "temptation," *peirasmos*, can refer to tests that challenge the integrity of one's faith (as in 1 Peter 1:6) or to "temptations," things that appeal to our sinful tendencies and challenge our moral integrity (Luke 4:13; see comments on this term in the discussion of James 1:1–4). It refers specifically to the coming tribulation period of the end time, described in Revelation 3:10. In that passage, Jesus, like Peter, promises that believers will be kept from the coming judgment: "I also will keep you from the hour of testing [*peirasmos*], that hour which is about to come upon the whole world, to test those who dwell on the earth." Paul refers to the same kind of rescue from the coming end-times judgment when he says that believers wait for the return of Jesus, "who rescues us from the wrath to come" (1 Thess. 1:10). And in the context of the rapture, when believers will be transformed and caught up with Christ in the clouds (1 Thess. 4:17), Paul reiterated this promise: "God has not destined us for wrath, but for obtaining salvation through our Lord Jesus Christ" (5:9).

Based on Peter's argument, we can conclude with confidence that New Testament Christians — like Noah and Lot in the Old Testament — are not going to suffer the wrath of the coming end-time judgment. That judgment is meant for the ungodly false teachers. Instead, believers can look forward to God's rescue of the righteous. Though Peter does not clearly spell out how that rescue will take place, his references to Noah and Lot suggest that believers will be removed from the place of wrath before that judgment falls. In fact, Paul's teaching concerning the rescue of believers from the coming wrath in 1 Thessalonians 5:9 and Christ's promise to believers in Revelation 1:10 all point to the rapture of the church as the means God will use to rescue believers prior to the day of the Lord.

— **2:10–11** —

Peter ends this section with a further description of the nature of the false teachers. He has already painted a disturbing picture in the first several verses of this chapter. The false teachers ...

- deceptively introduce heresies
- deny the Master who bought them
- invite destruction upon themselves
- indulge in sensuality
- cause the truth to be maligned
- greedily exploit believers

To his list of already dismal descriptions, Peter adds a number of other ugly attributes. These false teachers stand under condemnation because they indulge the flesh in corrupt desires and despise authority (2:10). The first summarizes the kind of sinfulness illustrated by the sexual immorality of the days of Noah and the times of Lot. The second relates to the false teachers' general disposition toward those who have been placed in positions of authority.

The Greek word *kyriotēs* generally refers to angelic authorities (Eph. 1:21; Col. 1:16), but in this context it appears to allow for both human authorities as well as angelic. Peter describes them as "daring" and "self-willed," dispositions opposite the humble and submissive spirit Peter elsewhere desires believers to exhibit. In his first letter, Peter exhorted his readers to submit to "every human institution" (1 Peter 2:13). Yet the false teachers described in 2 Peter 2 do not hesitate even to revile angelic beings (2:10).

We get the picture of cocky, defiant, indulgent, and out-of-control leaders willing to say or do anything to feed their own appetites of lust and greed. Such people are not among God's people. And such people, Peter says, can expect to receive wrath, not mercy, from the God of justice when Christ returns to rescue His people and judge the world.

Application

Rescued from Wrath

Is God a frightening Judge, or is he a good and gracious Father? Is He the source of wrath and destruction, or the fount of eternal blessing? The answer to this question depends not on who God is, but on who you are. God does not change. Because He is holy, He stands against wickedness; and because He is just, He will judge sinners justly. Yet God is also merciful and gracious, forgiving and blessing those who have placed their faith in Christ, whose death and resurrection bring forgiveness and new life. God justly condemns sin and justly forgives it on the basis of Christ's death. This leads me to two important facts.

First, God's compassion will result in the rescue of all believers. Because He is just and faithful, He will never forget even one of His children. This promise applies to *all* His children — the stubborn and the submissive, the weak and the strong, the mature and the adolescent. If you are a child of God by having placed your faith in Christ alone to save you from your sins — past, present, and future — then God's grace covers you. And if that's you, then God's promise to rescue you from the coming wrath applies to you. You won't be overlooked. He won't accidentally sweep you up with the wicked and send you into and through their judgment.

Second, God's judgment will result in the punishment of all unbelievers. Just as God is faithful in His compassion toward believers who have been declared "righteous" by His grace, God will be faithful in His judgment toward unbelievers whose guilt remains on them because of their rejection of Him and His gift of eternal life. Those who turn up their noses at God's gracious offer of forgiveness will not evade the consequences. Those who turn their backs on Christ's death and resurrection will endure the wrath of God.

How should we respond to these two truths? If you are a Christian, you should respond with both praise and prayer. Praise God for His great mercy toward you! Though we all deserve the same just punishment for our sinfulness, God has placed our sins on Christ, who bore the punishment for us. And He has placed Christ's righteousness in us, so we can partake of His life and blessing. None of this has anything to do with your keen insight, personal holiness, or any earned merit. It is all because of His matchless grace. By God's grace we have been redeemed and can stand with humble confidence before Him as our loving heavenly Father. And what a day that will be!

But you should also pray. Pray for those who don't yet know Christ. Peter has vividly described their destination—judgment. Pray for friends, loved ones, coworkers—people you know who already stand before God as a just Judge. Petition God to intervene in their lives, to bring about the circumstances necessary to soften the hardness of their hearts, to break through the shackles of sin that bind them, to shine a light of hope in the darkness of deception. Then think of ways you can become the answer to your own prayer. Ask God to reveal ways you can help bring them closer to the cross and the good news of salvation.

Disobedience Gone to Seed (2 Peter 2:12–22)

---

[12]But these, like unreasoning animals, born as creatures of instinct to be captured and killed, reviling where they have no knowledge, will in the destruction of those creatures also be destroyed, [13]suffering wrong as the wages of doing wrong. They count it a pleasure to revel in the daytime. They are stains and blemishes, reveling in their deceptions, as they carouse with you, [14]having eyes full of adultery that never cease from sin, enticing unstable souls, having a heart trained in greed, accursed children; [15]forsaking the right way, they have gone astray, having followed the way of Balaam, the *son* of Beor, who loved the wages of unrighteousness; [16]but he received a rebuke for his own transgression, *for* a mute donkey, speaking with a voice of a man, restrained the madness of the prophet.

[17]These are springs without water and mists driven by a storm, for

whom the black darkness has been reserved. ¹⁸For speaking out arrogant *words* of vanity they entice by fleshly desires, by sensuality, those who barely escape from the ones who live in error, ¹⁹promising them freedom while they themselves are slaves of corruption; for by what a man is overcome, by this he is enslaved. ²⁰For if, after they have escaped the defilements of the world by the knowledge of the Lord and Savior Jesus Christ, they are again entangled in them and are overcome, the last state has become worse for them than the first. ²¹For it would be better for them not to have known the way of righteousness, than having known it, to turn away from the holy commandment handed on to them. ²²It has happened to them according to the true proverb, "A dog returns to its own vomit," and, "A sow, after washing, *returns* to wallowing in the mire."

Think for a moment of the kinds of Scripture passages people hang on their walls.

Psalm 23 — "The LORD is my Shepherd, I shall not want . . ."
Matthew 6 — "Our Father which art in heaven . . ."
Numbers 6 — "The LORD bless thee and keep thee . . ."
Romans 8 — "In all these things we are more than conquerors . . ."

These and countless other scriptural scenes are lovely beyond description. We frame them in gold and set them against a background of peaceful gardens or natural landscapes, brilliant colors, gently rolling hills, fleecy clouds that add their own comfort to the words themselves. Such visual feasts leave us nourished with peace and hope.

But then there are the "unframable" Scriptures. Equally inspired and just as packed with truth. Yet the paintings that would fit these passages would be unwelcome in any room. If they were a musical score, everything would be written in a minor key. Those verbal portraits make us frown, disturb our peace, and cast dark shadows of rebuke over our lives. They vividly express the ugliness of unbelief and the dreaded results of shameless sin.

I love the fact that God doesn't fake, feign, or flatter. He is not a politically correct Being. When His Spirit moved various prophets and apostles to take up their pens and write the words we would one day read as inspired Scripture, God never once said, "Now, go easy. Don't offend anybody. Keep it mild." Never! God shoots straight. If He paints the portrait of a person's life, He includes the warts and scars and scabs. From Noah's drunkenness to David's adultery, from Jacob's conniving to Peter's hypocrisy — God's Word presents people as they are, not as later mythmakers wish they would have been.

These aren't the Bible stories that fill the pages of our kids' Bible storybooks, are they? Noah's ark, David and Goliath, Jacob's ladder to heaven, and Peter walking on water—these all find a place in our polite retelling of biblical stories. But God's Word doesn't shy away from the bad or the ugly of biblical history.

So, when God describes the condition of the human heart, He doesn't leave us with a one-sided presentation of its God-given potential for creativity, goodness, and love. Instead, God tells us, "The heart is more deceitful than all else and is desperately sick" (Jer. 17:9). The apostle Paul bluntly describes just how sinful and depraved we humans are:

> There is none righteous, not even one;
> There is none who understands,
> There is none who seeks for God;
> All have turned aside, together they have become useless;
> There is none who does good,
> There is not even one. (Rom. 3:10–12)

As one of my mentors used to say, "If depravity were blue, we would be blue all over." The words of Romans 3 are "blue all over." Not the kind of words you'd highlight in a mat and frame and hang on your study lounge, are they? Yet the truth they proclaim is just as vital to a balanced theology as "For God so loved the world, that He gave His only begotten Son" (John 3:16).

As rough as these personal episodes and as harsh as these passages may appear, the lurid details regarding false teachers in 2 Peter 2:12–19 seem even less sparing. Whereas the Bible's biographies present snapshots of human sin and Paul's words paint depravity with broad brushstrokes, the apostle Peter projects a detailed and dramatic picture of human corruption. The scene is neither pleasant nor encouraging. Rather, it is dark and foreboding. The tone feels more like a walk through the sleazy back alleys of a foul-smelling ghetto—where shameless gutter conditions accost our moral senses like putrid waste in a gutter.

Why does Peter delve so deeply into these depths of depravity? Remember that Peter is writing this letter to remind believers of the source of sound teaching, to encourage diligence in the faith, and to strengthen biblical foundations of beliefs and practices. To encourage the positive, Peter sets it against the black backdrop of the negative. In chapter 1, he described in brilliant hues the useful and fruitful image of a growing believer and pointed to the hope they have through embracing God's Word as their standard of unfailing truth. In chapter 2, he describes the useless and fruitless unbeliever in dark, drab colors, pointing to their future judgment for rejecting God's Word and God's Son and for leading others astray.

— 2:12–14 —

These first three verses present a desperate portrait of animal appetites taking full charge of human beings. When these subhuman impulses take control, the result is self-condemnation and destruction.

When God created Adam and Eve and placed them in the garden of Eden, He gave them authority over all the animals (Gen. 1:26–27). This dominion over animals is part of what it meant for human beings to be created in the image of God. Satan took the form of a serpent in order to deceive the human race, but instead of exercising their dominion over that animal, the human pair submitted to it, listened to his deceptive words, and abdicated their position (Gen. 3). Ever since that tragic fall, humans have continued to abandon their place of dignity over creation in exchange for behavior that puts them on par with the very beasts God meant them to dominate.

Though divinely endowed with superior reason, such people become, as Peter says, "like unreasoning animals." Instead of exercising dominion, they act like "creatures of instinct to be captured and killed." Instead of submitting to the divine power to lift them up to a place of dignity and glory, they mock and revile things they don't understand. With their animalistic mentality, a corrupt morality follows. Such people are constantly on the prowl for fornication or adultery. They size up every situation for opportunities to sin. They greedily bite at every baited hook, unconcerned about the disastrous consequences.

Like carnivorous predators, they hunt for naïve, weak, and unstable victims to devour. In fact, Peter says they have "a heart trained in greed"—masters at conning, extorting, stealing, blackmailing. They know how to jerk at the heartstrings and sound so sincere. Jesus described such monstrous humans well: "Beware of the false prophets, who come to you in sheep's clothing, but inwardly are ravenous wolves" (Matt. 7:15). It's no wonder Peter calls these false teachers "accursed children" (2 Peter 2:14)!

— 2:15–17 —

The false teachers, having known God's straight Way, have veered off to cut their own paths through the wilderness of wickedness. Instead of following Christ—the true Prophet—they follow in the footsteps of Balaam, a quintessential false prophet. Peter alludes to this Old Testament figure to illustrate a hireling prophet who peddled his gift (Num. 22–24; 31:1–16). That man loved money, and because of his greed, he led Israel into sin. He used his eloquence to fulfill his own lusts rather than faithfully represent the truth. In a similar manner, the false teachers in Peter's day led people astray for personal gain by persuasive false prophecy.

False prophets today are no different. In fact, every modern-day Balaam has his or her price. They may appear on the outside to be in it for the ministry, but it doesn't take long to realize they're in it for the money. And when the price is right, make no mistake, they exchange principle for profit.

This reminds me of the story of a crooked bank officer who approached a junior clerk and whispered to him one quiet afternoon, "Hey, if I gave you $25,000, would you help me, well, let's just say 'fix' the books? You know, make a few lucrative adjustments?"

The clerk responded, "Yeah, I suppose I could do that for $25,000."

His boss leaned in. "Would you do it for $100?"

Insulted, the clerk replied, "No way! What do you think I am? A common thief?"

The bank officer answered, "We've already established that. Now we're just negotiating the price."

The point of this story is that every fake has a price. Those who lack integrity will do anything to feed the greed. Peter calls this the "wages of unrighteousness" (2:15). But too often these false prophets forget that though their exploits can seem profitable in the short term, the work of wickedness will ultimately earn the wages of sin—death (Rom. 6:23). God Himself miraculously rebuked Balaam through a donkey, a sign of the depths of the prophet's animalistic madness. And Joshua 13:22 includes a brief note in its description of the conquest of the Promised Land that illustrates the ultimate end of false prophets who find themselves on the wrong side when judgment finally falls: "The sons of Israel also killed Balaam the son of Beor, the diviner, with the sword among the rest of their slain." The wages of sin was death.

Peter then uses three vivid word pictures to describe such apostates. First, as "springs without water" (2:17) they appear to have something refreshing to offer, but when you get close, you realize it's just a spiritual mirage. Second, they are "mists driven by a storm." Normally storms drive rain clouds bursting with water to nourish crops and prevent drought. But apostates deceive people with thunderous claims and flashy appeal—bringing with them not spiritually nourishing doctrine, but useless mists. Third, they may claim to lead people into the light through their "enlightening" teachings, but they and those who follow all end up in the same place: "black darkness."

— 2:18–19 —

Irenaeus of Lyons grew up in Polycarp's church in Smyrna before being sent to

From My Journal

A Dose of Discernment

My high school speech teacher made us memorize a Persian proverb. It goes like this:

He who knows not, and knows not that he knows not, is a fool; shun him.
He who knows not, and knows that he knows not, is a child; teach him.
He who knows, and knows not that he knows, is asleep; wake him.
He who knows, and knows that he knows, is wise; follow him.

Since high school I've learned the true meaning of those lines. I've discovered that all four "types" can be found on every campus, in any business, in all neighborhoods, and within every church. They don't wear badges marked "fool," "child," "asleep," or "wise." And you'll never have somebody walk up to you, shake your hand, and say, "Hi, I'm Donald. I'm a fool." Chances are, the last thing he will want you to discover is the deep-down truth that "he knows not that he knows not."

Then how in the world are we to know whom to shun, to teach, to awaken, or to follow? The answer, in a word, is *discernment*—the skill and accuracy in reading character and the ability to detect and identify the real truth, to see beneath the surface, to read between the lines, and to sense by intuition that something is not right. Hebrews 5:14 calls discernment a mark of maturity. It gives a person the proper frame of reference, a definite line of separating good and evil. It acts as an umpire in life and blows the whistle on the spurious. It's as particular as a pathologist peering into a microscope.

Discernment doesn't fall for fakes, flirt with phonies, dance with deceivers, or kiss counterfeits goodnight. In fact, discernment would rather relax alone at night with the Good Book than mess around with the gullible gang. The reason? Because it's from that Book that discernment learns to distinguish the fools from the children ... and the sleeping from the wise.

Before you start in on the bromide, "But that doesn't sound very loving!" better take a look at the apostle John's counsel. You remember John? He's the man known for his tender love for Jesus. Well, he wrote, "Beloved, do not believe every spirit, but test the spirits to see whether they are from God, because many false prophets have gone out into the world" (1 John 4:1). In today's talk: "Stop believing everything you hear! Quit being so gullible. Be selective. Think!" Lack of discernment spawns and invites more heresy than any one of us is ready to believe. One of the tactics of survival when facing "the flaming arrows of the evil one" (Eph. 6:16) is to make certain we are tightly holding on to the shield of faith.

A Christian without discernment is like a submarine plowing full speed ahead without radar or periscope. Or a loaded 747 trying to land in dense fog without instruments or radio—lots of noise, a great deal of power, good intentions ... *until*. I don't have another Persian proverb to describe the outcome, but who needs it? It happens day in, day out with disastrous regularity.

Second Peter reminds us with vivid words that false teachers are on the prowl. The moment they find a chink in the armor of the unsuspecting believer, their hidden stiletto of heresy will strike. To keep your discernment high, go to your *knee*; James 1:5 promises wisdom to those who ask for it. Go to the *Word*; Psalm 119:98–100 offers insight beyond any earthly source. And go to the *wise*; discernment is better caught than taught. Stay close to those seasoned saints, that is, the proven men and women who overflow with wisdom.[12]

Rome, then to Lyons in modern-day France. Throughout his life he encountered numerous false teachers and wrote a five-volume refutation of their teachings. Regarding the devious nature of false teachers' compelling yarn-spinning, Irenaeus wrote, "Error, indeed, is never set forth in its naked deformity, lest, being thus exposed, it should at once be detected. But it is craftily decked out in an attractive dress, so as, by its outward form, to make it appear to the inexperienced (ridiculous as the expression may seem) more true than the truth itself."[10] Indeed, false teachers entice others with arrogant, swelling words that leave a powerful impression on unsuspecting victims. They have an answer for everything. They express bold criticisms against the "simple" truth, quote hidden or forgotten sources, provide clever arguments, and twist reason. The gullible gobble it up.

Peter makes the point that the impressive words of the false teachers don't point us to the truth; rather, they point us to the teacher. We are wise to be suspicious of those who seem too smooth, too polished, too attractive. Those telltale signs often indicate that such teachers promise more than they deliver. We must be especially wary of preachers or teachers who constantly put down other ministers of the gospel and try to make themselves look like the best—or even the only—source of truth.

Though they promise freedom, the lifestyles of these false teachers drag others into the enslavement of corruption (2:19). They love to flaunt their freedom. To them, it means the liberty to sin as much as they want, unrestrained by truth, unafraid of repercussions in either this life or the life to come. Please don't misunderstand. I'm a preacher of grace. And I believe Christ has set us free from the Law and delivered us from man-made legalism. But uninformed and unspiritual believers often fail to realize that we have been set free from the Law *to live as loving children of God rather than beaten-down slaves of a brooding master.*

God never meant His grace and mercy to provide us with a license to sin. As Paul says in Romans 6:1 – 2, "What shall we say then? Are we to continue in sin so that grace may increase? May it never be! How shall we who died to sin still live in it?" The false teachers, ripping the doctrine of grace from its larger context of truth, distorted the Christian faith into an unrecognizable monstrosity. In the words of Dietrich Bonhoeffer, they offered "cheap grace."[11]

— **2:20 – 22** —

Throughout his description of the false teachers, Peter has hinted at the future judgments they will reap (2:1, 3, 9, 12, 13, 17, 19). In the last few verses of this chapter,

Peter zooms in on the lot of those who, having known the way of righteousness through Christ, have turned their backs on it and have gone their own way.

The false teachers Peter has in mind are not merely confused Christians, doubting Thomases, or backslidden believers. These are false professors—people who appear for a time to be authentic but are, in fact, like counterfeit bills amidst a pocketful of the real thing. They can pass themselves off as true Christians for a while, but eventually their words and deeds give them away.

These false teachers, Peter says, have "knowledge of the Lord and Savior Jesus Christ" (2:20). By their fruit, however, we can discern that they don't have a true, saving knowledge of Christ that has genuinely transformed their lives. Peter describes fruitful, saving knowledge of Christ in other parts of this letter:

- Grace and peace be multiplied to you in the *knowledge* of God and of Jesus our Lord. (1:2)
- His divine power has granted to us everything pertaining to life and godliness, through the *true knowledge* of Him who called us by His own glory and excellence. (1:3)
- For if these qualities are yours and are increasing, they render you neither useless nor unfruitful in the *true knowledge* of our Lord Jesus Christ. (1:8, italics mine)

In these passages, we see the results of the true, saving knowledge of Christ—multiplication of grace and peace, life and godliness, and increasing fruitful and useful virtues. This doesn't mean that every day, or every week, or even every month of a believer's life will be a bountiful harvest of quality spiritual fruit. But it does mean that the personal knowledge of Jesus Christ as Lord and Savior will result in the bearing of fruit over the lifetime of a believer. It's helpful to remember that fruit bearing is seasonal. Peter writes to believers assuming that they all need encouragement in their spiritual growth to regain or remain fruitful and useful (1:8).

Peter has in mind the kinds of people Jesus referred to when he said that Satan would sow "tares among the wheat"—deceptive look-alikes that become evident only as the genuine wheat bears its grain (Matt. 13:25–26). These are also the caliber of false teachers John described as "antichrists" who "went out from us, but they were not really of us; for if they had been of us, they would have remained with us; but they went out, so that it would be shown that they all are not of us" (1 John 2:19). This doesn't mean that true believers can lose their salvation. In fact, just the opposite! It means that false believers never had salvation to begin with—a fact demonstrated by their failure to remain in the Way of truth.

These people were intellectually aware of the truth but had never allowed it to transform their hearts. As a result, they are in a worse condition than those who had never heard (2:20–21)! They knew enough about the Christian faith to conduct themselves in ways that appear genuine. But eventually their cloaks of deception fell away and their malicious intentions became obvious to everybody.

How did it become obvious?

Returning to his earlier analogy of false teachers who conduct themselves like "unreasoning animals" (2:12), Peter likens their behavior to dogs and pigs. In Peter's day, dogs were regarded as unclean animals that ran in packs, wild and vicious. Don't think of the pampered, well-groomed pets of our day. Think of scavenging beasts no more appealing than giant rats. Quoting Proverbs 26:11, Peter says these false teachers who turn their backs on the truth are like dogs who return to their own vomit. He also says they are like a freshly bathed pig that cannot pass up the opportunity to return to its stinking muck. There's just something in the nature of undomesticated animals to act like animals. No matter how well you treat them, no matter how you pretty them up, in the end their instincts kick in and their true natures as beasts will be revealed.

In this way, Peter makes the stunning argument that ignorance of the truth is better than apostasy from it. How can he say that? I can think of three reasons. First, somebody who is ignorant of the truth can be won to the Lord, but somebody who has rejected it is seldom open to correction and change. They think they've "been there, done that." It's not impossible, but it's difficult to remove the baggage, clear the confusion, and help them unlearn what they have chosen to believe.

Second, those who are ignorant of the truth don't have the influence over others that the "learned" have. Those who think they know it all, teach as if they do. They influence others and lead them astray. In my experience, the most damaging critics of Christianity are those who claim to have been believers but were suddenly "enlightened" by a different religion ... or by no religion at all. The testimonies of apostates can be very influential and extremely persuasive.

Third, in the final judgment, the severity of punishment will be less for the ignorant than for the apostates. The Bible states that those who die without having a true, saving knowledge of Christ will be condemned to eternal separation from God. But according to Jesus' parable in Luke 12:41–48, those who never knew Him will suffer a lesser degree of punishment than those who were exposed to the truth but turned away from Him. Jesus said:

> And that slave who knew his master's will and did not get ready or act in accord with his will, will receive many lashes, but the one who did not know it, and

committed deeds worthy of a flogging, will receive but few. From everyone who has been given much, much will be required; and to whom they entrusted much, of him they will ask all the more. (Luke 12:47–48)

NOTES:

1. Christopher Edwards, *Crazy for God* (Englewood Cliffs, NJ: Prentice-Hall, 1979), preface.

2. Walter Bauer et al., eds., *A Greek-English Lexicon of the New Testament and Other Early Christian Literature*, 2nd rev. ed. (Chicago: Univ. of Chicago Press, 1979), 23–24.

3. Warren W. Wiersbe, *Be Alert* (Wheaton, IL: Victor, 1984), 38.

4. See Irenaeus, *Against Heresies* 1.16; Tertullian, *On the Soul* 34.

5. Irenaeus, *Against Heresies* 1.26.1.

6. See Oskar Skarsaune, *In the Shadow of the Temple: Jewish Influences on Early Christianity* (Downers Grove, IL: InterVarsity Press, 2002), 246–53.

7. William Barclay, *The Letters of James and Peter*, 2nd ed., The Daily Study Bible Series (Philadelphia: Westminster, 1960), 377.

8. Bauer et al., *A Greek-English Lexicon*, 666.

9. See the parallel in Jude 6 as well as the in-depth discussion of this understanding of Genesis 6 in my comments on 1 Peter 3:19–20, pages 204–7.

10. Irenaeus of Lyons, *Against Heresies* 1.1.2, in *The Ante-Nicene Fathers: Translations of the Writings of the Fathers down to AD 325*, ed. Alexander Roberts et al.; vol. 1, *The Apostolic Fathers, Justin Martyr, Irenaeus*, American reprint ed. (New York: Charles Scribner's Sons, 1899), 315.

11. Dietrich Bonhoeffer, *The Cost of Discipleship*, rev. ed. (New York: Simon & Schuster, 1995), 44–45.

12. Adapted from Charles R. Swindoll, "Think with Discernment," in *Come before Winter and Share My Hope* (Grand Rapids: Zondervan, 1985), 18–19.

ANTICIPATION OF CHRIST'S RETURN (2 PETER 3:1–18)

As the menacing clouds begin to break and Peter's loud storm of condemnation of false teachers subsides, a beam of light pierces the gloominess. This great apostle decides that now is the time to inject a ray of hope into his otherwise frightening portrayal of the future. Though the threat of false teachers is real and imminent, he wants us to lift our eyes beyond the immediate landscape and see the bright horizon that is yet to come. It's important to remember that between the rough period of false prophets and the coming restoration of creation, two unforgettable events intervene — the great tribulation, by which the present world and all its wickedness will be destroyed, and the return of Christ, by which a new era of righteousness will begin.

Before we follow Peter forward through these important topics, let's take another quick look back at where he's led us. The pointed message Peter wants to leave as his legacy can be summed up in two commands: "Beware!" and "Be ready!" The first chapter of the letter has addressed the issue of moral purity in the last days. He urged us to avoid the corruption of the world (1:4), reminding us of the fruitful Christian life expected of those who have been equipped with everything necessary for godliness (1:5–13). As the sure foundation for faith, Peter directed believers to Scripture as the Spirit-breathed, inerrant Word of God, encouraging us to stand strong in the truth (1:16–21). Such an exhortation for doctrinal and moral diligence was necessary as Peter transitioned to a stern warning about the presence of false teachers.

Chapter 2 shifts from a description of godliness and confidence in the truth to wickedness and peddlers of falsehood. The entire chapter describes the moral and doctrinal horrors of deceitful heretics (2:1–3). Because of their cunning deception, they will be formidable foes to the church. But Peter has reminded us that apostates who flirt with the truth, then turn their backs on it, will incur great judgment (2:21–22). When this judgment comes upon the world in the future, however, true believers in Christ will be rescued from wrath (2:9), while false prophets will find themselves caught in the fires of judgment. Behind this tirade against false teachers stands a warning to us all: avoid their deceptions by being discerning and remaining strong in the truth.

This now leads to Peter's finale in chapter 3. He further develops the issue of the end times, which he has mentioned several times in the first two chapters. In

KEY TERMS

μακροθυμέω [*makrothymeō*] (3114) "to persevere, be patient, wait long"

This word comes from two Greek words: *makros*, meaning "large," and *thymos*, meaning "intense anger, burning wrath, explosive rage." Together these words refer to the act of holding back one's anger. We might say such a person has a long fuse and can avoid sudden outbursts of rage. In 2 Peter 3:9, together with its noun form in 3:15, it refers to God's patience exhibited through holding back His wrath in order for more to be saved.

ἡμέρα κυρίου [*hēmera kyriou*] (2250 + 2962) "Day of the Lord"

Though simple to translate, the biblical phrase "day of the Lord" is complicated and rather difficult to sort out. It is a general title for any time of judgment followed by blessing. It usually refers not to a single twenty-four-hour period, but to a distinct period of judgment. In the Old Testament, it referred to any period of time when God sent judgment on the wicked, so there were many historical "days of the Lord." In Peter's usage, though, it has a more technical meaning relating to the final judgment yet to come.

ἐπαγγελία [*epangelia*] (1860) "promise, guarantee"

This term, often used in covenant contexts (Eph. 2:12; Heb. 6:17; 11:9), generally refers to various guarantees made by God that believers have not yet fully experienced, but in which they hope. Among these are included the Holy Spirit (Gal. 3:14; Eph. 1:13) and eternal life (2 Tim. 1:1; 1 John 2:25). Peter focuses on specific future events — the promise of Christ's return in judgment (2 Peter 3:4, 9) as well as the following "new heavens and new earth" (3:13). We can be confident that God will not break His promises. His track record for keeping promises is impeccable.

these, his final written words to the churches prior to his martyrdom, Peter answers the question, "How will all this end?" He gives us a final *warning*: avoid worldly corruption and false teachers (3:11, 17–18). He presents a last *reminder*: God's testimony is trustworthy (3:1–2). And he proclaims a glorious *promise*: a new creation is coming in which righteousness dwells (3:13).

A Warning to Skeptics and Sinners (2 Peter 3:1–7)

¹This is now, beloved, the second letter I am writing to you in which I am stirring up your sincere mind by way of reminder, ²that you should remember the words spoken beforehand by the holy prophets and the command-

ment of the Lord and Savior *spoken* by your apostles. ³Know this first of all, that in the last days mockers will come with *their* mocking, following after their own lusts, ⁴and saying, "Where is the promise of His coming? For *ever* since the fathers fell asleep, all continues just as it was from the beginning of creation." ⁵For when they maintain this, it escapes their notice that by the word of God *the* heavens existed long ago and *the* earth was formed out of water and by water, ⁶through which the world at that time was destroyed, being flooded with water. ⁷But by His word the present heavens and earth are being reserved for fire, kept for the day of judgment and destruction of ungodly men.

After writing a tirade against the despicable doctrines and practices of false teachers in chapter 2, in my imagination Peter takes a break to calm his Galilean fury. Standing up and taking a deep breath, he closes his eyes and reviews what he wrote in his first letter and considers the ground he has already covered in this second. Then, with bold resolve, he addresses his readers with a term of endearment, "beloved." The word hasn't appeared in this letter since 1:17, but he will repeat it four more times before ending his final written words to the churches (3:8, 14, 15, 17).

Peter clearly states his purpose for writing this second letter: to stimulate our "sincere mind" (3:1) by reminding us of things we should already know. Note that he writes to those already characterized by wholesome thinking, free from deception and corruption. They are "innocent" in thought and deed. But innocent doesn't imply impervious. These believers need to stay on the alert.

This reminds me of the mood in the United States in the months following the horrific events of 9/11. You remember. Fighters patrolled the skies. Police were on constant alert. Nobody dared ignore suspicious activity. Airline security reached its all-time peak. Everybody knew the threat of unexpected attack was real and pervasive. It could come at any time, anywhere, from anybody. But as months and years separated Americans from those devastating events, the original vigilance cooled, then virtually chilled.

Few people knew what threat level the Department of Homeland Security had set, and later on, most didn't care. Countless grew tired of hearing about terrorist cells. And many have grown weary of military actions against havens of terrorism worldwide. Though nobody wants their country attacked again, few keep up the state of alert necessary to prevent it. Vigilance has waned. We are back to business as usual.

The same kind of thing was happening in Peter's day with regard to false teachers. Intellectually believers knew the dangers, the risks, and the threats. They had kept themselves pure and undefiled. But they needed a reminder, a wake-up call—

something to stir them up and sound the alarm again. Peter knew the first waves of deception had come, and his readers had maintained their sincerity. But a tidal wave of truth-twisters was about to arrive, and believers needed to brace themselves for the devastating blow.

— 3:1–2 —

Peter spells out exactly what he wants his readers to keep at the forefront of their minds in light of the lingering threat of false teachers. First, we should remember *the words spoken beforehand by the prophets* (3:2). This includes all of the Old Testament writings. With this statement Peter returns to the topic he introduced in 1:19–21. There he urged his readers to "pay attention" to the prophetic word "as to a lamp shining in a dark place" (1:19). That shining lamp had been illuminated by the Holy Spirit, who moved the authors of Scripture to compose — without error — God's written and inspired Word. We are told that these prophetic writings looked forward to the coming of Christ. In fact, Christ Himself said, "You search the Scriptures because you think that in them you have eternal life; it is these that testify about Me" (John 5:39). The writings of Moses, the Prophets, and the Psalms all point to Jesus Christ (Luke 24:27, 44; John 1:45; Acts 28:23; Rom. 1:1–4; 1 Cor. 15:3–4).

Second, we should remember *the commands given by the Savior* (2 Peter 3:2). Most of these words come to us through the Gospels — Matthew, Mark, Luke, and John. Jesus called His hearers first and foremost to a belief in Him as equal to the Father: "Believe in God; believe also in Me" (John 14:1). In fact, because Jesus is the way, the truth, and the life, no one can come to the Father except through Him (14:6). In light of this fundamental conviction about the person of Christ, Jesus reiterated the Old Testament command to love God with all our heart, soul, and mind (Matt. 22:37). Yet along with this command Jesus emphasized the horizontal love both of our neighbors in general (22:39) and of fellow believers in particular (John 13:34).

Third, implied in Peter's reminder is a call to remember *the teaching of the apostles* (2 Peter 3:2). The apostolic doctrine formed the firm foundation of the church, of which Christ is the cornerstone (Eph. 2:20). Their ministry did not point to themselves, but back to Christ's person, work, and words. At the same time, Jesus' own words point forward to His second coming, when His work will be fulfilled and His glorious person will be universally revealed.

Peter's brief statement in 3:2 encompasses the entire Old and New Testaments — the prophets, Jesus, and the apostles. No other source of truth has the power to give us lasting stability and constant assurance. After this strong reminder for the godly to stand firm on the teachings of Scripture as the foundation for their faith, Peter offers a series of sober warnings to the ungodly. In verses 3–7, he communicates three dimensions of thought related to the present, the past, and the future.

— **3:3–4** —

First, Peter informs us of *something to know about the present.* He writes, "In the last days mockers will come" (3:3). Now, from Peter's perspective, near the end of his earthly life, this statement is prophetic. Yes, false prophets had already begun to challenge the apostles and offer their own counterfeit christs. Yes, many believers had already abandoned the faith, being led astray by heresy, lust, or greed. But Peter has in mind a different class of contrarian—those who will reject the faith by mocking, teasing, and poking fun at its claims. Those mentioned in chapter 2 were the false brethren who claimed to be believers but were not. Those described in chapter 3 are the cynical scoffers who make fun of the faith from the outside. Sometimes these categories overlap, but much of the time they are two distinct forces to be reckoned with.

Though Peter casts this warning about mockers as a prophecy, within a few years the first wave of these mockers already began to arrive on the scene. In fact, it may be that Jude's brief letter, written just a few years later, quoted Peter's prophecy as already coming to pass:

> But you, beloved, ought to remember the words that were spoken beforehand by the apostles of our Lord Jesus Christ, that they were saying to you, "In the last time there will be mockers, following after their own ungodly lusts." These are the ones who cause divisions, worldly-minded, devoid of the Spirit. (Jude 17–19)

Beginning in the first century and continuing to our own day, cynics have come and gone. Their shrill mockery and accusing fingers pointing at Christianity draw a lot of attention. The sum of their scoffing is, to paraphrase Peter, "How in the world can you believe this stuff? You think Jesus is going to come back? He lived, taught, and died. That's it. And everything stays just the same. Nothing's changed! In fact, history keeps plodding along, just as it has for thousands of years."

You see, the mockers, observing the historical and natural events of the present, assume that everything that has been will continue to be. The fancy term for this is "uniformitarianism." Now, that's a mouthful! It assumes an unbroken continuity of cause and effect in history and that this chain of events will continue unbroken into

From My Journal

Scoffed Up

As a preacher in the public square, rarely do I hear firsthand the mocking I know is out there. For most preachers, it's the same. I know "preacher roasts" are usually held regularly on Sunday afternoons, but most of the time, those snide remarks don't make it back to the pastor's ears. I say *most* of the time, because sometimes they do.

I'll never forget the first time I witnessed a bona fide mocker have his day during a sermon (it wasn't the last). I wasn't a preacher, just a member of the congregation sitting in the pew of a small church. Behind me sat a man in obvious disagreement with the preacher's words. After a while the fellow couldn't take it any longer. He actually stood up, shook his fist, and shouted, "That is ridiculous!" And he walked out. I must say to the credit of the preacher, he never blinked; he just kept right on preaching!

The first time I personally encountered public ridicule regarding the gospel of Christ occurred back in the early 1960s when I was a seminary student. A friend of mine and I drove up to Norman, Oklahoma, where I stood on a free-speech platform and spoke openly about the Lord Jesus Christ. Most people showed no interest in my message. But several took the opportunity to provide feedback—in the form of mocking jabs and sarcastic remarks directed not so much at me, but at Jesus Christ. In fact, a few of them even threw things! (Up until that point in my life I thought such things happened only in movies!) They delighted in mocking the Lord who died for them.

Those two episodes occurred decades ago. Since that time I've seen the tempo and volume of mockery intensify in America. On TV, in movies, over the airwaves, and on the Internet, the scoffers have become bolder as American culture in general has become more secular (I'm tempted to say "pagan"). Atheism, humanism, materialism, and antisupernaturalism have become the norm among the intelligentsia, and it doesn't seem to be changing.

Not surprisingly, Peter was right. Mockers have come.

the future. Wedded to this idea is the notion of *materialism*—that the physical universe is all that exists. And one more oversized word, *antisupernaturalism*, assumes that no supernatural beings (especially God) has or will interrupt the course of human history to make changes, either large or small. This is often coupled with *atheism*—the belief that such an active God doesn't exist at all.

Today scoffers like this—atheists, materialists, antisupernaturalists, uniformitarians—have loud voices. They write popular and academic books, travel the talk-show circuits, and influence the minds of the masses. The details may be new and certainly the favorable media coverage has increased—but the basic tone and intention mirrors the scoffers of Peter's day. This condition of mockers challenging the claim that a day of reckoning is at hand describes our own day well.

— **3:5–6** —

After telling us something to know about our present—the arrival of scoffers (3:3–4)—Peter addresses *something to remember from the past* (3:5–6). Peter says that when these mockers maintain that Jesus will never return to transform this world through judgment and restoration, they forget that God has done *exactly* this sort of thing before.

Scoffers almost inevitably reject two bedrock foundations of a Christian view of history: creation out of nothing and a global flood. Verse 5 provides a brief summary statement reminding us that God not only created the earth's atmosphere ("heavens") by separating water from water, but that He also formed the habitable world ages ago by a process of separating water from land. Genesis 1 describes both acts:

> Then God said, "Let there be an expanse in the midst of the waters, and let it separate the waters from the waters." God made the expanse, and separated the waters which were below the expanse from the waters which were above the expanse; and it was so. God called the expanse heaven …
>
> Then God said, "Let the waters below the heavens be gathered into one place, and let the dry land appear"; and it was so. God called the dry land earth, and the gathering of the waters He called seas; and God saw that it was good. (Gen. 1:6–10)

That was the first creation of heaven and earth. This is the kind of special creative act of God that atheists, materialists, and other skeptics openly reject. In fact, Peter says that the truth of creation "escapes their notice." That phrase is best translated, "But they deliberately forget" (NIV). It is not simply a matter of having never heard that God ordered everything. Instead, they come up with all sorts of theories and reasons to push the notion of a sovereign Creator out of their minds. They banish Genesis 1 to the category of myth or an antiquated worldview, favoring instead a billions-of-years process of astronomical and geological evolution.

Peter emphasizes God's acts of separating water in creating the sky and earth because the judgment of the earth that followed at the time of Noah involved a reversal of that separation, by means of a flood. The world at that time—that is, the world originally created in Genesis 1—was destroyed by those same waters. This judgment of the flood is described in Genesis 7:11–12.

> In the six hundredth year of Noah's life, in the second month, on the seventeenth day of the month, on the same day all the fountains of the great deep burst open, and the floodgates of the sky were opened. The rain fell upon the earth for forty days and forty nights.

I find it interesting that the same people who reject the evidence of God's design and creation of the world also reject the evidence of a global flood. They look at the same geological evidence and read the same accounts of a flood found in almost every ancient culture around the world, but they conclude it's all legend or myth, or at most, an exaggerated account of a local calamity like a tsunami or hurricane.

But Peter makes it perfectly clear that God destroyed the original heaven and earth through the flood. The new order of things that arose after the floodwaters subsided differed dramatically from the former world of wickedness. Peter means that just as God catastrophically intervened with water during the flood thousands of years ago, so He will one day intervene again—but next time, with fire.

— **3:7** —

Peter has told us something about our present—that mockers will come (3:3–4); then he reminded us of something about ancient history—that God judged the world of mockers during the days of Noah (3:5–6). Now Peter puts these two facts together, pointing forward to *something to count on in the future*—the coming judgment of the present world order (3:7).

Peter says that the present "heavens and earth"—the world order in which humans have lived since the flood of Noah—are being reserved for fire. This fire will come on the day of judgment, when God destroys the world and the works of ungodly people. No doubt this will include the false teachers of chapter 2, as well as the scoffers of chapter 3. It corresponds with Peter's repeated warnings of coming judgment in which the wicked will perish and the righteous will be saved (2:1, 3, 9).

What comes after the judgment by fire? Peter will address this topic in verse 13 — the ushering in of a "new heavens and a new earth" rising from the conflagration of the present order. Just as the world of Genesis 1 had been judged and was restored after the flood, so the present heavens and earth will be judged and restored after the fire. We can chart Peter's understanding of the various phases of the world in three distinct periods of "heaven and earth" — before the flood, after the flood, and after the fire.

It is interesting to note that in chapter 2, when Peter referred to biblical illustrations of God's rescuing the righteous and judging the wicked, he used the examples of the flood of Noah and the fire of Sodom and Gomorrah. These correspond to Peter's reference to the past judgment by flood and the coming judgment by flame. In fact, Peter even said that God made the people of Sodom and Gomorrah "an example to those who would live ungodly lives thereafter" (2:6).

FLOOD FOR THOUGHT

The Bible isn't the only ancient book that describes a worldwide flood. From South America to Asia, from Africa to Australia, ancient peoples recall a disastrous flood in their songs, poems, traditions, and legends. Scholars have long known of "flood stories" from widespread ancient cultures — epics of gods flooding the world to destroy wicked or annoying humanity, with only a handful of humans surviving.

The Sumerian account, for example, tells of a king, Ziusudra, who is told by the god, Enki, that the other gods plan to destroy humanity with a flood. The reason? Because people are too noisy and they keep the gods awake day and night![1] Ziusudra promptly builds a great boat and loads it with his family and animals to escape the destruction.[2] After the rain subsides, the king presents himself before the gods, An and Elil, and kisses the ground to beg them for his life.[3]

The Babylonian Epic of Gilgamesh mentions an old man named Utnapishtim, who escaped a flood sent by the gods to destroy humanity. One of the gods, Ea, had alerted him to the plan and prompted him to build an ark. When the rain ceased and the ark had come to rest on a high mountain, Utnapishtim sent a raven and a dove to make sure he could leave the boat. At once he sacrificed to the gods to gain their favor.[4]

Further east, the Hindu flood myth follows the main character Manu, who is informed by a fish that he must build a boat to escape a coming flood that will destroy his region. Manu heeds the warning of the talking fish. When the rain begins to fall, Manu enters the ark, and the fish tow the boat to the top of a mountain. The flood destroyed all creatures except Manu.[5]

These few examples of embellished flood stories suggest that the events described in Genesis 6–9 and reiterated by Peter in 2 Peter 3 rest on actual historical events. Yes, the various cultures modified the true version of events recorded in Scripture. They replaced Yahweh with gods (or a fish!), and they replaced Noah with characters like Ziusudra, Manu, or Utnapishtim. But the basic story reminds us of a historical truth humanity often forgets: that "the world at that time was destroyed, being flooded with water" (2 Peter 3:6).

Peter's message couldn't be more clear: regardless of the way things appear day in and day out, despite the mockery of scoffers poking fun at the idea of Christ's return and the coming judgments, *in the end, God wins*!

Application

Rethinking the Return

Yes, critics have denied it. Cynics have laughed at it. Scholars have ignored it. Liberal theologians have explained it away (they call it "demythologizing"), and fanatics have perverted it. "Where is the promise of His coming?" (2 Peter 3:4) many still shout sarcastically. The return of the Savior will continue to be attacked, misapplied, and denied. But there it stands, solid as a stone, soon to be fulfilled, ready to offer us hope and encouragement amid despair and unbelief.

"Okay, great. But what do I do in the meantime?" I can hear a dozen or more pragmatists asking that question in unison. Fair enough. If the doctrine of the second coming of Christ doesn't actually affect how we live, then does it really matter if mockers scoff at it? Shouldn't we just sweep that little embarrassing, irrelevant doctrine under the carpet and focus on more important things? What *should* we do in light of Christ's sure return?

First, it might be best for you to understand what you *don't* do. You don't dress up in a white robe and gather with like-minded fanatics in a commune or on some roof. You don't quit work and move to the highest mountains to be the first to meet the Lord when He descends. And you don't try to set dates for His return, based on cockeyed calculations or harebrained interpretations of the "signs of the time." In other words, don't join the unbiblical quacks who have overreacted and brought *deserved* ridicule on themselves by those ever-ready scoffers poised with rotten fruit in hand.

You *do*, however, get your act together . . . and keep it together. You *do* live every day as if it's your last, for His glory. You *do* work diligently on your job and in your home, as if He isn't coming for another ten years, for His name's sake. You *do* shake salt out every chance you get; you *do* shine the light and remain balanced, cheerful, winsome, and stable, expecting His return day by day. You *do* continue sharing the good news with those who are "blue all over." Other than that, keep looking up with hope and give a cold shoulder to the cool skeptics.

Oh, one more thing. If you're not absolutely ready to fly when Christ comes to snatch His own into the air (1 Thess. 4:17), you'd better get your ticket. *Fast.* As long as they are available, they're free. But don't wait. About the time you finally make up your mind, the whole thing could have happened, leaving you looking back instead of up. And instead of taking a high-speed trip to heaven to spend eternity with the Savior, you'll be left here—surrounded by "wise" skeptics who suddenly look, well, pretty stupid.

The Day of the Lord (2 Peter 3:8–13)

---

⁸But do not let this one *fact* escape your notice, beloved, that with the Lord one day is like a thousand years, and a thousand years like one day. ⁹The Lord is not slow about His promise, as some count slowness, but is patient toward you, not wishing for any to perish but for all to come to repentance. ¹⁰But the day of the Lord will come like a thief, in which the heavens will pass away with a roar and the elements will be destroyed with intense heat, and the earth and its works will be burned up. ¹¹Since all these things are to be destroyed in this way, what sort of people ought you to be in holy conduct and godliness, ¹²looking for and hastening the coming of the day of God, because of which the heavens will be destroyed by burning, and the elements will melt with intense heat! ¹³But according to His promise we are looking for new heavens and a new earth, in which righteousness dwells.

When I was a young believer, Bible prophecy was the hottest of all topics. If you wanted to increase attendance at the local church, you just scheduled a prophecy conference or announced your plan to start a sermon series on the book of Revelation. It seemed like dozens of books on prophecy were coming out every year! It felt hard to keep up. Interest has cooled over the decades, but you'll still find fervent fans of end-times teachers.

In light of this curiosity about prophecy and the tendency for some to go overboard on the issue, let me interject a few general facts about the future. I want briefly to share a few important points of counsel, at no extra cost. First, while God has revealed some things about the future, much still remains a mystery. One mark of immaturity in the Christian life is to read more into the biblical text than is actually there. We can be sure of the big picture when it comes to Bible prophecy, but a lot of details remain shrouded in obscurity.

Second, when searching for answers, continue to leave room for questions. Try not to make agreement on the particulars of future events a basis for fellowship with other believers. If you agree on the fundamental, saving truths of the faith related to the triune God, the person and work of Christ in His incarnation, death, resurrection, and ascension, then cut each other some slack on just how Christ's return is going to pan out. Be tolerant of those who don't see things as clearly as you do.

Third, though no one knows all the details, don't hesitate to stand firm on those clearly set forth in Scripture:

- Christ will physically return.
- There will be a final judgment.
- Heaven and hell are real.
- The resurrection of our bodies is a certainty.

These things are set forth plainly in the Bible and therefore can be counted on. In recent years the pendulum seems to have swung from obsession with details to ignorance of even the big picture. Balance is needed here, as always. Ultra dogmatism is unhealthy, but endless indecision on doctrinal views is unwise. If we don't have at least tentative answers, the seekers will find cults that do.

Prophetic events never fail to pluck the strings of our imaginations. Curious about the future, we are forever on a search for what lies just beyond the horizon. Scientists, philosophers, historians, politicians, and even fortune-tellers all make their forecasts and gain their followers, but no source of information compares to the Bible. When it comes to trustworthy, inspired truth we can count on, this Book not only stands out; it stands absolutely alone.

Peter already has established the authority of the Bible as a source for truth about the past and present (1:19–21). He has warned of the coming judgment that will catch unbelievers by surprise (chap. 2) and put scoffers in their places (3:1–7). Peter has reminded believers of sound teaching, to encourage diligence in the faith and to strengthen biblical foundations of beliefs and practices. Through his warnings, reminders, and promises, Peter urges diligence in light of the future hope of the coming of Christ and the glory that will come when the wicked are judged and the righteous rewarded. In 3:8–13, Peter further develops this encouraging hope.

— **3:8–9** —

Peter's original readers faced tough times: persecuted by emperors and governors, threatened by false teaching, belittled by scoffers, tempted to sin, swayed to defect from the faith. Hoping to calm their spirits, Peter reassures them that just as God put a stop to the wickedness of the world in the days of Noah, so He will do again (3:3–4). He reminds them that a day is coming when wrong will be righted and when the right will rule (3:4–7). The "present heavens and earth" (3:7) are marked for judgment.

At the beginning of verse 8, Peter urges us to take note of one thing in response to the mocking of skeptics who doubt that God will judge them. When Peter says that, for God, a day is like a thousand years and a thousand years like a day, he's not giving us some secret key to unlock prophecy in which we interpret every day as a thousand years and set some kind of date for the end of the world. Rather, he alludes to Psalm 90:4 — "For a thousand years in Your sight are like yesterday when it passes by, or as a watch in the night." The idea is that as far as God is concerned, our finite perception of time is irrelevant.

What comprises time on earth in no way impacts God's master plan. He is timeless — that is, He dwells above and apart from the cause-and-effect flow of time as we perceive it. Isaiah wrote: "'For My thoughts are not your thoughts, nor are your ways My ways,' declares the LORD. 'For as the heavens are higher than the earth, so are My ways higher than your ways and My thoughts than your thoughts'" (Isa. 55:8–9).

Why does Peter mention this theological truth? Because the scoffers rest their point on the basis of earth time, suggesting that a long delay in Christ's coming implies that God doesn't keep His promises. To be sure, from the perspective of finite human beings, God often appears to take His time to intervene. He often seems slow. We would love to push Him into fulfilling His promises or rush His plan. But God does things according to His own mysterious timetable. This doesn't mean that God doesn't care about rescuing and rewarding the righteous. Just the opposite! Peter claims that God's "delay" of judgment, in fact, makes room for His mercy!

Verse 9 refers to God's patient plan. He's not negligent about His promises. God is deliberately holding back the events of the end times in order to give as many people as possible an opportunity to turn to Christ and be saved. Seen from this perspective, the Lord is not slow … He's patient. He's not tardy … He's deliberately delaying. He's not indifferent … He's merciful. His plan is unfolding exactly as He has ordained it. The apostle Paul wrote that God "desires all men to be saved and to come to the knowledge of the truth" (1 Tim. 2:4).

To make this personal, imagine if Christ had returned just two weeks before you came to faith. Or two days. You would have missed salvation before the fires of judgment fell! Now apply this fact to others you know who do not yet know Christ. Put their names in verse 9 instead of Peter's "any" and "all": "[God] is patient toward _____, not wishing for _____ to perish but for _____ to come to repentance." That changes the perspective, doesn't it?

But God's patience doesn't benefit unbelievers alone. As He delays the coming judgment, He gives straying believers the opportunity to get their lives back on track. He leaves room for us to repent — not from damnation to salvation, but from a spiritually barren life to a life of spiritual fruit. Not only is God waiting patiently for non-Christians to believe, but He is also granting us time to share the good news of salvation with the lost (see Rom. 10:17).

—3:10–13—

Yet God will not delay forever. An unrevealed limit exists to this present period of patience. It's true that God, in His generosity and mercy, is holding back judgment. But Peter assures us that this mercy will come to an abrupt end when "the day of the Lord will come like a thief" (3:10).

"The day of the Lord" is a general title for any time of judgment. The term "day" is used figuratively; as we might say, "Back in grandpa's day, people didn't have computers." The phrase "the day of the Lord" refers to any period of time when God sends judgment on the wicked. This means there have been many historical "days of the Lord"—like the flood of Noah or the judgment of Sodom and Gomorrah.

But all these days had common features. Isaiah's words describe this well: "Behold, the day of the LORD is coming, cruel, with fury and burning anger, to make the land a desolation; and He will exterminate its sinners from it" (Isa. 13:9). Yet in the midst of the judgment, God promises that the righteous will be saved, as Peter preached on Pentecost, quoting the prophet Joel: "The sun will be turned into darkness and the moon into blood, before the great and glorious day of the Lord shall come. And it shall be that everyone who calls on the name of the Lord will be saved" (Acts 2:20–21).

Peter answers several big-picture questions for us in 3:10–12, but not always in the precise detail we might want.

- When will the day of the Lord come?
- What will happen when the day of Lord comes?
- How will the day of the Lord come?
- So, what should we do in response to the coming day of the Lord?

First, *when?* Peter dodges the *when* question by saying that the day of the Lord will come unexpectedly—"like a thief." This is a vivid word picture used by Christ to describe His own arrival in judgment in Matthew 24:43. Paul uses the analogy, too, when he says, "For you yourselves know full well that the day of the Lord will come just like a thief in the night" (1 Thess. 5:2). Just as a thief comes suddenly and unexpectedly, without announcement or warning, so the end-times judgment will begin when people least expect it.

Second, *what?* Three phrases in verse 10 tell us what will happen when this judgment comes. The "heavens will pass away," the "elements will be destroyed," and "the earth and its works will be burned up." Verse 12 further details this devastating picture, describing the heavens burning and the elements melting with intense heat. That's not a pleasant picture. Just as the former world in the days of Noah was wiped clean with all-consuming floodwaters, so the present world will endure greater purging by fire through intense heat.

Third, *how?* Peter describes the coming destruction with three terms in verse 10: "roar," "destroyed," and "intense heat." The images all refer to the familiar sounds and sensations that come with a disastrous fire. As a forest fire builds from mere cracklings to an uncontrollable ocean of flames, it sounds like a violent wind roaring through the trees. But instead of stripping off leaves and branches or felling several trees, forest fires leave behind a charred, barren wasteland, devoid of life. With this familiar analogy, Peter pictures the obliteration of the present world. In fact, Peter describes the destruction of the "elements" as melting (3:10, 12). In the ancient world, this expression did not refer to atomic particles as it does in modern science, but to the basic building blocks of the perceivable, material world—the earth, water, wind. All of these things, Peter says, will be wiped clear to make way for something new.

Finally, *so what?* What should we believers do in light of the end of all things? Peter answers this question in verses 11–13. Because everything will be destroyed with fire, we should live "in holy conduct and godliness" (3:11). There is no room for becoming attached to the material things of this world—putting our hope in them, investing in them, relying on them. They will all be burned to nothing!

At the same time, we should be "looking for and hastening the coming of the day of God" (3:12). In a certain sense, as we do the work of evangelism and share the gospel, we participate in speeding the return of Christ. God already knows how many and who will be saved, and when that number is fulfilled, the end will come (Matt. 24:14; Rom. 11:24–25). Don't go overboard on this, though. There's no way for us to know who or how many, so even though it's true that our work of evangelism hastens the end, we may be doing our work in the middle of His timetable!

Peter also says we should be "looking for new heavens and a new earth, in which righteousness dwells" (3:13). That is, our focus should be outside this present, temporary world as we look forward to the perfect eternal state, free from wickedness. The term "new heavens and a new earth" is first used in Isaiah to describe the new condition after the tribulation period, when Christ sets up His kingdom on earth (Isa. 65:17; 66:22). It also refers to the eternal state, after the millennium and great white throne judgment, when the new creation will replace the old (Rev. 21:1). Peter seems to refer generally to both, with an emphasis on the final, ultimate state of things, after the wicked of this world are judged in the tribulation and after the dead are judged in the lake of fire. Peter compresses these two end-times events in a general description. He does not intend to set out a time line but to assert that the present world is temporary; only the future world is eternal.

Reflecting the same kind of thought as Peter, the apostle Paul sums up the Christian hope this way: "For momentary, light affliction is producing for us an eternal weight of glory far beyond all comparison, while we look not at the things which are seen, but at the things which are not seen; for the things which are seen are temporal, but the things which are not seen are eternal" (2 Cor. 4:17–18).

Application

Clean Up, Look Up, Speak Up

Our marching orders as believers awaiting the Lord's return can be summed up in three commands: *Clean up* your life. *Look up* and expect His coming. And *speak up* every chance you get. Let's spend a little time reflecting on each of these applications of the end times.

First, what areas of your life require some cleanup? Don't rush through this; it's serious business. All of us have sin in our lives. In fact, John wrote, "If we say that we have no sin, we are deceiving ourselves and the truth is not in us" (1 John 1:8). Even the most mature believer has areas he or she needs to address. To help prick your conscience, study Paul's contrasting lists of the "deeds of the flesh" and the "fruit of the Spirit" in Galatians 5:19–23. Mark the fleshly deeds in your life … and the absent spiritual fruit. Then go to God. The apostle John continued in his discussion of sin, "If we confess our sins, He is faithful and righteous to forgive us our sins and to cleanse us from all unrighteousness" (1 John 1:9). Confess your sin, seek forgiveness, and ask for strength to overcome sin in this area.

Second, how can you live each day in constant expectation of His return? What can you do to remind yourself of the reality that this present world is temporary, but that He will usher in an eternal kingdom of righteousness? You might test your perspective by examining how you spend your time and money. Do you invest in eternal things that will survive His coming and gain a reward? Or are you merely acquiring things that will burn up in the end? Study 1 Corinthians 3:10–15. I suggest you go through your checkbook, review your expenses, and take note of your donations to God's work. Take a close look at your calendar. Are the things you're building made of temporary stuff like wood, hay, and stubble, which won't survive the flames? Or are they good quality, spiritual elements that will survive the coming judgment? Don't stop there, though. How can you adjust your budget and your schedule to focus more often on the important things in anticipation of His return?

Finally, with whom can you share Christ before it's too late? Imagine if Christ returned tomorrow and the judgment began. Whom would you miss in heaven? Whom would you leave behind? Whom would you feel grieved to see at the great white throne judgment because you failed to share with him or her the simple gospel that could have spared them from eternal condemnation? Pray for this person. Swallow your pride and lovingly share the truth with him or her. Communicate your concern. They may not listen. They may mock you. On the other hand, your words may be just the thing that nudges them one step closer to God's eternal kingdom.

So, what should you do in light of the coming day of the Lord? Clean up. Look up. And speak up. These three commands alone will keep us plenty busy until the Lord returns.

Living in Troubled Times (2 Peter 3:14–18)

---

¹⁴Therefore, beloved, since you look for these things, be diligent to be found by Him in peace, spotless and blameless, ¹⁵and regard the patience of our Lord *as* salvation; just as also our beloved brother Paul, according to the wisdom given him, wrote to you, ¹⁶as also in all *his* letters, speaking in them of these things, in which are some things hard to understand, which the untaught and unstable distort, as *they do* also the rest of the Scriptures, to their own destruction. ¹⁷You therefore, beloved, knowing this beforehand, be on your guard so that you are not carried away by the error of unprincipled men and fall from your own steadfastness, ¹⁸but grow in the grace and knowledge of our Lord and Savior Jesus Christ. To Him *be* the glory, both now and to the day of eternity. Amen.

Peter has written this letter to remind believers of sound teaching, to encourage diligence in the faith, and to strengthen biblical foundations of beliefs and practices. As he transitions to his final words to believers everywhere, we see him emphasize the need to read Scripture rightly, rejecting the destructive, heretical interpretations of the false teachers. Only in this way will we remain stable in the face of false teaching and fruitful in our spiritual growth.

In these five verses, Peter leaves his readers with four pointed commands:

- Be diligent (3:14).
- Be confident (3:15).
- Be on guard (3:17).
- Be fruitful (3:18).

In that order, let's let Peter fill in the blanks and firm up his final words.

— **3:14** —

The first thing we notice about Peter's clear command to *be diligent* is that he ties it in with his previous discussion. He begins with the logical connector, "therefore," pointing us back to his exhortation to live in light of the coming judgment and Christ's return. He has just finished writing of the Christian hope for new heavens and a new earth, in which righteousness dwells (3:13). In light of our anticipation for these things, we should be diligent today.

The verb "to be diligent," *spoudazō*, means to be zealous or to take great pains at accomplishing a task. In this case, Peter emphasizes the need for peace. Instead of squirming in panic and writhing in anxiety, we should exude peace. This kind of psychological tranquility comes through being "spotless and blameless"—being free from moral stains and without nagging guilt.

When we have a clear conscience by keeping short accounts with God and as we work hard to grow in our faith, we can face present troubles and future judgment with greater confidence. Peter has in mind the condition in which Christ finds us when He returns. The apostle John echoes the same kind of exhortation: "Now, little children, abide in Him, so that when He appears, we may have confidence and not shrink away from Him in shame at His coming" (1 John 2:28).

— **3:15–16** —

Whereas scoffers and mockers had declared that the Lord's delayed return implied He wasn't coming at all, Peter called His delay an expression of His mercy (3:8–9) that gives unbelievers an opportunity for "salvation" (3:15). Peter wants to encourage his readers to *be confident* that Christ's delay is purposeful.

Now, some might consider this kind of response a verbal dodge—an excuse for the Lord's tardiness. But to support his claim that all informed Christians believe this about the delay in Christ's return, Peter appeals to the parallel teaching of his counterpart, the apostle Paul. He reminds his readers that Paul also wrote that the patience of the Lord meant salvation. We saw this related in 1 Timothy 2:4—the desire for all to be saved and come to a knowledge of the truth. But Paul also said in Romans 2:4, "Or do you think lightly of the riches of His kindness and tolerance and patience, not knowing that the kindness of God leads you to repentance?"

Peter acknowledges that in some of Paul's letters we encounter things "hard to understand." This can encourage those of us who have spent a lifetime trying to decipher Paul's meaning in particular passages! If Peter himself noticed some difficult passages, how much more should we approach the Holy Scriptures with humility and patience.

But in the wrong hands, unclear passages in Paul's writings can have a disastrous effect. Peter says that some people — "the untaught and unstable" — distort Paul's writings as well as the rest of the Scriptures and thus bring destruction upon themselves. What does it mean to be "untaught"? The Greek word for this, *amathēs*, appears only here in the New Testament. One lexicon defines the word as describing "one who has not acquired a formal education, and hence with the implication of being stupid and ignorant."[6] And the term "unstable," *astēriktos*, refers to somebody who tends to change and waver in his or her views.[7]

These terms describe the false teachers Peter has dealt with in detail in chapter 2. Now they're back on his mind as he describes the way some mishandle the Old

THE EARLY NEW TESTAMENT CANON

Nowhere else in the New Testament do we find a passage like 2 Peter 3:15–16, where a New Testament writing refers to another New Testament writing as "Scripture," on the same level as the Old Testament. In the second generation of Christians, we see an increased awareness of apostolic writings as inspired Scripture; but in the first century, the term "Scripture" referred to the accepted canon of authoritative Jewish holy writings — the Old Testament. Peter's reference to Paul's work contains helpful insights about the apostle Paul and his letters.

First, Peter shows that Paul's letters already had begun to be collected by various churches. This is an indication of an early development of a "canon" or standard "collection" of New Testament writings within a decade of their composition. Of course, New Testament books were still in the process of being written, and no single church or teacher likely had a complete collection of everything composed to that date. It took time in the ancient world for these books to be copied, collected, and confirmed as authentic. But Peter's reference to "all [Paul's] letters" indicates that Peter, in Rome around AD 66, knew of a growing collection of Paul's writings.

Second, Peter clearly aligns Paul's writings with accepted Scripture. He says false teachers twist Paul's writings "as they do also the rest of the Scriptures." Peter saw Paul's writings as a smaller set of a larger category that included the Old Testament Scriptures. The word "Scriptures" here is the Greek *graphē*, the same word used by Paul in 2 Timothy 3:16, "All Scripture is inspired by God." This indicates an early awareness that God was in the process of adding a New Testament to the Old — a collection of distinct but equally inspired and authoritative writings to be used as a sure source of truth in the progress of revelation.

Some critics have alleged that the early Christians did not regard the writings of the apostles as "Scripture" and that this process of assembling a New Testament canon took several generations. What do they do, then, with the clear evidence from 2 Peter 3:15–16 that shows Peter assumed the scriptural authority of Paul's writings? Quite simply, they assume 2 Peter must have been written much later — a classic case of forcing the evidence into one's preconceived conclusions!

In fact, Peter's reference to Paul's writings is an early and important indication that, already in the first century, the concept of a "New Testament" was firmly established.[8]

Testament Scriptures, as well as the burgeoning New Testament writings. Because they lack the humility to submit to formal discipleship—and because they waver in their beliefs—these false teachers "distort" the Scriptures.

The Greek word "distort" is *strebloō*. It means to twist, wrench, or torture. The noun form of this word is used for the torture device known as "the rack." On this cruel device, a man would be fastened, then twisted and turned, often dislocating limbs as his interrogator attempted to draw information out of him. Peter's analogy is apt. The false teachers, Scripture in hand, would wrench and torture a text until it said what they wanted it to say. They ripped passages out of context, forced and twisted otherwise clear passages to conform to cloudy texts, concealed or exaggerated evidence, and used every other trick in the book to deceive people into accepting their teachings as "biblical."

This should serve as a warning to us all. Before we jump on a bandwagon and follow somebody's clever treatment of Scripture, we need to take a closer look at what's being taught. Does their "new discovery" of some undiscovered doctrine fit with the central truths of the Christian faith? Do their novel insights mesh with the rest of Scripture? False teachers thrive on being unique, nuanced, and novel. They often claim to find things in the Bible nobody has ever noticed ... *ever*! And they don't care that fine Christians and learned scholars disagree with them. In fact, they wear their deviant teaching and divisive doctrine as a badge of honor!

This is why we must filter what we hear through the whole counsel of God—the unified voice of all the Scriptures, not just isolated texts. We cannot allow a preacher's style or a teacher's charisma to lure us into accepting concocted arguments and endorsing clever conclusions. We must think critically, comparing a person's teaching with what Christians have believed from day one and with what can be demonstrated clearly in Scripture. Unlike the flimsy flap of false prophets, reliable interpretations of Scripture will stand under God's Word, stand up to challenges, and stand the test of time.

—**3:17**—

The third command in Peter's closing words is to *be on guard*. Because we know beforehand that false teachers carry Bibles, we must stand watch. Peter uses a military term for taking charge of a post, keeping our eyes peeled for approaching enemy combatants. Because they will sneak up on us through the dense fog of deception, wearing our uniforms, carrying our weapons, and speaking our language, we must be alert. From this day on, nobody can plead ignorance. Perhaps negligence, irresponsibility, and laziness ... but not ignorance.

The price of failing to be on guard is twofold. First, we will be dragged away by the errors of the false teachers. Like a soldier who turns his back on his post, the enemy will pounce and take us captive. Second, we will fall from our steadfast position. Peter does not refer here to losing salvation, but to losing *sanctification*—stumbling backward from the progress made in spiritual growth. Recall that at the beginning of this letter, Peter listed the virtues we must develop between faith and love—godly habits that mark us as useful and fruitful believers in Christ (1:5–8). With this exhortation to diligence in spiritual growth came a promise: "As you practice these things, you will never stumble" (1:10). Peter acknowledges in 3:17 the possibility of slipping backward—losing spiritual stability and being rendered useless and unfruitful.

Don't let your guard down for one moment. The results could mean disaster.

— **3:18** —

In contrast to slipping backward toward spiritual decline due to instability, Peter states his final command—*be fruitful*. He exhorts us to "grow in the grace and knowledge of our Lord and Savior Jesus Christ." With this command, Peter returns to the opening blessing of the letter: "Grace and peace be multiplied to you in the knowledge of God and of Jesus our Lord" (1:2). He also called for spiritual growth in his first letter: "Like newborn babes, long for the pure milk of the word, that by it you may grow in respect to salvation" (1 Peter 2:2). The overall goal of Peter's letter is that believers will continue to grow, to multiply in grace, and to be fruitful in their spiritual lives.

In 3:18, Peter exhorts believers to grow in both grace and knowledge. The challenge for us is to keep these two pursuits in balance. They may sometimes appear to be mutually exclusive categories. It can be easy to take one to an unhealthy extreme, but we must maintain both.

Grace	Knowledge
… keeps you tolerant and loving.	… keeps you strong and confident.
… gives you mercy and compassion.	… gives you discernment and discrimination.
… helps you believe and accept.	… helps you question and critique.
… results in vulnerability.	… results in stability.

To monitor your own spiritual growth, continue to ask yourself some probing questions. Am I keeping grace and knowledge in balance? Do others notice a measurable change in my character? Have I come to the place where past temptations no longer have the same, strong appeal? Am I demonstrating more discernment when it comes to counterfeit claims?

Peter's very last words — recorded for Christians living in both the first century and the twenty-first century — offer praise to Jesus Christ. This final doxology to His Savior stands as a profound testimony from a man who had once fallen from his own steadfastness, only to be restored to a place of spiritual strength unmatched by most believers since. Peter grew from a headstrong Galilean to a humble apostle — from a simple fisherman to a legendary fisher of men. We, too, can follow him on his remarkable journey of spiritual growth as we heed his warnings, recall his reminders, and embrace the divine promises he describes, applying diligence and hope and relying on the provision of the Holy Spirit. When we do this, we will be able to defeat false doctrine, avoid moral compromise, and join Peter in his passionate praise of our Lord and Savior Jesus Christ:

"To Him be the glory, both now and to the day of eternity. Amen." (2 Peter 3:18)

NOTES:

1. James D. G. Dunn and John W. Rogerson, eds., *Eerdmans Commentary on the Bible* (Grand Rapids: Eerdmans, 2003), 36.
2. Thorkild Jacobsen, "The Eridu Genesis," *Journal of Biblical Literature* 100, no. 4 (1981): 524.
3. Ibid., 525.
4. John H. Tullock, *The Old Testament Story*, 6th ed. (Upper Saddle River, NJ: Prentice Hall, 1981), 43.
5. James George Frazer, *Folk-Lore in the Old Testament: Studies in Comparative Religion, Legend and Law* (New York: MacMillan, 1923), 1:183–84.
6. Louw and Nida, eds., *Greek-English Lexicon*, § 27.24.
7. Ibid., § 31.79.
8. On the history of the New Testament canon, see F. F. Bruce, *The Canon of Scripture* (Downers Grove, IL: InterVarsity Press, 1988); Bruce M. Metzger, *The Canon of the New Testament: Its Origin, Development, and Significance* (Oxford: Clarendon, 1987).

Share Your Thoughts

With the Author: Your comments will be forwarded to the author when you send them to *zauthor@zondervan.com*.

With Zondervan: Submit your review of this book by writing to *zreview@zondervan.com*.

Free Online Resources at
www.zondervan.com

Zondervan AuthorTracker: Be notified whenever your favorite authors publish new books, go on tour, or post an update about what's happening in their lives at www.zondervan.com/authortracker.

Daily Bible Verses and Devotions: Enrich your life with daily Bible verses or devotions that help you start every morning focused on God. Visit www.zondervan.com/newsletters.

Free Email Publications: Sign up for newsletters on Christian living, academic resources, church ministry, fiction, children's resources, and more. Visit www.zondervan.com/newsletters.

Zondervan Bible Search: Find and compare Bible passages in a variety of translations at www.zondervanbiblesearch.com.

Other Benefits: Register yourself to receive online benefits like coupons and special offers, or to participate in research.

ZONDERVAN

ZONDERVAN.com/
AUTHORTRACKER
follow your favorite authors